DIVINE MUSIC IN ARCHAIC AND CLASSICAL GREEK ART

In this volume, Carolyn M. Laferrière examines Athenian vase-paintings and votive reliefs depicting the gods most frequently shown as musicians to reconstruct how images could suggest the sounds of the music created by the gods. Incorporating insights from recent work in sensory studies, she considers formal analysis together with literary and archaeological evidence to explore the musical culture of Athens. Laferrière argues that these images could visually suggest the sounds of the gods' music. This representational strategy, whereby sight and sound are blurred, conveys the "unhearable" nature of their music: because it cannot be physically heard, it falls to the human imagination to provide its sounds and awaken viewers' multisensory engagement with the images. Moreover, when situated within their likely original contexts, the objects establish a network of interaction between the viewer, the visualized music, and the landscape, all of which determined how divine music was depicted, perceived, and reciprocated. Laferrière demonstrates that participation in the gods' musical performances offered worshippers a multisensory experience of divine presence.

CAROLYN M. LAFERRIÈRE is Assistant Curator of Ancient Mediterranean Art at the Princeton University Art Museum and Associate Editor for the journal *Greek and Roman Musical Studies*.

DIVINE MUSIC IN ARCHAIC AND CLASSICAL GREEK ART

SEEING THE SONGS OF THE GODS

CAROLYN M. LAFERRIÈRE
Princeton University Art Museum

CAMBRIDGE
UNIVERSITY PRESS

CAMBRIDGE
UNIVERSITY PRESS

Shaftesbury Road, Cambridge CB2 8EA, United Kingdom

One Liberty Plaza, 20th Floor, New York, NY 10006, USA

477 Williamstown Road, Port Melbourne, VIC 3207, Australia

314–321, 3rd Floor, Plot 3, Splendor Forum, Jasola District Centre, New Delhi – 110025, India

103 Penang Road, #05–06/07, Visioncrest Commercial, Singapore 238467

Cambridge University Press is part of Cambridge University Press & Assessment, a department of the University of Cambridge.

We share the University's mission to contribute to society through the pursuit of education, learning and research at the highest international levels of excellence.

www.cambridge.org
Information on this title: www.cambridge.org/9781009315944

DOI: 10.1017/9781009315906

First published 2024

Printed in the United Kingdom by TJ Books Limited, Padstow, Cornwall

A catalogue record for this publication is available from the British Library

Library of Congress Cataloging-in-Publication Data
NAMES: Laferrière, Carolyn, author.
TITLE: Divine music in archaic and classical Greek art : seeing the songs of the gods / Carolyn M. Laferrière, Princeton University Art Museum.
DESCRIPTION: Cambridge, United Kingdom ; New York, NY : Cambridge University Press, [2023] | Outgrowth of the author's thesis (doctoral)–Yale University, 2017, under the title: Complex sensations of divine music in archaic and classical Greek art. | Includes bibliographical references and index.
IDENTIFIERS: LCCN 2023022471 (print) | LCCN 2023022472 (ebook) | ISBN 9781009315944 (hardback) | ISBN 9781009315913 (paperback) | ISBN 9781009315906 (epub)
Subjects: LCSH: Music in art. | Music, Greek and Roman–History and criticism. | Gods, Greek, in art. | Art, Greek–Themes, motives.
CLASSIFICATION: LCC ML85 .L23 2023 (print) | LCC ML85 (ebook) | DDC 780/.073–dc23/eng/20230605
LC record available at https://lccn.loc.gov/2023022471
LC ebook record available at https://lccn.loc.gov/2023022472

ISBN 978-1-009-31594-4 Hardback

Publication of this book has been aided by a grant from the von Bothmer Publication Fund of the Archaeological Institute of America

To Cliff, whose love of music inspired these pages

CONTENTS

FIGURES

ACKNOWLEDGMENTS

As with the composition of a musical score, this book has been a labor of love over many months and years, the arc of its melody ebbing, flowing, and changing in response to the conversations held and questions posed over the past decade. This project first began its life as a dissertation, written in the collegial and supportive community of the Departments of the History of Art and Classics at Yale University. I am profoundly grateful to Milette Gaifman for her guidance and mentorship when I first embarked on this project, and for her continued encouragement in the years afterward as I gradually transformed it into its current state. Her sharp interrogation and keen eye are apparent throughout these pages, whether in noticing the small, strange details that enliven a scene or in asking bigger questions, to which my answers now tie this project together. My thanks also go to Verity Platt, Pauline LeVen, and Diana E. E. Kleiner, who each offered careful and thoughtful advice on this project; their support over the years has been invaluable. I thank my colleague Susan Matheson for her continued support, for giving me the opportunity to work closely with objects in the Yale University Art Gallery, and for sharing her deep appreciation for the complexities and nuances of Athenian vase-painting. I am also grateful to Jaś Elsner, for thought-provoking discussions about Pan and divine music during the summer of 2015 at Oxford. Later in this project's life, I received support from Edward Kamens, Joseph Manning, and Irene Peirano Garrison, all with Archaia at Yale, and from Timothy Barringer, in the History of Art at Yale. In spite of working remotely during the pandemic, Jay Rubenstein made me feel welcome and supported at the University of Southern California (USC) and the Center for the Premodern World. Likewise, Ann Marie Yasin's constant guidance and encouragement as a colleague, mentor, and co-instructor have meant so much. Finally, I am grateful for my colleagues at the Princeton University Art Museum and the Department of Art and Archaeology, and especially Juliana Ochs Dweck and Nathan Arrington, who have supported me in these final phases of the manuscript's preparation.

I am thankful to all those who read drafts, chapters, and sections of this book and offered their comments and suggestions. While I was a postdoctoral associate at Yale, funding from Archaia allowed me to host a junior scholar's book colloquium; I am grateful to Michael Squire, Guy Hedreen, Barbara Graziosi, and Timothy Power for being such careful readers, each offering invaluable suggestions and comments that have made their way into this final version. It was a privilege to speak with J. J. Pollitt about scenes of Apollo and I am appreciative of the time he took to read what is now Chapter 3. Lauren Curtis, Sarah Olsen, and Naomi Weiss have read every chapter across multiple versions, each time offering astute guidance and support. My thanks must also go to Nathaniel Jones, who graciously read the entire manuscript and sharpened my thinking in the final stages. I am grateful to the audiences at the University of Southern California and the Center for the Premodern World, MOISA, AIA/SCS, CAA, Yale University, Oberlin College, the University of Toronto, King's College London, the Epichoreia meeting at New York University, Duke University, the University of North Carolina at Chapel Hill, the Canadian Institute for Mediterranean Studies, Carleton University, and the Swedish Institute at Athens for their attention and questions; it is always a privilege and a pleasure to be able to share my work and ideas. I thank Chelsea Gardner for hosting a fun and engaging interview about caves and music on the *Peopling the Past* podcast. I would like to thank my friends – too many to name – who have been with me on this journey, whether it was precariously venturing into a dark cave, listening to a talk on gods and music, visiting yet another museum room of vases, or simply having dinner together, on both sides of the Atlantic.

A book is never the product of one sole person, and it is truly a pleasure to thank my wonderful editor, Beatrice Rehl, and her entire team at Cambridge University Press. She has championed this book and offered words of encouragement and advice throughout the entire process. I am so grateful for her guidance. My thanks, too, go to the two anonymous reviewers, whose careful reading and astute comments have made this a better book. I also thank the Archaeological Institute of America, whose von Bothmer Publication Fund has enabled the publication of color images. Funding for image permissions and color printing was also generously provided by the Center for the Premodern World at USC and by the Princeton University Art Museum. A grant from the Center for Hellenic Studies supported additional research that was undertaken during the pandemic.

I am also profoundly grateful to the curators, scholars, librarians, and staff who have helped me arrange collections visits, study permits, and image permissions from the American School of Classical Studies at Athens, Art Resource, AKG images, the British Museum, the Museum of Fine Arts in Boston, the Antikensammlung in Berlin, the Getty Villa, the National Archaeological Museum in Athens, the Delphi Archaeological Museum, the Athenian Agora, Harvard Art Museums, the Kimbell Art Museum, the Metropolitan Museum of Art, the Antikensammlungen in Munich, the

Ashmolean Museum, the Cabinet des Médailles, the Louvre, the National Archaeological Museum in Naples, the Petit Palais, Sotheby's, the Thorvaldsen Museum, the Virginia Museum of Fine Arts, the Vatican Museums, the Martin von Wagner Museum der Universität Würzburg, and the Yale University Art Gallery. I would especially like to thank Ioanna Damanaki for her help in securing permissions in Greece, Hans Goette for giving permission to reproduce his plan of the Vari Cave, and Rossana di Pinto for her help and patience in securing permissions from the Vatican Museums.

It is perhaps fitting for a book on musical performance that I end these words of thanks with those who have patiently listened to me speak about this project over the many years since its inception. My parents, Dianne and Claude, have been unfailing in their support, offering words of encouragement and guidance at every break and pause, and often across great distances. I am more grateful to them than I suspect they know. My sister Anik has traveled with me on this book's journey, whether by working side by side at the Bodleian, humoring me by joining in my frequent trips to museum collections in London and Athens, or simply by offering a funny story or word of encouragement, bolstering my spirits along the way. My little dog Clio, my companion from a time before this project existed, has probably heard me prattle on about it more than I care to admit, but has always been ready for a walk or a peaceful moment at home, getting me out of my head when I needed it most. My daughter, Charlotte, came into this world in the midst of this project's revisions and, just by her mere presence, gave me some much-needed perspective on the necessity of being in the moment and of looking and listening carefully. Her joy in music and dance is a delight, and I hope that I have conveyed even the merest trace of her love of song with my words. My biggest debt of gratitude is owed to Cliff Robinson, without whom this book would never have materialized. His constant support, careful reading, willingness to talk yet again about another thorny problem, and, above all, his deep love of music, are apparent on every page, in every image, in every detail. As he so beautifully wrote many years ago, what good are words between those who share love? So, it is to him that I dedicate this book, with love and endless thanks.

ABBREVIATIONS

AA	*Archäologischer Anzeiger*
ABV	J. D. Beazley, *Attic Black-Figure Vase-Painters* (Oxford, 1956)
AEph	*Archaiologike Ephemeris*
AJA	*American Journal of Archaeology*
AJP	*American Journal of Philology*
AM	*Mitteilungen des Deutschen Archäologischen Instituts, Athenische Abteilung*
AntK	*Antike Kunst*
AR	Archaeological Reports (supplement to *JHS*)
*ARV*²	J. D. Beazley, *Attic Red-Figure Vase-Painters*, 2nd ed. (Oxford, 1963)
BAPD	*Beazley Archive Pottery Database* (www.beazley.ox.ac.uk)
BCH	*Bulletin de correspondance hellénique*
Beazley Addenda	Lucilla Burn and Ruth Glynn, *Beazley Addenda: Additional References to ABV, ARV² and Paralipomena.* (Oxford, 1983)
*Beazley Addenda*²	T. H. Carpenter et al., *Beazley Addenda: Additional References to ABV, ARV² and Paralipomena*, 2nd ed. (Oxford, 1989)
BICS	*Bulletin of the Institute of Classical Studies*
BMCR	*Bryn Mawr Classical Review*
BSA	*British School at Athens Annual*
CAJ	*Cambridge Archaeological Journal*
CJ	*Classical Journal*
ClAnt	*Classical Antiquity*
CP	*Classical Philology*
CQ	*Classical Quarterly*
CVA	*Corpus vasorum antiquorum*
CW	*Classical World*
DK	H. A. Diels and Walther Kranz, eds. Die Fragmente der Vorsokratiker. 5th ed. (Berlin 1934–7)
GaR	*Greece and Rome*
GRBS	*Greek, Roman and Byzantine Studies*
GRMS	*Greek and Roman Musical Studies*
HSCP	*Harvard Studies in Classical Philology*
HTR	*Harvard Theological Review*

IG	*Inscriptiones graecae*
JdI	*Jahrbuch des Deutschen Archäologischen Instituts*
JHS	*Journal of Hellenic Studies*
JRGZM	*Jahrbuch des Römisch-germanischen Zentralmuseums, Mainz*
LIMC	*Lexicon iconographicum mythologiae classicae* (Zurich, 1981–2009)
MAAR	*Memoirs of the American Academy in Rome*
MdI	*Mitteilungen des Deutschen Archäologischen Instituts*
NM	*National Archaeological Museum, Athens*
Paralipomena	J. D. Beazley, *Paralipomena* (Oxford, 1971)
PastPres	*Past and Present*
PMG	Denys L. Page (ed.), *Poetae Melici Graeci* (Oxford, 1962)
RA	*Revue archéologique*
RBPhil	*Revue belge de philologie et d'histoire*
RE	A. F. Pauly and Georg Wissowa, eds. *Real-Encyclopädie der Classischen Altertumswissenschaft* (1893–1978)
RÉA	*Revue des études anciennes*
RES	*RES: Anthropology and Aesthetics*
RhMus	*Rheinisches Museum*
SEG	*Supplementum epigraphicum graecum* (Leiden 1923–)
TAPA	*Transactions of the American Philological Association*
ThesCRA	*Thesaurus Cultus et Rituum Antiquorum* (Los Angeles: Getty, 2004–)
WürzJbb	*Würzburger Jahrbücher für die Altertumswissenschaft*
YaleBull	*Yale University Art Gallery Bulletin*
ZPE	*Zeitschrift für Papyrologie und Epigraphik*

N.B. the abbreviations are taken from the *AJA* list of standard reference works.

INTRODUCTION

Seeing Divine Music

Sometimes, a visual image almost seems to sound, its evocative rendition of a performance provoking its viewers to imagine that they hear the music that the figures are shown playing. Ancient Greek visual culture abounded with images of men and women engaging in musical practice, so much so that scenes of music-making are pervasive among the material evidence that survives from Athens in particular, appearing across various media throughout the Archaic, Classical, and Hellenistic periods. Not only do the images establish the importance of music within Athens during this time, but in depicting the possible range of responses to musical performance, they also offer us a glimpse into the profound effect that the sounds of music could have had on the listening audience. Beyond the repeated attention given to representations of men and women playing music, the visual material also depicts the gods performing on their instruments, so that both human and divine are regularly shown engaging in musical activities. As with scenes featuring their human musical counterparts, images of divine music explore both the act of making music and its subsequent effect on the listening audience, as we may see on one especially compelling image, where Apollo and Artemis stand close together, their bodies contrasting with the vase's red background as the image focuses our attention on the performance that is underway (Fig. 0.1).[1] The god stands just slightly off center, dressed as a professional musician while he pulls a *plektron*, a long pick, across the strings of his large stringed instrument.[2] He faces Artemis, who lowers her bow and arrow with her left hand while

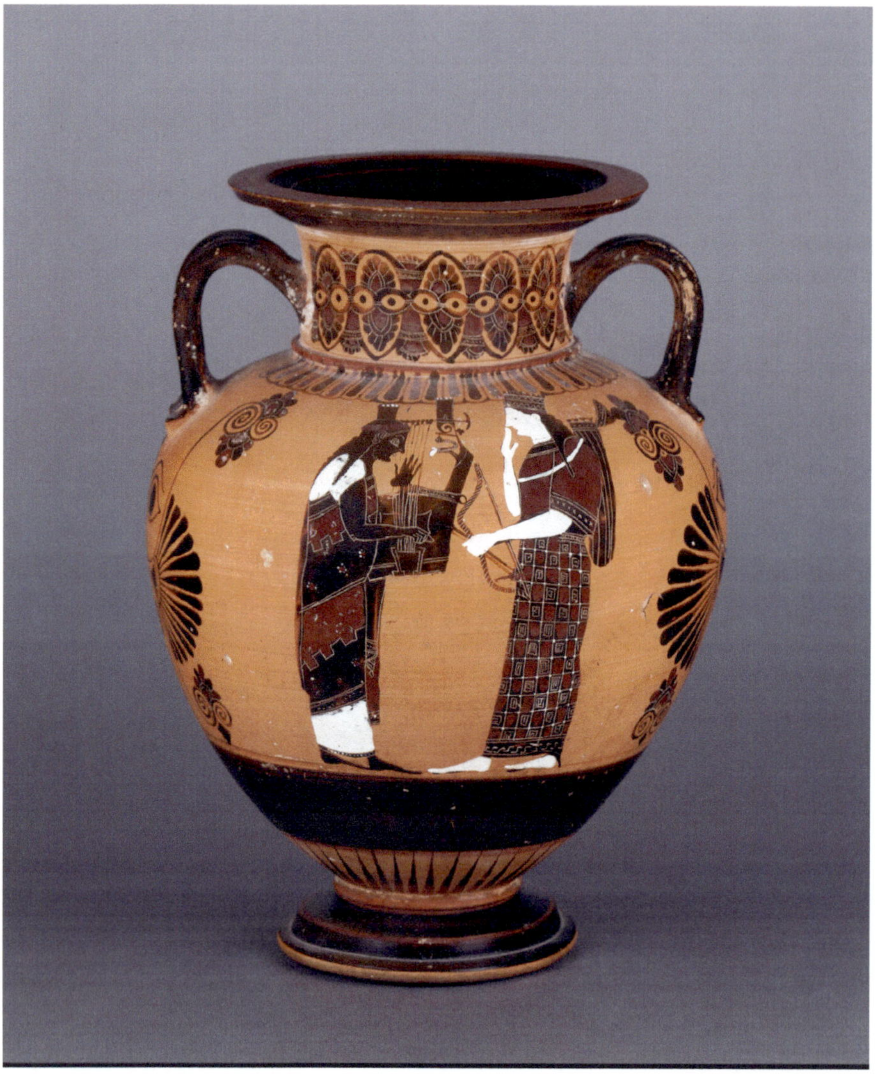

0.1. Possibly from the workshop of Group E, *Apollo Playing the Kithara Beside Artemis* (side A), Attic black-figure neck *amphora*, ceramic, h. 39.5 cm, *c.* 550 BCE. London, British Museum, 1843,1103.98 (B260). © The Trustees of the British Museum.

she raises her right to her mouth, echoing the physical composition of Apollo's body. Upon first encountering this image, the scene of the two deities seems very much in keeping with the larger repertoire of Athenian representations of the gods in each other's company. Indeed, this and other similar scenes are depicted throughout the surviving material culture from Archaic and Classical Athens, whether it is in mythological scenes that adorned pediments, metopes, and friezes on temples, in painted images on ceramic vases, in devotional scenes carved into shallow votive reliefs, or in sculptural groups that were displayed throughout ancient cities and sanctuaries. And yet, despite its inherent silence as a work of art, there is something powerfully evocative, or even contemplative, about this particular image of Apollo and Artemis: there is no obvious myth at work here, no sequence of events that the two divine siblings perform together that would account for the connection the image develops between the two figures. What, then, has brought the gods together and captured their attention – and our own? It is, the image suggests, the beautiful sounds of Apollo's music.

In its depiction of a musical performance, the painted scene of Apollo and Artemis asks us to reflect upon how the sounds of music could be captured by a visual image. In other words, it offers us a compelling example with which to consider how an otherwise silent visual representation could communicate the ebbs and flows of a melody, the underlying rhythms of its progress, the crescendos that punctuate its conclusion. Playing with the relationship between auditory music and visual image, the Austrian poet Rainer Maria Rilke offers a tantalizing poetic vision of music as the breath of statues, "Musik: Atem der Statuen, Vielleicht: | Stille der Bilder. Du Sprache wo Sprachen | enden."[3] Invoking both music and painting, the poet draws an implicit connection between the shared, powerful effect that both music and the visual arts can exert upon their audiences. Long before Rilke noted the profound relationship between music and art, the Archaic poet Simonides articulated a similar link between art and music, evocatively stating that ζωγραφίαν ποίησιν σιωπῶσαν ... τὴν δὲ ποίησιν ζωγραφίαν λαλοῦσαν, "painting is silent poetry... and poetry is talkative painting."[4] In each instance, there exists the potential for sound to slip into art and art, in turn, to slip back into sung poetry, suggesting a permeable aesthetic boundary between the two, where one medium could provoke its audience to perceive it as another. In considering Greek representations of music, there is thus something powerfully evocative about the visualization of music: not only do the images invite their viewers to see the music, but they also position this experience of looking at music within a musical culture in which sounds were performed, heard, and felt by the looking and listening bodies of the audience.

Scenes of musical performances that adorned the sides of Athenian vases or were sculpted into stone reliefs can thus offer us a fleeting, though inherently silent, glimpse into the musical culture that so pervasively characterized ancient Athenian society.[5] Within the music and performance context of Archaic and Classical Athens, images of the gods engaging in musical practice, such as the one with which we began, have often been interpreted as representing the ideals to which men and women aspire. As Sheramy Bundrick has persuasively shown, artists created images that "expressed the ideals and values permeating Athenian culture," so that, rather than taking such scenes as "mere illustrations and interpreted as photographic documents of actual practices," we should instead position them within the broader range of musical practices that would have been familiar to Archaic and Classical Athenians.[6] By situating images of music-making within their ancient context, Bundrick compellingly weaves together historical, political, and social change with Athenian *mousikē*, the combination of instrumental music, poetic song, and choral dance that, together with *gymnastikē*, or physical athletics, constituted elite *paideia*, or education.[7] Following her approach, we might interpret our scene of Apollo and Artemis within the context of the Peisistratid tyrants and their reorganization of the Panathenaic festival in 566 BCE, when greater prominence seems to have been placed on musical contests.[8] In depicting Apollo dressed as a mortal musician ready to perform in public, the image suggests that even he could participate in the newly instituted festival contests, although his divine status all but assures his victory over all possible competitors. The inclusion of another musician on the other side of the vase underscores the potential festival context for this image, since the lyre player is similarly dressed in his performance robes (Fig. 0.2). That he stands between two columns points to his future success in the competition, as they recall other such monuments that were set up to commemorate individual victories.

Although this and other images of both human and divine music-making suggest where, how, and often why Athenians practiced music, how they could have responded to musical performances is less clear.[9] How did an ancient Athenian audience react to music? Can we infer from the surviving visual material how the music of a *kithara* was meant to make its listeners feel, as opposed to that of an *aulos*, or a harp, or a *syrinx*? It is also unclear what relationship existed between the men and women who were depicted playing their instruments and the gods who were shown playing the same instruments, not least since the two performed in very different ways, in different spaces, and for different audiences. Our image of Apollo and Artemis presents us with precisely this tension, in that the performing musician is a god, capable of actions unheard of for men and women. Would such an image of the musical Apollo, or indeed of the Muses, Dionysos, or Pan, have been seen as an ideal representation of a human counterpart? Was it even thought to be possible to hear divine music? What did it mean to see divine performances on vases and reliefs, but not to be able to hear them? In many ways, we are doubly removed from the sounds of the gods' music, since we not only encounter a visual rendition of a sonic performance, which puts us at a sensory distance from the music being depicted, but the musician is himself divine and thus exists outside of the musical culture of ancient Athens, even as his representation was created within that cultural framework. Despite this distance, there has been a concerted effort here to make the human musician on the vase's other side appear similar to Apollo (Fig. 0.2): both wear highly decorated robes with a white *chitōn* underneath, both have long hair that curls down their back, and both are depicted in the same moment of having just drawn the *plektron* across the *kithara*'s strings while the left

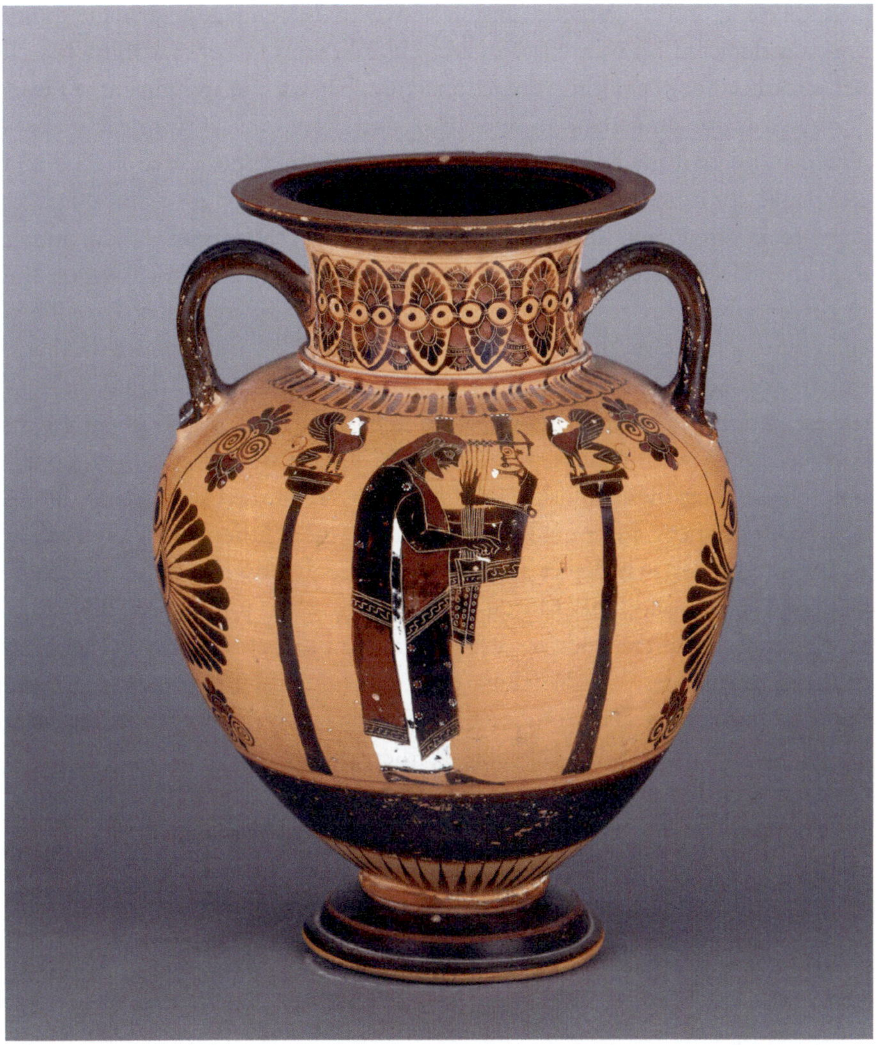

0.2. Possibly from the workshop of Group E, *Kitharoidos Between Two Columns* (side B), Attic black-figure neck *amphora*, ceramic, h. 39.5 cm, *c.* 550 BCE. London, British Museum, 1843,1103.98 (B260). © The Trustees of the British Museum.

hand stabilizes the large instrument. Indeed, it has even been suggested that the solo musician is once again Apollo, although his beard and hairstyle more likely mark him off as a human performer.[10] However, this visual repetition, where the body of the god blurs into that of the mortal musician, and that of the musician blurs back into the body of the god, allows the image to mediate between human and divine, or even between visual image and audible sound. Not only is music shown to be an activity that is shared by men, women, and gods, but the image presents one way by which to engage with Apollo, that is, through the musician and Apollo's shared performance of music, especially on the *kithara*, the god's instrument of choice.

In focusing on this aesthetic tension between visual image and divine sound as it was depicted on painted vases and carved reliefs in Archaic and Classical Athens, this book explores the connection between how ancient viewers perceived image and sound, how human and divine music were each represented in a visual medium, and how images depicted music that both could and could not be heard. It also is concerned with where these musical images were seen, used, and interacted with, and how those sites of encounter fundamentally affected how divine music was perceived. By focusing on the spaces in which images of the gods' musical performance may have been encountered and how their ancient audience may have interacted with them, this book offers a new model for how to understand the significance of representations of divine music within the social and religious culture of Archaic and Classical Athens. To explore the intersection of visual representations of the gods, divine music, and the viewers' response to the sounds of the gods' performances, I examine Archaic and Classical Athenian sculpted reliefs and painted vases that depict the gods most frequently shown as musicians, namely Pan, Apollo, the Muses, and Dionysos. In prioritizing the visual evidence in which the gods are shown playing musical instruments, listening to the performances of their fellow gods, and physically responding to these sounds, I argue that scenes of divine music cannot be understood as idealized extensions of human music-making. Rather, the images mark the difference between human and divine music through the divergences in their respective audiences, their sites of performance, and the specific manner in which the auditory aspect of divine music is communicated in a visual medium.

This book thus advances a new methodology for interpreting Archaic and Classical scenes of the gods' music-making by positioning them within the larger framework of ritual interaction between human and divine. Working between the visual images, the ancient contexts in which they were encountered, and the potential sensory responses that they elicited, I suggest that the images offered their viewers the possibility of an epiphanic encounter of the gods that is mediated through their sensory engagement with the visualized sounds of divine music. Throughout this book, I develop a theoretical framework for articulating the relationship between visual representations of divine music, the viewer's memory and perception of musical sounds, and the viewer's subsequent imaginary enlivening of the god's performance. To ground my discussion of divine music and the effect that scenes of the gods' musical performances could have had on their audiences, in this introduction I outline some of the theoretical methodologies and scholarly work that underlies my analysis, and define the key terms and scope of my discussion. I also elaborate upon the important points of difference between human and divine music, ultimately demonstrating why representations of the gods' music-making require their own analysis and interpretation.

MUSIC AND THE GODS

The vase featuring Apollo as a musician and Artemis as his audience offers us a new model for interpreting visual representations of music-making, or indeed of any image that invokes the viewer's senses. If we focus our analysis on scenes of music-making specifically, we find that not only are scenes of musical performances extremely common in the surviving visual material from Archaic and Classical Athens, but within this corpus, the gods' musical skills are particularly emphasized, whether it is Apollo playing his instrument to his divine family, the Muses creating euphonic music together as a chorus, Dionysos dancing ecstatically to the music played by his followers, or Pan playing his pipes for dancing Nymphs. We can see, for instance, the important place given to music on a red-figure storage vessel that depicts the gods gathered together in celebration. Here, in the center of the image, stands Apollo, once again holding up his *kithara* (Fig. 0.3).[11] The *kithara* has been put on display and it commands our attention both through its size and through its frontal depiction, the only object or figure in this scene to have been shown in this way.[12] As the god holds the instrument, he touches the strings with his left hand as he draws the *plektron* across them, producing, as we are invited to imagine, a beautiful flurry of musical notes. Our musician is joined by a number of other figures. On the far right is Dionysos, the god of wine who here holds up a *kantharos*, the drinking cup the god typically uses. Two female figures, possibly maenads, the followers of Dionysos, stand on either side of Apollo;[13] the figure next to Dionysos also holds *krotala*, or castanets, that she plays while she lifts her robes to dance to the rhythmic music. The final figure on the far left is Hermes, the messenger god, who holds a *syrinx*, the pipes he invented at the end of the *Homeric Hymn to Hermes*;[14] he holds the instrument up to his mouth, about to play it and lend its shrill sounds to the music of the lyre and *krotala*.

In this image, Apollo is depicted as the stable and immobile center, the point around which the other figures move: the maenads each turn their heads toward Hermes and Dionysos, creating dynamic pairs, even as their feet point toward Apollo, ultimately directing their movement toward the source of music. By positioning Apollo's musical performance in the center, the image suggests that his music expands out toward his companions. Perhaps in response to Apollo's performance, Hermes seems about to play his own instrument, so that the two streams of music issuing from the two instruments are here joined together with apparent disregard or lack of concern with what the combination of musical sounds depicted in the image might sound like. Instead, the gods are presented as virtuoso musicians who are capable of impressive feats of musical skill that are unachievable by men and women. The overall effect of this otherwise strange musical combination is that of a

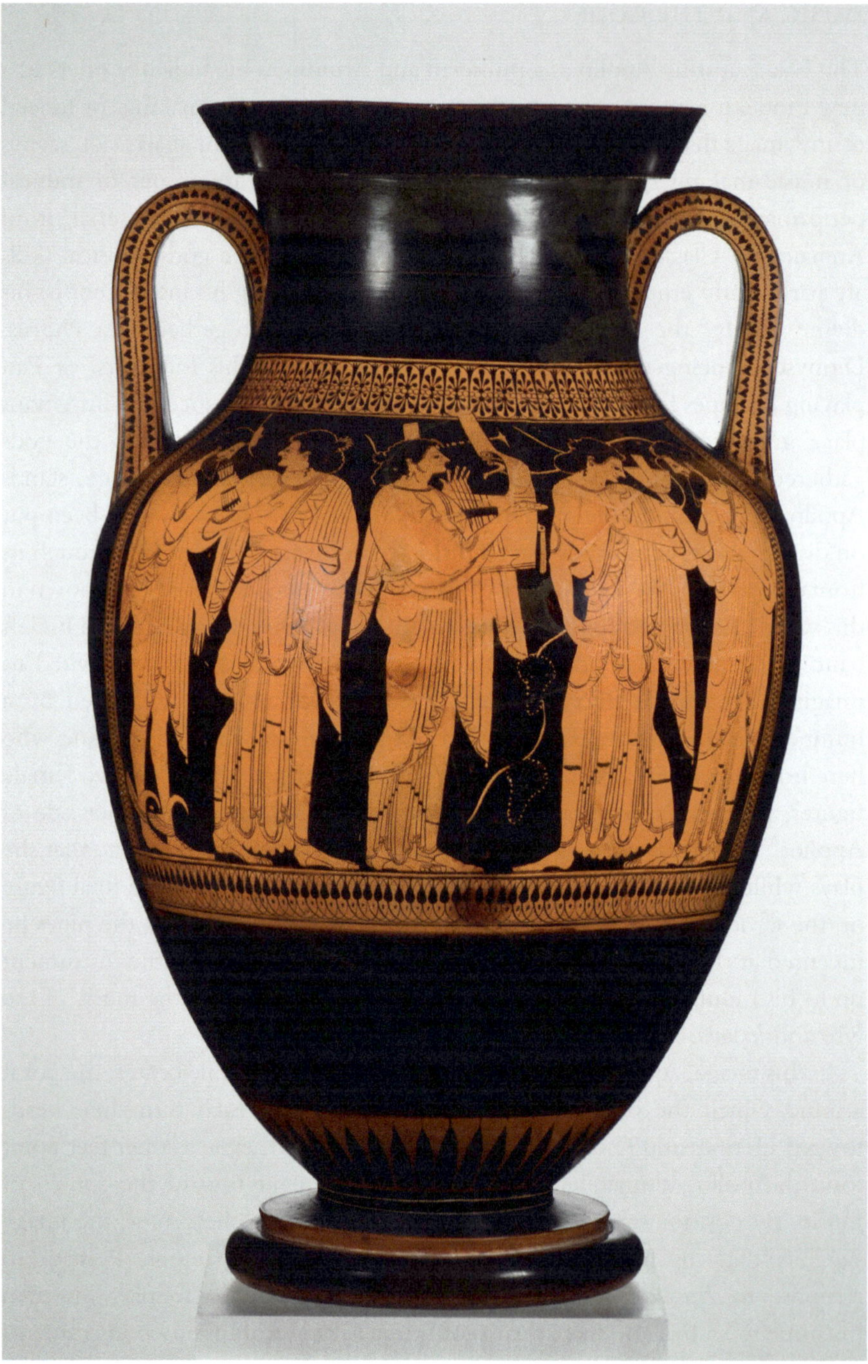

0.3. The Nikoxenos Painter, *Gathering of the Gods* (side A), Attic red-figure *amphora*, h. 65 cm, *c.* 500 BCE. Munich, Antikensammlungen, 2304 (J405). Staatliche Antikensammlungen und Glyptothek München, photograph by Renate Kühling.

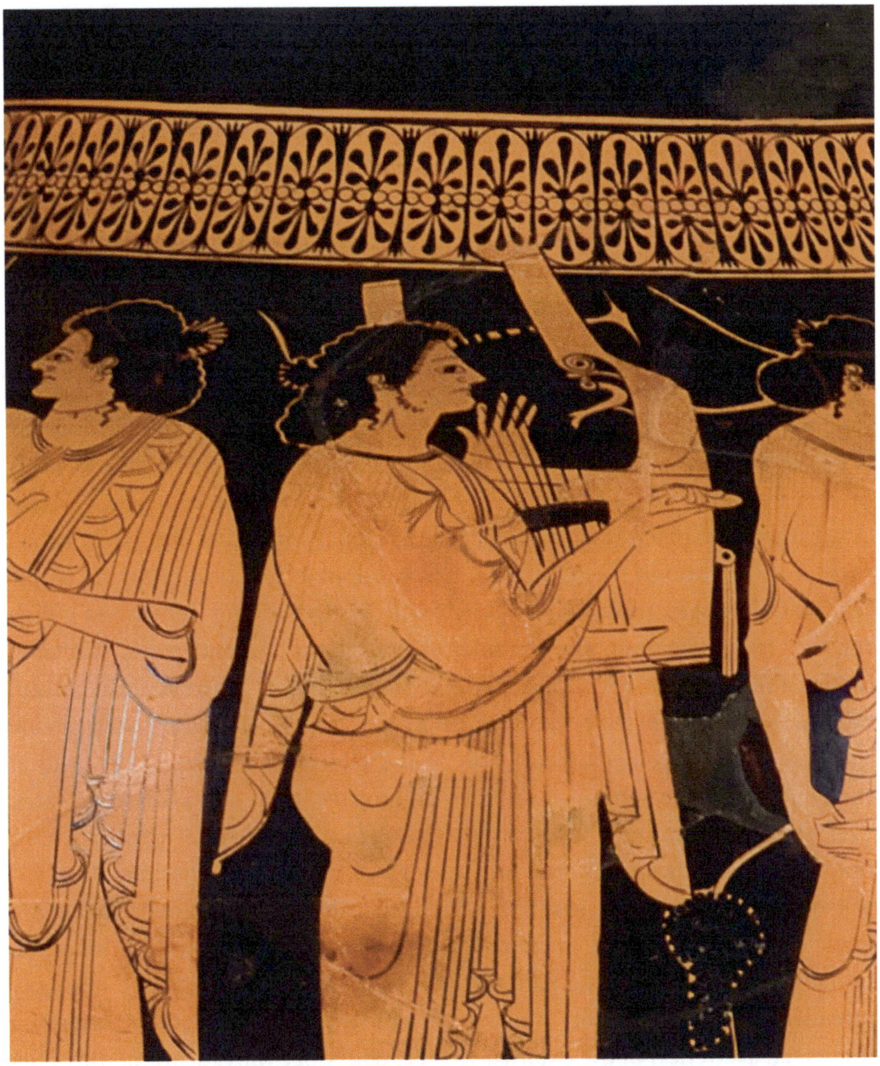

0.4. Detail. The Nikoxenos Painter, *Gathering of the Gods* (side A), Attic red-figure *amphora*, ceramic, h. 65 cm, *c.* 500 BCE. Munich, Antikensammlungen, 2304 (J405). Staatliche Antikensammlungen und Glyptothek München, photograph by Renate Kühling.

divine celebration that does not adhere to human musical preferences.[15] The expansive and compelling nature of the gods' music can even be seen in the rendering of Apollo's *kithara*, which has been shown as so large that it erupts through the decorative border that frames the scene, effectively suggesting that his music is capable of moving beyond the image (Fig. 0.4).[16] Moreover, even though many of the figures who move around Apollo, especially Dionysos and the maenads, are not associated with calm and orderly music, here they are shown as somewhat subdued, as if they have adapted their movements to the particular kind of music that Apollo creates on his lyre.

Scenes of divine music collectively attest both to the importance of music within the Greeks' conception of their gods and to how the gods could play, enjoy, and respond to music. Above all, in depicting the gods enthusiastically engaging in musical practice, the images that are painted onto vases or sculpted into shallow reliefs function in two distinct ways that are relevant to our discussion. First, in visually rendering the gods' musical performances, the images link the musical activities of mortals to those of the gods, so that music-making becomes a shared activity between them. Music is thus established as a point of contact between these groups, a common endeavor to which both humans and gods devote themselves, even if the spaces and occasions in which music is performed differs between them. Second, as visual representations of the gods, the images are capable of communicating the presence of the divine to their human viewers. Broadly, within the context of Archaic and Classical religion, the *eikōn*, literally the icon, of a god acts both as an image of that divine being even as it also embodies the god's actual presence.[17] Although the significance of this double function of divine representations has been most fully explored with respect to cult statues and votive reliefs,[18] images painted onto the sides of vases should be understood similarly, so that the gods are not simply mythical characters in a narrative scene but, rather, they are also embodiments of divine presence.[19] Music and divine presence come together on the sides of the first vase we saw where, within the swirl of abstract patterns, palmettes, and foliage, there are two pairs of large eyes, staring directly out at their beholders (Fig. 0.5). Much work has been done on the significance of eyes on Greek vases, particularly with respect to so-called eye cups, where it has been argued that the eyes could have acted as a mask of a mythological creature or even a god, particularly during the symposium.[20] Although the patterns here seem, at first glance, to be primarily intended as mere ornament, the eyes that emerge from within their patterning suggest an awareness of the external viewer, who once moved around this vase, perhaps held it in his or her hands, and looked back at the eyes, meeting the vessel's gaze. We might even take the eyes as suggestive of the presence of the divine, so that the sounds of Apollo's music, so powerfully depicted on one side, have potentially made the god both aware of and available to his human audience. But we could also interpret the eyes as belonging to the vase itself, so that they act as extensions of the vessel, the clay and colored slip reaching out to engage with the viewer.[21] Though the vase is a work of art that features elaborate paintings on its body, it nevertheless acts on its viewers, looking at and acknowledging its audience members who listen simultaneously to Apollo's divine music and to the mortal kitharode's performance. The very material of the vase, together with its painted decoration, are thus essential to the work of mediating the visual sounds of music to the viewer and of blurring Apollo's music together with that of the mortal *kitharoidos* on the vase's other side.

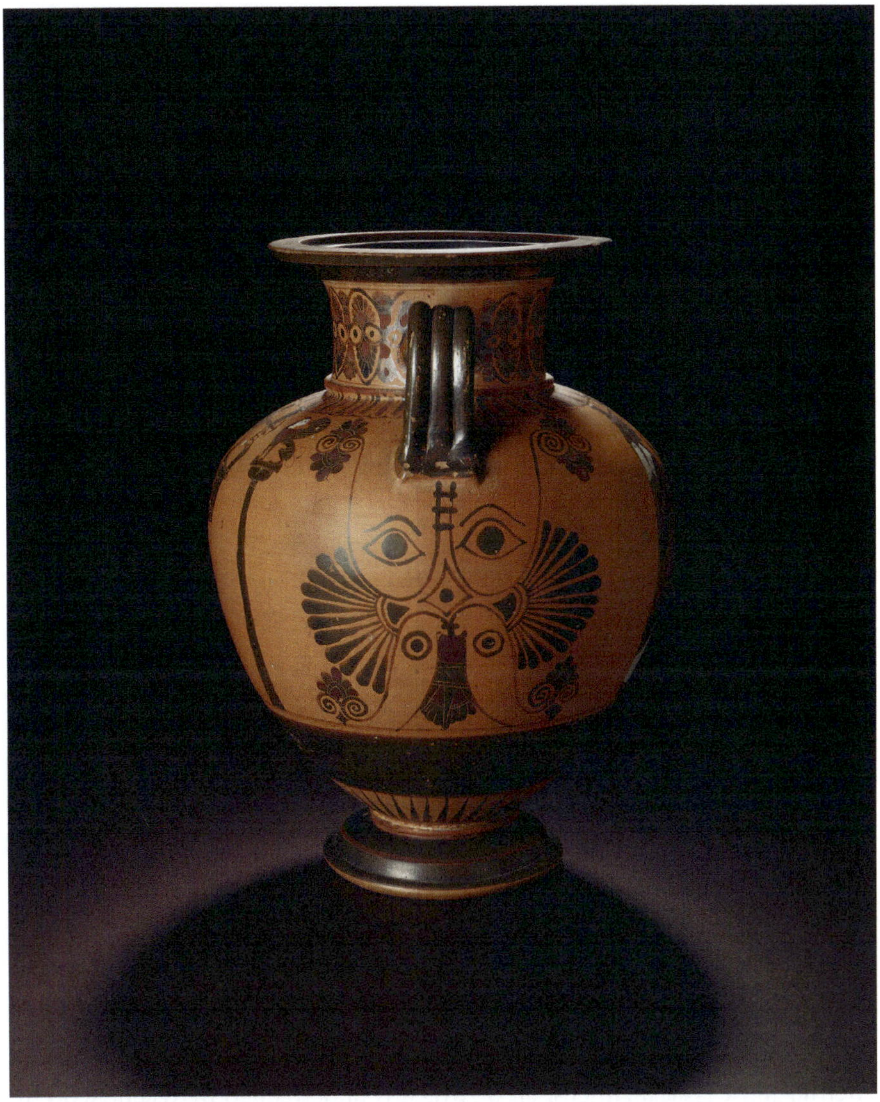

0.5. Side view. Possibly from the workshop of Group E, *Apollo Playing the Kithara Beside Artemis* (side A), *Kitharoidos Between Two Columns* (side B), Attic black-figure neck *amphora*, ceramic, h. 39.5 cm, *c.* 550 BCE. London, British Museum, 1843,1103.98 (B260). © The Trustees of the British Museum.

Moreover, in ascribing superlative musical skills to the gods, each image also offers a point of origin for the seemingly otherworldly effect that music can have on its audience.[22] Many of us have had those experiences where a piece of music can move us to tears, give us goosebumps, or cause the hairs on the back of our necks to stand up. Our bodies and emotions respond to music in such a way that is beyond our control – it is as if the music itself pulls these responses out of us as we lose ourselves to the melody. Throughout this book, I argue that it is precisely this powerful and profound effect that music can have that was believed to have been caused by the gods, so that each bodily response ancient viewers experienced when they encountered representations of divine music could have been further understood as experiencing the felt presence of the gods themselves. Within this framework, then, I suggest that the point of contact between human and divine music-making is not simply their shared engagement with musical practices. Rather, each image suggests that divine presence may be felt in those moments of extreme physical and emotional response to the visual depiction of music.

MUSIC, THE VISUAL, AND THE SENSES

How can we see sound? And, even more, how can we see, hear, and experience divine sound? These questions are at the heart of this book, that is, how these Archaic and Classical images of divine music invited their viewers not only to see the gods' performances, but to imaginatively hear them as well. In their absence of audible sound, scenes of divine music represent the opposite phenomenon to acousmatic sound, or sound without a visual referent.[23] Instead, the images are stubbornly silent, despite their evocative depictions of music-making and appreciation. How then are we, or were ancient viewers, meant to glimpse the sounds of these divine performances? Given the sheer number of Archaic and Classical scenes that feature representations of divine music, it would seem that there was clearly some sense that not only did the gods play music for themselves, but that it was possible for the men and women who saw these images to experience, in one way or another, the sounds created by the gods.

To analyze how images of divine music communicate their embedded musical sounds and how ancient viewers might have responded when confronted with these scenes, I work within a methodology that brings together close formal analysis with the poetry, physical contexts, and musical culture of Archaic and Classical Athens, all of which is underpinned by recent work in sensory studies, with respect to both the ancient and modern worlds. Building upon Richard Neer's formalism, where "images and texts produce meaning,"[24] and Verity Platt's claim that "the material stuff of antiquity can be most effectively yoked to the thinking and sensing body that inhabited it . . . if we believe that objects *mattered*,"[25] throughout this book I show how each image of a divine musician engaging in his or her craft visually evokes the sounds and effect of the god's music through the repetition of formal elements among the musicians, instruments, and audience. In other words, careful visual analysis offers a path by which to draw out the synesthetic experience, or as James Porter stresses, the *sun-aisthēsis*,[26] the conflated aesthetics, of sight and sound.

Let us return to the Nikoxenos Painter's *amphora* on which Apollo plays his *kithara* among the gods (Fig. 0.3). Here, the inclusion of the lyre aids in affirming Apollo's identity, as does his youthful appearance, his hairstyle, and his choice of divine and mythological companions. Attributes are a powerful tool for identifying gods and other mythological or heroic figures in Archaic and Classical Greek art, and indeed more broadly in Greco-Roman visual culture. This scene is no exception, and despite the absence of any inscriptions, we are still able to identify Apollo through his instrument, Dionysos through his *kantharos* and grape vines, and Hermes through his *syrinx*, winged boots, and hat. Here, however, as with all scenes of music-making, both human and divine, Apollo's intentional use of the instrument for his musical performance also imparts an impression of the musical sounds present in the image. As such, in depicting the god actively engaging in music-making, the image makes visible the sounds of his music, so that the structure and design of the composition together impart the rhythm, timbre, and affective quality inherent to the god's music. The aesthetic conflation of sight and sound thus manifests through the forms and shapes that the lines and curves make as they are rhythmically repeated across the surface of the vase or relief, coming together to create a unified musico-visual composition.

Images, in other words, can create visual soundscapes by asking their viewers to imagine the presence of sound. Throughout this book, I build upon the important work done on this topic, notably by James Porter, Tilman Seebass, and Dimitrios Yatromanolakis.[27] Whether addressing musical instruments or painted inscriptions, each has argued that the inclusion of these visual objects or words, as well as their placement within the composition, would have suggested specific sounds for the viewer. Let us look again at the divine celebration (Fig. 0.3) to see the consequences of this new way of seeing and listening to images, moving beyond noting the inclusion of inscriptions or instruments. Instead, we may see how the entire composition is structured in such a way as to indicate to the viewer that sound is present, is being heard, and is eliciting a powerful response. In the image, we see that the curving lines that constitute the body of Apollo's instrument are repeated in his tightly curled hair, in the sweep of his drapery as it wraps around his torso, and in the undulating forms that create his body. Similarly, vertical lines make up the arms and strings of the instrument, the god's hanging drapery, and even his tall, erect posture.[28] Apollo and his instrument are thus shown to be in harmony with each other, unified by the music they create together. We may also start to understand the effect that the god's music has on his audience: the bodies of Hermes, Dionysos, and the two maenads are also composed with similarly curving and straight lines, so that in addition to the attention they give to Apollo's performance, their very bodies are shown to be in tune with his music. Moreover, although the maenads turn their heads toward the gods on either side of the scene, their bodies and feet point toward Apollo, as if his music were physically drawing them in despite the other activities in which they are engaged. In isolating the particular representational mode associated with the sound of each god's musical performance, this and other images impart to their human viewers a sense of the sonic quality, or the "sonic persona" as Timothy Powers terms it,[29] that is associated with the sounds of each god's music, whether it is Apollo's rhythmic and harmonious performances, the Muses' unifying and inspiring chorality, Dionysos' ecstatic revelry, or Pan's piped melody that echoes off of cave walls.

In communicating sound visually, an aesthetic tension emerges between the evocative visual depiction of each god's performance and what I call the "unhearable" sound that divine music possesses for the human audience. Unlike manmade music, when the musician is Apollo, the Muses, Dionysos, or Pan, the sounds of the gods' music cannot be physically heard by a human audience, but must instead be provided by the imagination in response to external phenomena. The conditions that might make it possible to hear the sounds of divine music rarely manifest; only in moments of profound ritual choral performance do the ancient sources suggest that a communal musical and danced performance might begin to evoke the presence of the gods. The *Homeric Hymn to Apollo* presents one such instance, where the Cretans perform a paean with Apollo, who leads their procession. This event, however, is remarkable in the surviving literature, and, importantly, it is set in a mythic and heroic time where such interactions with the gods were believed to have been possible.[30] Crucially, these physical experiences of divine presence seem to have been restricted to the mythological past; in the historical period, it was precisely the growing distance between men and women and their gods that rendered epiphanies so powerful and striking.[31] Moreover, the visual material, in contrast with the episode from the *Homeric Hymn to Apollo*, rarely, if ever, shows men and women playing their instruments together with the gods, further demarcating the distance between the two. This remoteness inherent to divine music marks an essential point of difference between images of the gods' music, which cannot be easily heard, and scenes of human music-making, which depict performances that could potentially be experienced by men and women in the home, the theater, the sanctuary, or in other public gatherings. As a result, there exists a palpable tension between the visual medium in which the gods' performances were rendered and the implied sounds of divine music that we, as the audience, are meant to hear. Throughout this book, I argue that representations of the gods playing their instruments were so powerful precisely because they offered a path by which to experience divine presence.

In examining of scenes of divine music, I look beyond that which is purely visual, that is, the god's performance, and instead I bring to the fore each image's suggestion of imaginary sound, a tantalizing visual hint of the texture of each god's music and the manner in which it may have been perceived by an ancient viewer.[32] We find similar discussions of perception among the Presocratics, most notably on the role of music in creating harmony within the bodies of its listeners, and in aligning those harmonic bodies with the cosmos.[33] Herakleitos, for instance, claims that sensory experience is essential for facilitating knowledge, while Parmenides suggests that sense perception can, when paired with the ability to think and understand, offer human beings the potential to grasp the truth of the cosmos within their imaginative minds.[34] Later in the fourth century BCE, Aristotle, drawing in part on the earlier work of the Presocratics, developed a theory of the senses and perception in *De anima* and *De sensu*.[35] In *De anima* in particular, Aristotle posits that both the human subject and the external object are agents in the process of perception. The object emanates sensory emissions, be it through sight, sound, taste, touch, or smell, that travel through the medium of air, to the individual, who then actively perceives these sensory emissions with his or her own body.[36] Human subjects further enhance their perception through their *phantasia*, the process by which they contribute any previous general knowledge of the object and the manner in which one might perceive it, creating effectively a blended perception that brings together both real and imagined sensation.[37] For instance, when encountering an image of a *kithara*, the viewer is prompted to recall or to imagine those sounds that are generated by the instrument. It is through this system of passive and active modes of viewing that the Greek experience of visualized sound is made intelligible.

We may also see a similar blending of sensations – and especially of sight and sound – in the technical vocabulary used in the sixth and fifth centuries for the visual arts and musical theory. *Rhythmos*, for instance, denotes so much more than our modern 'rhythm': as I discuss more fully in Chapter 3, rather than noting simply the regular pacing and tempo of a melody, in the late sixth and fifth centuries BCE, *rhythmos* was used more specifically to describe a form, that is, an individual component of an object or a musical composition.[38] Similarly, various technical terms are especially rich, such as *poikilia*, which refers to beautifully crafted objects that entice their viewers through variegated surfaces that are particularly animated by the vibration, gleaming, and shivering of light.[39] Moreover, as LeVen notes with respect to *poikilia*, it was used for both visual and aural phenomena, so that the two sensory perceptions are conflated and confused in order to offer an especially vibrant and evocative description.[40] Music, therefore, was not simply a powerfully affective medium in Archaic and Classical Greece, but it was also one that spilled over into other modes of perception, and especially into the visual and kinesthetic, so that it could be heard, or felt, not only with the listeners' ears, but also with their eyes, their bodies, and their minds.

In suggesting that the visual arts in Archaic and Classical Athens could provoke a range of auditory sensations in their viewers, I inevitably draw upon my own sensory responses to the objects, anchoring my analyses in how I, as a perceiving and sensing agent, experience the sweep of Apollo's *plektron* as it glides across the lyre's strings, or the Muses' choral performance, or Pan's piped melody. While my sensory responses to these representations are my own, they are both grounded in the formal compositions offered by the images themselves and in our current scholarly understanding of the vibrant musical culture that characterized ancient Athens. As Betts acknowledges in a recent volume on phenomenological approaches to Roman culture, a methodology that engages with sensory studies "has the capacity to acknowledge the inevitability of subjectivity whilst aiming to record sensations, emotions, and experiences objectively within that caveat [of potential] interpretations."[41] For Betts, and generally for the phenomenological study of ancient material culture, "a core principle of sensory archaeologies and histories must therefore be to make clear where imagination, simulation, or cognitive techniques have been used in order to gain an insight into the subject of study."[42] Moreover, following D'Angour, "the musical sounds to which [the Athenians] sang and danced . . . need not wholly bypass the taste and musical understanding of modern observers and listeners."[43] This approach, which posits that it is possible for us to gain an understanding of how music could affect ancient listeners, necessarily involves the sensing bodies of the viewers, since both music and art are experienced by and felt in one's physical body, as further noted by both D'Angour and Porter.[44]

Such an approach also requires us to be aware of the spaces in which these images were encountered, since they too would have had a profound effect on the ancient viewer's experience of divine music. The importance of context for the interpretation of ancient music has received much attention recently, and is so fundamental to any interpretation of the importance of music in Greek antiquity that studies are broadly categorized according to where and how music was performed.[45] However, images of divine music are not simply mimetic representations of performances that occurred in the theater or at a sanctuary; rather, as visual renditions of the gods' musical activities, the representations are necessarily tied to where and how ancient viewers could have encountered them. The range of original contexts is particularly broad, especially for the vases I consider in Chapters 2–5, and includes the domestic sphere and associated areas, the symposium and the subsequent revel outdoors, the cemetery and the grave, and the religious sanctuary. In his seminal volume on the Greek symposium, for instance, François Lissarrague positioned vase-paintings within that powerfully evocative space, so that the images and inscriptions that adorned their sides collectively establish the closely linked sensory apparatus that Greek artists developed between image and space.[46] Thus, expanding upon Lissarrague's work, we should consider the possibility that the sensations displayed in an image could invoke or expand upon similar sensations present in the object's context of use.

The particular location in which these images were encountered mattered for the effect they could have on their audience: we need only think of how we ourselves act differently in distinct spaces to understand how profoundly an image's context could determine how it might act upon its viewers. A crucial component of my approach, therefore, is the image's ability to interact with its viewer, a process of engagement that may be amplified by the context in which the image was encountered and by the content of the composition itself. We are able to say something about the contexts in which these objects were seen and used because of the inherent functionality of both vases and relief sculpture. With respect to Athenian ceramics, each vase was shaped into a specific form that was tied to a correspondingly specific task, so that its very shape assumes that the vase was used, or at least that it had the potential to be used, within certain contexts, such as the domestic sphere, the symposium, the sanctuary, or the cemetery. As physical, three-dimensional objects, vases could be picked up, carried from one place to another, stacked one on top of the other, or set up to be displayed. Votive reliefs, by contrast, were less mobile, not least because the marble with which they were created did not lend itself to easy transport. Moreover, their function was, above all, to be dedicated and set up on display within a sanctuary, so that even as they offered a profoundly sacred experience to their viewers, the sites of these encounters remained relatively stable. Both ceramics and reliefs, however, could nevertheless be moved and relocated at any given time. Vases could be easily shifted between their initial Athenian context and the Etruscan or South Italian tombs in which they were later discovered. Marble reliefs also traveled, especially in the Roman period, when they were often exported to Rome where they could be set up primarily as aesthetic art objects in elite villas. Viewers, then, could have experienced these objects in multiple contexts. However, that the vases and reliefs were created by Athenian artists, potentially with an Athenian audience in mind, suggests that they can be studied both in their Athenian context and in their later Italian landscape.[47] I have thus proceeded from the hypothesis that considerations of the vases and reliefs within the sphere of Archaic and Classical Athenian life and within the later Etruscan or Roman context in which they were discovered are equally valid for the scope of this study and represent different aspects of their lives as objects.[48]

In foregrounding the importance of the object and its contexts, I work within a methodology that posits the possibility of recovering how the visual arts could provoke a range of aesthetic and religious responses in ancient viewers and, in turn, how these responses were tied to the ritual, political, or social spaces in which the objects were encountered.[49] Crucial to this model of interaction and viewer response is my understanding of images of the gods as being evidence of ancient worshippers' engagement with the divine as well as acting as visual tools by which to shape and determine the nature of that ritual interaction.[50] Timothy Power adopts a similar framework in his exploration of the connection between music and religious contexts. Music, he argues, should be situated "as a material presence within the lived acoustic experience of cult, as ritualized sound which, alongside other, non-musical sounds, makes certain psychological and even physical impressions upon the worshippers who perform and listen to it."[51] Following Power, then, sound – and music more specifically – should be considered an integral element in the worshippers' experience of cult activity, essential for ensuring the perceived ritual success of the worshippers' actions.[52] We should take a similar approach to our images of divine music, which consistently offer their viewers the possibility for experiencing the sounds of the gods' music, even as the nature of that experience could change depending on where the image was encountered. Given the variety of musical affects offered by the ancient contexts in which vases and reliefs were seen and used, I work between the sensory experiences offered by the images themselves, the physical spaces in which these images may once have been seen, and the musical culture that so pervaded ancient Athens, as well as more broadly within Greek culture generally. In putting the evidence gained from each of these sources – visual, archaeological, literary, and philosophical – together in productive dialogue, throughout this book I establish a network of interaction between the viewer, the visualized music, and the landscape, all of which determined how divine music was depicted, imaginarily perceived, and even reciprocated.

It is especially within particularly evocative contexts that I show that the ancient viewers' sensory experiences of images of divine musicians were associated with music's almost otherworldly power over its audience, capable of moving them to extreme states of emotion. Images of musical performance thus facilitate encounters between human and divine in a similar way as described by Verity Platt with respect to visual encounters with representations or poetic descriptions of the divine.[53] Throughout her study on epiphany in Greco-Roman culture, Platt argues that depictions of the gods allowed viewers to comprehend the image not just symbolically as a visual representation, but also as the epiphanic presence of the divine. Images thus played an essential role in mediating between human and divine: not only did they depict successful scenes of ritual, but they also presented the image of the god to the worshippers, giving them another point of access to the divine for whom they performed their rituals. I expand upon Platt's theoretical model to address visual representations of sound, and more specifically of divine sound, ultimately arguing that the scenes of divine musicians invited their viewers to hear imaginatively the sounds of the music through each act of looking. In positing the importance of music as a mediating force between human and divine, I also draw from studies that explore the relationship between divine epiphany in the performance of hymns within ritual, particularly with respect to the commonalities shared between surviving texts and visual representations.[54] As such, I work between the human performance of hymnic song and the divine audience for whom the hymns were sung, ultimately establishing a network of participation between human and divine that is mediated by music.[55] In bringing together these divergent approaches, throughout this book I show that images of divine musicians ask their audiences to participate in the manifestation of the divine through their sensory engagement with the musical and visual representations of the gods' performances.

THE LIMITS OF HUMAN AND DIVINE MUSIC

Although representations of both human and divine music-making cannot be taken as simple reproductions of reality, they nevertheless offer a glimpse into how the Athenians perceived and depicted their musical culture, as well as how they conceived of their gods as engaging in similar actions. Nevertheless, important distinctions exist between each group's musical activities, and these differences have, I suggest, specific consequences for how divine music was

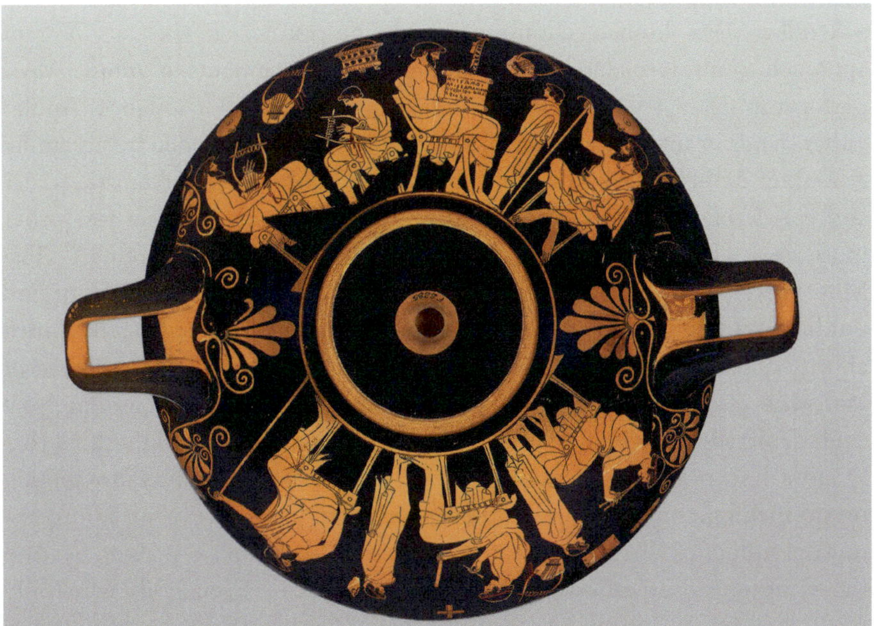

0.6. Douris, *School Scene* (sides A, B), Attic red-figure *kylix*, ceramic, h. 11.5 cm, d. 28.5 cm, *c.* 490–480 BCE. Berlin, Antikensammlung, F 2285. bpk Bildagentur/Antikensammlung / Johannes Laurentius/Art Resource, NY.

represented, perceived, and experienced by the human audience. Above all, scenes of the gods engaging in musical practice suggest that these divine activities were often imagined and depicted as distinct in form and appearance from those of human men and women. Such a delineation between human and divine music finds a compelling parallel in the clear distinction that existed, as Ford notes, between specific genres, where "songs to the gods belonged to a separate category from songs for mortals."[56] Expanding upon Bundrick's categorization of the contexts in which music-making was depicted on Classical vases,[57] we can say that while both human and god play the same instruments, they do so in dramatically different contexts, with little overlap between the locations, styles, and audiences of their performances. Young men are often shown learning to play the *aulos* and the lyre in school scenes, where they are taught by older men who have already mastered their instruments (Fig. 0.6).[58] Both young and mature men may also play the *kithara* and *aulos* on a low stage, possibly suggesting that they perform in musical competitions held during religious festivals (Fig. 0.7).[59] Women, for their part, play a similarly wide range of instruments, including the *barbitos* lyre, the *aulos*, various types of harps, and *krotala*. Moreover, regardless of their social status or profession, women seem to perform predominantly indoors, whether in domestic or symposium scenes (Fig. 0.8).[60] They do, however, occasionally accompany men outdoors when they play music as part of the *kōmos* procession that often followed a symposium.

Unlike their human counterparts, divine musicians take a different approach to music-making and often play their instruments in unique ways, perform in distinct spaces, and for different audiences. For instance, Apollo either stands or sits still while he plays his lyre, often surrounded by his family and other deities, as we saw at the beginning of this introduction (Figs. 0.1 and 0.3).[61] He can even play his instrument one-handed, a feat few other musicians, whether human or divine, are rarely shown attempting.[62] The Muses play a vast array of instruments in similarly wide-ranging indoor and outdoor settings, where they may perform either alone or together in a chorus (Fig. 0.9).[63] Perhaps the most stark distinction is with the figure of Pan, who plays his pipes in his cave, whereas men and women are rarely, if ever, depicted playing music of any kind in such a space. We might think that Dionysian scenes of music would offer the closest parallel to human sympotic music-making, but even here there are clear differences, for Dionysos' musical influence also spills over to determine ecstatic music-making beyond the symposium, in otherwise indeterminate spaces. Even gods who only rarely pick up an instrument, such as Athena, Eros, or Nike, play in distinct ways from human musicians, whether by striding powerfully toward an altar with a large *kithara* (Fig. 0.10)[64] or flying next to the scene singing while playing a *tympanon*.[65]

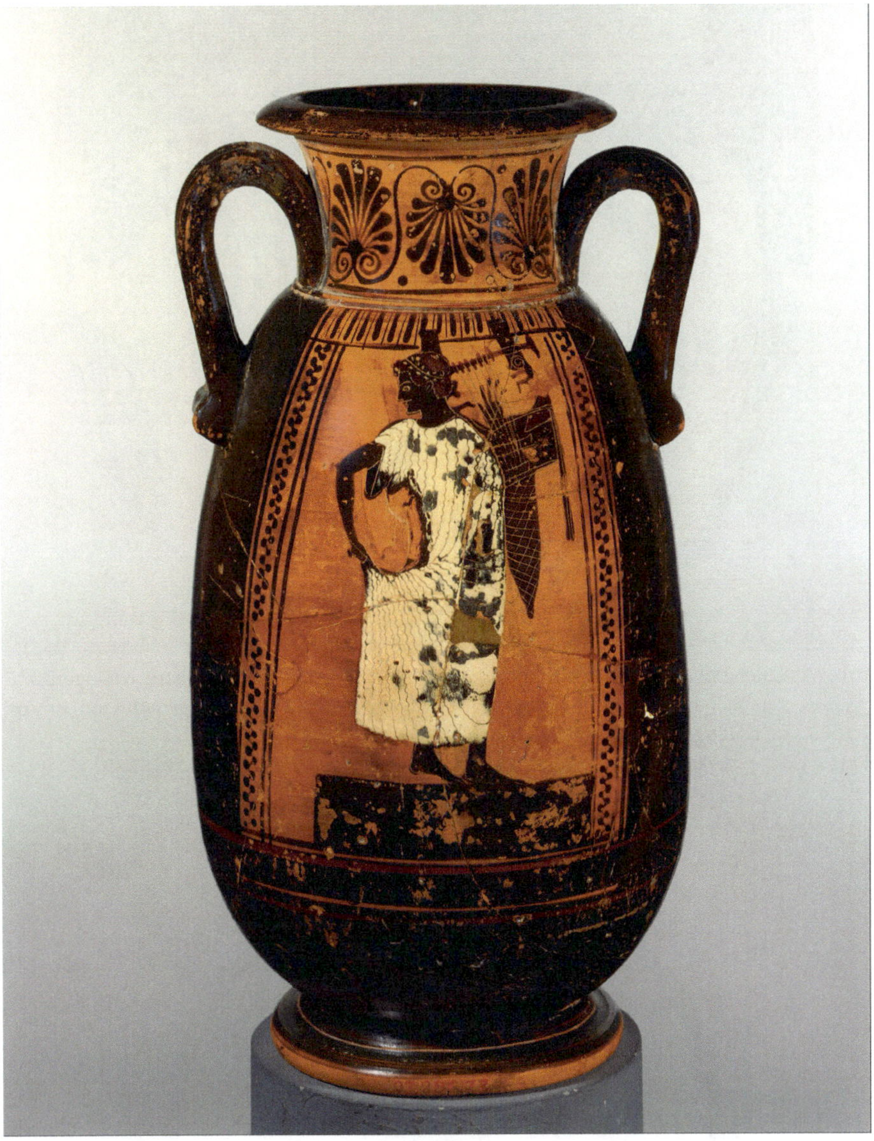

0.7. *Musical Contests* (sides A, B), Attic black-figure neck *pelikē*, ceramic, 26.7 x 15.3 cm, *c.* 500 BCE. New York, Metropolitan Museum, 07.286.72. Rogers Fund, 1907. Creative Commons CCO.

The character of each type of music and the training it required also seems to differ between humans and gods. Both literary and visual sources attest to the importance of musical education within Athenian society, where it was one of the essential elements in Athenian *paideia*, that is, the combination of training in *gymnastikē* and *mousikē*, which consisted of music, song, and choral dance.[66] Given *paideia*'s importance in the late Archaic and early Classical periods, it is not surprising that students are regularly described in literary texts

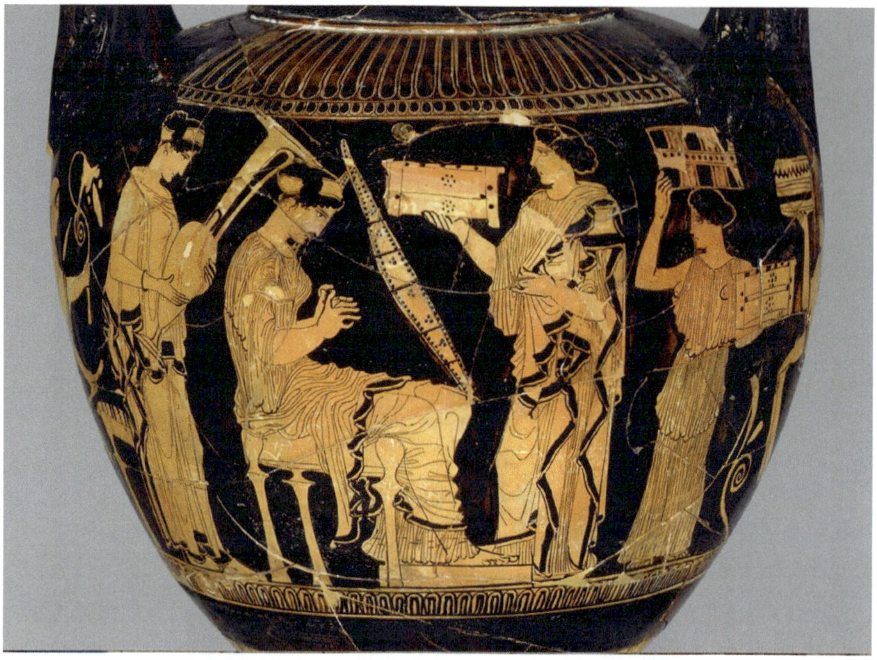

0.8. Attributed to the Washing Painter, *Seated Bride Playing an Instrument*, Attic red-figure *lebēs gamikos*, ceramic, h. 51.1cm, *c.* 430–420 BCE. New York, Metropolitan Museum of Art, 07.286.35a, b. Rogers Fund, 1907. Creative Commons CCO.

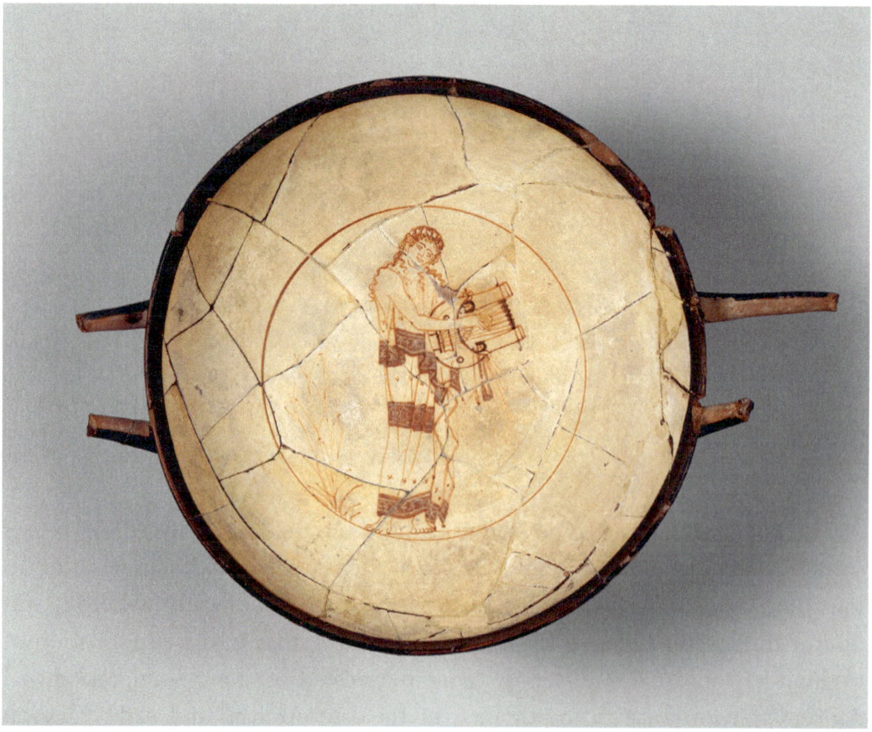

0.9. The Hesiod Painter, *Standing Muse Playing the Phorminx*, Attic white-ground stemless *kylix*, ceramic, h. 3.6 cm, d. 15 cm, *c.* 470–460 BCE. Paris, Musée du Louvre, CA 483. Photo: Hervé Lewandowski. © RMN-Grand Palais/Art Resource, NY.

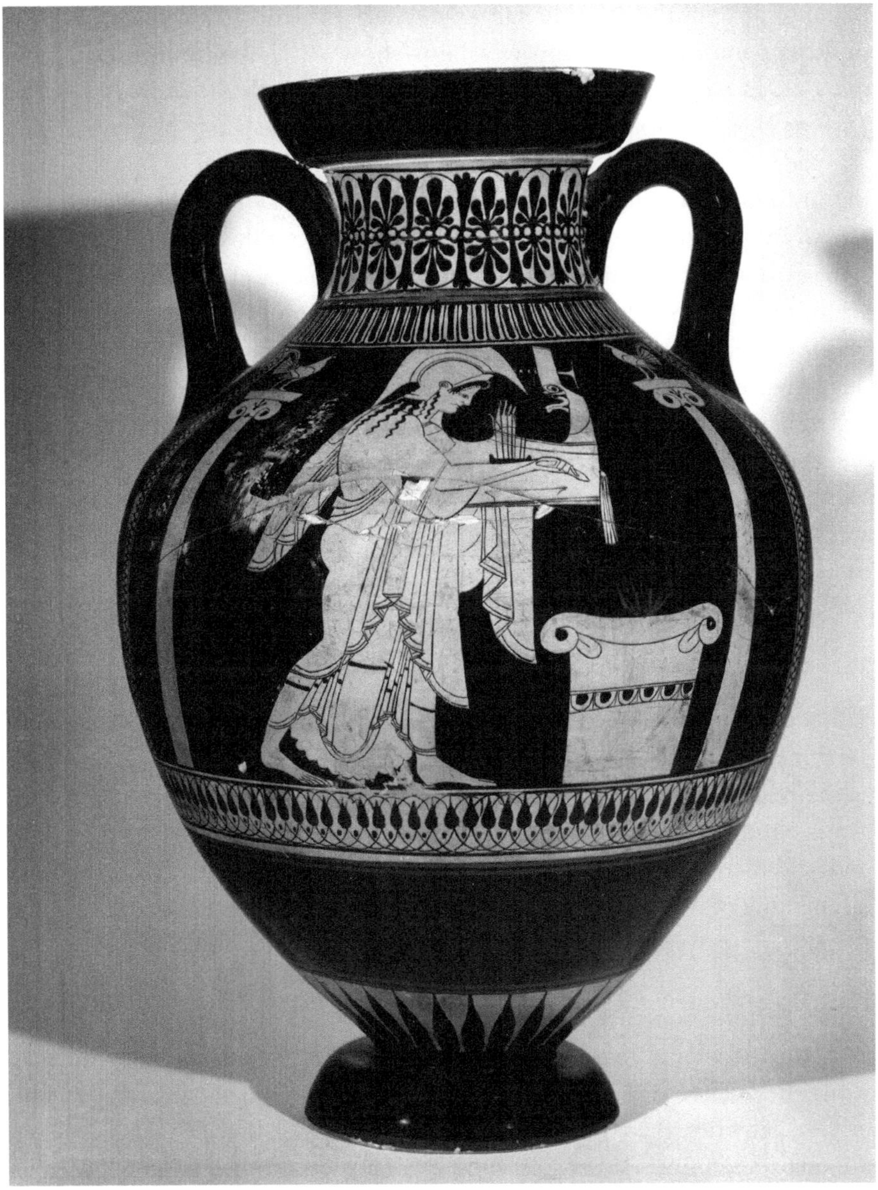

0.10. The Nikoxenos Painter, *Athena with Kithara* (side A), Attic red-figure *amphora* in a Panathenaic shape, ceramic, 39.9 x 26.2 x 26.2 cm, *c.* 500 BCE. Berlin, Antikensammlung, Preussischer Kulturbesitz, F 2161. bpk Bildagentur/Antikensammlung/Art Resource, NY.

and depicted in the visual arts with their teacher, learning to play their instruments, to sing poetry, and to dance together in a chorus.[67] The gods, however, have a different relationship with their music: absent from Archaic and early Classical literature and images of divine musicians is the emphasis on the musical education and training that is so crucial for human music-making. Indeed, the gods seem to have no need for instruction, practice, or regular training, and instead both literary and visual evidence shows them as fully proficient musicians who innately know how to play beautiful music. For instance, in recounting Hermes' first performance with the *chelys* lyre in the *Homeric Hymn to Hermes* (54–64), the young god immediately plays music that is superlatively beautiful while he sings a hymn, even though he only invented the instrument moments before. Later in the hymn, when Hermes gives his lyre to Apollo with the statement that he will "learn it this very day" (σήμερον εἰδήσεις, 466), Apollo instead is immediately capable of playing the instrument with great skill. Similarly, there are no representations of Apollo learning to play the lyre; rather, he is shown as a skillful *kitharoidos*, as we have seen above, delighting his divine companions with his music.[68] Although ancient literary and visual sources regularly speak to the importance of Athenian *paideia*, what seems clear is that divine musicians play their music entirely outside of this social structure. In its absence of training, different contexts of performance, and superlative quality of sound, divine music-making is, at every stage, shown to be fundamentally distinct from human musical practices.

THE GODS, THEIR MUSIC, AND THE VISUAL ARTS

The surviving visual material thus presents a full and rich picture of the gods' enjoyment of music, a claim that is supported by Hesiod's *Theogony*, in which, as the poet makes clear, the gods love music. The Muses dance as a chorus across Mount Helicon, singing beautiful songs that recount the histories of gods and men alike. Zeus delights in the songs sung by his nine daughters. And it is because of Apollo that, together with the Muses, men and women learned to sing and play music.[69] Such emphasis on the gods' proclivity for music abounds in the visual arts, where Apollo plays his lyre to Artemis and Leto, the Muses perform together as a chorus, Pan pipes on his *syrinx* while Hermes leads three dancing Nymphs forwards, or satyrs play both the lyre and *aulos* while they dance with Dionysos. Despite their shared emphasis on the gods' musical activities, there is nevertheless a felt difference between the visual and the textual accounts, so that the visual evidence cannot be explained solely in terms of the literary narratives.[70] There is nothing inherently conclusive in the literary narratives themselves that makes them a sure guarantee that Hermes and Apollo may both be associated with the lyre, that Hermes and Pan are each linked with the *syrinx*, and that satyrs must necessarily use the *aulos*. Moreover, if the visual record does show something different, such as Dionysos watching a satyr play the *kithara* or the Muses playing the *aulos*, these differences cannot be rejected as a failure to portray the true story about each mythical figure. Within the association of certain gods with specific instruments, it becomes possible to identify specific gods through their representation, much as we did with Apollo earlier, where his lyre acts as a marker of his divine persona.

But even more than establishing identity, the inclusion of instruments within scenes of divine musicians adds an affective dimension to the visual image in their association with musical sounds. It is precisely this affective element inherent to representations of divine musicians that I examine throughout this book.

Given the cultural, religious, and historical frameworks in which I discuss the creation of scenes of divine music as well as the range of possible responses to them, I restrict my corpus to painted vases or sculpted reliefs that were made in Athens and Attica during the Archaic and Classical periods. I further restrict my focus to representations of those gods who are the most frequently depicted engaging in musical activities, namely Apollo, the Muses, Dionysos, and Pan. I do not discuss those gods who are less commonly shown playing an instrument, such as Hermes, who may occasionally play a *syrinx* and, less frequently still, a *chelys* lyre; similarly, Eros, Nike, and Athena are not examined.

Working within these parameters, my argument develops over five chapters, which are each devoted to a distinct style of music performed by a specific god, focusing on the divine "sonic persona" they each exhibit.[71] The book begins by examining a specific space in which images of divine music were displayed: the Attic cave shrines sacred to Pan and the Nymphs. Here, votive reliefs featuring Pan's music-making and the Nymphs' choral dance were once displayed throughout the rocky, subterranean landscapes, offering us a tantalizing glimpse into how the sounds of the god's music were made visible as well as how they potentially affected the ancient audience. Represented on reliefs that evoke the physical caves in which they were displayed, Pan's music not only inspires the Nymphs' *choreia*, but also reaches out to involve the worshippers, inviting them to participate in the musical and danced performance. Having thus established divine music's rich potential to engage with its human viewers in particularly evocative contexts, I turn to similar scenes of the musical gods that were painted onto ceramics, a medium that often lacks a specific context in the ancient world largely because it was a more portable and versatile object. I begin with scenes of Apollo in order to explore the typical characteristics and modes of representing divine music within the visual vocabulary of painted vases. In Chapter 2, I focus on images where Apollo plays his lyre while he also pours a libation, in order to isolate each gesture and thus determine how these scenes communicated Apollo's music-making. In their suggestion of coordinated visual and musical rhythms, I discuss how Apollo's music could have been perceived within the context of the elite symposium. Chapter 3 also looks at Apollo, but focuses on the god as a masterful *kithara* player. By determining how divine music could be conveyed in a visual medium, I bring together terms shared between the discourses of ancient music theory and art criticism, such as *rhythmoi*, *symmetria*, and *harmonia*. In considering these terms together with the elite sympotic contexts in which these objects were encountered, I examine how ancient viewers in Athens could have physically responded to the sounds of Apollo's orderly music. Moving beyond an elite, male sympotic setting, in Chapter 4 I turn to the Muses, the goddesses responsible for inspiring music and poetry, in order to investigate how ancient viewers' interactions with scenes of divine music were dramatically altered depending on the various contexts in which the goddesses and their music were experienced. I end with Dionysos, returning once again to the symposium. Dionysos' mode of performance is unique among the gods I consider: the god himself rarely plays an instrument. Instead, he seems to inspire those around him to take up their own instruments, eliciting a wild, erratic response to the sounds of that music. As such, when considered within the musically infused and intoxicated world of the symposium, representations of this god offered his human viewers the opportunity to respond with their own bodies to the music, ultimately losing themselves in the wild revel.

This is, above all, a book about divine music, but it is just as much about the human viewers who once experienced the gods performing, whether by seeing images of divine music, imaginatively hearing its beautiful and at times seductive sounds, reciprocating with their own music-making, or even responding to the sounds through an embodied dance. When put into dialogue with the continued efforts made throughout Athens during the Archaic and Classical periods to paint and sculpt the gods engaging in musical practice, the range of experiences offered by the images are lasting testaments to the profound effect such images could have. Moreover, not only are divine musicians continuously represented in the visual arts, but they operated within a culture filled with musical hymns, choral dances, and festival performances, all experiences that constituted so much of Athenian public and private life. Within the musical life of the city of Athens, images of divine music-making mediated the interaction between human and divine, and did so by positioning music as a shared activity between the two, a practice that each could engage in, experience, and enjoy. Ultimately, the human experience of participating in the gods' musical performances offered worshippers a point of contact with the gods even as it established bonds among viewers through their shared act of venerating the divine.

NOTES

1 *BAPD* 7848; *LIMC* s.v. Apollon no. 668a; Walters 1928: III.He.9, pl. 654.1A–C; Shapiro 1992: 65–66.

2 The costume of the professional *kitharoidos* consisted of the *epiporpama*, which was a long robe, highly decorated, and fastened at the shoulders with a brooch. On *kitharoidia*, see generally Power 2010.

3 Rainer Maria Rilke, *An die Musik*, 1–3. "Music: breathing of statues. Perhaps: | Silence of paintings. You language where all language | ends." Translated by Mitchell 1989: 146–47.

4 Plut. *De glor. Ath.* 3; *Mor.* 347a. For further discussion, see Sprigath 2004: 243–80; Männlein-Robert 2007: 20–22; Squire 2016b: 12, 18–19.

5 For more on the song culture of ancient Athens, see especially Herington 1985.

6 Bundrick 2005: 2–3.

7 For more on musical education, see Hagel and Lynch 2015: 401–12; Laferrière 2023.

8 This reorganization may have been in response to similar efforts made to incorporate musical contests at the Pythian Games at Delphi around 586 BCE. Shapiro 1989: 1–16, and especially 48–59; Bundrick 2005: 7–8; Power 2010: 440.

9 As noted by Butler and Nooter 2019: 1–2.

10 Walters 1928: 654.1A–C; Shapiro 1992: 65–66.

11 *BAPD* 202095; Lullies 1956: 19–20, pls. (556–59, 66) 178.1–2, 79.1–2, 80.1–2, 81.1–2, 88. 8; *ARV*^{2} 220.1; *Paralipomena* 346; Beazley 1925: 91.1, 469; *Beazley Addenda* 98; *Beazley Addenda*^{2} 198; Furtwängler and Reichhold 1904–32: pl. 158; Simon 1969: 31, fig. 20; Paquette 1984: 67, S4; Haas 1985: 150, figs. 13–13A; Maas and Snyder 1989: 78; Shapiro 1989: pl. 64A; Vierneisel and Kaesar 1990: 367, 436; Le Dinahet and Étienne 1991: pl. 78E.

12 Frontal faces are much discussed throughout this book. In general, important work on frontal figures in ancient art has been carried out by Korshak 1987; Frontisi-Ducroux 1995; Mackay 2001; Mack 2002; Hedreen 2007: 217–46; Hedreen 2017: 154–87. I also follow Meyer Schapiro's argument (1973, 38f.) that these frontal faces actively look at their viewers.

13 For more on the complexities surrounding maenads, see Chapter 5.

14 *Hymn. Hom. Merc.* 512.

15 The *kithara* was fundamentally a performance instrument and seems to have been played only by highly trained musicians in competitions or public performances. The *syrinx*, by contrast, was a shepherd's instrument, formed out of reeds and played to soothe the flocks. Despite their different contexts of use, see Weiss' discussion (2018: 212–24) of the third stasimon in Euripides' *IA*, where the *kithara* and *syrinx* are played together, along with the Libyan *lōtos* (pipe).

16 I discuss the importance of objects breaking through the frame throughout this volume. For more on frames in ancient art, see Hurwit 1977: 1–30; Platt and Squire 2017c; Marconi 2017: 117–53.

17 Vernant 1985a; Vernant 1985b; Vernant 1990; Platt 2011: 119–23.

18 In addition to Platt's important 2011 volume on epiphany, which explores the significance of images' double function, see also Donohue 1997.

19 Although the images of the gods are necessarily smaller when they are depicted upon vases, I follow Vernant (1985a; 1985b) in asserting that variations of size are an essential characteristic of divine images.

20 On the significance of the eyes painted onto cups, see especially Hedreen 2007; Squire 2016b: 20–25; Grethlein 2016; Neer 2019: 8–10. Bundrick (2015) has argued that Etruscan tombs were the primary archaeological context for many of the eye cups.

21 On materiality and Greek vases, see Gaifman and Platt 2018; Gaifman 2018b.

22 On the relationship between music's effect on the body and the social act inherent to listening to music, see especially Bicknell 2009. On the connection between memory and musical effect, see Curtis and Weiss 2021.

23 On acousmatic sound, see especially Kane 2014.

24 Neer 2002: 7.

25 Platt 2016: 74.

26 Porter 2010: 45–47; Porter 2013.

27 Porter 2010: 405–50; Seebass 2011; Porter 2013; Yatromanolakis 2016.

28 For a more general study on the repetition of specific compositional elements across vases, see Steiner 2007, as well as a nuanced critique of her work in Squire 2009: 86–87 and *BMCR* 2007.11.19.

29 Power 2018: 24.

30 For more on this episode in the *Homeric Hymn to Apollo*, see Olsen 2019: 327–34.

31 On epiphanies in Greco-Roman religious culture, see Platt 2011; Petridou 2015.

32 For a similar approach, see generally Grethlein 2017: 191–248.

33 Seaford 2013: 18, 26, 31–33; Podlecki 2014: 1–3.

34 For example, DK 22B55; DK 28B4. For further discussion, see Curd 2013 and 2019.

35 For further discussion, see especially Griffith 2021.

36 Arist. *De an.* 419a, 425b–426b. On the discussion of the perception of sound in particular, see 419b–421a.

37 Arist. *De an.* 417a–418a, 419b. On perception and *aisthesis* in Aristotle, see especially Porter 2010: 99–102.

38 Pollitt 1974: 218–28.

39 Grand-Clément 2015: 407.

40 LeVen 2013: 231. On the aesthetic consequences related to *poikilia*, see Grand-Clément 2013; Grand-Clément 2015.

41 Betts 2017b: 195–96. For the practical implementation of this methodology, see, for example, Warford 2019.

42 Betts 2017b: 195–96. Apart from the substantial treatment of phenomenology in twentieth-century continental philosophy, the rise of sensory archaeology owes much to earlier discussions of phenomenology. See Fahlander and Kjellström 2010; Day 2013; Hamilakis 2013; Pellini, Zarankin, and Salerno 2015. Current work on the senses and material culture includes Betts 2017a, 2017b; Hamilakis and Meirion Jones 2017; Harris 2017; Hamilakis 2013: 6–12; Hamilakis 2017: 171–75; Laferrière 2019b. On the senses and classical antiquity more generally, see Butler and Purves 2013; Bradley 2015; Squire 2016a; Rudolph 2018; Purves 2018; Butler and Nooter 2019.

43 D'Angour 2019: 33.

44 Porter 2010: especially 435–40; D'Angour 2015.

45 A context-based approach to ancient music largely begins with Murray and Wilson 2004a. Subsequent studies have focused upon technical aspects of music theory and notation, particularly as they relate to actual performance techniques (e.g., Pöhlmann 1960; Pöhlmann 1976; West 1981; West 1982; West 1992; D'Angour 1997; Mathiesen 1999; D'Angour 2006; D'Angour 2007; Hagel 2009), the aesthetic appreciation of music in antiquity (see Porter 2010 in its entirety, as well as Peponi 2012; LeVen 2013; Budelmann and LeVen 2014; D'Angour 2015; Gurd 2016; Creese and Destrée forthcoming), a socio-cultural approach, examining music and poetry as they relate to the theater (see especially Kurke 2000; Peponi 2009; Power 2010; Bierl 2012; Nooter 2012; Kowalzig and Wilson 2013a; LeVen 2014; Weiss 2018), or more broadly within religious ritual (Nordquist 1991; 1992; Shapiro 1992; Kowalzig 2007b; Power 2018).

46 Lissarrague 1990b.

47 Indeed, the vessels' shape and imagery are consistent with the artistic styles and objects discovered in Athens, so that it is not inconceivable that some or many of the Attic vases discovered elsewhere in the Mediterranean were initially created with an Athenian audience in mind. On this issue, I generally follow Richard Neer, who states that "Attic vases were exported throughout the Mediterranean world … yet their iconography remained resolutely Athenian … indeed their exotic Hellenism seems to have been part of their value to Etruscan and other 'barbarian' consumers." Neer 2002: 9. Similarly, see Topper 2013: 11–12.

48 Tyler Jo Smith (2014c) clearly lays out the problems of working with Greek vases:

> The growing concern for the exact find-spot of each and every vessel has turned scholarship towards context and away from function. Inevitably, this makes problems for the vases, their decoration, and for us. How do we account for all those Athenian imports in Etruscan tombs, or indeed for those found in the Greek cities of Magna Graecia, or even those from the sanctuaries and cemeteries of nearby Corinth? Such questions loom against the backdrop of claims that Athenian vases reflect local social significance or home-grown psychological concerns. Vases travelled and so did their images.

For a similar approach, see Marconi 2004: 27–28. On the importance of studying vases within the context of their export, see Bundrick 2015; Langridge-Noti 2015; Bundrick 2019.

49 See especially Elsner 1996: 515–31; 2007; Gaifman 2008: 85–103; Platt 2010: 197–213; Platt 2011; Gaifman 2013: 39–52; Elsner 2017: 457–99; Gaifman 2018a.

50 Elsner 1996; Platt 2011; Gaifman 2016; Mack 2018.

51 Power 2018: 15. For more on lived experience within an ancient religious context, see Rüpke 2011; Raja and Rüpke 2015a; Raja and Rüpke 2015b; Rüpke 2016.

52 On the specific instruments shown in representations of religious ritual, see Nordquist 1992.

53 Platt 2011.

54 Peponi 2009: 39–70; Platt 2011; Kurke 2012; Kurke 2013b; Weiss 2018.

55 In this focus on human–divine interaction, my approach complements recent work by Manon Brouillet, in which she independently develops the argument that men and gods were co-participants in the performance of the epic narrative, so that the gods became present both through men's actions within the narrative and through the poet's performance of the epic. Brouillet 2016: especially 398–99, 435–38.

56 Ford 2011: 76. As Ford notes (74), in *Laws* 700A–E, "Plato fantasizes that in the good old days people regarded prayers to the gods as a distinct kind (*eidos*) of song and kept them apart from anything having to do with songs for mortals." Ford goes on to demonstrate that we may see a similar distinction between categories of song intended for gods and men in the fourth chapter of Aristotle's *Poetics*.

57 Bundrick 2005. This volume first categorizes fifth-century vase-paintings by instrument and then thematically by the specific Athenian social practice that is depicted, taking into account the social class or gender group that would have engaged in such activities.

58 *BAPD* 205092; *ARV*^{2} 426, 31.48, 1653; *Paralipomena* 374; *Beazley Addenda* 117; *Beazley Addenda*^{2} 237.

59 *BAPD* 2460; Becker 1977: 49, cat. 1393; West 1992: pl. 20; Christie's London, 28 April 1993, cat. 17; Bundrick 2005: 167. Cf. the *amphora* by the Pan Painter, New York 20.245, Richter and Hall 1936: no. 66, pl. 72; *ARV*^{2} 522.30; *Beazley Addenda*^{2} 257. On musical contests generally, see Shapiro 1992.

60 *BAPD* 214881; *ARV*^{2} 1126.1; *Paralipomena* 453; *Beazley Addenda*^{2} 332; Yatromanolakis 2007: 270; Bundrick 2005: 188–89, with previous bibliography.

61 *BAPD* 301790; *ABV* 331.12; *Beazley Addenda*^{2} 90; Walters 1928: III H e Pl. 64, 3.

62 To my knowledge, there are only two other examples where a musician plays an instrument while undertaking another task, one by the Berlin Painter and one by the Pan Painter. The first by the Berlin Painter is the name vase, where the satyr Orochares plays his *barbitos* and holds up a *kantharos* (*BAPD* 201809); the second, by the Pan Painter, is a fragmentary *amphora* of Panathenaic shape where Herakles holds a *kantharos* in his right hand while the left plays the *barbitos* (*BAPD* 41237).

63 *BAPD* 209556; *ARV*^{2}: 774.3; *Paralipomena*: 416; *Beazley Addenda*^{2}: 287; Pottier (1895); Wehgartner 1983: 72, no. 85; Queyrel 1992: no. 2; Robertson 1992: 180.

64 *BAPD* 202065; *ARV*^{2} 221.7; *Beazley Addenda* 98; *Beazley Addenda*^{2} 198; Demargne 1984: no. 585; Neils 2001: 148; Bundrick 2005: 20.

65 *BAPD* 218007; *ARV*^{2} 1414.18; *Paralipomena* 490; *Beazley Addenda*^{2} 375; Walters, Forsdyke, and Smith 1893: E129.

66 On *mousikē*, see especially Murray and Wilson 2004a and 2004b.

67 Hagel and Lynch 2015; Laferrière 2023.

68 For analysis of the structure and significance of the *Homeric Hymn to Hermes*, see Clay 2006. The hymn may be dated between the late sixth and early fourth centuries BCE: Kirk 1985: 74; to the late sixth century: Janko 1982: 133–50; Shelmerdine 1995; to the early fifth century: Radermacher 1931: 216, 222; Eitrem 1906: 282; to the seventh century: Allen, Halliday, and Sikes 1936: 275–76. Johnston (2002: 109) takes the chronological range from the late sixth to the early fifth as the most likely.

69 Hes. *Theog.* 1–11, 35–52, 63–67, 93–95.

70 Castaldo 2000: 5–9.

71 Power 2018: 24.

ONE

SCULPTING DIVINE MUSIC

Pan, the goat god child of Hermes, is a nimble musician, playing his *syrinx* as he jumps and leaps across the craggy mountainside, at least according to the *Homeric Hymn to Pan*. However, among the Greek gods associated with music and dance, Pan is not an immediately obvious figure to include. He appeared late to the Athenian pantheon, having apparently arrived from Arcadia within the broader context of the Persian Wars in the early fifth century BCE and, according to Herodotos, for this reason he seems to have been initially associated with torch races and sacrifices.[1] However, by the end of the fifth and beginning of the fourth century in Attica, Pan came to be depicted and described predominantly as a capable musician. He not only is described in the Homeric hymn as piping a tune in the rural countryside for the Nymphs who accompany him (5–18),[2] but in Athens there seems to have been considerable and deliberate effort put toward depicting Pan as a musician. It is especially on the series of late Classical Attic votive reliefs, as we see on an example discovered in a cave at Eleusis (Fig. 1.1),[3] where we see Pan represented as a musician who actively plays his pipes while the Nymphs dance beside him.[4] As a corpus, these reliefs were deposited in cave shrines located in the Athenian *chōra*, the *polis*' surrounding territory, and may be dated fairly precisely since they were mostly excavated from closed contexts. Even more, their original place of display within the caves is often known, so that in many cases, the evidence allows for a preliminary reconstruction of the appearance of the cave sanctuaries together with the rituals that were once performed within them.

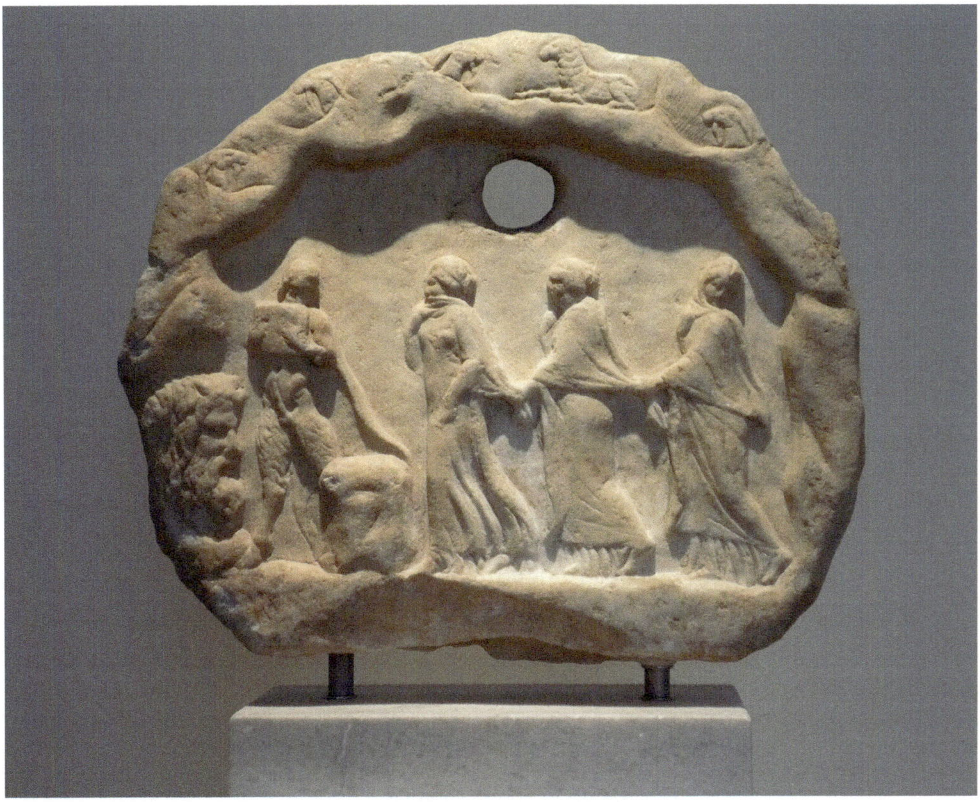

1.1. Votive relief depicting Pan and the Nymphs, from a cave of Pan in Eleusis, white marble, 28 × 35 cm, 325–300 BCE. Athens, National Archaeological Museum, NM 1445. Author's photograph. The rights of the depicted monuments belong to the Hellenic Ministry of Culture and Sports/Hellenic Organization of Cultural Resources Development (Law 4858/2021).

As a result, the votive reliefs on which Pan is depicted as a musician can be collectively positioned within clearly defined ritual spaces, so that both the images and the cave sanctuaries situate Pan's music within a particular mode of experience that was potentially open to ancient worshippers.

The relief from Eleusis, as is typical for the corpus, focuses entirely upon Pan's musical performance and the Nymphs' corresponding choral dance. Three female figures take up most of the available visual space; although it is often difficult to identify groups of mythical or divine female dancers, the figures should be understood as Nymphs, given their association with Pan and the frequent presence of dedications to the Nymphs in the majority of the caves in which the reliefs were discovered.[5] On this relief, the figures grasp tightly onto their companions' robes and move together across the visual field, their drapery floating out behind them. Pan strides forward in front of the Nymphs, separated from his companions by the large, rectilinear stone altar. He holds in his hands an extremely large *syrinx*, roughly the size of the god's torso.[6] The size and nature of his instrument hint at the type of music that the god plays, so that the visual prominence the instrument holds within the image suggests a corresponding acoustic dominance. As viewers, then, we are invited to imagine a loud musical sound emerging from Pan's pipes, which then fills the space, enveloping the three Nymphs. The four figures, bound together in their collective experience of music and corresponding bodily response, move as a unit throughout the cave in which they reside. The Nymphs' restrained movements, heavy clothing, and downturned gazes suggest that they perform for themselves and for Pan, dancing to the sounds of the pipes that have filled their cave. They nevertheless have an attentive audience: nestled throughout the cave walls are Pan's goats and sheep, and along the left side sits the protome, or mask, of Acheloös the river god. Although the animals and the god do not participate in the Nymphs' dance, their rhythmic placement on the rocky frame that encloses the central performance nonetheless retains a sense of movement and chorality.[7]

We may see a similar conception of Pan as musician advanced in Euripides' *Ion*, where, with evocative language, in lines 492–502, the tragedian paints for his audience a vivid picture of a divine celebration, as the chorus of Creusa's servants sing that:

ὦ Πανὸς θακήματα καὶ
παραυλίζουσα πέτρα
μυχώδεσι Μακραῖς,
ἵνα χοροὺς στείβουσι ποδοῖν
Ἀγλαύρου κόραι τρίγονοι
στάδια χλοερὰ πρὸ Παλλάδος
ναῶν συρίγγων
ὑπ' αἰόλας ἰαχᾶς
ὕμνοῦσ' ὅτ' ἀναλίοις
συρίζεις, ὦ Πάν,
τοῖσι σοῖς ἐν ἄντροις...

Oh resting place of Pan
and cliff that lies near
the Long Rocks full of caverns!
There they tread the dance,
Aglauros' daughters three,
over the verdant grass before the temple
of Pallas and sing
to the shimmering sound of piping
when in your cave
shaded from the sun, O Pan,
you play your pipes... [8]

Here, in a dark cave, nestled into the slopes of the Acropolis, the haunting sound rises from Pan's piping to accompany the young girls' dance that takes place just outside. The ode teases and entices its listeners, painting an aural picture of the brilliant grass outside Athena's temple, the clear sounds of the god's pipes, the dark, mysterious recesses of Pan's cave, and the beautiful sight of the young girls' dance. The use of αἰόλος in line 499 goes even further in creating this image, since the adjective elusively evokes both visual and acoustic qualities with respect to Pan's music.[9] The ode thus asks of its audience that they imagine a sound that shimmers as it emerges from Pan's pipes, perhaps a high-pitched song, easily flitting about from note to note under the masterful hands of the goat god. Indeed, at every turn, the tragedian invokes and involves the audience's senses, absorbing them in the scene through his description of lush, green grass (στάδιον χλοερόν), or the dark cave in which Pan resides (ἀνήλιον ἄντρον). Euripides' description of the mythical music and dance, fittingly, constitutes part of the choral ode in his tragedy, so that a visual doubling occurred before the audience who watched the chorus sing and dance on stage, while at the same time the chorus performed the mythical music and dance of the ode. Human and divine music and choral dance blend together in this theatrical context, so that the audience at once witnessed the performance of a tragedy and gained a privileged vision of the mythical revel that could occur on the other side of the Acropolis.[10]

In both the votive relief from Eleusis and the tragic choral ode, Pan and his female companions are presented as musician and dancer, each interacting with the others through his or her movements. In depicting divine music and the danced response to it, the votive reliefs in particular offer us the opportunity to situate Pan's visual music and the Nymphs' danced response within the ancient contexts in which they would have once been encountered and within the ritual practices that once occurred around them. In this chapter, then, I consider divine music together with the visual effect the reliefs may have had on the worshippers who once saw these scenes within the Nymphs' sacred caves. Even more, I explore how ancient viewers may have interacted with the reliefs when they encountered them in the immersive, evocative context of the cave shrines. Such an emphasis on the gods' music and dance and the subsequent effect their performance could have had upon their viewers is suggested, above all, by the images themselves. If we return to the relief from Eleusis, we can say with certainty that the Nymphs' dance stands out as a captivating and striking element of the composition, capturing the viewer's attention as the three female divinities move elegantly across the visual field. And indeed, the Nymphs' dance, which takes up the majority of the visual field, hints at the profound response they have to Pan's music, which fills the space of the cave with the sounds of the *syrinx*. The Nymphs' bodily response to the sounds of Pan's music, therefore, acts as one of the primary ways by which we can access the presence and effect of divine music on its listening audience. To draw out compositional elements that hint at the visualized presence of Pan's music and the Nymphs' response, throughout this chapter I focus on the reliefs' particular mode of representing Pan's music-making and the Nymphs' danced response, as well as the images' overall composition; such an approach also allows for an exploration of the relationship between image and context, and between divine musician and mortal audience.[11] By looking both within and outside each votive relief, I argue that when these images were encountered within the cave shrines sacred to Pan and the Nymphs, the reliefs invited their worshippers to have a fully embodied, multisensory experience of divine music and dance.

MUSIC IN STONE

The *Homeric Hymn to Pan* presents a particularly Athenian persona of the goat god, one where he is associated with the Nymphs, for whom he plays his pipes while they dance.[12] The hymn, which was probably composed in the first half of the fifth century BCE,[13] takes place in a wild, rural setting where Pan roams about the wooded fields and mountainous hills, accompanied by the dancing Nymphs (2–3).[14] As each day draws to a close, Pan returns from tending to his sheep and plays "sweet music," μοῦσαν νήδυμον (15–16), with his *syrinx*. Pan's music echoes across the landscape while the Nymphs accompany him with their song, so that, together, Nymphs and god dance to their collective performance.[15] A later Hellenistic hymn from Epidauros also conceives of Pan as the musical and dance companion of the Nymphs. In this evocative song, Pan is described as the "star of the dance-floor," χρυσέων χορῶν ἄγα[λ]μα (3), and the "prince of popular music," χωτίλας [ἄ]νακτ [α μ]οίσα<ς> (4), who may "coax heavenly notes from his sweet-sounding pipes," εὐθρόου σύριγγος εὐ[θὺς] | ἔνθεον σε[ι]ρῆνα χεύει (5–6).[16] Moreover, the hymn posits that Pan also acts as the leader of the Nymphs, or νυμφαγέτης (1), suggesting that it is he who guides the Nymphs in their dance. Together, they provide musical entertainment for the gods.

Pan is similarly shown playing his pipes while the Nymphs dance on Attic votive reliefs. Despite the consistency with which he performs on his instrument across the corpus, the compositional placement of the divine musician within each relief is surprisingly varied. While the Nymphs generally dance in the center of the image, Pan may instead be found in numerous positions, moving from left to right, top to bottom, inside the image to superimposed on the frame. His ever-changing location thus suggests that the god was thought to be capable of moving freely throughout his cave, jumping nimbly from one rocky perch to another, much like we hear in the Homeric hymn. Given the moveability of his performance, the location from which Pan's music emanates has a correspondingly different visual effect on the composition of the scene and the viewer's encounter with the object.

When the god is included within the main scene, Pan often sits on the extreme side of the relief (e.g. Fig. 1.7), where he acts much as the musicians in an orchestra do when they accompany a modern opera or ballet, in that he contributes the music that provides the rhythmic foundation for the performance but does so from the periphery. Pan may also occasionally participate in the Nymphs' dance, as we saw on the relief from Eleusis (Fig. 1.1).[17] Here, Pan acts as the *nymphagetēs*, much like he is described in the hymn from Epidauros, as he leads the Nymphs in their dance, moving with them across the floor of the cave while he plays his instrument. The composition of the relief draws further attention to the importance Pan and his music hold for this scene: not only does Pan play a singularly impressive *syrinx*, which suggests a correspondingly large and expansive sound, but the god is also the only standing figure on the left side of the altar, so that the viewer's attention is immediately drawn toward his performance. As he plays his pipes, he moves to its music, his *chlamys* billowing out behind him. The curving lines of his legs are echoed by the undulating rock frame, almost as if to suggest that the music that emanates from him fills the space of the cave and the surrounding landscape.

Pan's movements are not restricted to the main visual field, however, and he may also leave the scene altogether to occupy a position on the relief's frame. On a triangular relief discovered in the Vari Cave (Fig. 1.2), Pan perches cross-

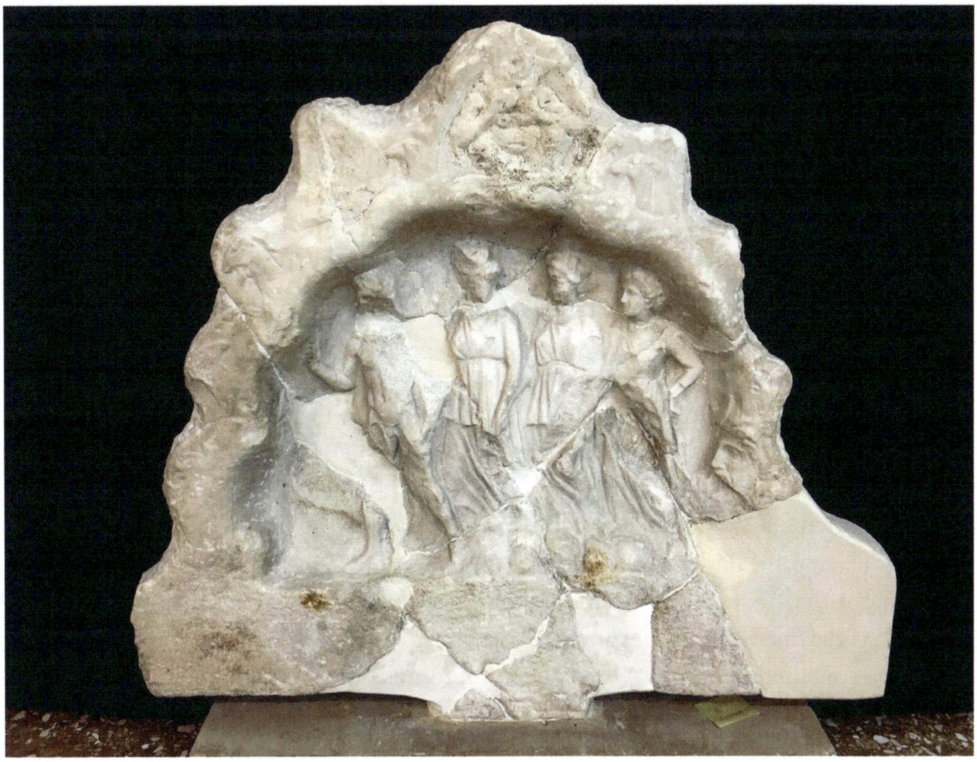

1.2. Votive relief depicting Pan and the Nymphs, from the cave to the Nymphs (Vari Cave) on Mount Hymettos, probably Hymettian marble, 68 (including tenon) × 70 cm, 320–300 BCE. Athens, National Archaeological Museum, NM 2009. Author's photograph. The rights of the depicted monuments belong to the Hellenic Ministry of Culture and Sports/Hellenic Organization of Cultural Resources Development (Law 4858/2021).

legged upon the stylized cave frame while he holds his *syrinx* to his mouth.[18] Depicted frontally, he sits at the apex of the triangular relief that invokes the shape of Mount Hymettos, into which the Vari Cave descends. Sheep and goats populate this rocky landscape, drawing a visual connection with the actual mountainous and cave landscapes in which ancient viewers would have found themselves. The curvilinear border of the relief rises up in a broad arc at the top of the votive, as if to suggest that Pan himself has forced the rock of the relief to move outwards to create space for his body. Even when Pan is depicted outside of the central scene, nestled on his hilltop at a distance from the dancing Nymphs, their beautifully moving bodies nevertheless make clear to the viewer that they both hear and respond to the god's music.

Such moveability in the rendition of Pan's body is common across the corpus of reliefs. In depicting the god in many possible locations throughout the image and its frame, each image plays with and tests its own borders, pushing back on the limitations of the relief sculpture to communicate something distinct about the representation and cult of Pan, and his relationship with the Nymphs.[19] The specific mode of representing Pan and his music as crossing boundaries is thus a consistent and perplexing feature of the reliefs: although he may occupy many positions on the frame, in each he interacts with the main visual scene in a distinct way. For instance, on two reliefs discovered in the cave to Pan and the Nymphs on Mount Parnes (Figs. 1.3 and 1.4),[20] Pan appears at the top left corner of the frame. Yet, even though his position with respect to the rest of the relief is similar in both of these images, his appearance differs greatly between the two. On the first, a relief dedicated by Telephanes (Fig. 1.3), Pan sits cross-legged and is depicted frontally so that he stares at the viewer while lifting his pipes to his mouth to play the instrument. Conversely, on the second relief (Fig. 1.4), Pan is shown in profile as he perches among the rocks and peers down at the rest of the image; the god also holds his *syrinx* and, despite some damage to the relief, the Nymphs' dance suggests that he too plays it here. Pan can even intrude into reliefs dedicated to other gods, such as on a relief to Kybele, where the goat god is shown halfway up the *naiskos* frame, seemingly suspended mid-air, playing his pipes (Fig. 1.5). Such organizational and representational freedom for the figure of Pan within the corpus of votive reliefs suggests, through a visual medium, a prevailing conception of the god as being able to appear spontaneously to his worshippers and to unsuspecting individuals, taking them by surprise much in the same manner as do the goats who roam the rocky faces of mountains.[21]

Pan's short stature and changeable position across the reliefs enhance our interaction with his music and the Nymphs' dance. First, with the majority of the reliefs, the viewer's eye is immediately drawn to the large and imposing Nymphs. It is only after we recognize that the Nymphs dance that we must

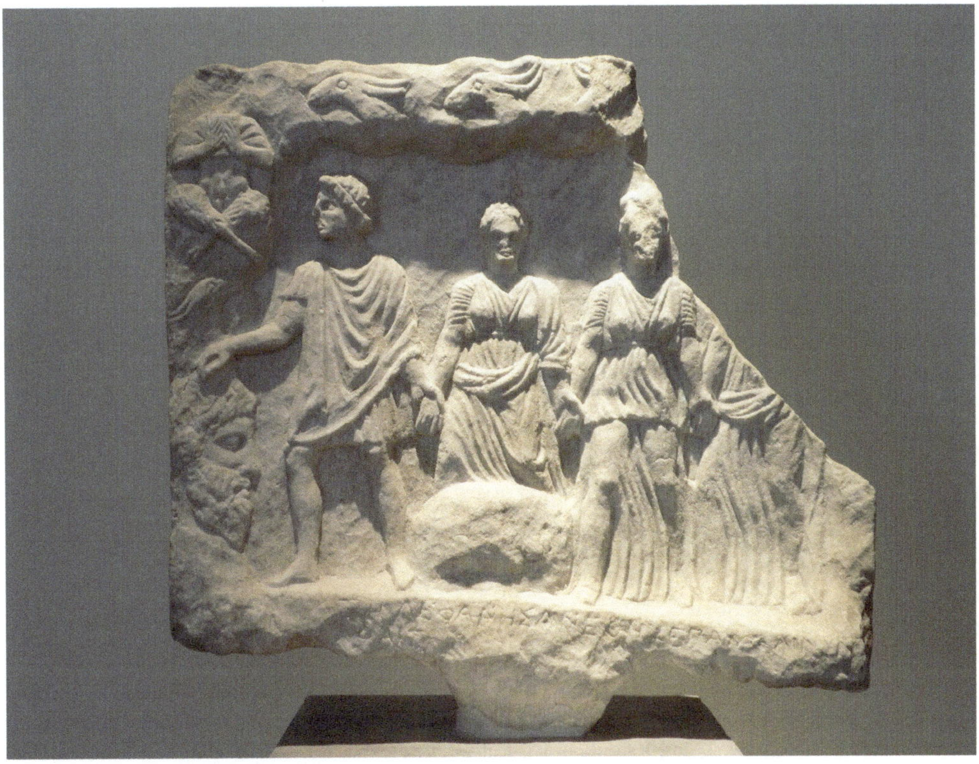

1.3. Votive relief dedicated to Pan and the Nymphs by Telephanes, from the cave of Pan on Mount Parnes, white marble, 43 × 47 cm, 310–290 BCE. Athens, National Archaeological Museum, NM 1448. Author's photograph. The rights of the depicted monuments belong to the Hellenic Ministry of Culture and Sports/Hellenic Organization of Cultural Resources Development (Law 4858/2021).

also search for Pan, the source of the music, in order to make sense of the image. Second, Pan's inconsistent position from image to image, moving throughout the main visual plane and the frame, has the potential to have a profound effect upon the viewer: each time we come across a relief dedicated to the Nymphs, we must look anew to find the inspiration for the Nymphs' movements. In other words, we must deliberately seek out Pan and his music in each image. Moreover, if we were to consider the reliefs broadly in their original cave setting, for the ancient worshipper, who also stood in a cave and looked up at reliefs, the effect is such that Pan almost seems able to appear anywhere in the undulating masses of rocks, the deep stalagmites, and the hundreds of tiny crevices of the cave's walls. By encouraging the viewer to imagine that Pan moves throughout the cave shrine in this way, the votive reliefs could manipulate the viewer's senses: by showing that Pan and his music could be present at multiple times and in multiple places, each image suggests the possibility that Pan and his music might invade the space of the cave and surround the worshippers.

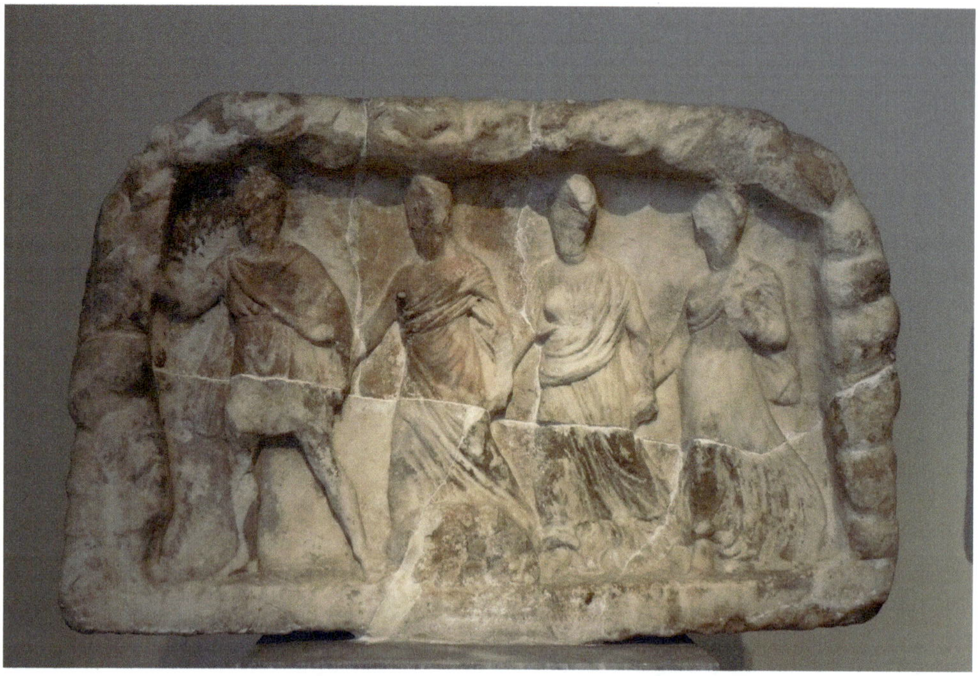

1.4. Votive relief depicting Pan and the Nymphs, dedicated by Aristokles, Polystratos, Phaulos, Pausias, Diopeithes, Theotimos, Stratos, Archias, Pytheas, Phaidon, Eucharides, Aristonikos, Pythodoros, Thrasyllos, Kallisthenides, from the cave of Pan on Mount Parnes, white marble, 52 × 82 cm, 330–320 BCE. Athens, National Archaeological Museum, NM 1859. Author's photograph. The rights of the depicted monuments belong to the Hellenic Ministry of Culture and Sports/Hellenic Organization of Cultural Resources Development (Law 4858/2021).

SCULPTED DANCE

In attributing such transformative power to Pan's music, his performance on the votive reliefs and its effect upon the dancing Nymphs takes on added significance. As with Pan's music-making, the Nymphs' dance is consistently depicted on the fourth-century votive reliefs, on which they hold hands or their companions' mantles and move forwards together as a unified group, their drapery swirling around their feet and flowing out behind them. For instance, the triangular relief from the Vari Cave (Fig. 1.2) offers us a clear example of how the Nymphs exhibit features of choral dance: the figures move forward together in unison, holding each other's hands, their steps carefully coordinated. As they move together, the Nymphs' drapery falls in similar folds across their bodies, sweeping diagonally down around their outstretched legs and trailing out behind them. This particular mode of representation is typical within the Greek visual vocabulary for indicating that the figures are engaged in *choreia*.[22] The gesture of Nymphs holding hands during a choral dance is not restricted to the visual material, and it also appears, for instance, in the *Homeric Hymn to Apollo*, where the "lovely-haired Graces

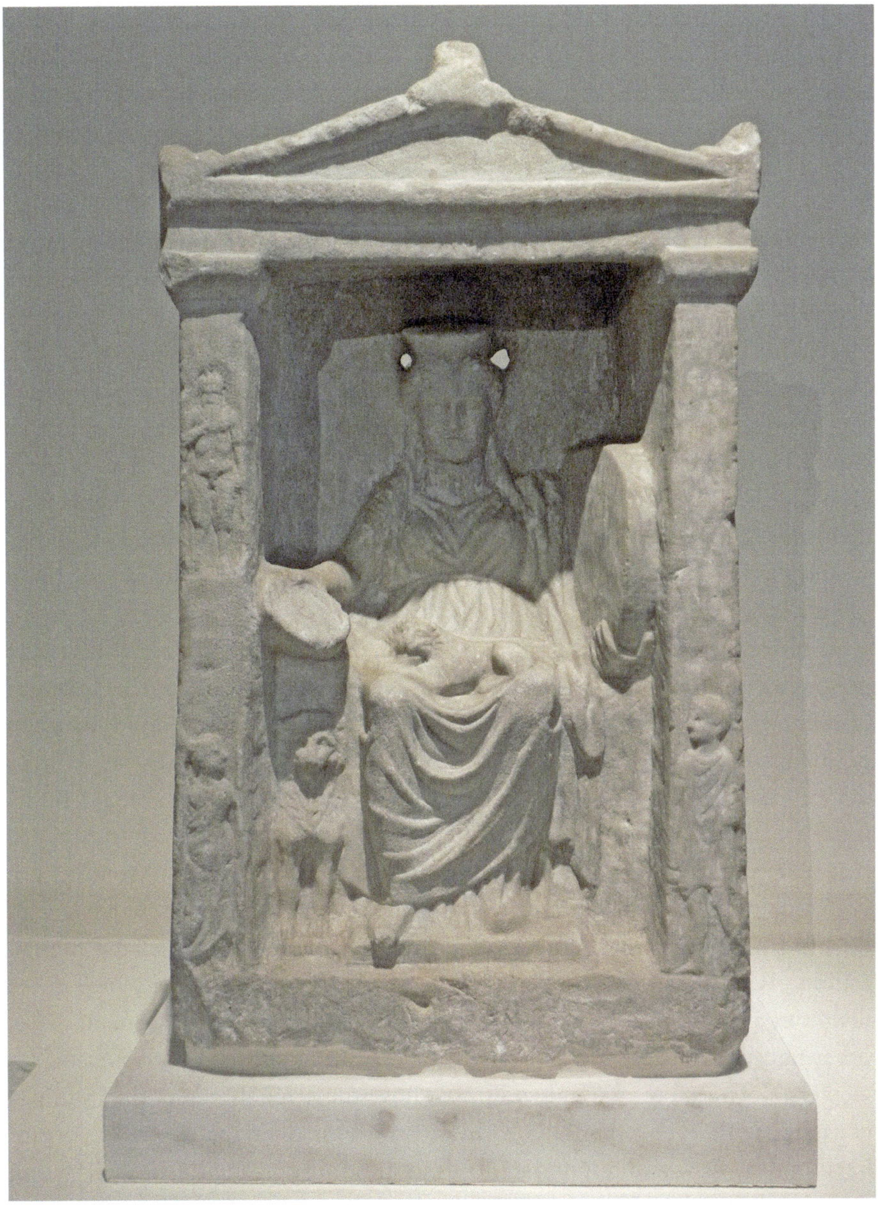

1.5. Votive relief dedicated to Kybele, found near the Enneakrounos fountain, Athens, Hymettan marble, 45 × 27 cm, late fourth century BCE. Athens, National Archaeological Museum, NM 3538. Author's photograph. The rights of the depicted monuments belong to the Hellenic Ministry of Culture and Sports/Hellenic Organization of Cultural Resources Development (Law 4858/2021).

and the cheerful Horai, and Harmonia, Hebe, and Zeus' daughter Aphrodite, dance, holding each other's wrist" (194–96).[23] Within Greek mythology, the Nymphs are often characterized as chorus dancers. The *Homeric Hymn to Aphrodite* introduces dancing Nymphs when Aphrodite narrates her abduction by Hermes, stressing that just beforehand, she was in the forest where "nymphs and marriageable maidens," νύμφαι καὶ παρθένοι ἀλφεσίβοιαι, danced together in the wild forest with Artemis (117–41). Aphrodite returns to the Nymphs at the end of the hymn, where she uses dance as a feature that is distinctive to these particular divinities, saying that they "tread the lovely dance (καλὸν χορόν) among the immortals" (254–76). Dancing Nymphs similarly appear in the *Homeric Hymn to Dionysos*, where they move alongside Dionysos (10–11). Perhaps the clearest discussion of dancing Nymphs in relation to Pan occurs in the *Homeric Hymn to Pan*, where the "clear-voiced mountain Nymphs" (Νύμφαι ὀρεστιάδες λιγύμολποι, 19), "moving nimbly" (φοιτῶσαι πύκα, 20) beside Pan as they sing and dance (μέλπονται, 21). Later fifth-century comedy similarly develops the idea of choral Nymphs, who dance in caves with the chorus in Aristophanes' *Birds* (1099), or who dance in a chorus with Socrates in *Clouds* (271). The inclusion of dancing Nymphs on the fourth-century votive reliefs, therefore, would have immediately evoked for the viewer the *choreia* with which these divinities were associated.[24]

In visually emphasizing the divinities' *choreia*, the votive reliefs collectively present a consistent understanding of the Nymphs. Importantly, the portrayal of these divinities throughout the corpus does not necessarily imply that it is possible, or even desirable, to reconstruct a sequence of danced steps or to determine to which performance or ritual these sculpted dances may allude. Indeed, it has already been argued by Naerebout and Smith, among others, that such endeavors are not only difficult but probably futile.[25] Moreover, as with our discussion of divine music throughout this book, these images of divine dance cannot be understood solely as ideal versions of related human actions. Rather we must take seriously the particular way in which these divinities are shown responding to Pan's music, how their movements affect other figures in the scenes, and how they may have engaged with the ancient viewers.[26] Therefore, we must examine how these reliefs depict the Nymphs engaging with each other and with Pan through their shared experience of hearing the music and responding to its sounds through their dance, all within the cave shrines in which the images were once displayed. For instance, if we look again at the triangular relief (Fig. 1.2), we may see that while the repetition in their clothing emphasizes the dancers' connection with each other, the individual variation that occurs in each Nymph's dress, where one pulls her *himation* to her face, or another twists in her dance so that her drapery pulls tightly across her torso, also suggests distinct personae among them. Far from undermining the strength of their chorality, the distinctions made among each figure further underscore their unity, as each individual Nymph works with the others for their performance, responding as a unified group to the sounds of the music that they hear.

Similarly, if we return to the relief from Eleusis (Fig. 1.1), we may further see how interrelated Pan's music is with the Nymphs' dance, so that together, the gods are shown as a spectacle to be enjoyed. The relief makes clear that the divinities' dancing is essential to its composition and perhaps even to a broader theological conception of the Nymphs as choral dancers. Together, Pan and the Nymphs complement the meaning of each other's gesture: the visual sounds of Pan's music are suggested by the Nymphs' embodied response to it, physically moving to the sounds of the pipes. This close connection between musician and dancer is particularly drawn out here as the Nymphs' swirling drapery echoes the curvilinear line of Pan's *chlamys*, indicating that they hear his song and dance to his music. The left-most Nymph stares directly at Pan, as if captivated by his music, while the second looks down, absorbed in her dance. The final Nymph appears to have been startled mid-dance step by her foot hitting the cave wall (Fig. 1.6). Her surprise at her surroundings hints

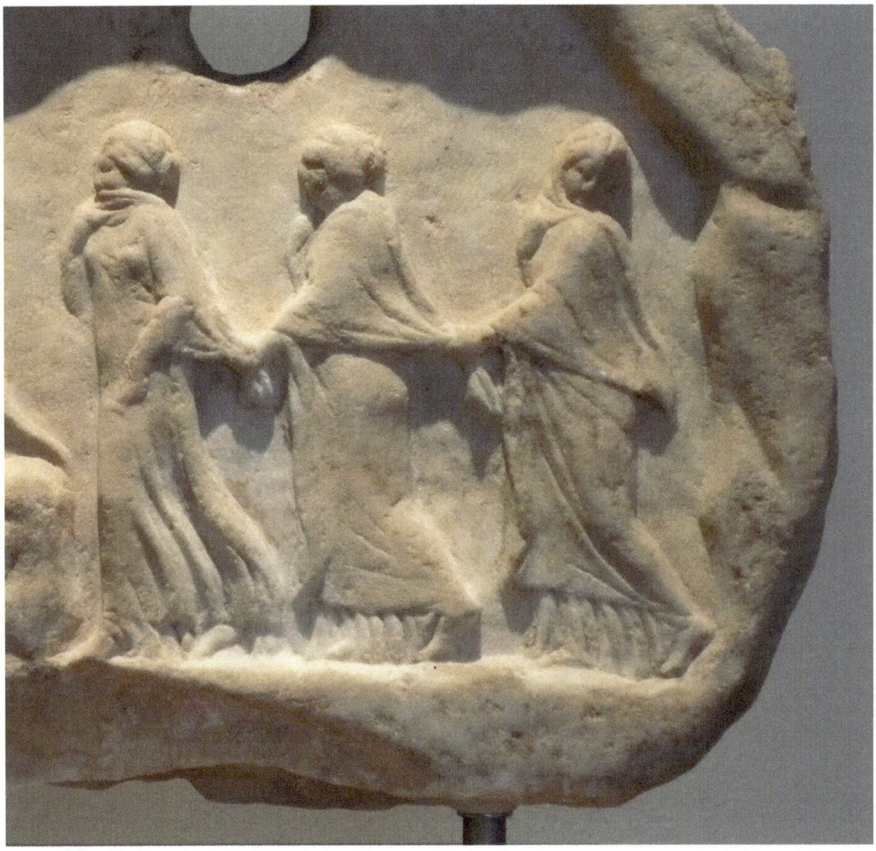

1.6. Detail of a Nymph. Votive relief depicting Pan and the Nymphs, from a cave of Pan in Eleusis, white marble, 28 × 35 cm, 325–300 BCE. Athens, National Archaeological Museum, NM 1445. Author's photograph. The rights of the depicted monuments belong to the Hellenic Ministry of Culture and Sports/Hellenic Organization of Cultural Resources Development (Law 4858/2021).

at the music's ability to consume the full attention of whomsoever hears it. This subtle detail also points to the spaces in which the reliefs were displayed, as it potentially evokes the worshippers' experiences within similar caves, where they may have also moved carefully throughout the dark landscape, hitting their feet against the rocks that jut outwards.

We should also consider the space in which the Nymphs dance. Although in the literary sources the Nymphs typically dance outdoors in the wilderness, whether a forest or an open field, in the votive reliefs their dance always takes place in a cave. The reliefs thus clearly establish where these Nymphs dance and, by extension, where the viewer could expect to encounter the divinities. The relationship between landscape and dance is developed on a votive relief deposited in a cave sanctuary to Pan and the Nymphs at Megalopolis in Arcadia; although the relief was discovered outside of Attica, it largely adheres to the Attic style of representing these divinities, hinting at the broader dissemination of the Athenian theological conception of the divinities (Fig. 1.7).[27] Here, the three divinities again take up the majority of the visual plane as they move within a shallow rocky frame that surrounds the image.

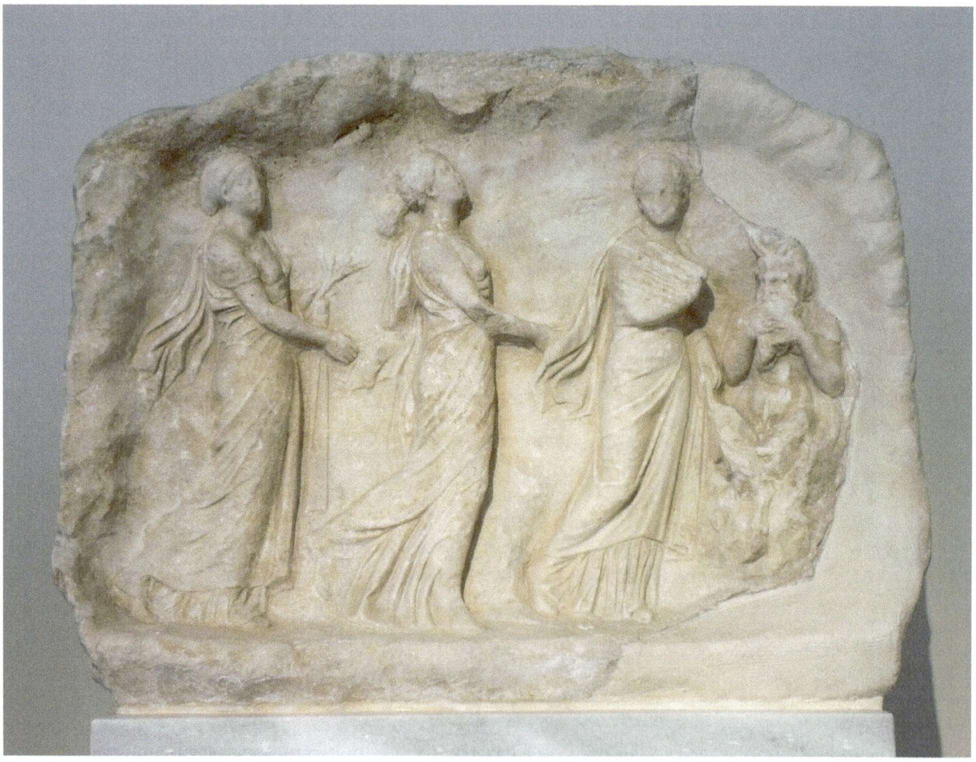

1.7. Votive relief depicting Pan and the Nymphs, from Megalopolis, Pentelic marble, 55 × 73 cm, 330–320 BCE. Athens, National Archaeological Museum, NM 1449. Author's photograph. The rights of the depicted monuments belong to the Hellenic Ministry of Culture and Sports/ Hellenic Organization of Cultural Resources Development (Law 4858/2021).

Each is dressed similarly in a *chitōn* and *himation*, with her hair elaborately braided and pulled back. They move across the visual field while they hold onto each other's robes. Their collective forward movement is made clear by the treatment of their drapery: deep incised lines reveal each dancer's body by twisting and folding around her form. Their complementary movements and gestures thus establish their unified chorality.

The image also develops a close relationship between the dancers and Pan. The musician sits adjacent to the dancing chorus and holds his instrument up to his mouth, his nearly frontal position confronting the external viewer with his musical performance. The dancer closest to Pan most clearly exhibits the influence his music has on her. The broad sweeping lines of her drapery echo the rigid parallel lines of Pan's *syrinx*. The deep, incised folds of her clothing gradually become animated as they near her ankles, where her drapery gently twists out behind her as she internalizes his music and expresses it through her movements. She also maintains a physical connection with Pan through her hanging drapery, which falls on his leg. A strong diagonal thus extends from her arm, down through her drapery, and continues with the line of his leg. A similarly formed diagonal intersects with this line, beginning with Pan's right arm and continuing through the dancer's outstretched right leg, creating a chiastic effect between these two figures that exemplifies the integration of their movements. The divinities are thus shown not only dancing within their cave to music that originates from Pan's *syrinx*, but they are depicted as having been completely absorbed by his performance.

Beyond locating the divine musical and dance performance within the walls of a cave, this relief also displays an awareness of the relationship between the divinities and the natural landscape.[28] For instance, the dancer furthest away from Pan, the tallest of the three, holds out a sheath of wheat, as if displaying the grains to her external audience. The plant's curvilinear stalks and leaves repeat the lines of their drapery that move and twist around their bodies as they dance, suggesting a deep connection between the plant's growth and the choral performance. While this relief is unique in its inclusion of plant life and may draw from other representations of the Horai,[29] the image provides what is perhaps the most overt reinforcement of the Nymphs' fundamental connection with nature, which is not elsewhere seen in the votive reliefs but which, as we have seen, is a recognizable element of their divinity as it is presented in literary evidence. For the ancient worshipper, who would have probably travelled to a cave to venerate the Nymphs, this relief from Megalopolis would have brought to mind the entire semantic range of meaning associated with these particular divinities. In other words, when confronted with the image of Nymphs dancing, worshippers may have recalled the reasons for which they had come to worship the Nymphs: the growth and prosperity of plants and animals, the continuation of natural fertility, and the regeneration of human life.

Further nuancing the Nymphs' dance on the votive reliefs is the close syntactical relationship between divine Nymphs and mortal young women. Their name, *nymphai*, hints at their ambiguous status, where the term refers both to the nature spirits and to young women.[30] In Euripides' *Ion*, discussed above, the tragedian conflates the mortal Aglaurids, who are young, unmarried virgins, or *nymphai*, with the dancing Nymphs.[31] However, despite their shared actions, the Aglaurids are not divine nor can they expect to have the Nymphs' long lifespan.[32] Rather, Euripides' elision of the two groups establishes a link between young female figures and the physical landscape of Athens, in which the Nymphs are "almost omnipresent."[33] The young girls in Euripides' tragedy are thus at once representative of an ever-present potential for future regeneration, much as we see with the Nymphs or Horai on the relief from Megalopolis, but as the daughters of King Erechtheus, who was born from the earth itself, they also maintain a link with the Athenian landscape through their genealogical heritage. In front of Athena's temple, with the patron goddess of the city as their audience, the three young women dance with Pan, continually celebrating the Athenian landscape in order to ensure the continual prosperity of the *polis* and its citizens. We might consider the female visitors who travelled to the cave sanctuaries of Pan and the Nymphs as similarly engaged with the full semantic understanding of Nymphs, so that they could venerate the Nymphs even as they were themselves *nymphai*. The potential for an embodied response to the scenes of divine music and dance, and even the embodied participation in the divine celebration, was thus built into the very framework of cult worship for the Nymphs.

GODS AND SACRED CAVES

Pan's choice of musical instrument and his moveable location within the votive reliefs owes much to his genealogical ties with his father Hermes, who invented the *syrinx* at the end of the *Homeric Hymn to Hermes* (512) and who, as the messenger god, was thought to be capable of moving through disparate spatial realms.[34] It is perhaps unsurprising, then, that Hermes is included in the majority of reliefs. Unlike Pan, however, Hermes' position within each composition is much more consistent: in the majority of votive reliefs, the messenger god holds a Nymph's hand and acts as the dominant male *koryphaios* (κορυφαῖος) as he leads the dancing divinities forwards.[35] The only major point of change in Hermes' representation is the position of his body, which can range from a profile position, such as on a relief from Megara (Fig. 1.13), to a three-quarters view as on a vertically oriented relief from the Vari Cave where the god stands in *contrapposto*,[36] or a frontal position as on another relief from the Vari Cave (Fig. 1.12). In each instance, however,

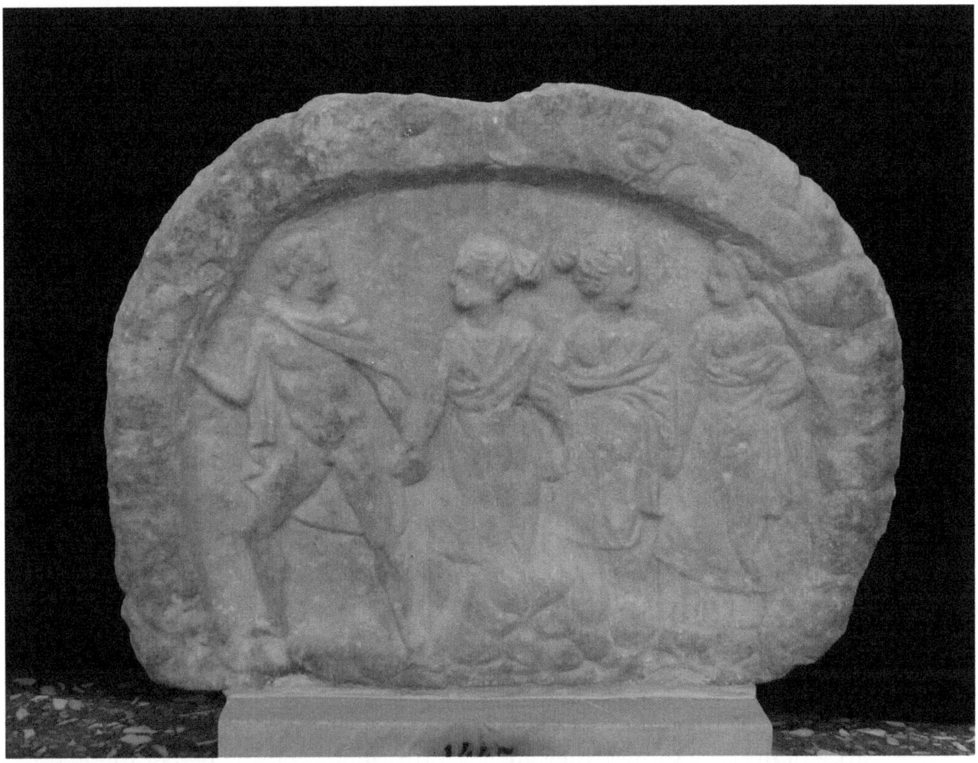

1.8. Votive relief depicting Hermes, Pan, and the Nymphs, found in the foundations of a private house in Piraeus, white marble, 27 × 38 cm, 320–300 BCE. Athens, National Archaeological Museum, NM 1447. Author's photograph. The rights of the depicted monuments belong to the Hellenic Ministry of Culture and Sports/Hellenic Organization of Cultural Resources Development (Law 4858/2021).

Hermes maintains close physical contact with the Nymphs, evoking the theological relationship that existed among the divinities.[37]

Hermes' role as a messenger god, responsible for transporting figures across borders, is underscored by his actions in the reliefs, where he directs the Nymphs' dance.[38] His function as leader of their choral dance is particularly emphasized on a relief found in the Piraeus, where the god carries his *kērykeion*, his messenger staff, as he dances, guiding the chorus' path (Fig. 1.8).[39] Hermes here does not simply guide the Nymphs' movements within their cave, directing them around the altar, but as he moves forward, his hand and *kērykeion* overlap with the rocky frame. By intruding upon the physical boundary that encloses the image, Hermes' actions draw attention to the distinct framing device that is unique to this corpus of votive reliefs. And, if we were to consider Hermes' boundary-crossing movement together with Pan's frequent appearance on the frame, the reliefs as a group seem to play with their physical boundaries, exploring that point of tension where the sculpted image begins and ends.

The figure of Hermes thus draws repeated attention not only to the cave frame and setting in which the gods perform, but also to the actual caves in which the reliefs were displayed and in which ancient viewers would have encountered their imagery. Such engagement between the scene, the object, and the landscape thus suggests that there was an awareness of the potential for interaction between the image and the cave shrine in which the reliefs were deposited and displayed. Indeed, the surviving Attic cave sanctuaries that housed dedications to Pan and the Nymphs offer an entirely unique opportunity to situate visual representations of divine music and dance within their ancient context.[40] It is thus worth taking a closer look both at the *Dyskolos*, a fourth-century comedy by Menander, and at the surviving cave shrines sacred to Pan and the Nymphs, in order to gain a better sense of how a cave landscape may have affected the ways in which ancient viewers encountered and experienced the votive reliefs and the cult more broadly. Moreover, in attempting to position the reliefs within their original landscape, we must also posit active and willing viewers, who were eager to engage with the experience of the divine that the caves offered, since they deliberately had to leave Athens and travel to the cave shrines.[41]

As we have seen across a number of examples, while the votive reliefs consistently introduce the presence of divine music and dance to the sacred space of the cave shrines, they are less forthcoming about whether music was a feature of human ritual activity in those spaces. While there is, unfortunately, little evidence that speaks to human musical activities in the caves, Menander's *Dyskolos*, a comedy performed in 316 BCE, offers an example of cult activity for Pan and the Nymphs, where a small community convenes outside of a cave at Phyle, located to the northwest of Athens.[42] The religious gathering, which would have been staged in the center of the orchestra between the houses of Knemon and Gorgias,[43] takes on the qualities of a raucous celebration, during which the worshippers play music, dance, pour libations, eat the meat of a sacrificed sheep, and drink wine, all within the sacred cave where couches for the participants have been set up.[44] Though no clear archaeological evidence has survived attesting to these actions in actual ritual practice, Menander's comedy provides invaluable evidence for the effect that Pan's music was understood to have on his mortal audience, as well as for how music may have functioned more generally within the context of cult for Pan and the Nymphs.[45]

While this dramatic performance of the ritual took place on stage, so that its costumes, sets, and songs presented their own sensory experiences to the audience, Menander's clear portrayal of the setting and actions nevertheless allows for an imaginative reconstruction of the participants' potential experience. In this scene, the worshippers are described as having gathered within the small enclosure of Pan's cave,[46] where each sensory element of the ritual would have been amplified. In addition to the smell and taste of food, we might also imagine the participants listening to the rich, resonant sounds of the *aulos* that would have filled the cave. In fact, Menander places particular emphasis on music, and Sostratos' mother, whose dream inspired the sacrifice, instructs a young girl named Parthenis to "play Pan's song, [since] this god, they say, should not be approached in silence," αὔλει, Παρθενί, | Πανός σιωπῇ, φασί, τούτῳ τῷ θεῷ | οὐ δεῖ προσιέναι (432–34).[47] At one point, the sounds of the instruments, the women's dance, and general merriment were so loud, that one character, Getas, remarked to Sikon that the worshippers "are making such a racket in there, carousing – no one will notice," θόρυβός ἐστιν ἔνδον, | πίνουσιν· οὐκ αἰσθήσετ᾽ οὐδείς (901–02).[48] Getas' remark also points to the extent to which the human, ritual, and musical sounds could echo throughout the cave. We may further imagine, then, that the particular blending of sounds from the music, the women's dance, and the feasting produced a cacophony appropriate to Pan's musical nature.[49] In Menander's comedy, while the cave provides the setting for the ritual celebration and feast, it is the amplified sounds of music that seem to facilitate a possible encounter with the gods themselves.[50]

Menander's *Dyskolos* thus gives detailed attention to the sensory experience offered by the performance of music and dance within the cave shrine, so that the natural sounds produced by the cave accompany those created by the worshippers. We might expect, then, that a group of worshippers approaching a cave to Pan and the Nymphs could also potentially have played music. Although no surviving evidence can establish that humans performed music within the caves, it is clear from the votive reliefs that these spaces were conceived as having been infused with musical sounds and, when considered together with the *Dyskolos*, that these sounds could have been partially produced by the cave itself and partially by human musicians. Within this framework, Pan joins his worshippers in performing his own music, while the Nymphs depicted in the reliefs dance to both human and divine musical sounds. This mimetic repetition between a god making music and his human worshippers playing their instruments suggests a high degree of participation required of the viewers when they encountered these votive reliefs. Not only did they look actively at the scene, but they may even have lent their own music to their experience of viewing, so that they could have engaged with the image both visually and sonically.

If we turn our attention to a particularly well-preserved cave in Attica, the Vari Cave on Mount Hymettos, we find that it similarly offers a powerfully evocative experience within its walls.[51] Moreover, given its relatively intact state and the archaeological work previously undertaken there, this cave also offers a compelling example for reconstructing the appearance of the ancient religious site and the rituals that would have occurred within it. Familiar to local shepherds who used it to find shelter for themselves and their flocks,[52] the cave became known to scholars after Richard Chandler came across it in 1765.[53] It was subsequently visited by European travelers throughout the nineteenth century and first excavated in 1901 by a team of American archaeologists.[54] The site and its finds have been re-examined by J. M. Wickens in 1986, and more recently by Günther Schörner and H. R. Goette, who significantly add to our understanding of the cave, which is not otherwise mentioned in surviving ancient literature.[55] In addition to studying the finds discovered in the cave, they also attempted a reconstruction of ancient worshippers' movements within the space based on the surviving inscriptions, the physical landscape of the cave, and initiation cults involving the Nymphs.[56]

Together with other surviving caves sacred to Pan and the Nymphs, such as those at Phyle and Penteli, the Vari Cave presents a clear picture of the typical appearance of late Classical cave shrines.[57] Regular features in these caves include small springs with fresh water, terracotta figurines of Pan and, occasionally, Silenos, pottery fragments of *loutrophoroi*, and wall inscriptions. The body of each cave could also be manipulated and adapted by particularly devout individuals; at Vari, a certain Archedemos from Thera claims to have renovated it and the work that he apparently undertook seems to have transformed the cave into its current state (Fig. 1.9).[58] In each instance, the votive reliefs were set up throughout the cave: at least seven complete reliefs have been reconstructed from the cave at Phyle, with additional fragments, while another seven, with additional fragments, were found in the Vari Cave.[59] Importantly for my discussion, the Vari Cave was discovered in a relatively intact condition, and because of the amount of evidence that has survived from it, it is a site that lends itself to a rich, sensory interpretation of the archaeological evidence.[60] Moreover, given the cave's high level of preservation, it offers an exciting opportunity to situate the ancient worshipper's potential religious experience within a distinct and defined landscape.[61] Indeed, the thorough excavation and subsequent publications of the Vari Cave, as well as its excellent state of preservation, provide the most complete picture of what probably occurred within cave sanctuaries to Pan and the Nymphs. Although it is difficult to be certain as to how an ancient visitor to the cave would have experienced its features, the cave's landscape has changed little since antiquity,[62] so that certain traces in the archaeological site expose what must necessarily have been visible to ancient visitors. Much of my analysis thus foregrounds both the worshippers' potential interactions with the reliefs that would have been displayed in the cave and the suggestion of music within the cave and the reliefs.[63]

Since the Attic cult for Pan and the Nymphs was regularly located in caves, consistent across the worshippers' potential experience of the votive reliefs was

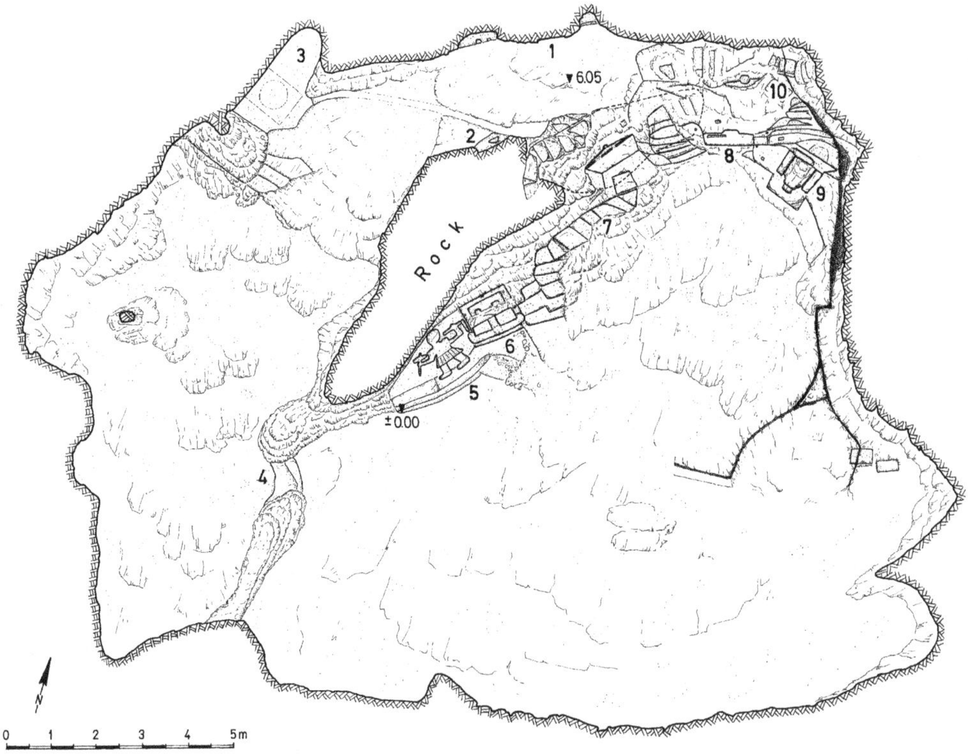

Legend:
1- Dedicatory inscription
2- Charitos inscription
3- Basin
4- Steps and entrance of the main chamber
5- Relief of Archedemos
6- Altar
7- Staircase
8- Votive niche of Pan
9- Seated statue
10- Pan inscription

1.9. Plan of the Vari Cave. Courtesy of H. R. Goette.

the way in which the dramatically different environmental conditions of the subterranean shrines amplified the senses, bent sounds, and introduced a unique sensorial environment into the context of religious ritual.[64] The Vari Cave, with its dark rooms, dripping water, and echoing sounds, offers this particular range of sensorial experiences and, as a result, its physical landscape becomes much more than a simple delineation of sacred space that passively hosts the rituals performed within it. Rather, by acknowledging its role in enhancing visitors' sensory perception, we allow for the possibility that the cave actively contributed to the ancient worshippers' experience of religious ritual for Pan and the Nymphs.[65] Moreover, the specific experience the cave offers to its visitors is as essential a part of the ritual as are the actions performed or offerings given.[66] The Vari Cave, in other words, works upon all those who entered, exerting its own material presence upon them. The cave's rocks, earth, moss, and water, as well as the gradual darkness and echoing sounds that it creates, all would have contributed, and indeed still do, to one's experience of its landscape. The entirety of the cave could thus actively affect the worshipper's perception of that space.[67]

The Vari Cave adheres to the general trend for these cave shrines in that it is located far outside the city limits of Athens.[68] Most of the journey from the city to this specific shrine is steadily uphill and becomes increasingly rural; in antiquity, worshippers would probably have passed shepherds and their flocks along the way. One's sensory experience on this isolated mountain walk would have been, and indeed still is, one of relative silence except for the noises of animals, the rustling of plants and trees, and the crunching of grass underfoot.[69] The cave itself is not immediately visible from the slope of the mountain, since its small entrance opens almost directly downwards into the earth, where it divides into two rooms separated by a large, rocky barrier wall.[70] The cave, in contrast with the mountainside, thus presents a very different sensorial field that is determined by its cavernous nature.[71] It was, and remains, a dark, damp space: the western room descends quickly, engulfing its visitors in darkness, while throughout both rooms water continuously drips from the stalactites that cover the ceiling. There is even a small pool in the western room, upon which is inscribed ΧΑΡΙΤΟΣ, indicating that the pool belonged to one of the Graces, or possibly to a single nymph (Fig. 1.10).[72] Though the basin is now empty, in antiquity the water's own material nature not only would have conditioned its movement within its rocky container, but the sounds it would have created as it flowed around the small basin would have contributed to the other sounds already present within the cave. Moreover, the presence of the manmade basin suggests deliberate human activity in the space: in antiquity, the continuous stream of water dripping from the stalactites and the gurgling of water in the spring located on the far side of the eastern room may have prompted worshippers to carve out this small pool.[73] This attention to the cave's landscape and a deliberate attempt to enhance its natural features amplifies the auditory presence of water in the cave, and may even suggest that within it, the sound produced by the abundance of water was conceptualized as an auditory manifestation of a divinity.[74]

Indeed, water's pervasive presence throughout this particular cave may be associated with the similarly ubiquitous presence of Acheloös, the god of the large river in northern Greece who is included in the majority of the late Classical votive reliefs.[75] The sound of the water as it drips and falls from the stalactites or moves within the spring thus is more than the material presence of naturally occurring water and, instead, it becomes almost indistinguishable from the god.[76] The omnipresence of water, combined with the repeated depiction of Acheloös on the reliefs where he emerges from the cave walls, reinforces the visitor's impression that the god is eternally present and hints at the way that watery sounds moved throughout the space. The water that

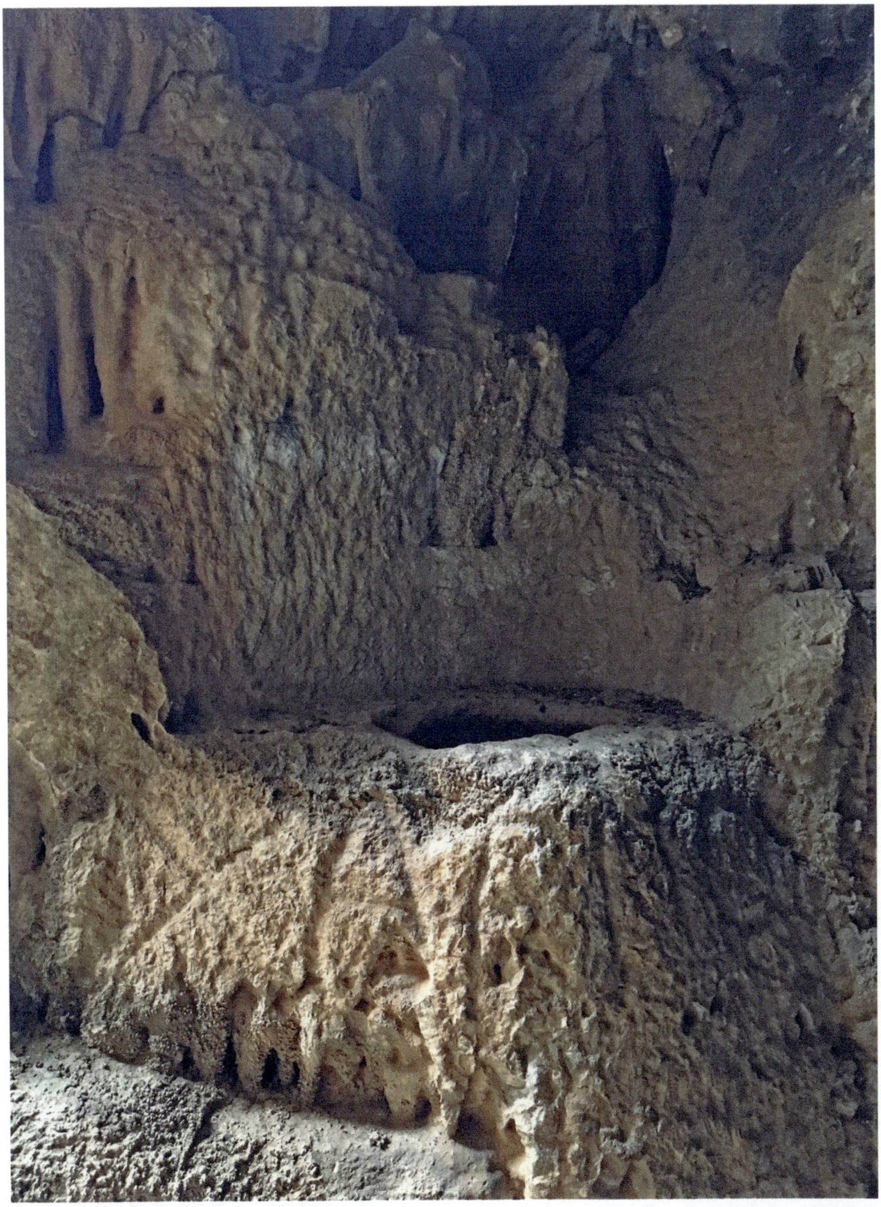

1.10. Basin with ΧΑΡΙΤΟΣ inscription. Author's photograph. The rights of the depicted monuments belong to the Hellenic Ministry of Culture and Sports/Hellenic Organization of Cultural Resources Development (Law 4858/2021).

Acheloös embodies may thus be conceived as dripping from the rocky material of the Vari Cave, so that each time visitors heard the water or felt it drip upon them, they experienced the physical presence of the river god. Above all, by drawing out the connections between the reliefs and the water and rock of their physical surroundings, the images establish the environment of the Vari Cave as one that is materially divine.

Further enhancing the relationship between the carved reliefs that were deposited in this and other cave shrines and the landscape of the caves themselves is the rocky frame that surrounds each votive; as we have seen, almost the entire corpus of votive reliefs dedicated to Pan and the Nymphs exhibits this feature.[77] The sculpted cave thus refers both to the cave in which the relief was deposited and to the rocky material substance from which the image was made. The ancient viewers who looked at the reliefs within the actual, physical space of the Vari Cave would have perceived a clear repetition, a visual doubling, between the frame and the walls of the cave. We have already encountered one relief from the Vari Cave that was carved into a roughly triangular shape (Fig. 1.2), while yet another was shaped into a tall, rounded hill, each echoing the shape of the very mountain into which the cave descended.[78] As a group, therefore, the reliefs are intimately linked with their environment in their shared material and form.

Within the Vari Cave, the votive reliefs were once set up on the hill in the southern room (Fig. 1.11). Importantly, their mode of display in this particular cave differs from contemporaneous practices in open-air shrines, where votive reliefs were typically set up on top of *stēlai*; instead, based on the surviving

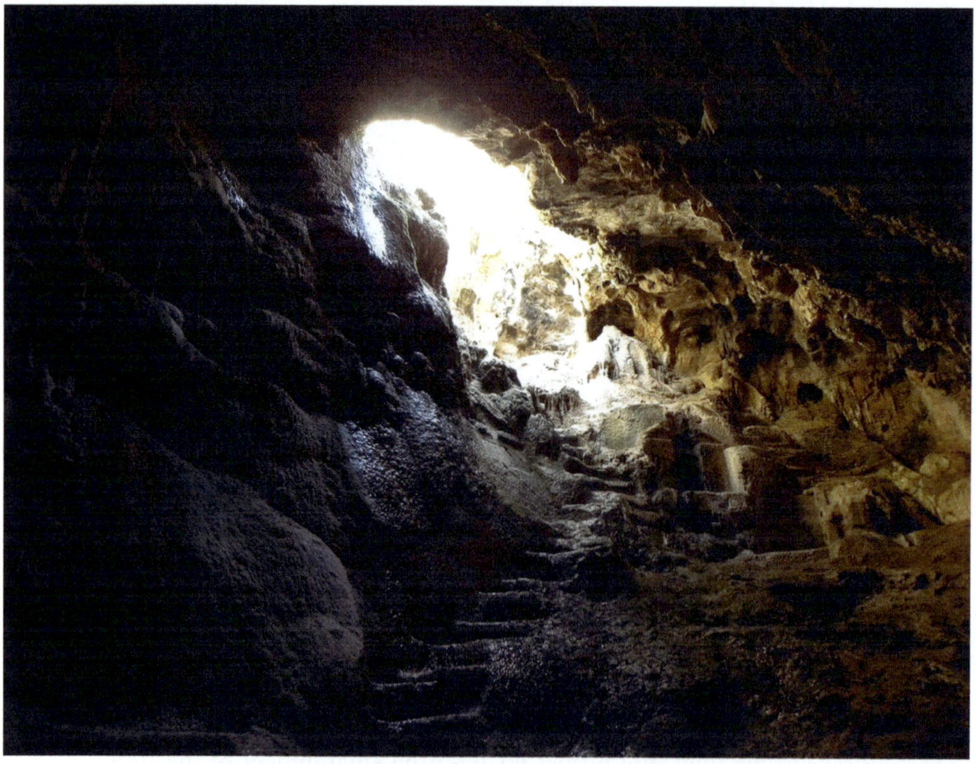

1.11. Southern room, Vari Cave. Author's photograph. The rights of the depicted monuments belong to the Hellenic Ministry of Culture and Sports/Hellenic Organization of Cultural Resources Development (Law 4858/2021).

cuttings in the rock, here they seem to have been inset into holes drilled down into the hill or inserted into recesses carved directly in the walls of the cave.[79] Set into the cave's upward incline in this way, the images would have loomed over the visitors as they entered the southern room and stood on the flattened platform at the base of the hill.[80] However, as the worshippers approached the reliefs, the gods would have been visible at eye level or even slightly below. Each relief would probably have also been brightly painted, so that the divine bodies would have stood out against the rocky landscape, almost appearing to dance and play music in the cave itself. When looking at the reliefs, perhaps even walking among them on the hill, the ancient worshippers encountered a mimetic echo between the actual, physical cave in which each relief was dedicated and the sculpted cave that surrounds the gods. This perceived blurring, encouraged by the rock frames and subterranean setting of each relief, allows the images to fold into the cave's own landscape, the visitor's sensory experience of the reliefs collapsing into their physical experience of the cave.[81] The repetition between landscape and image, sanctuary and icon, not only draws attention to the importance the physical cave had for the Athenians' conception of Pan and the Nymphs, but also suggests that it both determined and created the conditions in which worshippers experienced the presence of the gods. The sheep and goats that are often depicted on the frame of the reliefs echo this visual blurring between divine image and sacred space, because they recall the animals that roam the slopes of Mount Hymettos, the shepherds who enter the cave to rest with their flocks, and the goats that run with Pan in the countryside.

The corpus of votive reliefs thus presents a consistent portrayal of the divinities within their cave: Pan plays his music while his sheep and goats hop across the rocky landscape, the Nymphs dance across the relief and are often led forward by Hermes, and Acheloös watches over the performance. Given that a clear context exists for these objects, it becomes possible to analyze the imagery presented on the reliefs within potential ancient experiences in the cave sanctuaries. It thus remains to discuss how the images could communicate the sounds of divine music to the viewer within visually similar spaces, and also what experience ancient worshippers might have sought to engender by depositing reliefs that consistently depicted the gods playing music and dancing. How, in other words, did the reliefs create a landscape that invited the possibility of human participation in Pan's musical performance and the Nymphs' dance within these caves?

DIVINE MUSIC AND DANCE IN THE CAVE

Above all, scenes of the gods' music and dance invite us to think about how worshippers were invited to interact with, and even amplify, the divine performance within the cave shrines of Pan and the Nymphs. Beyond the deliberate evocations of the physical space around them, the consistent depictions of divine music in the votive reliefs point to the importance of music within the space of the cave, as we see with an inscription left by Archedemos near the entrance to the Vari Cave.[82] It reads:

Ἀρχέδημος ὁ Θ-
ηραῖος ὁ νυμφ-
όληπτος φραδ-
αῖσι Νυμφῶν τ-
ἄντρον ἐξηργ-
άξατο.

Archedemos of
Thera, the nympholept,
at the instructions
of the Nymphs
worked out this cave.[83]

With this inscription, Archedemos clearly establishes his identity as a Theran, isolating himself from any particular Attic deme or tribe, though he may have been a metic in Athens.[84] He further describes himself as a nympholept, someone possessed by the Nymphs.[85] The ritual consequences of using this loaded term, however, are unclear, as it could imply that an individual was caught up in a frenzy, had oracular capabilities, or experienced heightened awareness and clarity of thought, as occurs in Plato's *Phaedrus*. There, when Socrates responds to Phaedrus, who has noted that an unusual rhetorical eloquence accompanies Socrates' sentences, he says: "Then be quiet and listen to me. For the place seems truly inspired by a god (θεῖος ἔοικεν), so do not be surprised if I perhaps become possessed by the nymphs (νυμφόληπτος) as my speech progresses. You see at the moment I am also at the point of breaking out into dithyrambs (διθυράμβων φθέγγομαι)" (238d).[86] As the philosopher comes under the influence of the Nymphs, present at their nearby shrine on the Ilissos river, he demands silence in his audience, so that his musical, and even dithyrambic, performance can be clearly heard.[87]

There is thus something inherently musical, or at the very least poetic, in the term nympholept. If we return to the inscription left by Archedemos in the Vari Cave, we may see a hint of a similar relationship between the Nymphs and poetic music, as well as some attempt to introduce music into the cave. Though the initial three lines are challenging to scan, the last three form an iambic trimeter.[88] While it is difficult to determine the precise character of these lines' musicality, at the very least the inscription evokes a sonic quality, as it could have been read out loud within the cave, almost confirming the Nymphs' power in their cave by infusing that space with the sounds of testimony to divine presence.[89] If we take the attempt at metrical composition seriously, then we have a rudimentary song, which could be sung out into the cave, possibly for the Nymphs, the divine audience for this performance. Thus, already at the entrance to the cave, this inscription provides a connection among worship for the Nymphs, music, and sung poetry.[90]

The votive reliefs to Pan and the Nymphs, together with the landscapes of the cave in which they were displayed and the suggestion of music within them, thus suggest a mode of interacting with divine music that was available to the ancients themselves. If we return to the relief where Hermes' *kērykeion* intrudes upon the rock wall of the frame (Fig. 1.8) with a deeper understanding of the context in which the relief was displayed, the image suggests that the god could continue walking forwards, up to, and through the frame. Moreover, his assertive grasp upon the Nymph's hand raises the possibility that as the god moves through the frame, so too will the Nymphs join him on his journey. The relief thus presents Hermes both as a leader of the Nymphs' dance within their cave, as well as a god capable of moving individuals, whether human or divine, across otherwise solid boundaries, since both spaces are infused with music.

Pan's moveable position throughout the corpus of reliefs further nuances our understanding of the effect of divine music within the ancient caves and the particular ways in which space, both in the image and within the physical caves, was manipulated to make divine music more accessible to the worshippers. Moreover, the god's changeable position at the limits of each image, whether on the frame or the edge of the visual field, confers a sense of liminality to the god's presence, so that the peripheral Pan acts not just as the source of music, but also as a mediator between human viewer and dancing Nymph.[91] On a relief dedicated to the Nymphs by Eukleides, Eukles, and Lakrates (Fig. 1.12),[92] the main visual field is taken up by the three dancing Nymphs and Hermes, who holds his *kērykeion* in his left hand while he guides their dance forward, while Pan stands to the right, overlapping with the rocky frame that encloses the image. As he stands in this visually indistinct space, he lifts his *syrinx* to his mouth and creates the music to which the Nymphs dance. The rightmost Nymph takes a step to the left, and as she passes by Pan, her foot overlaps with his, emphasizing the connection between her dancing steps and his music. The central Nymph is almost frontal facing and is carved in the deepest relief, suggesting that she is the closest to the viewer as she weaves back and forth. The Nymph at the beginning of the line, depicted in profile, takes a step to the left, which creates the forward momentum that pulls her companions with her past the altar. Her robes sweep out behind her and frame the entire altar.[93] The group's movement is directed toward a frontal mask of Acheloös, embedded in the rounded arch of the cave wall where he evokes the water that drips down throughout the space. As the Nymphs dance to Pan's music and follow Hermes, they twist their way through their dark cave,

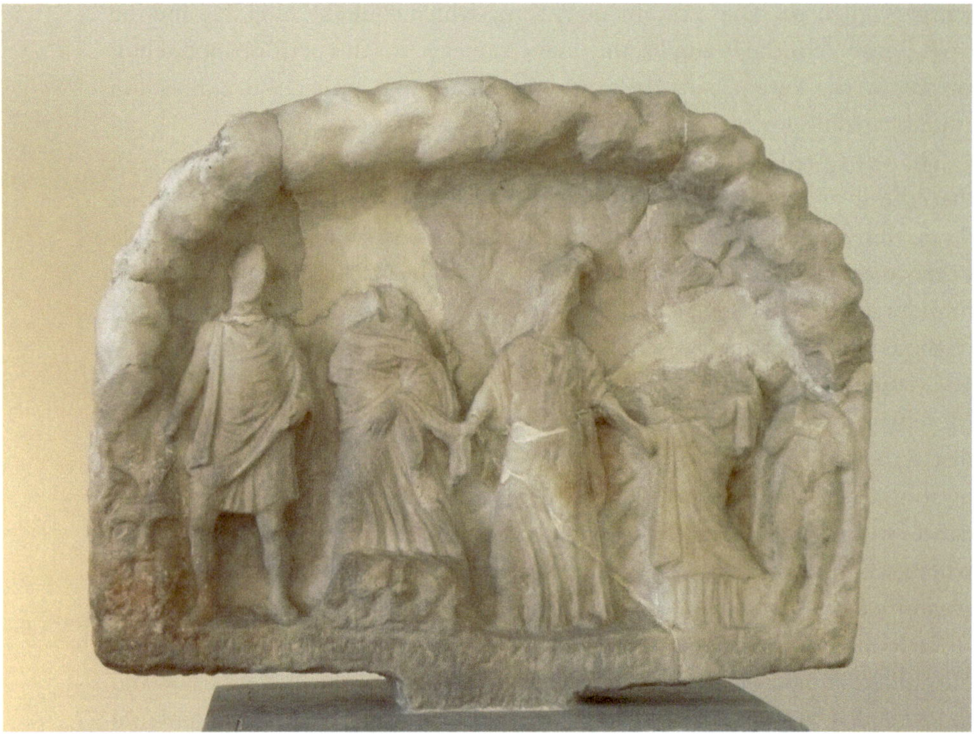

1.12. Votive relief dedicated to the Nymphs by Eukleides, Eukles, and Lakrates, from the cave to the Nymphs (Vari Cave) on Mount Hymettos, white marble, 40 × 50 cm, 340–330 BCE. Athens, National Archaeological Museum, NM 2008. Author's photograph. The rights of the depicted monuments belong to the Hellenic Ministry of Culture and Sports/Hellenic Organization of Cultural Resources Development (Law 4858/2021).

passing by the altar and emerging on the other side.[94] But more than simply dancing across the space occupied by the altar, in this scene the group transgresses the spatial boundaries of the image itself: Hermes, with his right hand, touches Acheloös' horn and bores through the wall of the cave.[95] The dancing divinities follow him, moving dynamically to the sounds of Pan's music as they walk toward and, presumably, through the frame.

We see another instance where Pan's musicality and moveability act as essential compositional elements of these reliefs, together preparing viewers to experience the god's music by inviting them to search visually for the god, to enliven both his actions and his performance. Looking beyond the corpus of reliefs to Pan and the Nymphs to a late fourth-century votive dedicated to the goddess Kybele, we see Pan and his music acting as intermediaries between human and divine. On the relief, the goddess sits on a throne, holding a tambourine, or *tympanon*, in one hand and a libation bowl in the other (Fig. 1.5).[96] At her feet sits a lion, mimicking the frontal posture the goddess maintains, while a young lion stretches across her lap. Meanwhile, Pan is suspended against the left column of the *naiskos* framing the seated goddess.

Positioned in a manner similar to Kybele, Pan is depicted in a frontal stance, echoing the goddess' own confrontation with her viewers. Pan's stillness on the frame, where he stands with one hand straight down by his side, is offset by a single gesture: as on the reliefs dedicated to Pan and the Nymphs, he raises his *syrinx* to his mouth to play the instrument. He is joined on the relief's frame by two other individuals, possibly intended to depict human worshippers.[97] They are represented in profile, turning their heads and bodies toward the enthroned goddess.

In locating Pan's musical performance on the relief's frame, the image explores how divine presence manifests within the experience of worship and, even more, how divine music is essential to that process. Positioned on the frame, Pan's music surrounds and encloses Kybele, following the architectural barrier established by the relief itself. In this way, both he and his music at once act as a barrier and a mediator between human and divine. Indeed, the image hints that Kybele betrays an awareness of the unifying effect of his melody. The specific manner in which Kybele holds out her libation dish, tilting it to pour out its contents, suggests that she may soon put the vessel down, her ritual having been completed,[98] and will devote her attention to the other object she holds, her tambourine. The large size of her instrument further draws attention to the potential music that the goddess might soon create, so that the viewer is invited to imagine the percussive sounds of the tambourine blended with the piped music from the *syrinx*.[99]

The musical potential built into her representation here adds a sense of energy to her entire appearance, as if she might, at any moment, be animated through the sounds of Pan's music to devote her attention to musical performance and to move her body to its music. Indeed, the image hints at the kinetic potential bound up in her figure: as the goddess leans forward, her right leg follows the movement of her body, and her foot slips over the podium upon which her throne stands, as though she is about to stand and take a step outward into the space beyond the relief. Yet her body position is ambiguous, for while her lower body suggests forward momentum, her upper body remains firmly within her *naiskos*. Her head betrays no movement, and she continues to stare directly ahead. The two figures depicted on the frame, possibly a man and woman who have come to worship Kybele, are similarly depicted in a moment of transition between action and stillness. They are each shown with one leg outstretched behind, as if to suggest that they are in the act of walking past Pan and toward the goddess. Furthermore, just as Kybele's foot encroaches upon the surface of the relief, as if emerging from the stone, so do the worshippers' hands intrude deeper into the relief as they reach around the side of the pilasters, their outstretched limbs coming ever closer to the goddess. In depicting the effect of Pan's music in this way, the relief thus captures in stone a crucial element in our understanding of the significance of Pan's music for his human audience, for whom the act of hearing his music could have the ability to bring them closer together through the shared act of listening. Pan's frontal position in this image, so reminiscent of his appearance on the votive reliefs to Pan and the Nymphs, thus continually offers this possibility to his audience, inviting them to hear his music through looking at his image.

DANCING WITH THE GODS

The visual repetition between the sculpted cave that surrounds the votive reliefs and the actual, physical cave in which the reliefs were displayed blurs the image into its surroundings, so that Pan's music and the Nymphs' dancing bodies seem to slip easily from the cave carved into the marble slab to the one made up of the living rock. In this way, as the viewer is invited to imagine the sounds of Pan's music and see the Nymphs dancing to the piped music within their cave, each image also suggests that this divine performance takes place in the very space in which the worshippers stand, so that god and mortal occupy the same landscape. Further obscuring the limitations of each relief are the frontal faces that are regular compositional features of the reliefs.[100] The Nymphs, for instance, often betray an awareness of the space beyond the image by the direction of their gazes. Not only may they be depicted frontally, as if piercing the surface of the image with their movements, but the central Nymph, positioned second in the line of dancing women, is also frequently shown gazing out into the space beyond the carved relief.[101] Their direct gazes may thus be conceived as connecting with those of the worshippers, bringing about an epiphany through ritually conditioned modes of looking.[102]

The concept of kinesthetic empathy is particularly relevant here since it allows us to examine how ancient viewers may have engaged with these scenes of dancing Nymphs – how, in other words, they might "feel when [they] watch dancing."[103] The term, which developed from current work in dance studies, may be defined following Deidre Sklar as "the process of translating from visual to kinesthetic modes," so that the viewer gains the capacity "to participate with another's movement or another's sensory experience of movement."[104] The importance of sight within a dance, whether the gazes exchanged among the figures who dance or between the spectators who look upon a performance, should not be underestimated: in each instance, bodily movement or physical responses to the dance are encouraged through these acts of looking and, by extension, of imaginatively hearing the sounds of Pan's music and feeling it move through one's physical body. Such embodied seeing that is encouraged by the Nymphs' awareness of their audience is thus further complemented by the viewing audience's potential response to Pan's music, as well as to the sights and sounds of the cave itself. As a result, whether or not visitors to the cave sanctuaries of Pan and the Nymphs played their own musical instruments, their encounter with the votive reliefs still remained a multisensory one. Not only would they have seen the figures carved into the reliefs, but they would also have smelled the dampness of the cave and heard the torches snapping and crackling in the dim lighting, all of which affected their encounter with the image. Adding to the distinct sensoryscape offered by each cave was the worshipper's potential enlivening of Pan's musical performance, so that he or she imaginatively listened to his pipes by drawing on their previous experiences with what type of melody a *syrinx* produces, how it felt to participate with one's peers in a communal dance, and what it meant to internalize a melody and respond to it with one's body.[105] Therefore, while music may have been made within the caves, and may even have been required of the worshippers as they approach the sanctuary, musical sounds already were virtually present in the cave through their inclusion in the votive reliefs. Each image thus invites the viewer to search for the source of music to which they dance: Pan's moveable position in the image works in tandem with the Nymphs' dance, so that the worshippers would need to actively search for the musician and, upon discovering him, imaginatively listen to the sound of his music. By activating the images in this way, they might 'hear' Pan's music within themselves as they watch the Nymphs perform their dance.

Mortal worshippers are shown as the audience for Pan's music and the Nymphs' dance on two reliefs, suggesting a potential model for human engagement with the divine within the space of the sacred caves. The first of the two, from Megara, located near the boundary of Attica, depicts a man, woman, and two children who stand near a stone altar while they look up at a chorus of dancing Nymphs who are being led forward by Hermes (Fig. 1.13).[106] A small Pan is perched high up on the cave wall and holds his *syrinx* up to his mouth.[107] Pan's placement in the scene shows one possible way in which his music could affect the mortal worshippers. He sits directly above the human family, and his legs dangle below him, almost reaching the man's head. While the family does not hold any instruments, it is nevertheless visually linked with Pan's musical performance through its close proximity to him. Together, as musician and audience, the family and Pan complete the Nymphs' dance, whether by playing the *syrinx*, watching the dance, or, for those worshippers who encounter this relief in their own cave, by imaginatively supplying the music to which the divinities move. The image thus suggests that the sculpted cave has been filled with divine and mortal music, creating a musically infused space in which the Nymphs freely dance.

A similar scene may be found on a relief from the deme of Hekale, located to the northeast of Athens (Fig. 1.14).[108] Once again, Pan sits above the mortal worshippers and plays his *syrinx*. Below, the three Nymphs hold hands and, as a chorus, dance forwards. Their flowing drapery, suggested by the curvilinear lines used to demarcate their clothes, marks the unison of their physical

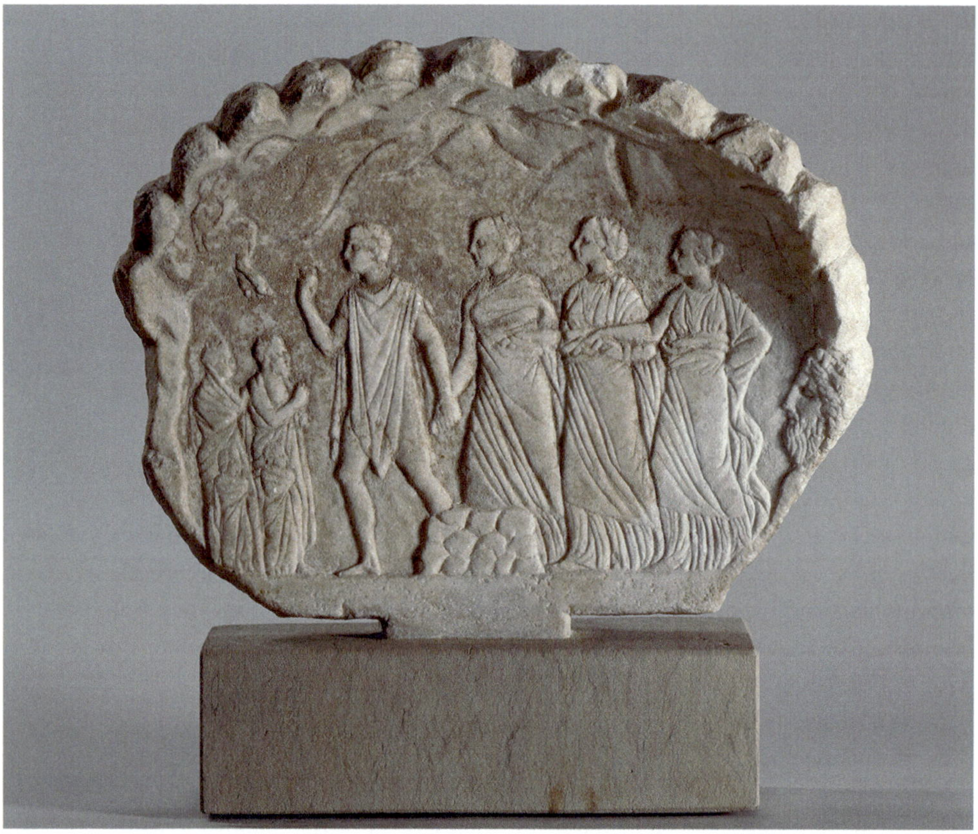

1.13. Votive relief depicting Pan, the Nymphs, Hermes, and worshippers, from Megara, white marble, 40 × 31 cm, 320–300 BCE. Berlin, Antikensammlung, SK 711. bpk Bildagentur/Antikensammlung/Johannes Laurentius/Art Resource, NY.

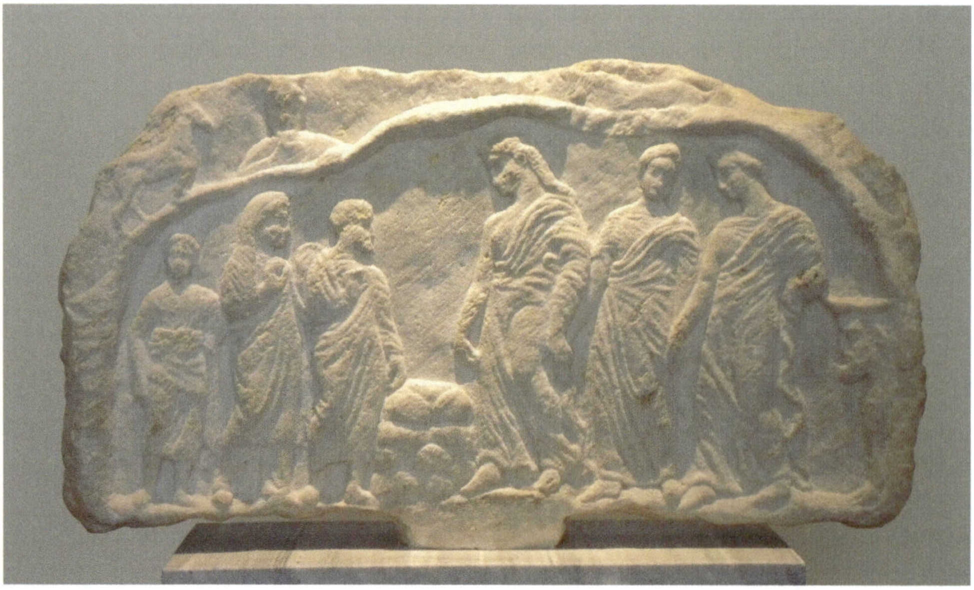

1.14. Votive Relief Depicting Pan, the Nymphs, and Worshippers, from Hekale, white marble, 28 × 52 cm, 325–300 BCE. Athens, National Archaeological Museum, NM 3874. Author's photograph. The rights of the depicted monuments belong to the Hellenic Ministry of Culture and Sports/Hellenic Organization of Cultural Resources Development (Law 4858/2021).

movements. Immersed in their physical response to Pan's music, the Nymphs' dance draws them out of the deep cave, away from Acheloös and the water trickling down the walls, moving toward the altar. In front of this altar stand an older man, a woman, and a younger man, two of whom raise their hands in recognition and prayer as they watch the Nymphs' performance. The mortal worshippers and Pan are again linked through their close visual proximity, suggesting that both are actively engaged in the Nymphs' dance, whether by contributing the music that fills the cave or by watching the spectacle unfold. Moreover, there are a number of visual cues in this relief that suggest that it could have deliberately provoked its external audience to participate as well. Pan not only is depicted frontally, but even rests his arms on the image's border line, suggesting that he exists at once outside of and within the image, in the space of the worshipper and of the dancing Nymphs. The young man to the far left mimics Pan's frontality, directing his attention to his viewer. The central Nymph also betrays an awareness of the external cave in which the relief was deposited as she throws her head back and seems to look through the surface of the stone votive. In the figures' awareness of the external world, the relief thus seems to invite its viewers to engage with the depictions of the dancing divinities, to imaginatively hear Pan's music and to join the choral dance.

Through his frontal position and the way in which his music surrounds the scene as it moves through the frame, Pan in this relief acts as a mediator between Nymph and mortal worshipper. He not only performs for those who have gathered in the cave, but he establishes them as the attentive audience for the Nymphs' dance. Moreover, as we have seen, Pan's marginal position on the frame infuses both spaces with his divine music. On the relief dedicated by Telephanes (Fig. 1.3), Pan sits on the top left side of the rectangular frame where he is surrounded by his goats as he plays his pipes. Just as the frame encloses the central scene, so too does Pan's music, which cascades down and reverberates across the rocky frame, surround it with music. By occupying this liminal position on the frame, Pan is depicted in the parergonal space that belongs both to the image and to the external rocky cave.[109] As such, he marks the dividing point between the figures depicted within the relief and those mortal viewers who exist beyond it. His frontal stare and bodily organization confront the visitor to the cave, establishing, in much the same way as a herm, a visual boundary that marks the distance between two spaces. The Archaizing style used for the depiction of his body also points to a visual relationship established between Pan and herms, drawing a formal connection between his rigidly formed body and that of a herm's rectangular support, erect phallus, and Archaic facial features.[110] The image thus suggests that Pan acts as an extension of Hermes, helping here to maintain the boundaries separating the human from the divine, even as he renders this barrier permeable through his music. In his liminal position on the frame, between the image and the outside world,

Pan's music oscillates between the two spaces and infuses the larger external cave with its sounds. Within the shared sensory experience offered to the sculpted figures in the relief and the worshippers standing in the cave, the formal boundaries between image and reality break down in the shared experience of listening to Pan's music. Inside the frame, the three Nymphs hold hands and sway to the music as their drapery swirls around their legs. At the same time, within the dim lighting of the cave, the ancient viewer could see Hermes guiding the Nymphs' dance to the left, out from their dark cave, passing from the image to the cave. Yet, as we can see in Telephanes' relief, while Hermes leads the Nymphs to the left, the image depicts them taking small steps forwards, around the altar, and toward the viewer. As they move closer to the human world, they stare out, engaging the worshipper's gaze and inviting them to join in their sacred dance.

While the depiction of Pan's music prompts its viewers to recall the sounds of his instrument and contribute that sound to their viewing experience, the Nymphs' embodied response to that music asks their audience to respond similarly, to feel the sound move through their own bodies. The significance of this shared sensory experience can be further explained if we return to Sklar's definition of kinesthetic empathy as "the capacity to participate with another's movement or another's sensory experience of movement."[111] In her discussion of *choreia* in the Greek theater, Olsen expands upon Sklar's work to suggest that though dance is "initially received visually by the audience, ancient and modern theories of kinesthetic empathy and proprioception would suggest that viewers can also have an embodied response to dance, a sensation of felt participation or inner mimicry."[112] While our reliefs would not have been seen in the theater, they do depict scenes that, as I have shown, are broadly associated with *choreia*, so that they collectively created a similar opportunity for the ancient viewer to have an embodied experience of the divine musical and danced performance.[113] For the viewer, who may have been standing in front of these reliefs, looking at them juxtaposed with the rocky cave landscape in which they were displayed, the Telephanes relief offers one way by which to experience, by way of kinesthetic empathy, the divine music, the divine dance, and the sacred space in which both occur. The image, in other words, repeatedly invites its viewers to see themselves in the same physical space as the gods, to imaginatively listen to Pan's music, and to jump up, assemble some companions, and dance around the cave, joining the Nymphs in their chorus.[114] Bodies thus come together through embodied seeing and listening, so that whether stone, human, or divine, all may dance together in a moment of visual and kinesthetic unity.

This kind of powerful, embodied provocation is particularly evident with the relief dedicated by Eukleides, Eukles, and Lakrates in the Vari Cave, discussed briefly above (Fig. 1.12). Here, three Nymphs follow Hermes as they dance to the left, while Pan stands on the right as he plays his *syrinx*. The first Nymph energetically follows Hermes by the altar, and the central Nymph throws open her body, facing the viewer in an almost complete frontal position as she dances to the left. The final Nymph takes a step into the relief, entering it on the diagonal as she holds her companion's outstretched hand with her left. Hermes is also frontally facing and takes a diagonal step outwards, toward the viewer. Together, the four figures almost seem to create a semicircle, where at the right of the relief the Nymph enters the relief, and on the left Hermes prepares to step out of it.[115]

But where do they step out to? Let us return to the Vari Cave, where our ancient worshippers stand together at the base of the southern room, where there extends a large, flattened-out terrace. As they look up at the reliefs, they would have seen Hermes leading three dancing Nymphs while Pan plays his *syrinx*, whose music the viewers imaginatively enliven. They might take in the relief, animated by the music they have imagined and heard, and then see Hermes step out of the scene and move toward them. Through their shared acts of listening to Pan's song and playing their own music, the worshippers could join in their celebration, and together, god, Nymph, and human dance across the floors of the cave. These images thus require the viewer to have a multisensory experience in which sight becomes confused with sound, and sound is then translated into a bodily response through dance. In this way, the human visitors to the cave do not merely see a god, but rather they experience an epiphany of Pan and the Nymphs in their own bodies by sharing in the Nymphs' physical response to Pan's music.

Just as Pan's music has an effect upon the Nymphs and inspires them to dance, so too could it have an effect on the human worshippers who travelled to the cave sanctuary and looked upon these reliefs. As we have seen, the god's music is repeatedly shown having the ability to elevate the human listener to the level of the divine or to break down the barriers separating god and man, thereby allowing the Nymphs to step out of the reliefs and into the actual, physical cave. The viewers in turn could facilitate the Nymphs' movement by contributing their own melody to the image when they respond cognitively to the representation of a musician playing his instrument; they hear the sounds of the pipes within their own minds by drawing on previous experiences of listening to the music produced by the instrument.

But more than simply witnessing the Nymphs dancing in their cave, these reliefs allowed for a fully embodied experience of the Nymphs: by imaginatively listening to the music that Pan plays, and perhaps even contributing their own music, ancient worshippers were repeatedly invited to join in the Nymphs' dance. Not only would they have seen the Nymphs dancing in their cave, but they might even have heard the music to which the divinities dance and responded to it with their own bodies. The reliefs show, in other words, that an epiphany of Pan and the Nymphs was not one that was experienced through sight alone but, rather, the images encouraged their viewers to feel the Nymphs' presence through their own bodies, so that Pan and the Nymphs became present to the worshippers when they listened to Pan's *syrinx* or when they danced in the cave. Pan and the Nymphs were thus revealed when the worshippers committed themselves to a fully sensory and bodily engagement with the reliefs, at which point they could experience an epiphany of the gods by feeling the divine music move through their own bodies.

NOTES

1 On Pan generally, see Borgeaud 1988. For Pan in Arcadia, see Jost 1985. Pan apparently helped the Athenians at Marathon in 490 BCE, then again at Salamis and Plataia in 480 BCE. On Marathon, see Hdt. 6.105. On Salamis, see Aesch. *Pers.* 447–49, the *Suda* s.v. ἀλίπλαγκτος, and Soph. *Aj.* 695; Borgeaud 1988: 232 n. 39. On Plataia, see Paus. 9.3.9. Pan's sanctuary in Athens was located on the north slope of the Acropolis (Kavvadias 1897: 1–32; Casson 1912: 248–50; Judeich 1931; Brommer 1938: 376–81; Brommer 1956: s.v. Pan; Fuchs 1959: 37–39; Travlos 1971: 93, 417–21). For a representation of Pan in the pose of a runner, which may allude to the cultic activity that took place at Pan's sanctuary on the Acropolis, see a black-figure vase published by Erika Simon (Würzburg, Martin von Wagner Museum, 44630; Simon 1976: 19–23, plate IV.1; Borgeaud 1988: 134, 244 n. 9). For early representations of Pan, see Brommer 1949: 5–42.

2 I discuss the *Homeric Hymn to Pan* in more detail in Laferrière 2019a.

3 Furtwängler 1878: 201; Pottier 1881:pl. 7; Thallon 1903: 301; Svoronos 1908–37: 443–49, pl. 73; Feubel 1935: xix, no. IIIa.A2, 54–56; Travlos 1960: 55, pl. 41.β; Fuchs 1962: 21, no. A2, 36, n. 75; Kahil 1965: 31; Isler 1970: 30–31, 42, 112, 17, no. 12; Edwards 1985: 565–69, no. 38; Güntner 1994: 121, A23, pl. 5.1; Kaltsas 2002: no. 455. The relief was later reused as a waterspout, at which point a hole was drilled into the background.

4 On this corpus of reliefs, see especially Feubel 1935; Fuchs 1959; Fuchs 1962; Edwards 1985; Güntner 1994: 10–25.

5 For more on the Nymphs in Greek religion, see especially Larson 2001.

6 The large size of the god's instrument evokes the splendor later attached to a similarly impressive *syrinx* in *Daphnis and Chloe*, 2.35.1.

7 As noted by Weiss (2018: 27–31, 236–41), animals are often imagined as dancing to music played by Apollo and Pan.

8 Eur. *Ion* 492–502. Translation adapted from Kovacs 1999: 376–79. With respect to lines 498–500 Kovacs accepts the authority of Page, whom I have also followed here. Diggle (1981: 327) retains ὕμνων in his edition, but marks it with daggers.

9 In its reference to both visual and aural qualities, it recalls the similarly multifaceted use of *poikilia*. For more on *poikilia*, see the introduction to this volume, and especially LeVen 2013; Grand-Clément 2015.

10 The scene described by Euripides takes place on the northeast side of the Acropolis. For more on an audience's experience of theater and dance, see Weiss 2023; Weiss forthcoming.

11 For this approach, I draw on recent work by Milette Gaifman (2008), Martina Edelmann (1999), and Anja Klöckner (2001; 2010), each of whom situates votive reliefs within a religious framework.

12 Generally on this hymn, see Thomas 2011.

13 Janko (1982: 184–85, 98) analyzes the linguistic peculiarities and ascribes the hymn to an Attic context. Moreover, both Janko and West (2003: 18) argue that the language is

consistent with the fifth century BCE, with Janko further arguing that the hymn probably does not date later than the mid-fifth century BCE.

14 *Hymn. Hom. Pan.* 2–3. ὅς τ' ἀνὰ πίση | δενδρήεντ' ἄμυδις φοιτᾷ χοροήθεσι νύμφαις. . .

15 *Hymn. Hom. Pan.* 20–25.

16 Text and translation from Furley and Bremer 2001a: 240–43; 2001b: 193–96.

17 A similar relief was discovered in the Athenian Kerameikos (K170). Gruben 1969: 39; Hoepfner 1976: 218; Camp 1977: 138; Edwards 1985: no. 52, 611–13.

18 *IG* II[2] 4650 (SEG 54 318); Thallon 1903: 290, 306, 12, pl. V; Svoronos 1908–37: 587, no. 238, pl. 100; Feubel 1935: xii, no. II.21, 38; Isler 1981: 34, no. 177; Edwards 1985: 572–77, no. 40; Schörner and Goette 2004: 64–67, pl. 39.3. The inscription has been most recently restored and translated by Schörner and Goette 2004: 64–67.

19 We might think here of Derrida's particularly evocative discussion of the parergonal frame (1987: 54) as well as generally Hurwit 1977: 1–30; Platt and Squire 2017c.

20 NM 1448: *IG* II[2] 4646; Svoronos 1908–37: 449–50; Feubel 1935: xiv, no. II.27, 42–43; Fuchs 1962: 243, 44 n. 14, 45 n. 21, 49, pl. 65.2; Isler 1970: 30, 112, 17, 26; Edwards 1985: 618–24, no. 54; Vikela 1994: 202 n. 59, 206, n. 90; Güntner 1994: 125, A44, pl. 9.1; Kaltsas 2002: 219, no. 456.

NM 1859: *IG* II[2] 4832; Svoronos 1908–37: 574–75, no. 228, pl. 96; Feubel 1935: xiv, no. II.26, 42–43; Fuchs 1962: 243, pl. 69.1; Brommer 1956: 981; Isler 1970: 30, 112, 17, 26; Edwards 1985: 503–09, no. 26; Güntner 1994: 125, A42; Kaltsas 2002: 221, no. 460.

21 On Pan and epiphany, see Meillier 1975: 121–31; Borgeaud 1988: 243 n. 3.

22 On dance in Archaic and Classical Greece, see, for example, Naerebout 1997; Calame 2001: 30–31; Shapiro 2004; Smith 2010b; Rocconi 2015; Naerebout 2017; Olsen 2020; Smith 2021. On *choreia* specifically, see Weiss 2020; Steiner 2021.

23 αὐτὰρ ἐϋπλόκαμοι Χάριτες καὶ ἐΰφρονες Ὧραι | Ἁρμονίη θ' Ἥβη τε Διὸς θυγάτηρ τ' Ἀφροδίτη | ὀρχεῦντ' ἀλλήλων ἐπὶ καρπῷ χεῖρας ἔχουσαι. Translation from West 2003: 87. While there is a distinction between holding hands and holding wrists, since the latter holds additional wedding connotations, nevertheless, in this passage it is clear, following Steiner (2021: 112) that this gesture of joined wrists is characteristic of the female figures' choral dance. For more on dance in the *Homeric Hymn to Apollo*, see Chapter 3 as well as Lonsdale 1994–95 and generally Steiner 2021.

24 Peponi 2009: 56–57, 60–68; Peponi 2013: 15–16.

25 For further discussion of visual representations of dance, see especially Naerebout 1997: 60–77, 112f.; Smith 2010a: 12f.; Smith 2010b; Smith 2014a: 231; Naerebout 2015; Smith 2016; Gianvittorio 2017: 26; Naerebout 2017: 60.

26 For more on representations and discussions of dancing gods, see Laferrière forthcoming.

27 Feubel 1935: XVII, no. IIIa.A1, 53, 58; Fuchs 1959: 21–23; Muthmann 1975: 95, 142; Edwards 1985: no. 86, 777–83; Güntner 1994: A9, 15–16; Kaltsas 2002: no. 454. The relief was possibly found in Sparta, although Megalopolis seems more likely, based on the stylistic similarities with Athens. Edwards suggests that the artist was probably Athenian, or at least was very familiar with similar Attic reliefs. Two similar, although fragmentary, images were found, one in the Kerameikos and another on the slopes of the Acropolis.

28 Nymphs could reside on the high mountains, in shady groves, in dark caves, on the flat plains, in trees, and by or in any body of water. Nilsson 1972: 14. *Loutrophoroi* and other items associated with marriage and childbirth have been found in most of their sanctuaries in Attica from the Archaic period onwards, hinting at their association with natural female fertility. See, for example, King and Wickens on the finds from the Vari Cave: King 1903; Wickens 1986: vol. 2, 90–121.

29 For a discussion on the inclusion of imagery related to the Horai, see Edwards 1985: 780–81.

30 Larson 2001: 3–4.

31 At the time this tragedy was performed, between 414 and 412 BCE, the association between Pan and the Nymphs in Attica was well known, and they shared cave sanctuaries throughout Attica.

32 On the meaning of *nymphē*, see Calame 2001: 26; Larson 2001: 3. Tragic choruses do, however, frequently assimilate themselves to dancing Nymphs. Weiss 2018: 69–70. On female choruses more generally, see Calame 2001; Budelmann and Power 2015.

33 Nilsson 1972: 14.

34 For more on the genealogical relationship between Hermes and Pan, see Laferrière 2019a. On the *Hymn to Pan*, see Thomas 2011. On the *Hymn to Hermes*, see especially Clay 2006: 95–151. On Hermes more broadly, see Versnel 2011: 309–78; Miller and Clay 2019.

35 Despite Aristid. *Or.* 53.4, "Hermes as *khorēgos* always leads the nymphs," the *khorēgos* was more typically the individual who financed the choral performance. Conversely, the *koryphaios* was a member of the chorus who was responsible for leading the other performers in their dance. However, as Wilson notes (2000: 130–36), it was not impossible for certain *khoregoi* to serve as *koryphaioi*. See also Lawler 1964: 80–81. In almost every surviving instance where the Nymphs dance on fourth-century votive reliefs, Hermes occupies the primary position in front of the dancing divinities.

36 Athens, National Archaeological Museum, NM 2011, *IG* II^2 4652. Thallon 1903: 312–13, pl. v; Svoronos 1908–37: 634, no. 342, pl. 137; Speyer 1932: 76, pl. 22–23; Feubel 1935: IV, no. 1.III, 6–8; Fuchs 1959: 36, n. 74 and 1962: 247, pl. 67; Edwards 1985: 439–46, no. 15; Güntner 1994: 120, no. A16, pl. 3; Kaltsas 2002: 218, no. 450; Schörner and Goette 2004: 69–71, pl. 41.1.

37 *Hymn. Hom. Ven.* 261–63. Hermes is elsewhere linked with the Nymphs. In the *Thesmophoriazusai* by Aristophanes (977–78), the chorus prays to "Hermes Nomios and Pan and the dear Nymphs" (Ἑρμῆν τε νόμιον ἄντομαι καὶ Πᾶνα καὶ Νύμφας φίλας). Hermes often acts as the leader of Nymphs, as seen at the end of the *Hymn to Hermes*, where Apollo gives Hermes control over oracular bee maidens, often associated with the Nymphs at Delphi (see Larson 2001: 12; 2011: 352). The *Hymn to Aphrodite* stresses the sexual connection between the two, who mate in sacred caves (261–63). Finally, Hermes is linked with the Nymphs in his role as *kourotrophos*, where he brings the infant Dionysos to the Nymphs for safekeeping after he was born from the thigh of Zeus.

38 I know of only three exceptions but, in each instance, Hermes still maintains an intermediary position between the Nymphs and the external world. Two of these exceptions are the unusual reliefs from Mount Penteli, where Hermes stands immediately adjacent to the Nymphs, and separates them from Pan and the mortal worshippers. In both instances, the god's role as *koryphaios* is evoked by his twisting posture and weight shift, as if he will soon take a step forward (Athens, National Archaeological Museum, NM 4465 and 4466). The third exception is a vertical relief from the Vari Cave, where Hermes once again stands beside the Nymphs, all of whom look at him (Athens, National Archaeological Museum, NM 2011).

39 Edwards 1985: no. 43, with previous bibliography.

40 I have explored this topic more in Laferrière 2019b.

41 The only exception to this general pattern is the cave to Pan on the north slope of the Acropolis.

42 As David Wiles has shown (1984: 170–74, 76), Menander's awareness of the technicalities of the earlier comedies at least makes it possible to approach his work with the same eye to satire and nuanced commentary on contemporary life. In foregrounding the ritual setting of the *Dyskolos*, I follow the model laid out in Bathrellou 2012.

43 Though there has been much debate on the location of the two houses, it is widely accepted that Pan's cave was located at center stage. For more, see Quincey et al. 1959: 3; Wiles 1991: 233 n. 41; Brown 1993; Rzepkowski 2012: 584–87.

44 Men. *Dys.* 419–421; Wickens 1986: 175–76; Borgeaud 1988: 239–40.

45 See also Yioutsos 2014: 59–61.

46 As Roy notes (1996: 114–15), though Menander took care to locate Pan's shrine within an actual, physical sacred cave, the cave at Phyle is on a steep, almost inaccessible mountain-side. In his comedy, Menander relocates the cave to a more accessible and less remote location, while he still maintains the name of its original site.

47 Translation adapted from Arnott 1979: 250–51. Borgeaud (1988: 166) suggests that "this remark most probably reveals a contrast between Pan's rite and normal cultic practice: when the baskets and the *chernips* approach the altar chosen for the sacrifice, the worshippers are generally completely silent." Whether or not rituals for Pan deviated from what constitutes "normal cultic practice," what is striking is Menander's emphasis on the importance of music within cult activity for Pan.

48 Translation adapted from Arnott 1979: 336–37. Though this scene may be intended to mock pastoral religious enthusiasm, this joke would only be comprehensible to a contemporary Athenian audience if it were not already generally understood that one could be expected to play music either outside of or within caves sacred to Pan. See also Bathrellou 2012.

49 Borgeaud 1988: 168.

50 Yioutsos 2014: 59.

51 I discuss the Vari Cave in more detail in Laferrière 2019b.

52 Weller 1903: 274.

53 Chandler 1776: ch. 32.

54 The 1903 site report was published as a series of articles under the guidance of Charles Heald Weller and the American School of Classical Studies in Athens. The original report includes: Weller 1903; Dunham 1903; Thallon 1903; King 1903; Baldwin 1903; Bassett 1903.

55 Wickens 1986: no. 20, 90–121; Schörner and Goette 2004. The cave is also mentioned in conjunction with studies on the Nymphs, nympholepsy, and the role of caves in Greek religion: Connor 1988: 166–74; Larson 2001: 14–16, 242–45; Ustinova 2009: 61–63; Pache 2011: 37–38, 44–52. For more on the cave's acoustics, see Yioutsos et al. 2018.

56 Schörner and Goette 2004: 60–77.

57 Although the Vari Cave was most active from the late fifth century into the fourth, there is evidence of cult activity in the Vari Cave already at the end of the sixth century BCE. On the cave to Pan and the Nymphs at Phyle see Wickens 1986: 245–69, no. 47. The cave at Penteli survived because its roof collapsed in antiquity, preserving its interior until its discovery in 1952. On the Penteli cave, see Zorides 1977; Wickens 1986: no. 39, 202–11, with earlier bibliography; Travlos 1988: 329–30, 332–34; Larson 2001: 246. Two large votive reliefs were also discovered in the cave (Edwards 1985: nos. 20 and 22).

58 The first sign of Archedemos' presence in the Vari Cave occurs on a block that is believed to have been set up outside of the cave, upon which two inscriptions were carved, one on either side. The first reads "Archedemos of Thera | cultivated a garden | for the Nymphs" Ἀρχέδαμος ὁ Θερ- | αῖος κᾶπον Νύ- | μφαις ἐφύτευσεν (*IG* I^2 784). The second side reads "Archedemos of Thera and *cholondcheste* built this house for the Nymph" Ἀρχέδεμος ὁ Θερ- | αῖος καὶ ΧΟΛΟΝΟΔ- | ΧΕΣΤΕ[.] Νύωφαι ἐχ- | σοικοδόμεσεν (*IG* I^2 785). The term *cholondches* is otherwise unknown, but it may relate to the term *cholos*, or bile. Translation from Pache 2011: 47–48; see also Weller 1903: 265; Schörner and Goette 2004: 51–54. As Squire suggests (2018: 444–47), Archedemos may also have created a rudimentary self-portrait on the walls of the southern room.

59 Thallon 1903; Edwards 1985: nos. 13, 15, 16, 21, 23, 26, 29, 33, 36, 37, 40, 51, 54, 76; Larson 2001: 242–47.

60 Inevitably, my description of the sensory experience offered by the Vari Cave depends upon my own experience walking through its walls. Although my sensory responses to the cave are both my own and, to some degree, culturally construed by the memory of my other experiences, they may still offer us a glimpse into the range of potential experiences open to the ancient visitor. I adopt a phenomenological approach to the Vari Cave more fully in Laferrière 2019b: 185–216. For more on this methodological approach, see in general Betts 2017b: 195–96 and, specifically with respect to Pan, Yioutsos 2014.

61 For a similar attention to one's sensory experience of the landscape, see Hamilakis 2013: esp. 1–16, 57–110. On the ancient viewing experience within a sanctuary, see Day 1994; Day 2000; Day 2010.

62 Chandler's detailed observations from 1765 (1776: chapter 32) allows us to compare what survives with what he described. Importantly, the same general appearance was preserved up until the time of the cave's excavation.

63 Schörner and Goette (2004: 60–77) rely upon Edwards' analyses of the reliefs.

64 For more on how caves could manipulate the senses within Greek ritual, see Sporn 2007; Ustinova 2009; Katsarou and Nagel 2021. On the acoustics of Greek caves, see Yioutsos et al. 2018. Synesthesia, the conflation of senses, has been discussed in relation to antiquity by Butler and Purves 2013: 1–8; Porter 2013 and 2010: 3, 45–47, 64–66, 355–56, 368, 417, 492, 511.

65 I draw here on Gell 1998: 66–72; Osborne and Tanner 2007. On ancient art's materiality see Bielfeldt 2014; Platt 2016; Platt and Squire 2017b; Gaifman and Platt 2018. For more on materiality and its modern consequences see Bennett 2010: 1–19, esp. 12–13.

66 Apart from the substantial treatment of phenomenology in twentieth-century continental philosophy, the rise of sensory archaeology owes much to earlier discussions of phenomenology. See Fahlander and Kjellström 2010; Day 2013; Hamilakis 2013; Pellini, Zarankin, and Salerno 2015. Current work on the senses and archaeology includes Hamilakis 2017: 171–75 and 2013: 6–12; Betts 2017a and 2017b; Hamilakis and Meirion Jones 2017; Harris 2017: 129–30. On the senses in antiquity see Butler and Purves 2013; Bradley 2015; Squire 2016a; Rudolph 2018; Purves 2018; Butler and Nooter 2019.

67 Hamilakis 2017: 171–72.

68 It takes four to five hours to walk the distance from the Acropolis in Athens to the Vari Cave.

69 As Wickens notes (1986: 93), in antiquity trees would have been more common on the hillside than they are today, "as the old name of the hill, Kapsala, derived from *kavsoxila* ('firewood'), suggests."

70 As Schörner and Goette show conclusively (2004: 17–20), this barrier only allows for one path forward: through the smaller and darker western cavern.

71 For an acoustic analysis of the Vari Cave see Yioutsos et al. 2018: 2170–72.

72 The invocation of the Charites (the Graces) does not preclude the worship of the Nymphs in the Vari Cave. Female pluralities, particularly triads, were extremely common in early Greek myth and cult; one may think of the Muses, the Charites, and the Horai as belonging to this phenomenon. On female pluralities in Greek myth, see Nancy 1996: 1; Nancy 2000; Larson 2001: 7–8; Porter 2013. While the precise identity of the recipient may remain unclear, this area was clearly intended as a focal point of worship, since there is a small ledge near the pool that seems intended to hold offerings. Weller 1903: 275–76; Schörner and Goette 2004: 44.

73 When the cave was excavated, Wickens (1986: vol. 2, 90–121) notes that miniature *loutrophoroi* were uncovered around the spring in the southern room, perhaps hinting at the spring's role in purification rites that took place before a marriage.

74 The possibility of experiencing an epiphany of the gods was an integral aspect of Greek religion. For more on epiphany broadly, see Platt 2011; Platt 2014; Petridou 2015.

75 For a comprehensive discussion of Acheloös and a catalogue of images depicting the god, see Isler 1970; Isler 1981.

76 The prominence of water in the cave was also noted by Wickens, who writes that "there is much dripping water in the cave" (Wickens 1986: 92).

77 A notable exception is the relief dedicated to the Nymphs by Telephanes, Nikeratos, and Demophilos, which is surrounded by an architectural frame. The relief, which can be dated to 350–320 BCE, was found in the Cave of Pan and the Nymphs on Mount Penteli. Athens, National Archaeological Museum, NM 4465, 4465a.

78 The vertical relief, already mentioned above, is in the Athens National Archaeological Museum (NM 2011).

79 Based on niches cut into the walls of the cave and the holes that run along the small terraces that would have supported the votives with their stone tenons, it seems likely that all the reliefs were once displayed in this area. Schörner and Goette 2004: 60–77.

80 This flattened platform and its retaining wall were visible during the initial excavations, but little now remains, as noted by Weller 1903: 281–82; Schörner and Goette 2004; Yioutsos 2013: 24, 31–41, 113. Despite Weller's suggestion that worshippers may have danced past an altar that was set up on this platform, there is no archaeological evidence, beyond the inclusion of an altar on the votive reliefs, to support this idea. The only altar that has survived in the Vari Cave was dedicated to Apollo Hersos, and was carved into the living rock adjacent to the sculpted image of Archedemos. The inscription here has traditionally been read as "Apollonos Hersou" (*IG* I² 783; Schörner and Goette 2004: 46–49; Pache 2011: 48–51). Dr. Alexandra Mari with the Greek *ephoreia* has also suggested that the sigma in the inscription may have been flipped on its side, since the inscription was running up against the wall of the altar; if this is the case, the inscription could read Apollo Hermes. She presented her work in a public lecture, *Cave Sanctuaries in Attica: The Cave of Pan at Vari*, on October 11, 2016, at the Athens Centre. As Schörner and Goette point out, it is unlikely that this altar was intended for the Nymphs, since it is clearly divided into two separate offering areas. An altar dedicated to the Nymphs has not been found. For more, see Weller 1903: 281–82; Yavis 1949: 214–15; Schörner and Goette 2004: 113.

81 The cave frame on each relief, therefore, is essential to the image's visual theology. On visual theology see Gordon 1979; Vernant 1985a and 1985b; Elsner 1996: 518; Tanner 2006; Gaifman 2017; Platt 2017: 384, 390; Mack 2018.

82 My discussion draws on Laferrière 2019b. A second inscription confronts the visitor shortly after passing by the basin and the Archedemos inscription. It appears to be the oldest of the inscriptions found in the cave, and mandates certain actions within the space. It reads: τἄντερ᾽ ἔχ- | σο κλύζετε | καὶ τὸν ὄν- | θον νίζετε (Wash the | intestines outside, | and wash out | the waste). When taken together with the basin full of water just across the passageway, the inscription suggests that visitors to the cave were meant to purify themselves, and anything that they might bring with them, before entering into the depths of the cave itself so that they would not pollute the shrine. This inscription, then, further establishes the Vari Cave as one that constitutes sacred space in which worshippers must follow certain designated actions. *IG* I² 789; Schörner and Goette 2004: 44–46.

83 *IG* I² 788; *IG* I³ 980. Translation lightly adapted from Pache 2011: 45–46; see also Dunham 1903: 299–300; Schörner and Goette 2004: 42–44.

84 Kansteiner et al. 2014: Archedamos.

85 Connor 1988: 156; Larson 2001: 16. He also clearly establishes his identity as a Theran, thus rendering him unaffiliated with any particular Attic deme or tribe, other than potentially as a metic within Athens itself. That he is not Athenian is of interest, since the cults of Pan and the Nymphs seem very much focused on the *chōra* around the city.

86 Translation adapted from Emlyn-Jones and Preddy 2022: 384–385. See also Connor 1988: 158; Emlyn-Jones and Preddy 2017: 446–47.

87 There are, of course, Dionysian overtones to dithyrambic performances, and Dionysos was thought capable of manifesting through the performance of a dithyramb. See Lavecchia 2013. For more on dithyrambs, particularly in Athens, see Kowalzig and Wilson 2013a, 2013b.

88 Schörner and Goette 2004: 43.

89 On epigrams and reader-interaction, see Meyer 2005; Männlein-Robert 2007; Tueller 2008; Day 2010: 26–75.

90 Pache 2011: 51.

91 Derrida 1987: 52–68; Platt and Squire 2017a.

92 Εὐκλείδης Εὐκλῆς Λακράτης Νύμφαις (*IG* II² 4651). Edwards notes that this seems to be the earliest representation of Pan standing. Thallon 1903: 304–05, pl. IV; Feubel 1935: 33–34; Fuchs 1959: 22; Fuchs 1962: 244; Isler 1970: 30, 106, 12, 14, 17, 24; Edwards 1985: 489–95, no. 23; Güntner 1994: 123, A35; Schörner and Goette 2004: 62–64, pl. 38.2. Another relief, NM 2007, quite similar in its organization, but carved with less skill, was also found here.

93 Superimposed behind the altar, her position also recalls the tradition in scenes of sacrifice on earlier fifth-century vase-painting, wherein the deity or a relevant symbol is located behind

the altar. Here, the Nymphs are clearly shown as the intended deities, a claim that is supported by the inscription below. For more on the relationship among god, altar, and worshipper, see generally Van Straten 1981, 1992, and 1995.

94 Vernant 1989.

95 The cave wall that surrounds the relief acts as the formal frame that encloses and delineates the image. On frames generally, see Hurwit 1977: 1–30; Derrida 1987: 52–68; Platt and Squire 2017a: 3–99.

96 Svoronos 1908–37: pl. 239.1; Vermaseren 1982: no. 182, pl. 36; Naumann 1983: 185, 186, 327, no. 270, pl. 27.2; Güntner 1994: 134, no. B36; Kaltsas 2002: 233, no. 491; Gaifman 2017: 417–22. Her frontal posture here recalls the position of a cult statue, positioned at the back of the *naos* and gazing out towards the door of the temple. Munn's volume (2006) on Kybele is an important study on the goddess and her journey from Asia to Greece. On cult statues more generally, see Donohue 1997.

97 Gaifman 2017: 419–21.

98 Gaifman 2017: 412; Gaifman 2018a: 117–50.

99 According to Herodotus (4.76), the *tympanon* or tambourine was used during the nocturnal rites for Kybele. For more on Kybele, see Munn 2006.

100 For more on frontal gazes in Greek art, see especially Korshak 1987; Frontisi-Ducroux 1995; Mackay 2001; Mack 2002; Hedreen 2007; Hedreen 2017.

101 Similar scenes may be seen on the votive from Hekale, Mount Parnes, and the Ilissos (Athens NM 3874; Athens NM 1859; Berlin, Antikensammlung 709). On those reliefs where the Nymphs stand rather than dance, the central Nymph still exhibits this behavior, as can be seen on a rectangular relief from the Vari Cave (Athens NM 2011). A notable exception is the relief from Megalopolis, where the Nymph leading the dance turns her gaze outwards towards the surface of the relief (Athens NM 1449), while the two surviving Nymphs on the relief dedicated by Telephanes both confront the viewer with a direct frontal stare (Athens NM 1448).

102 Day 1994; Day 2000; Day 2010; Platt 2011.

103 Foster 2011: 1.

104 Sklar 2001: 198–99, n. 3.

105 As discussed, for instance, at Arist. *De an.* 417a–418a. I develop this point further in Laferrière 2019b.

106 This particular relief has been much discussed, and an extensive bibliography may be found in Edwards' entry for this relief, but the most relevant sources are Rouse 1902: 86, fig. 22; Thallon 1903: 302; Feubel 1935: xi, no. II.19, 36–37; Brommer 1956: 981, no. 32; Fuchs 1962: 244; Muthmann 1968: 24, pl. 11.2; Isler 1970: no. 15; Blümel 1971: 66, no. 76, fig. 109; Muthmann 1975: 90, pl. 13.2; Edwards 1985: 737–42, no. 77; Güntner 1994: A37; Klöckner 2010: 115–17, n. 23.

107 For a comparable example of Pan perched on a ledge, see a relief in Berlin (Antikensammlung 709; Edwards 1985: no. 5).

108 This is now modern day Ekali, located in the municipal region of Kefisia. There is no known cave sanctuary to Pan and the Nymphs in this area, although this of course does not preclude the possibility of its existence. Most sources agree on the late Classical dating of this relief. Isler 1970: 30–31, 112, 17, 26; Güntner 1994: 121, no. A22; Kaltsas 2002: 220–21, no. 458. Edwards, supported by Fuchs, suggests that a Hellenistic date might be more plausible given the parallels between this votive and other Hellenistic examples (Fuchs 1962: 246, pl. 66.1; Edwards 1985: 716–20, no. 71).

109 Hurwit 1977; Derrida 1987: 1–30; Platt and Squire 2017c.

110 For more on the relationship between Pan and herms, see especially Gaifman 2008: 94, 96; Versnel 2011: 309–78; Laferrière 2019a: 34–37.

111 Sklar 2001: 199, n. 3. See also Foster 2008.

112 Olsen 2021: 158–59. See also Peponi 2015.

113 On the audience and *choreia*, see especially Weiss 2020; Olsen 2021; Steiner 2021; Weiss 2023.

114 Sklar 2008: 87–89.

115 I do not argue that the Nymphs dance in a circle, but rather that their movements on this and other reliefs suggest an awareness of the external world and a desire to incorporate the human viewer into their movements. For more on the circle dance in lyric poetry, see Calame 2001: 34–36. On the possibility of the Nymphs dancing in a circle, see Yioutsos 2017: 215–16.

TWO

POURING PERFORMANCES

In our discussion of Pan's music as it was represented on fourth-century BCE votive reliefs, the cave context in which the reliefs would have been encountered proved to be essential for animating the sounds of the god's music and enlivening the Nymphs' dance for the ancient worshippers. In many ways, the votive reliefs offer us the clearest picture of how scenes of divine music could have prepared their viewers to have a powerfully transformative experience by visually alluding to the sounds of Pan's music and by representing the Nymphs' danced response to those sounds, while, at the same time, inviting ancient viewers to imaginatively hear the sounds of divine music within specific cave landscapes. However, the vast majority of representations of the gods engaging in musical practice are found on late sixth- and fifth-century painted vases, which were, at least by nature of their shape, intended to be used in the symposium. However, vases were inherently moveable, making the possible spaces in which they were seen and used relatively wide-ranging, so that their audience might include both men and women, depending on where and how the objects were used. Let us now look at a different approach to representations of divine musicians not only with respect to the medium in which they were created, but also to the contexts in which they were encountered and the significance of the gods' music for the human audience.

We begin with the figure of Apollo, the quintessential divine musician within the Greek pantheon. Sitting alone on a low stool, the god stares

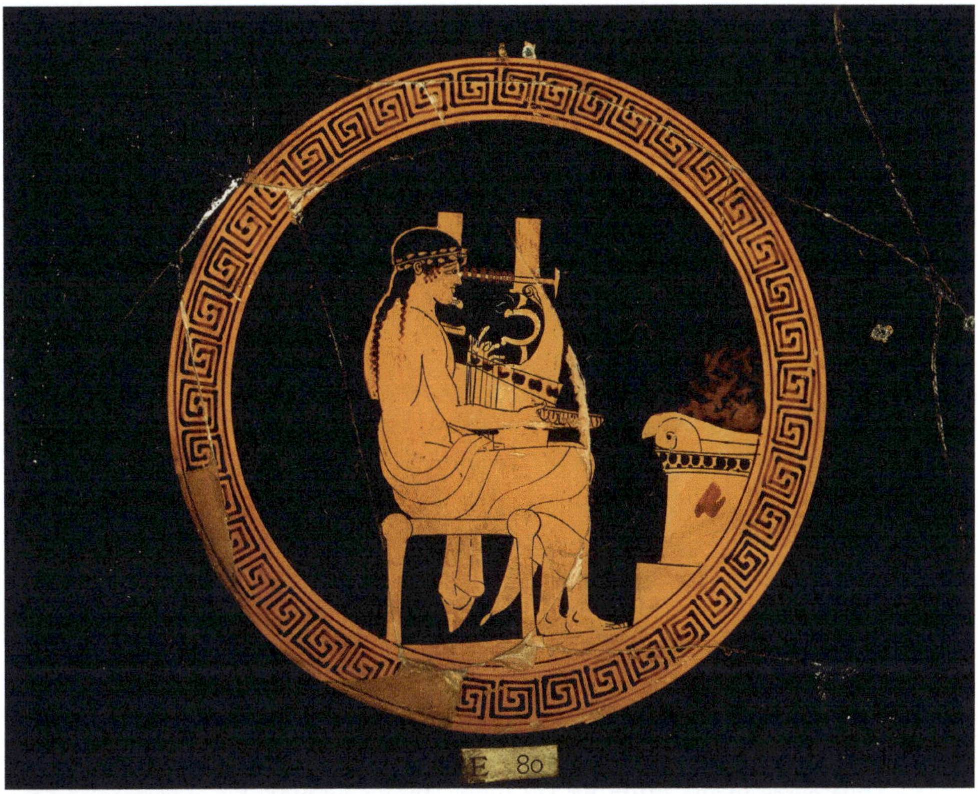

2.1. The Painter of London E 80, *Apollo Seated in Front of an Altar* (tondo), Attic red-figure *kylix*, ceramic, h. 8.89 cm, *c.* 480–470 BCE. London, British Museum, 1893,1115.1 (E80). © The Trustees of the British Museum.

intently to the right, directing his attention to the blood-spattered altar upon which a fire burns and crackles in front of him (Fig. 2.1).[1] In his right hand, he holds out a *phialē*, a shallow bowl he will soon use to pour out his liquid offering.[2] He has been depicted just moments before his ritual will occur, as he stretches out his arm to receive the liquid poured out by a companion who has not been included here. Partially overlapping with the libation dish is an enormous *kithara*, which rises up alongside the figure's torso, its arms reaching above the figure's head while its wide body almost extends the length of his seated form. Upon closer inspection, it is clear that he not only holds the instrument, but he plucks its strings with the fingers on his left hand. Despite the unusual technique the god uses to play his instrument, the image clearly depicts him creating musical sounds to accompany his libation. Within the scene, music blends and pours out together with his liquid ritual, both acting as the offering the young male figure leaves at the burning altar.

The image presents a distinct kind of musical performance: as the god plays his *kithara*, he also pours a libation, so that he undertakes both actions, one musical and the other ritual, in a single moment.[3] The simultaneity of these two actions is surprising, not least given the clear physical challenge involved in playing an instrument one-handed while also using the other hand to perform a separate action. Not only did a lyre typically require one hand to balance the instrument and manipulate the strings while the other pulled the *plektron* across the instrument to produce sound, but the libation itself also required two hands, one to pour the liquid into the *phialē*, and another to tip the contents of the *phialē* onto the ground.[4] Moreover, libations were typically undertaken by two individuals, with each participant performing one of the two actions. How, then, does Apollo achieve this distinctive balancing act?

As we have seen, images of divine musicians actively performing offered their viewers the opportunity to see the visual presence of divine music through the particular way in which the forms of the musician's body, drapery, and instrument echo each other. Although Apollo plays his instrument unconventionally in the tondo image, we may nevertheless see traces of the movement of sound throughout the painted scene. For instance, the god's body has been composed with long and short curving lines as his exposed torso rises up in a long sweeping line, while his long hair falls down on his back in tight curls. Anchoring his nude chest are the large curving folds of his drapery, which envelops his entire lower body. The curvilinear lines of varied tightness that constitute the god's body are repeated in the body of the god's *kithara*, which itself is composed of broad sweeping lines and more delicately curving decorative components. With his left wrist, Apollo supports his instrument by the decorated strap that wraps around its arm and body, while the middle finger of his hand pulls gently on the fourth string. The repeating pattern on the sash echoes the alternating forms of black and red on the god's head where his wreath encircles it, as well as the egg and dart pattern on the altar. In a similar manner, the curvilinear lines that make up the forms of the god and his instrument are echoed by the curved rim of the *phialē*, the intricately composed egg and dart decoration on the altar, and the broad sweeping lines of the volute on the altar's surface. In contrast to the mass of curving forms, the vertical arms and strings of the *kithara* stretch upwards, past the god's head. Straight and zigzagging lines also make up Apollo's fingers as he pulls on the strings. In engaging with these contrasting visual forms, the viewer's eye is repeatedly drawn to the center of the image, the spot at which the music is created and from which it emanates outward to fill the scene. Our gaze is then drawn down by the continuing line of the strings, and it is from this line that Apollo's arm extends the *phialē*, holding it out at the same level as the altar. All three elements of the scene, that is, the altar, *kithara*, and god, are thus joined together through the repetition of similar formal elements, creating a visual rhythm that implicitly references the musical sounds – and possibly even the melody – that emerge from the instrument. In this scene, the visual and the sonic have come together in musical harmony.

My reading of Apollo's performance in the tondo image depends on an essential detail: that the god's left hand does not simply support the instrument but, rather, that he actively plays the instrument by plucking at its strings to produce distinctive musical notes and sounds. The image confronts us, then, with a number of questions. How does Apollo play his instrument with one hand, when other musicians, both mortal and divine, are not shown doing so? Does his unique performance style affect the character of his music or the ritual he undertakes? And, perhaps most importantly, how did these scenes of Apollo's musico-religious performance interact with the human viewer, who might not only be invited to hear the sounds of Apollo's performance, but who could also sing his or her own hymns and pour his or her own libation? In other words, how could the sensory engagement with divine music have offered an experience of divine presence within a shared human and divine ritual, especially when the god's music was encountered within a sympotic context? By analyzing Apollo's two actions, I show that not only is Apollo represented as actively producing musical sound in these images, but that the images depict the god deliberately coordinating his two actions in order to draw in and involve his audience in his ritual and musical performance. Even more, by staging the related sensory experiences of his two performances, I argue that the images offered their viewers the possibility of a particularly powerful imagined experience of Apollo, one where coordinated action and musical rhythm encouraged a harmony between human worshipper and divine musician.

APOLLO'S MUSIC

The unique character of Apollo's simultaneous musical and ritual performance becomes particularly clear when it is compared with other examples where the god plays his lyre without engaging in another activity. For instance, if we look at one image that depicts Apollo's music-making (Fig. 3.9), discussed more extensively in Chapter 3, it is clear that the skill with which Apollo performs has captivated his audience, whose attention is directed toward Apollo, with little other movement in the scene to detract from his performance. Only the deer betrays any hint of movement as she takes a step forwards, walking from the source of music toward a member of the listening audience. Even Apollo himself is immobile, moving only his hands as he plays the instrument. His performance here acts as the focal point of the scene: in line with the god's face is his left hand, dampening various strings or plucking at others while his right hand holds the *plektron* and sweeps it across the strings. Apollo and his instrument are thus the point around which the image unfolds, so that the god's musical performance constitutes the active center to an otherwise inactive scene.

Yet within the corpus of red-figure vases in which Apollo both plays his lyre and pours a libation, each image is filled with movements that have been deliberately coordinated: as Apollo pulls gently on the lyre's strings, he might extend his *phialē* to his companion, or tip the vessel so that the liquid begins to fall down to the earth. The other figures and objects in the scene are also coordinated in their movements. For her part, Artemis, who, as we will see, is his most common companion, often lifts her jug to pour the liquid into her brother's *phialē*. At the same time, a deer might step toward Apollo or flames might crackle as they burn upon an altar. Above all, it is Apollo himself who distinguishes between scenes depicting exclusive musical performance and those in which music-making is joined by ritual action: he is the sole figure who performs both actions, and this particular mode of representing Apollo introduces a distinct conception of the god, that he is shown to be so proficient a musician that he can bring together music and ritual into one harmonious scene.

This synchronicity, that is, these two actions that have been coordinated musically, is distinct to visual representations of Apollo.[5] The other gods, conversely, are not shown pairing their music with another activity. For instance, when Pan plays his *syrinx* for the Nymphs, that is the only activity that he ever performs; he does not hunt for rabbits, nor does he undertake any other pastoral activity.[6] He might occasionally join in the Nymphs' dance, but that is the closest he is ever shown to engaging in multiple actions at once. Similarly, in a Dionysian revel, the satyrs and maenads play their instruments as prompted by Dionysos, but neither they nor he attempt to divide their attention by using one hand to undertake another action.[7] Perhaps it goes without saying that mortal musicians are not shown attempting this balancing act: they only ever engage in one activity, even when the performance depicted is clearly one of superior skill, as is the case for the Berlin Painter's masterful *kitharoidos* (Fig. 2.2).[8] Despite the clear skill with which the musician performs, there is no attempt in the image to suggest that he plays unconventionally or with innovation, at least in terms of his technique. With respect to representations of our musical Apollo, although careful attention is given to depicting the particular way the god handles his instrument, some have suggested that it is difficult to ascertain whether or not Apollo plays the lyre or if he merely holds the instrument without producing any musical sounds.[9] These arguments, which rely in part upon technical studies of musical theory and practice, observe that since Apollo holds a *phialē* in his right hand instead of a *plektron* and since his left hand is often ambiguously positioned upon the instrument, he does not actually play it.[10] According to this logic, therefore, Apollo cannot play his instrument since his right hand does not employ a *plektron*, despite the left hand's articulation upon the strings.[11] However, given the technique required to play the lyre one-handed, skillful human musicians

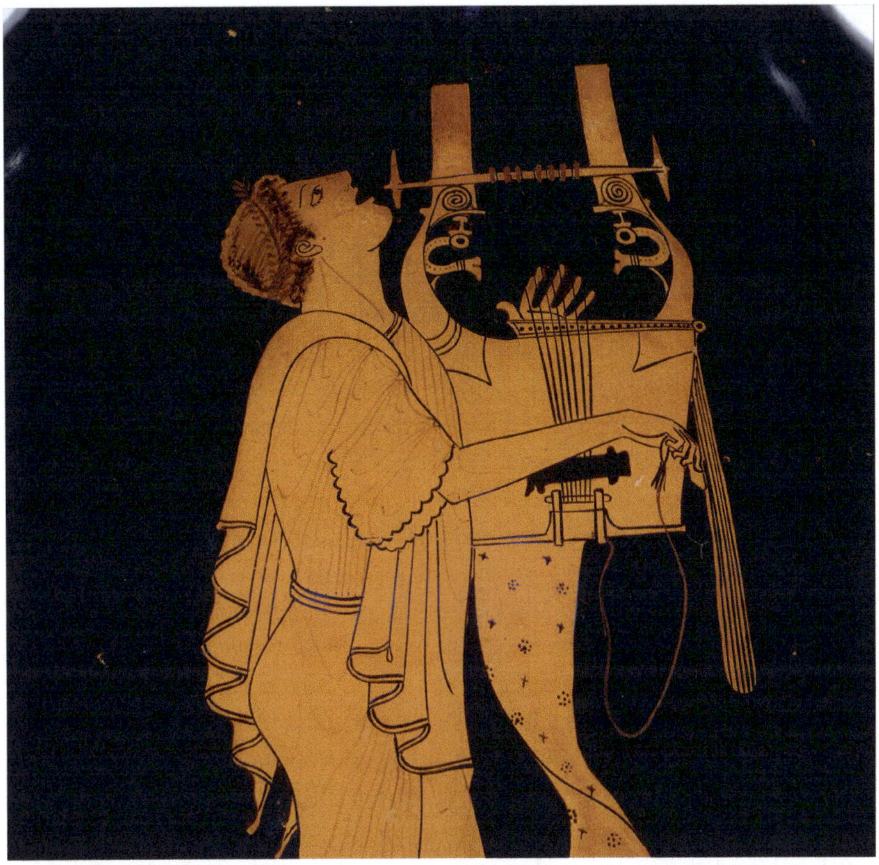

2.2. Detail. The Berlin Painter, *Young Man Singing and Playing the Kithara* (side A), Attic red-figure *amphora*, ceramic, h. 41.50 cm, *c.* 490 BCE. New York, Metropolitan Museum of Art, 56.171.38. Fletcher Fund, 1956. Creative Commons CCO.

should have been able to perform in this way, and indeed the literary sources confirm that left-handed plucking could be used to complement right-handed strumming.[12] Moreover, we can imagine that displays of technical virtuosity within musical performance would have prompted some experimentation with technique, much like we see in the modern world with contemporary musicians.[13] In the visual material, however, mortal musicians – or indeed even other divine musicians – are not shown engaging with their instrument in this particular way. Rather, this style of playing is specifically reserved for Apollo, arguably in order to suggest that he is a particularly skilled musician, beyond comparison with anyone else.[14]

To support the argument that Apollo plays his lyre in this distinct manner and produces some sort of musical sound, it is worth revisiting a select number of examples that feature scenes of mortal musicians, which are often cited in the arguments against the active nature of Apollo's performance.[15] As is made clear by the Berlin Painter's *kitharoidos* (Fig. 2.2), the musician's left hand can be held with fingers splayed out and thumb reaching back to lend support to the instrument, while the right hand pulls the *plektron* across the strings.[16] On another vessel, Paris, who leans back on a rock while he plays his *chelys* lyre, folds up his hand into a rounded ball, as if to push against the strings to dampen any sound they might produce.[17] Another variation occurs with the figure of Alkaios on a *kalathos*, where he plays his *barbitos* alongside Sappho (Fig. 4.17a). Here, he stretches out four fingers to touch separate strings while his thumb wraps around another string. Given the varied position the left hand is shown to have in the visual material, the images together suggest that the left hand was responsible for manipulating the strings in some way, whether it was to dampen certain strings, to pluck certain strings in between the strokes of the *plektron*, or, less likely, to create different harmonic lengths on the strings.[18]

In those representations where Apollo holds his *kithara* and pours a libation, his left-hand gestures on the instrument's strings recall those where the musician plays his lyre in a more traditional manner. In the cup tondo (Fig. 2.1), he bends his middle finger to pluck at a specific string, as if to produce a similarly specific musical sound. On a jug, he uses his left hand both to support the large *kithara* and to touch five distinct strings; his last three fingers are even bent and curved to wrap around strings (Fig. 2.17). Like Alkaios, Apollo may also hook a thumb around a string while the other fingers are splayed out.[19] He also occasionally makes a fist with his left hand, as if temporarily dampening the strings, preventing any sounds from occurring.[20] In each instance, there is a clear awareness of the musical sounds the god could potentially create with his left hand, and the variation that exists across the corpus points to the sonic possibilities inherent in these images. When compared with the scenes of human musicians, the only element that the god lacks is a *plektron* held in his right hand. Moreover, when Apollo is shown holding a string between two fingers or with a string wrapped around a single finger, as we saw in the tondo image with which we began, the image may even suggest that he plucks at certain strings to produce specific musical notes. Although the sounds the god creates with his lyre cannot be determined in terms of their complexity or acoustic level, at the very least the images invite us to imagine that Apollo plucks a single string at one time, producing individual notes at regular, rhythmic intervals.

The scene painted by the Villa Giulia Painter on a stand for a mixing bowl offers further support for the claim that Apollo actively plays his instrument on this and other similar scenes (Fig. 2.3).[21] Here, the gods have assembled together, many of whom hold libation dishes, as well as a male youth, possibly Ganymede or Ion, who is depicted on a smaller scale than the Olympians.[22] Since the youth holds a wine jug, he seems to have been included here to act as the cup bearer to the gods. However, rather than filling drinking cups, the image suggests that he must instead fill the gods' *phialai*.[23] Apollo stands

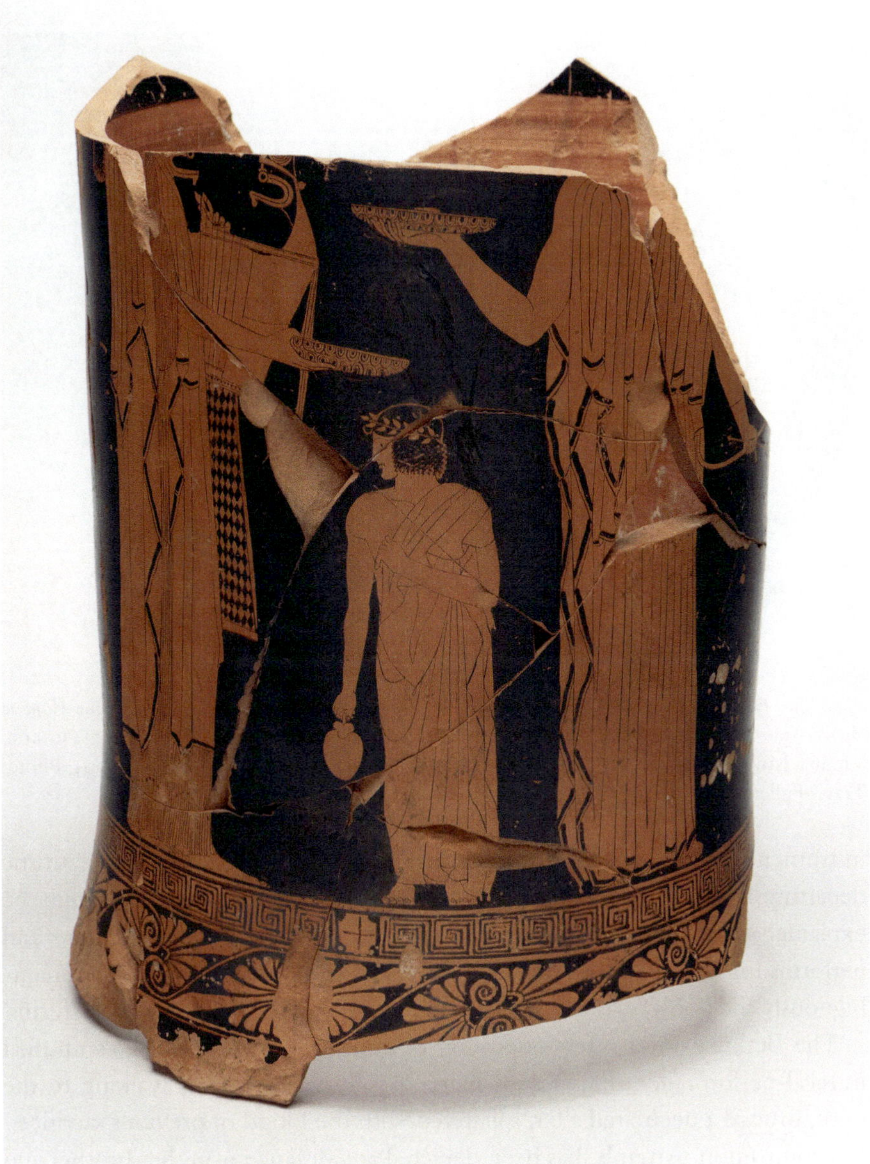

2.3. The Villa Giulia Painter, *Assembly of Gods*, Attic red-figure stand, ceramic, h. 29.5 cm, 460–450 BCE. Cambridge, Fitzwilliam Museum, GR.P.13. © Fitzwilliam Museum, Cambridge/Art Resource, NY.

directly adjacent to this youth; extending his *phialē* to the right, the god has been depicted moments before he tips the contents of his libation dish onto the ground. At the same time, he holds a large *kithara* with his left arm and, surprisingly, strikes its strings with a *plektron* held in his left hand. This is an extremely unusual, if not unique, depiction of a musician, since the *plektron* is always shown held in the musician's right hand while the left arm stabilizes the

(A)

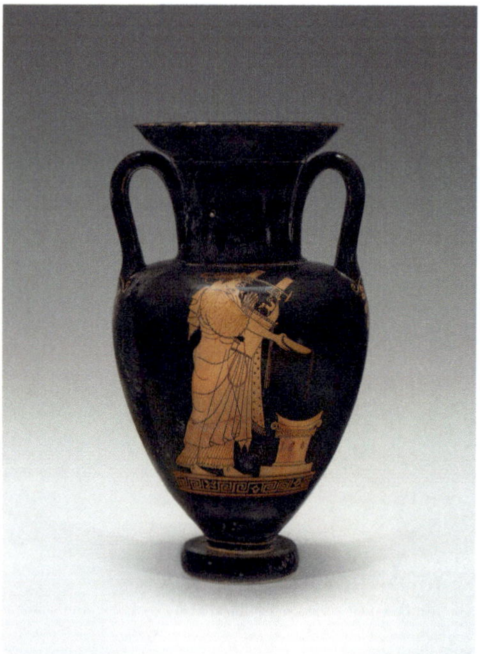

(B)

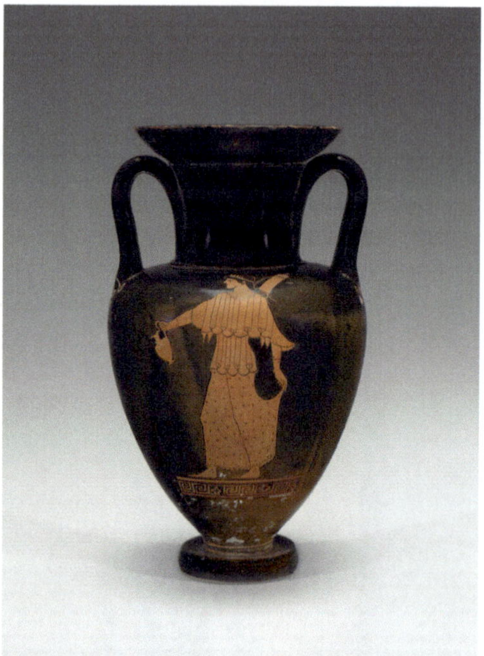

2.4. The Berlin Painter, *Apollo Pouring a Libation at an Altar* (side A), *Artemis Offering Wine to Apollo* (side B), Attic red-figured Nolan *amphora*, ceramic, 29.21 cm × 17.15 cm, *c.* 480 BCE. Virginia Museum of Fine Arts, Richmond. Arthur and Margaret Glasgow Fund, 82.204. Photo: Travis Fullerton. © Virginia Museum of Fine Arts.

instrument and the left hand manipulates individual strings.[24] Such an artistic departure from the proper mechanics of playing the instrument may only be explained through a desire to stress that the god clearly plays his lyre and performs his libation simultaneously. In other words, in this scene, it is unambiguously the god's own music that accompanies the ritual action he performs.

The Berlin Painter offers one other option for depicting Apollo's unusual musical performance (Fig. 2.4).[25] Here, Apollo stands alone, walking to the right, toward a decorated altar, splattered with the blood of previous sacrifices. His companion, Artemis, has been depicted at a distance from her brother and appears on the reverse of the vase with her bow and quiver of arrows strapped to her back. Despite her physical separation from her companion in the ritual, she nevertheless holds a jug and takes a step forward, as if to move around the surface of the vase toward her brother to help him complete his offering. Shown in the midst of his ritual, Apollo once again holds the *kithara* with his left hand, fingers splayed out, touching some of the middle strings, while his thumb gently hooks around the first string (Fig. 2.5). Unlike the Villa Giulia Painter's stand, where the normal technique of holding the *plektron* in the right hand was reversed so that the god could still play the instrument to its fullest extent, on this vessel the Berlin Painter instead manipulated the placement of

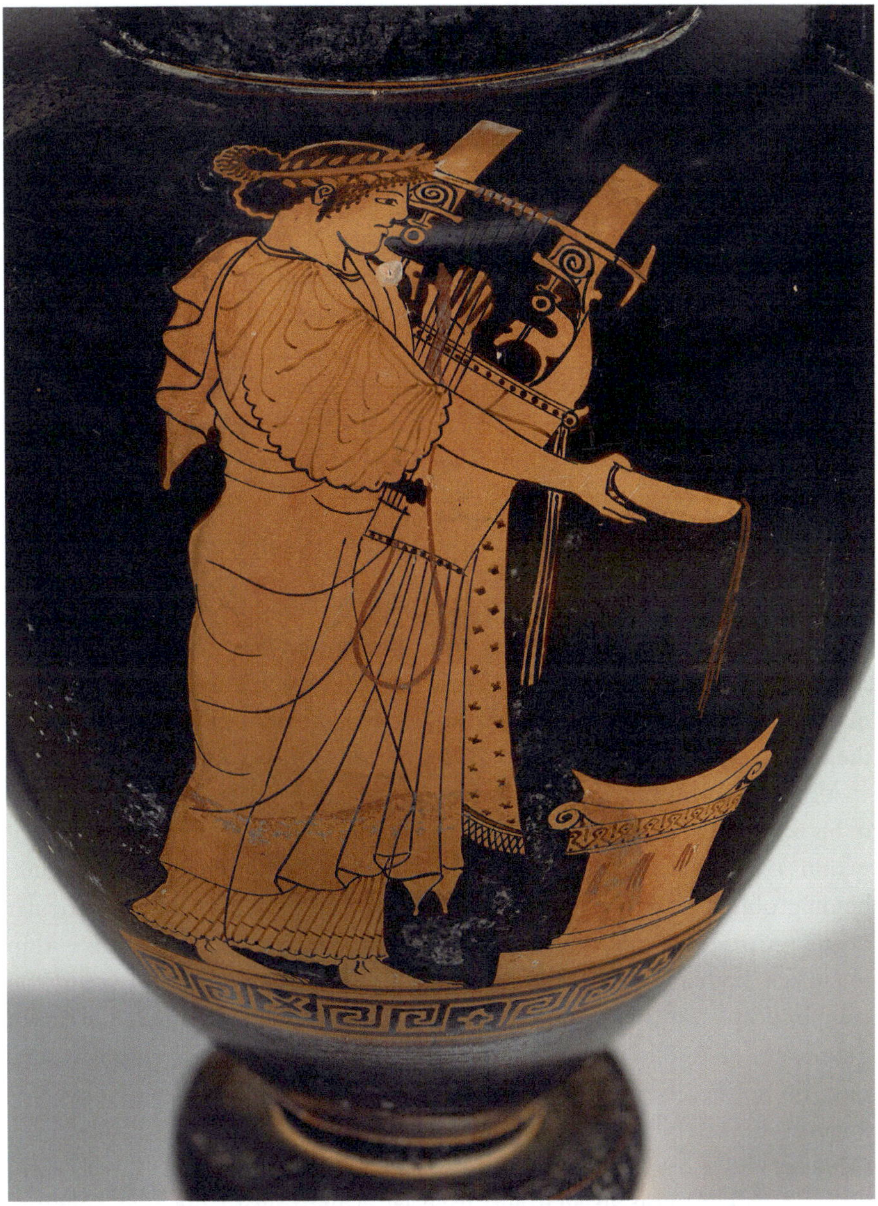

2.5. Detail of Apollo. The Berlin Painter, *Apollo Pouring a Libation at an Altar* (side A), Attic red-figured Nolan *amphora*, ceramic, 29.21 cm × 17.15 cm, *c.* 480 BCE. Virginia Museum of Fine Arts, Richmond. Arthur and Margaret Glasgow Fund, 82.204. Photo: Travis Fullerton. © Virginia Museum of Fine Arts.

the *plektron*. In one reading, we could interpret the placement of the pick as having been tucked between the god's left hand and the strings or, alternatively, as having been suspended between the strings. In either case, the image still stresses that musical performance was, or is about to be, underway, and that the god has merely paused in his music-making to pour out his libation.

Alternatively, we might also understand the *plektron* as having been suspended in front of the strings. If this is the case, then the otherwise inanimate *plektron* has been given its own agency: the added red used for its body clearly overlaps on top of the instrument behind it, so that the pick appears to float in front of the strings, unsupported by the god's hand. Angled in such a way that the tip of the *plektron* would catch the first string, it seems almost ready to draw itself across the instrument to create a sequence of musical sounds. It is as if the god's divinity has animated the device, which now acts in conjunction with Apollo to produce the music that accompanies his ritual act.

The repetition of rhythmically resonant visual forms further underscores the importance and presence of music within this scene. The vertical lines that comprise the decorated fabric and support band that hang from the instrument mimic those of the liquid that falls from the *phialē*, as well as those of the god's drapery, both on his diaphanous *chitōn* and heavier *himation*. Each element originates from Apollo's connection with his instrument and then moves outward to condition the depiction of the rest of the scene, so that as the liquid offering gently falls down to the altar, so too does Apollo's music rise up from the animated *plektron*, which strikes the instrument's strings, filling the space that surrounds the god.[26] Both music and libation are thus suspended in mid-air, repeatedly asserting the necessary simultaneity of the two gestures and the unique ability of Apollo to engage in both actions at once.

Although Apollo's coordinated musical and ritual performances are distinct to his particular mode of representation, they can also be situated more broadly within a fifth-century mode of depicting the gods pouring libations while holding objects that both identify them and elaborate upon their particular divine *personae*. The objects the gods hold thus have a double function within the image, both as identifying attributes and as enhancing their role within the composition.[27] However, there is an important distinction to make between the images of Apollo and those of other gods, namely that the objects they carry do not necessarily require any additional action on their part. Take, for instance, a votive relief discovered in the sanctuary at Eleusis that depicts Demeter and Kore standing in front of a group of worshippers, who have placed a basket upon an altar and have led a pig toward the two divinities (Fig. 2.6).[28] Standing adjacent to the altar is Kore, who holds two torches in her right hand. Her mother, Demeter, stands beside her; she lifts a small bundle of wheat in her left hand and holds out a *phialē* in such a way that suggests that she is tipping out its contents.[29] The wheat the goddess holds serves two purposes in this image: first, it helps us to identify Demeter, who would otherwise be recognizable only through her association with Kore, whose torches act similarly here.[30] Second, in displaying the wheat so prominently, Demeter invokes her own theology, that is, her role in ensuring the regeneration of agricultural crops each spring and the Mysteries that took place at

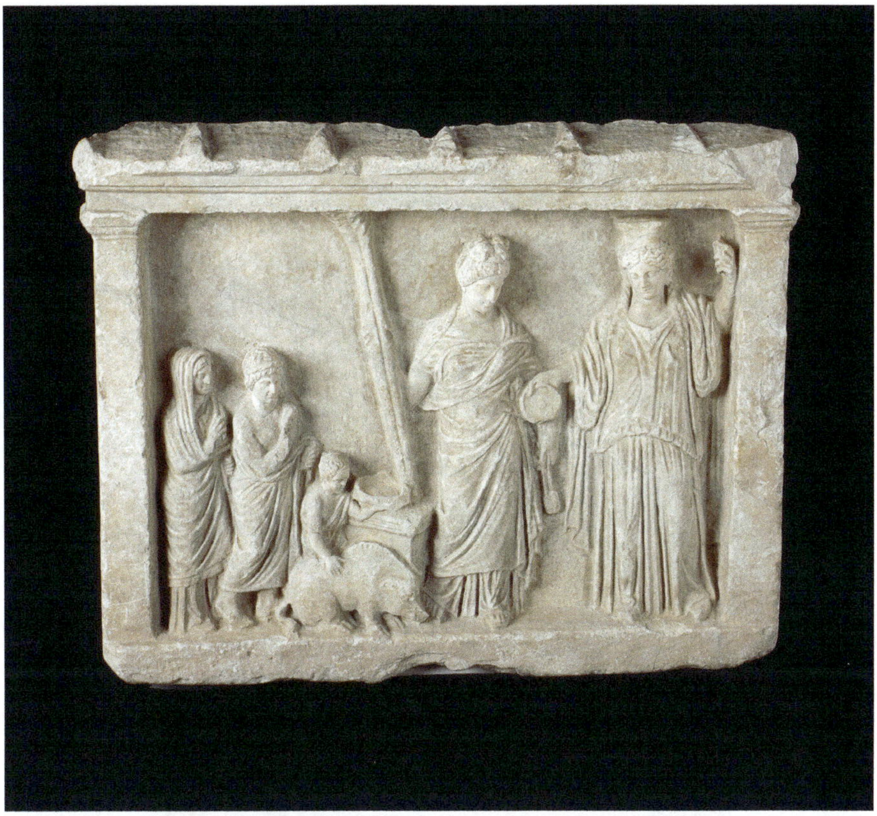

2.6. Votive relief depicting a Sacrifice to Demeter and Kore, from Athens, marble, 48 × 61 cm, *c.* 340–320 BCE. Paris, Musée du Louvre, MA752. © Musée du Louvre, Dist. RMN-Grand Palais/Daniel Lebée and Carine Déambrosis/Art Resource, NY.

Eleusis, which seem to have been involved in concerns about the cycle of human life and fertility more broadly.[31] The wheat thus at once identifies Demeter while it also invokes the reasons why the Greeks would be concerned to worship her.

Similarly, there are instances when Apollo pours a libation while he simply holds his lyre. In these images, such as a red-figure neck *amphora* by the Niobid Painter, it is clear that the god does not play his instrument, since he holds his tortoise shell *chelys* lyre by one of its arms (Fig. 2.7).[32] With his other hand, he extends the *phialē* across the altar toward Artemis, who holds her bow in one hand and a jug in the other.[33] Importantly, the instrument that Apollo holds hangs unused by the god's side and remains silent. However, for those images where Apollo does hold his lyre in such a way that suggests that he plays it, embedded within and layered upon the images are the sounds of the god's music and the theological significance of his divine performance. When Apollo holds the lyre in such a way that suggests an active musical

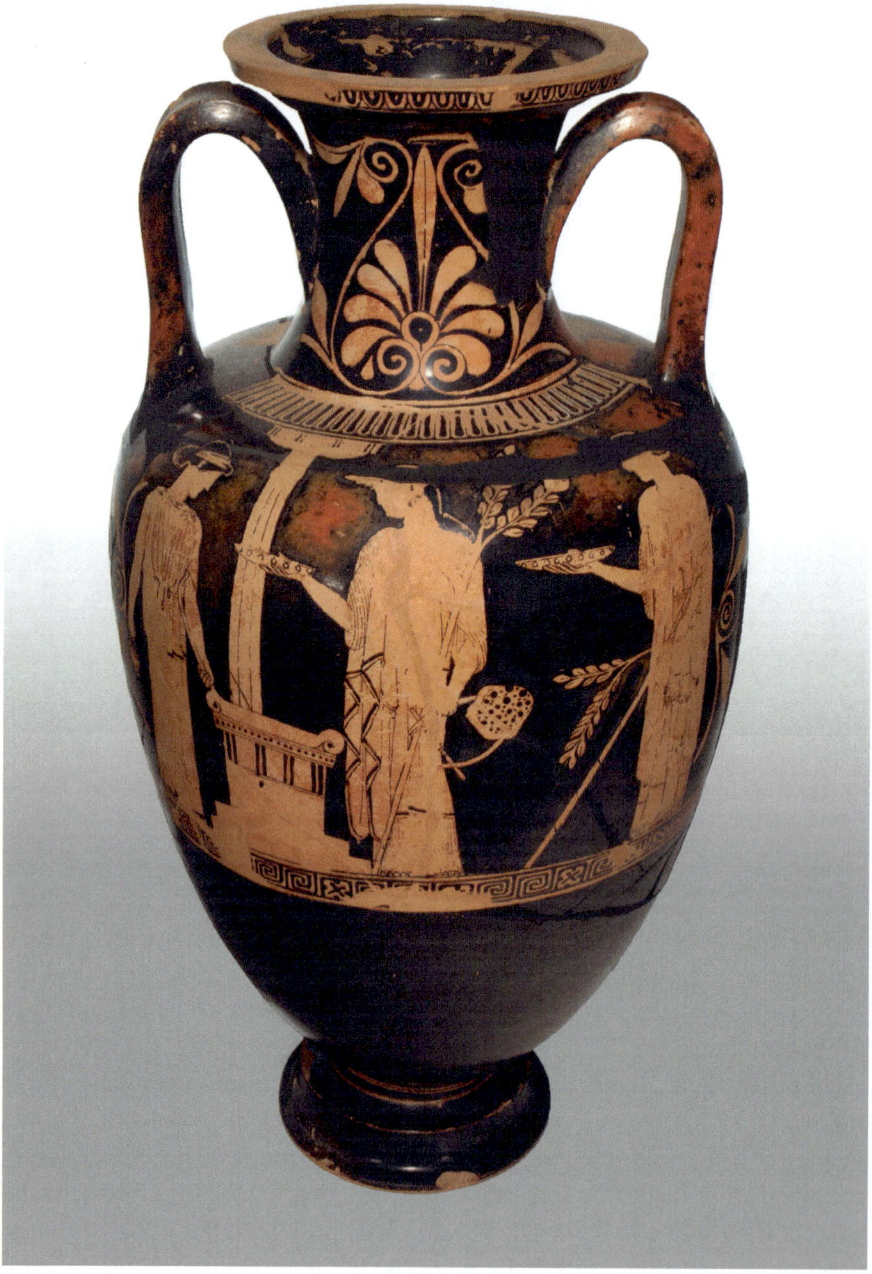

2.7. The Niobid Painter, *Apollo, Artemis, and Leto at an Altar* (side A), Attic red-figure neck *amphora*, ceramic, *c.* 450 BCE. Würzburg, Martin von Wagner Museum, H4533. Photograph © P. Neckermann.

performance, we must take that representational choice seriously. Apollo's lyre, in these instances, fulfills multiple functions within the image. It not only identifies Apollo for the viewer, but it also suggests the presence of visual sound within the image and the potential effect his music could have on those who listen.

APOLLO'S LIBATION

Thus far, I have argued that when Apollo holds a lyre in one hand, with or without a *plektron* in the other, the god actively plays his instrument. With our attention having been focused on the sounds of the god's music, our interaction with the tondo image on which Apollo sits in front of an altar is enhanced (Fig. 2.1). Aware of the god's performance, we are now invited to imagine the music emerging from the lyre as the god plucks one string at a time, repeatedly infusing the space around him with sound. Even if Apollo's music is nothing more than a slow-paced rhythm of single musical notes, the specific sounds the god creates are crucial elements within the scene and, moreover, are essential for his ritual.

It remains now to consider the significance of the god's second action, the libation he offers. That the god performs a ritual is made clear by a number of vases on which the god stands or, in a few instances sits, in front of a flaming and blood-splattered altar, as we have already seen in the tondo image with which we began. Moreover, on a number of vases, additional red paint has been added to render the liquid that falls from his *phialē*. In these images, the god both prepares for his ritual and, in fact, is already in the midst of it. As with the problematics inherent to Apollo's particular style of musical performance in this corpus, the god's libation also presents a complication to our understanding of the function of ritual. After all, why would a god need to pour a libation?

The vases on which gods are depicted pouring libations may be roughly dated between 500 and 450 BCE.[34] In addressing this corpus, scholars have tried to explain how the gods might perform religious rituals when they themselves are typically the intended object of cult activity, for whom they perform these actions, and what the images were intended to communicate about Greek religion. The resulting responses may be broadly categorized into five groups: the first focuses its attention on the *phialē* and its role in mediating between human and divine;[35] the second associates each scene with an episode from myth;[36] the third suggests that representations of the gods' libations should be understood as expressions of the gods' own divinity;[37] the fourth argues that scenes of the gods pouring libations advance a particular relationship with human ritual practice;[38] and finally, the fifth positions divine libations within the broader socio-religious context of fifth-century Athens.[39] Importantly, though each theory builds upon the work of previous scholars, there is much overlap among these five categories, so that any given interpretation may include elements of other approaches. Moreover, research on the topic of divine libations does not progress sequentially. Although scholars continually refute, nuance, or build upon previous work, often a scholar will return to a previously advanced theory, so that when taken together, modern research forms an interconnected network for understanding this complex topic.[40] In positioning these images of libating gods in dialogue with the rituals that define the context for their interpretation what follows, I draw upon the recent work undertaken by Milette Gaifman. As she convincingly argues, since the surviving Classical vase-paintings and votive reliefs unequivocally show that both men and gods could undertake this particular religious ritual, one should not dismiss the scenes as illogical.[41] Rather, we must take seriously the representational choice to depict the gods engaging in ritual libations, and consider the significance of such scenes within the context of Greek religion. By turning to the content of the images, to those scenes where gods have gathered together for the performance of a ritual, she argues that when these images are considered together with their human counterparts, they display similar interests in cultivating community and close bonds among participants.[42] Drawing on Gaifman's reoriented framework for the study of images of divine libations, in what follows I focus on how Apollo and his music establish relationships with his companions, and how his own simultaneous gestures similarly coordinate the actions of those who accompany him.

MUSICAL COMPANIONSHIP

In positioning scenes of Apollo's musico-ritual act within the framework of Greek religion, it is clear that the god is represented engaging in activities where the presence of the divine could be perceived. As such, we should discuss the significance of Apollo's libation within contemporaneous practices of Greek ritual, where relationships among worshippers and the god were strengthened through their shared actions, even as the particular way in which Apollo is shown performing those actions is distinct to his own image. For instance, a libation requires two discrete actions, one where the liquid is poured into the *phialē* and another where the contents are tipped out onto the ground or altar. In the images, however, Apollo instead both pours his own libation and plays his instrument. However, he is often joined by other divine figures, and especially by his sister Artemis, whose appearance creates a more intricate sequence of movements and responses.

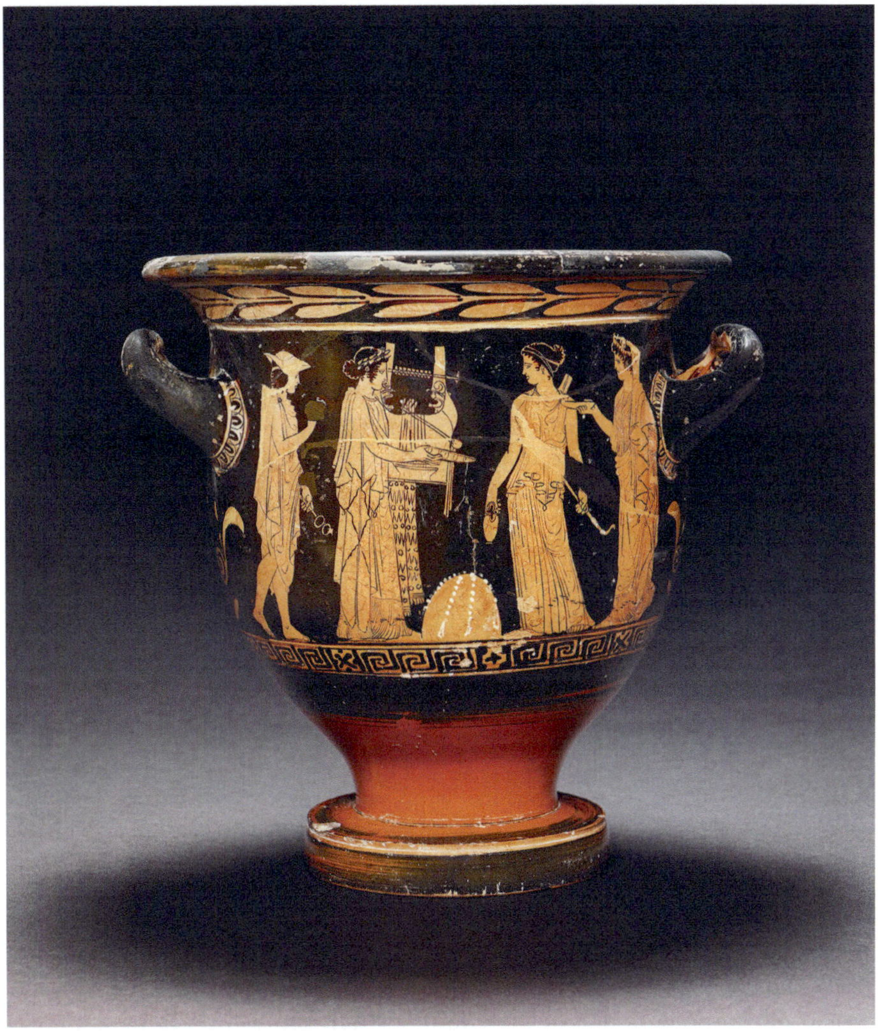

2.8. In the manner of the Dinos Painter, *Apollo, Hermes, Artemis, and Leto at the Omphalos* (side A), Athenian red-figure bell *kratēr*, ceramic, h. 33.02 cm, *c.* 425–410 BCE. London, British Museum, 1836,0224.4 (E502). © The Trustees of the British Museum.

In these scenes, Apollo's body regularly displays the physical effect of his music, as do the bodies of his companions, so that when taken together, they create a visual and musical unity. Moreover, when Apollo also undertakes a libation, as is demonstrated by the image on a red-figure mixing bowl in the manner of the Dinos Painter (Fig. 2.8), we may see a similar effort to establish a visual harmony between his body and his actions.[43] Apollo's performance here takes place upon the Delphic *omphalos*, believed in antiquity to be the navel of the world and which is here decorated with four white fillets that have been draped over its rounded surface. Apollo stands in profile, depicted again in the costume of a *kitharoidos*, with his long robes cascading down around his stationary form. As we saw with the tondo image with which we began, the god plays his *kithara* with his left hand and plucks at a string with his thumb, while with his right he extends his *phialē* and begins to tip it over. Together with the *omphalos*, which overlaps with his feet, Apollo acts as the stable focal point of the scene, while his large instrument, paired with the large *omphalos*, anchors the rest of the image and commands visual and sonic attention.

In contrast to Apollo's static pose, the other gods – Hermes, Artemis, and Leto – are shown in motion, as if they are moving toward the source of music. On Apollo's left is Hermes, who takes a step to the right while holding his staff. He raises his arm to greet the other gods, having even possibly helped their passage to Apollo's sanctuary at Delphi in his role as a messenger god. To the right of the *omphalos* is Artemis, who wears her quiver of arrows strapped to her back and holds a bow in her left hand and a small jug in her right. Her body is portrayed in an exaggerated curve, which visually suggests that she continues to move to face her brother.[44] At the far right of the image is Leto, who holds up a *phialē* to her daughter. As with Hermes, Leto is shown in the middle of taking a step forwards: by layering her voluminous drapery on top of the decoration around the vase's handle, Leto appears to have arrived suddenly on the scene to join her children and their ritual.

Having thus attracted his peers' attention through the musical sounds of his *kithara*, Apollo begins his libation. Indeed, Artemis is shown having already filled her brother's *phialē* so that the wine, rendered in added reddish-purple slip, trickles out of it and will soon reach the surface of the *omphalos*. The verticality of the falling liquid is picked up by the vertical lines of the *kithara*'s strings and the cloth that hangs from the instrument, reinforcing the connection between liquid offering and musical accompaniment. Moreover, the *phialē* overlaps with the lyre, occupying the place where Apollo's *plektron* would otherwise be found at the end of a strum across the strings; a kind of visual confusion emerges between the two, so that the object that produces musical sound overlaps with the vessel that is used for a ritual libation.[45] Those elements that provoke a sensory response emanate outwards from this central point of overlap, so that the sounds of the music spread out into the larger space, while the trickling of liquid falls down to the ground. Further blurring divine music with ritual, the image captures Apollo's libation suspended mid-fall, just as the musical sounds also hang in the air, suspended in a moment of arrested action. Music and liquid are captured in a shared moment of becoming, in which the libation has not yet been fully poured out and Apollo's music is in the midst of being created. It is in this transition, where liquid becomes libation and musical notes become a melody, that the significance of Apollo's ritual and musical performance begins to reveal itself: in placing the actualization of these two acts on display for the other gods, Apollo implicitly asks his fellow gods to watch and even participate in the simultaneous creation of music and ritual, an action unique to Apollo himself. The gods are thus joined into musical and ritual harmony through their shared experience of encountering Apollo's musical libation.[46]

This harmony, however, is not restricted only to the gods, but it also extends around to the other side of the vase, where three young and beardless men stand together. In visually associating the young, presumably elite, men of Athens with Apollo and the *omphalos*, the image evokes for the viewer the sanctuary at Delphi, where the Athenians sent *theōriai* to perform musical hymns, often the paean, for the god as part of their veneration.[47] Music, performance, and ritual are brought together through the evocation of contemporary practices of worship at the sacred site where the divine scene takes place. Moreover, in linking Apollo and the three young men on the other side of the mixing bowl, the image implicitly suggests that they might even share the same sacred space as Apollo. Within the image, then, perhaps the young men can begin to hear the sounds of the god's music, since they are already shown physically responding to its music. Drawn together in their musical harmony with the god, they even begin to mimic his appearance: they are all young and beardless, they have long, flowing drapery reminiscent of his, and they may even be the same size as the god, having similarly filled the vertical span of the image. Within the musically unified space created by Apollo's music, each youth may potentially act as a physical extension of the god, who has drawn them together through his song and ritual performance.

We have seen how Apollo's music not only coordinates his own music and ritual actions, but that it also brings his fellow gods and his mortal viewers into his harmony. The consequences of Apollo's music for his actions and for the bodies of those around him is even more pronounced in the scene on a red-figure storage vessel painted by the Chicago Painter (Fig. 2.9).[48] Here, Apollo and Artemis stand together, each depicted with elongated, elegant bodies.[49] Apollo holds his instrument, here delicately rendered despite its enormous size, while in his other hand he extends the *phialē* toward his sister, Artemis, who is here clearly identified through her bow. Her drapery echoes the appearance of Apollo's: a delicately creasing *chitōn* is covered partially by a heavier *himation* that has a dark border, which falls alongside the body in intricate folds. The only significant difference between their respective depictions is in their physical positions: Apollo is shown in strict profile, while Artemis faces the frontal plane of the image. Despite her *en face* position, Artemis still turns her head toward her brother and looks at him, her gaze passing across the instrument. From this profile position, we can see that even her hair echoes her brother's, as it is tied up in a style reminiscent of Apollo's when he is shown in the guise of a masterful *kitharoidos*.[50] As Apollo tilts the instrument forward slightly, angling it toward his companion, Artemis stretches out her wine jug, delicately holding its handle and lifting it to complete the ritual action begun by her sibling.

(A) (B)

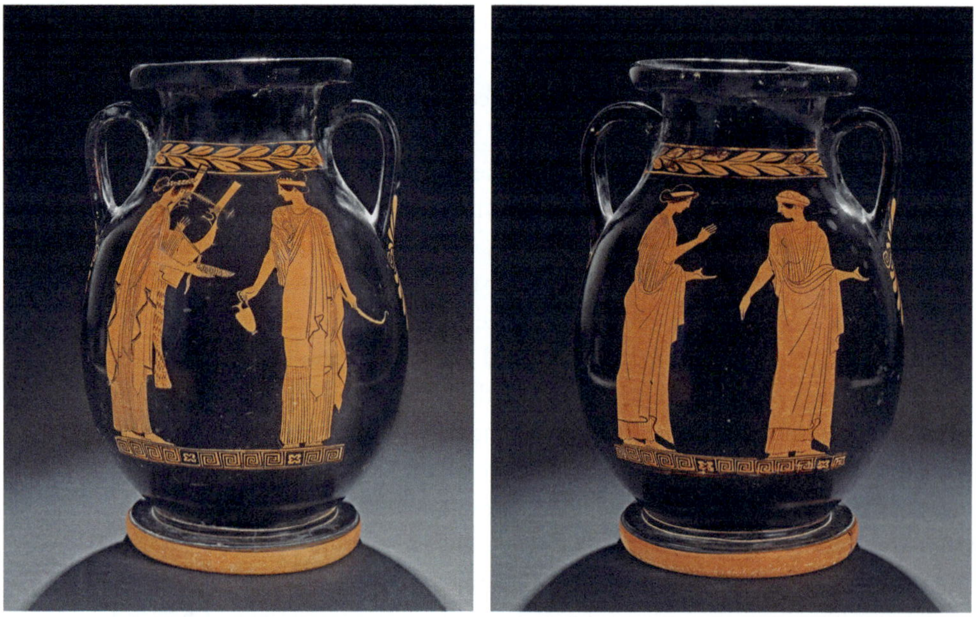

2.9. The Chicago Painter, *Apollo and Artemis* (side A), *Two Women* (side B), Attic red-figure *pelikē*, ceramic, h. 41.91 cm, 460–450 BCE. London, British Museum, 1843,1103.28 (E383). © The Trustees of the British Museum.

The libation itself has not yet begun, but instead the image explores the moments leading up to it, including the necessary preparations for the offering and the establishment of a coordinated unity between the participants.[51] Visually, each element in the scene has been depicted in such a way that they resonate with other forms and shapes. The verticality of the drapery and the forms of the two figures are contrasted by the downward-sloping diagonal lines created by those elements that occupy the space between them. The crossbar of the *kithara*, the hand strap on the instrument, the *phialē*, and the wine jug mimic each other through their similar orientation. Visual harmony is established in this scene not only between the resonances between the two figures, but also between the instruments, both musical and ritual, that they hold. Music and ritual have thus come together in this scene, where the synchronicity between animate and non-animate beings or objects creates the conditions in which Apollo's own harmonized offering may take place. Cutting across these visual resonances is the body of the *kithara* itself, which moves upwards on a diagonal, angling toward Artemis. The chiastic structure the instrument forms with the rest of the opposing diagonals draws attention to its importance within the scene. Further underscoring its importance is its clear upward movement, so that it, along with the heads of Apollo and Artemis, breaks through the upper line of the frame.[52] Together, music and the divine press up against the scene's visual boundary and move across it, challenging the visual limitations of the scene.

Apollo's music thus expands outside the image, where it may be heard by those positioned beyond the frame's borders.[53] That Apollo's presence and influence may be heard and felt by those outside the scene is suggested by the image painted onto the other side of the vase. There, two female figures, who here appear to be mortal women, stand next to each other in positions that mimic those of the two gods. The repeated bodily composition between divine gods and mortal women suggests that Apollo's carefully cultivated synchronicity, wherein he performs a libation and performs his music, as well as the synchronicity he has established with Artemis, has determined the composition of the two images, much as we have just seen between the mortal youths and the Delphic Apollo. As a result, the relationship between the two sides of the vase, one divine and the other human, is enhanced and nuanced through each figure's response to Apollo's music: not only have the regular, rhythmic sounds of Apollo's lyre fostered the gods' harmony with the objects they hold and with each other, but his music has even attuned the gods' bodies to those of their human worshippers. Above all, just as the two deities have come together for the ritual in a kind of coordinated performance, so too do the two mortal women reflect the divine harmony the gods embody. Even though the women do not perform a ritual of their own, in mimicking the poses and gestures of the gods, they embody the unifying potential inherent to Apollo and his music.

RHYTHMIC LIBATIONS

The vase-paintings that depict Apollo playing a lyre and pouring a libation visually link music with ritual. However, the context in which many of these vessels could have been encountered – namely, the Athenian symposium, itself filled with libations, music, dance, and poetry – also introduces human music and ritual into the ancient viewer's experience of the scenes of Apollo; indeed, we have already seen how these scenes reach out to their mortal viewers to draw them into Apollo's synchronizing musical and ritual performances. In each instance, visual and actual audible sounds come together with the libation, so that all three can be perceived at once by the viewer. If we look at the Pan Painter's vase (Fig. 2.10), we again encounter Apollo who plays his *kithara* and pours a libation; he is accompanied by Artemis and Leto.[54] The inclusion of the deer, however, further nuances how the god's music could have potentially affected the ancient viewer, since its position within the composition, directly below Artemis' vessel, presents the external, human viewer with the sequence of events about to take place. Upon looking at the image, one's eye follows the direction of the animal's gaze as she looks at Artemis. Similarly, the line of the deer's head extends up through the goddess' arrow, then

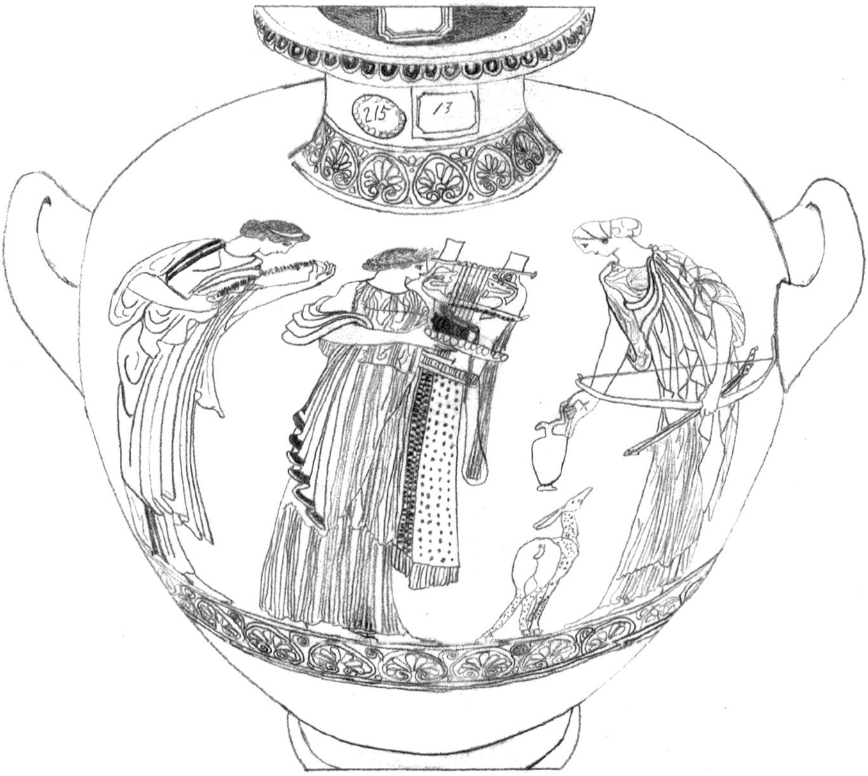

2.10. Line drawing by the author of the Pan Painter's *hydria* that depicts Apollo with a *kithara* and *phialē*, joined by Artemis and Leto. The original dates to *c.* 480–470 BCE, and is currently in the Museo Archeologico Nazionale, STG 192.

intersects with the line of her bow, which points to her wine jug. By drawing visual attention to the painted jug in this way, the image establishes the events necessary for Apollo's ritual, that Artemis must first pour the liquid into Apollo's *phialē* before he can make his libation. Moreover, only Artemis' arm and her vessel venture into the negative space between the two gods, so that the visual tension between her forward movement and Apollo's static pose makes clear that the ritual will soon begin. For his part, Apollo's activities similarly indicate that the ritual is imminent. The god has already begun playing his *kithara*: his fingers are splayed out on the strings while his thumb is hooked around the first two strings, as if at any moment he will sound out the notes of his melody that will accompany his ritual. The scene is filled with potential activity that will soon take place: the music will soon ring through the scene, the liquid will soon be poured from the jug into the *phialē*, and the *phialē* will soon empty its contents onto the ground, onto that negative space between Apollo and Artemis, where the deer stands. The viewer's eye thus returns to its place of entry, where, together with Leto, we wait for the ritual to begin.

The particular way in which the deer has been depicted here, in an unusual three-quarter angle, further involves the external viewer in the gods' ritual. In having been depicted from behind, as if the animal were walking away from the viewer, the deer seems to move toward the gods, where she looks up at Artemis as the goddess begins the ritual.[55] The animal's position can be equated, therefore, with the position of the viewer who gazes at the image, so that in engaging with the deer, we are given a point of entry into the scene.[56] If this is the case, then the image also invites us to consider how the external viewer might have responded to this particular presentation of Apollo's musico-ritual performance, especially within one potential context in which it was encountered, namely, the symposium. The Athenian symposium, associated both with the aristocratic male elite and, following the democracy, with the urban, democratic citizens,[57] was a ritual drinking party which began with libations to the gods,[58] and continued, often late into the evening, with drinking games, singing poetry, and performing music.[59] If the vessels upon which Apollo plays music and pours his libation were seen and used by elite male Athenians within the symposium, then the god's two activities, that is, his music and his ritual, are repeated between the visual, divine sphere and the actual, human symposium. The viewer, who was possibly an elite, male, Athenian citizen, would have drunk wine, played instruments, and poured libations, so that he similarly engaged with actions that were similar to the god's. Moreover, through the visual invitation to imagine the sound of the god's music, the image offers its sympotic viewers the opportunity to participate in the god's ritual. In this way, each individual present at a symposium could have enlivened the scene by imagining and creating its soundscape, providing the sounds of the music that the image suggests are already coordinating the actions of the gods. In so doing, the audience, external to the image, animates the god's actions, so that Apollo continuously performs, and reperforms, his music and ritual.

The relationship between Apollo and his male, citizen audience is further developed by the scene painted onto a storage vessel by the Sabouroff Painter (Fig. 2.11).[60] Here, Apollo sits on a plain chair while he holds an undecorated *phialē* and a *chelys* lyre, the instrument of choice in scenes of musical education.[61] The god, who wears a plain *himation* that wraps around his lower body, is shown here not as a performance *kitharoidos*, but rather he recalls the depiction of a youthful Athenian citizen who plays his instrument for his companions.[62] Accompanying the god is a female figure, who may be intended to depict Artemis, though there is little in her depiction that definitively identifies her. As with Apollo, her clothes have little additional adornment and instead she wears similar long, plain clothes. She faces Apollo while she holds up her wine jug, pouring out its contents. The three inanimate

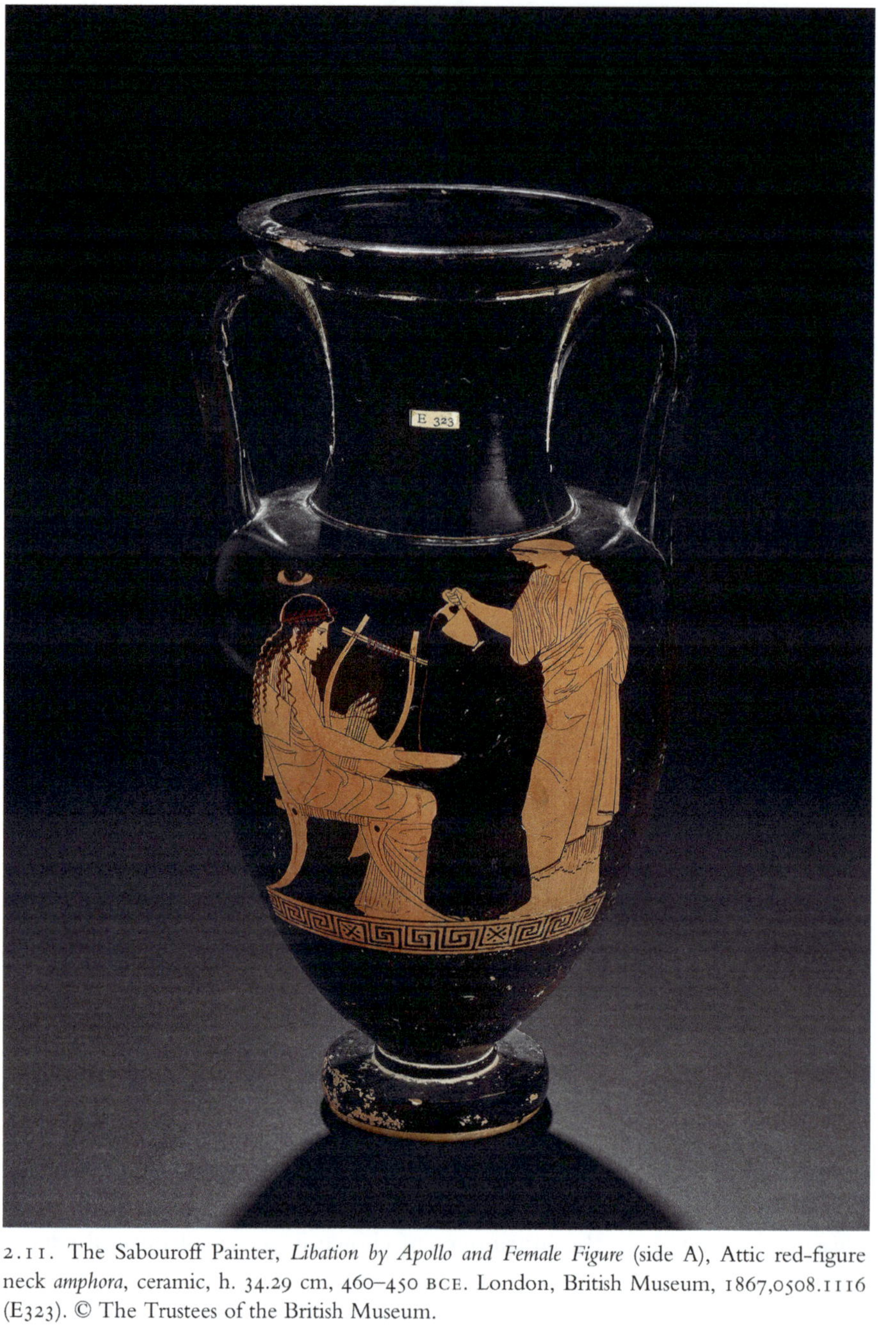

2.11. The Sabouroff Painter, *Libation by Apollo and Female Figure* (side A), Attic red-figure neck *amphora*, ceramic, h. 34.29 cm, 460–450 BCE. London, British Museum, 1867,0508.1116 (E323). © The Trustees of the British Museum.

objects in this scene – the lyre, the *phialē*, and the wine jug – together function as the image's focal points: both the *phialē* and the jug extend out into the central negative space created between the forms of the two gods, drawing attention to their importance within the scene. At the same time, Apollo's lyre, with its arms extending gracefully upwards, bridges the gap between the two

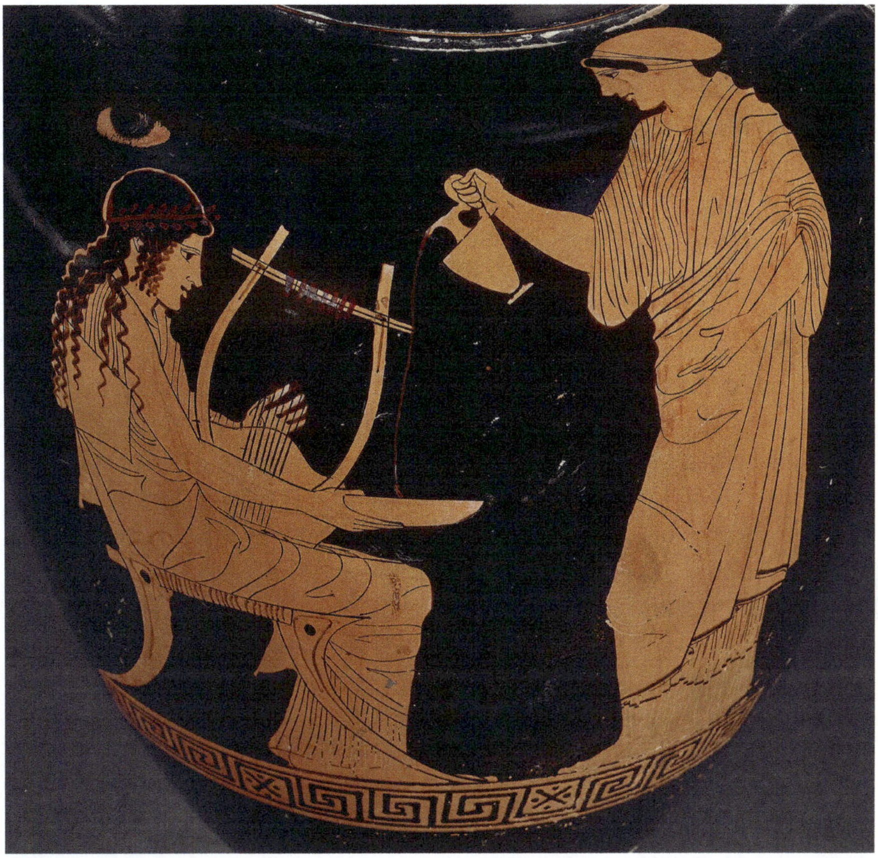

2.12. Detail. The Sabouroff Painter, *Libation by Apollo* (side A), Attic red-figure neck *amphora*, ceramic, h. 34.29 cm, 460–450 BCE. London, British Museum, 1867,0508.1116 (E323). © The Trustees of the British Museum.

vessels. Even at this basic, formal level, the image draws out the connection between the music the god plays and the ritual he performs.

The visual link between music and libation is emphasized by the liquid that the female figure pours, which bends and winds its way down, and reaches out at one point to intersect with the crossbar of Apollo's lyre (Fig. 2.12). In drawing together music with ritual, the image suggests that Apollo's music and his ritual must work together, so that each element, figure, and action is in harmony with the others to perform a perfectly coordinated musical libation. The Sabouroff Painter's composition has thus been carefully choreographed so that the gestures of each figure and the placement of the objects complement those of each other. The sounds of Apollo's music establish the rhythm to which the libation is poured; indeed, such coordinated flows of music and liquid recall the semantics of *rhein* and *rhythmos*, which, as I discuss further in Chapter 3, can describe 'flows' of various kinds, be they aquatic, temporal, visual, or musical. This visual, musical, and liquid *rhythmos* in turn extends outward to condition the symmetry between the god and his companion, the two participants in the ritual, as well as between the two figures and their musical and ritual objects. When encountered in a symposium that was itself filled with music, the image's invitation to its audience is easily realized as they could imaginatively hear the sounds of the god's music through the actual music that was performed. The viewer's active and imaginative engagement with the visualized sounds in the image thus allow the sounds in the two spaces to blend together, so that Apollo's performance takes place in the image even as it also accompanies the similar human activities in the symposium.

In connecting images of Apollo's musical performance with the sounds of human music-making, we are invited to imagine what quality of sound Apollo's music takes and how its particular sound and cadence might affect his companions.[63] The connection among music, rhythm, and ritual that I developed with respect to the Sabouroff Painter's vessel is not only a loose analogy asserting that a movement may be rhythmic in a manner similar to a musical melody. Rather, it exists within the very language used to describe both a libation and a metrical rhythm. A libation, for its part, was typically referred to as a *spondē*.[64] This term, *spondē*, was also used to denote one of the metrical feet of Greek poetry, where it described a foot composed of two long syllables.[65] The connection between the metrical and ritual *spondē* is particularly pronounced with spondaic hymns, which Martin West, in his discussion of Greek meter, notes occurred primarily within the Dorian religious tradition in the Archaic and Classical periods, when a hymn could be composed entirely from spondaic feet.[66] The example that West uses is, perhaps appropriately, a hymn for Apollo and the Muses:

> σπένδωμεν ταῖς Μνάμας παισὶν Μούσαις
> καὶ τωῖ Μουσάρχωι <τωῖ> Λατοῦς υἱεῖ.
>
> Let us pour a libation to the Muses, children of Memory
> And to the leader of the Muses, the son of Leto.[67]

He argues that this and other similar hymns were composed with long syllables in order to impart an effect of grandeur during the ritual action, so that each long syllable coincided with a step in the religious ritual.[68] While it is difficult to prove that such a strict synchronicity between action and syllable occurred, it seems plausible at least that within the context of a hymn, both the spondee and the particular words or syllables that occupy this particular point in the line are important features of the hymn's performance. The spondee not only ends the poetic line by demanding silence at regular intervals, almost as if asking its audience to contemplate the actions of the gods and heroes within the narrative, but it also can draw out specific moments, thus allowing for the potential coordination of the worshippers' religious actions with the musical prayer. In *Laws*, Plato even describes a particular kind of music that was intended to accompany a libation, the *spondeion*, which further suggests a connection between the specific composition of a spondaic hymn and the *spondē* itself.[69] Such malleability of genre and meter, wherein the song acts as a hymn offered to a god even as it recalls the *spondeia* offered at the beginning of a symposium, in turn allows for a blending of music and action, so that the two come together into a harmonic unit.[70]

There was thus a potentially powerful relationship that existed between religious action and musical rhythm, a connection that we also see developed in Theocritus' *Idylls*, where the poet notes that "songs are the finest of gifts to the gods," γεράων δὲ θεοῖς κάλλιστον ἀοιδαί.[71] If we return to the vases on which Apollo pours his libation while playing his lyre, we may see that similar attention has been given to their careful composition, insofar as the god's musical and ritual activities have been placed in close, rhythmic proximity with each other. This is the case on the storage vessel by the Sabouroff Painter where the musically coordinated actions necessary for the libation are further emphasized through the elongated distance the liquid must fall from the female figure's jug to Apollo's *phialē*, held just above the god's low chair (Fig. 2.12). The synchronized act of pouring a libation is thus a contrived activity that must be harmonized between the two participants in order to be performed successfully. In a similar way to a dance, where the sequence of each individual's movements is ordered according to a musical rhythm, so too can the libation, at least in this context, be treated musically as its fall from one vessel to another and then to the ground is determined by the rhythm of the music. Yet in this scene, Apollo creates both the music and rhythm according to which the libation will be performed. As a result, his movements and the movements of his companions are controlled by the music he himself plays. We cannot forget, either, that the specific technique the god uses to play his instrument, that is, producing sound only with one hand that plucks at individual strings, probably suggests that the tempo of the music he is shown creating is rhythmically slow, since only one musical note can be produced at any given moment, as opposed to strumming a sequence of strings with a *plektron*. The musical notes thus hang in the air, each distinct in its sound, having emerged from the instrument in a regular, punctuated rhythm. Coordinating their actions to the sounds they hear, Apollo and his companions move together, adjusting their actions to perform their tasks in rhythm with each other. This connection between music and religious action is further drawn out by the liquid offering itself, which reaches out in its descent to intersect with Apollo's lyre. Here, the *spondē* of the religious offering has fused with the spondee of Apollo's musical rhythm.

Similar attention is given to exploring the effects of an elongated, visual abstraction of the god's actions on a storage vessel in the style of the Chicago Painter (Fig. 2.13).[72] Apollo once again appears with a *kithara*, holding his

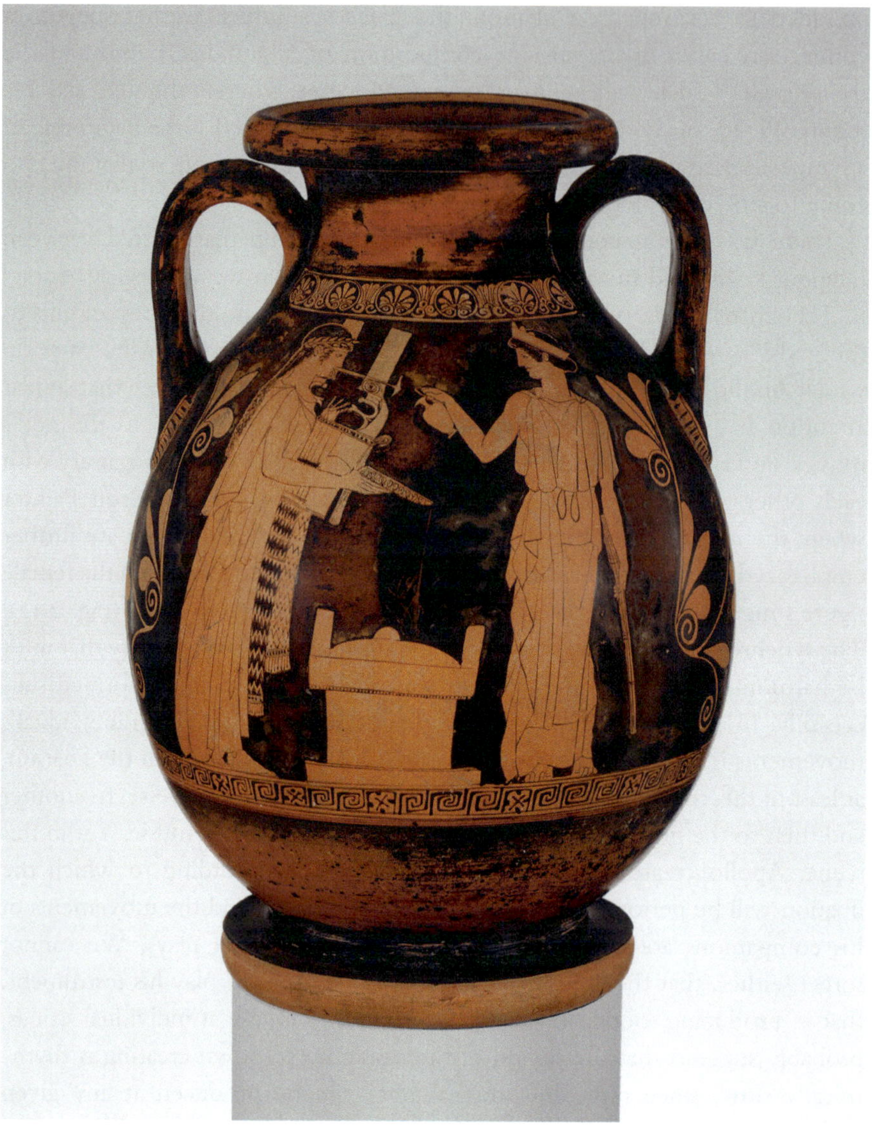

2.13. Attributed to an artist near the Chicago Painter, *Apollo and Artemis at an Altar* (side A), Attic red-figure *pelikē*, h. 41.9 cm, mid-fifth century BCE. New York, Metropolitan Museum of Art, 06.1021.191. Rogers Fund, 1906. Creative Commons CCO.

instrument in his left hand and the *phialē* in his right. Though Apollo's profile position stands out against the female figure's frontal pose, her drapery echoes the appearance of his, so that both wear long robes that flow and fold as they fall around their bodies. Visually, the image establishes a rhythm between the two, so that before they complete any action, they are already implicitly joined together. Set up between the two figures is an altar upon which a fire burns. The altar both separates the gods as they perform their ritual directly above it, while it also draws them together by acting as a focal point around which their shared activity occurs. As Apollo tilts the instrument forward slightly, angling it toward his companion, the female figure, possibly Artemis, holds out her wine jug, delicately holding its handle and lifting it to continue the ritual action begun by her brother.

The visual emphasis placed upon the god's actions once again invites its viewers to imagine the sounds associated with Apollo's musically infused libation, establishing Apollo as a god capable of moving his audience's bodies through his music. Apollo's close relationship with music is the subject of another hymn, namely, Callimachus' *Hymn to Apollo*, where Apollo's epiphany to the reader is conveyed through particularly evocative acoustic descriptions. Though the hymn is Hellenistic, and thus postdates the vases examined here, the poet's use of dactylic hexameter does explore a connection with the earlier *Homeric Hymn to Apollo* in which the god is similarly associated with music and dance. The hymn begins:

> Οἷον ὁ τὠπόλλωνος ἐσείσατο δάφνινος ὅρπηξ,
> οἷα δ' ὅλον τὸ μέλαθρον· ἑκὰς ἑκὰς ὅστις ἀλιτρός.
> καὶ δή που τὰ θύρετρα καλῷ ποδὶ Φοῖβος ἀράσσει·
> οὐχ ὁράᾳς; ἐπένευσεν ὁ Δήλιος ἡδύ τι φοῖνιξ
> ἐξαπίνης, ὁ δὲ κύκνος ἐν ἠέρι καλὸν ἀείδει.
> αὐτοὶ νῦν κατοχῆες ἀνακλίνασθε πυλάων,
> αὐταὶ δὲ κληῖδες· ὁ γὰρ θεὸς οὐκέτι μακρήν·
> οἱ δὲ νέοι μολπήν τε καὶ ἐς χορὸν ἐντύνασθε.
>
> How Apollo's laurel branch is shaking,
> How the whole house is. Away, away, you who are impious.
> Phoibos must now be kicking the doors with his beautiful foot.
> What! Do you not see? All of a sudden the Delian palm tree is nodding
> In joy, in the air the swan is singing sweetly.
> Fly apart yourselves, you bars of the gates,
> You bolts as well. The god is no longer far;
> Begin your singing and dancing boys.[73]

In Callimachus' poem, metrical rhythm is consistently blurred with divine epiphany. The *enargeia* characteristic of this passage vividly conveys the presence of the god, creating a powerful sense of anticipation.[74] Callimachus obliges his audience and Apollo soon appears in the third line as one of the metrical feet with which the hymn is composed: in the final spondaic foot of the third line, Callimachus draws out the sound that the god makes as he manifests before the reader. The god kicks down the door with his foot (ποδὶ), creating a loud booming sound extended in two long spondaic syllables ([ἀ]ράσ-σει). The double sigma at the end of the line thus creates a hissing noise, which in turn suggests that the god materializes in front of the poet and his audience.[75] The following line's exclamation – Don't you see? (οὐχ ὁράᾳς;) – further suggests the specific way that worshippers would have perceived the god, that is, through the conflated sensory experience that both sight and sound offer.

Apollo appears again with a physical form at the end of the hymn, when he confronts Envy, who has criticized the length of the hymn.

> ... ὁ Φθόνος Ἀπόλλωνος ἐπ' οὔατα λάθριος εἶπεν·
> οὐκ ἄγαμαι τὸν ἀοιδὸν ὃς οὐδ' ὅσα πόντος ἀείδει.'
> τὸν Φθόνον ὡπόλλων ποδί τ' ἤλασεν ὧδέ τ' ἔειπεν:
>
> ... Envy speaks furtively into Apollo's ear:
> I do not like that poet who does not even sing as much as the sea.
> Apollo drives Envy away with a kick and speaks as follows ...[76]

With one swift kick, a metaphor that revisits the notion of Apollo-as-metrical-foot from line 3, Apollo drives Envy away while also refuting her criticism with poetic verse. Thus, the foot with which he kicks her is at once his own physical foot and the metrical foot of the devotional hymn, so that god and poet work together to refute Envy's criticism. In blurring this distinction between physical and metrical feet, Callimachus makes it possible for the god to manifest at the beginning and the end of the hymn as the poetic meter itself, revealed to the listener or reader through each and every recitation of the hymn.[77] Apollo is presented here as almost interchangeable with the poetry. This blurring between god and metrical rhythm may remind us of a similar blurring that occurred between a god and his or her image, especially with the rise of naturalism in the visual arts.[78] In portraying the divinity not just as having an anthropomorphic body, but also as a likeness of a moving, living body, each image thus claims to represent the god accurately, as he or she might be encountered in the world. An image of a divine body thus acts as a mimetic *eikōn* of that same deity. It is between this tension between unseeable god and visually accessible representation that Callimachus similarly places Apollo in his poem. In the hymn, Apollo implicitly, and repeatedly, manifests as an auditory epiphany, appearing both as a character in the poem and as naturally occurring sound itself, easily heard in the world, or as the physical touch of another body, a sensation experienced within one's everyday life. The aural and tactile sensations that Callimachus associates with the god are thus presented to the audience, who then are invited to imagine hearing the god and, as a result, to experience his presence. In the hymn, Apollo is not simply a god associated with music who skillfully plays his instrument, but rather he is the sound itself, the music that emanates from the instrument he plays.

The vase by the Chicago Painter similarly offers the viewer a potential experience of Apollo as auditory sensation. Given how the god plays his instrument in the image, we might imagine that the sounds emerging from the god's lyre are slow and ponderous, perhaps like the long spondaic foot of poetic meter. Moreover, here, the visual music coordinates the actions of Apollo and Artemis, thus creating a visual rhythm between the gods and the musical and ritual objects that they hold (Fig. 2.14). The verticality of the drapery and the

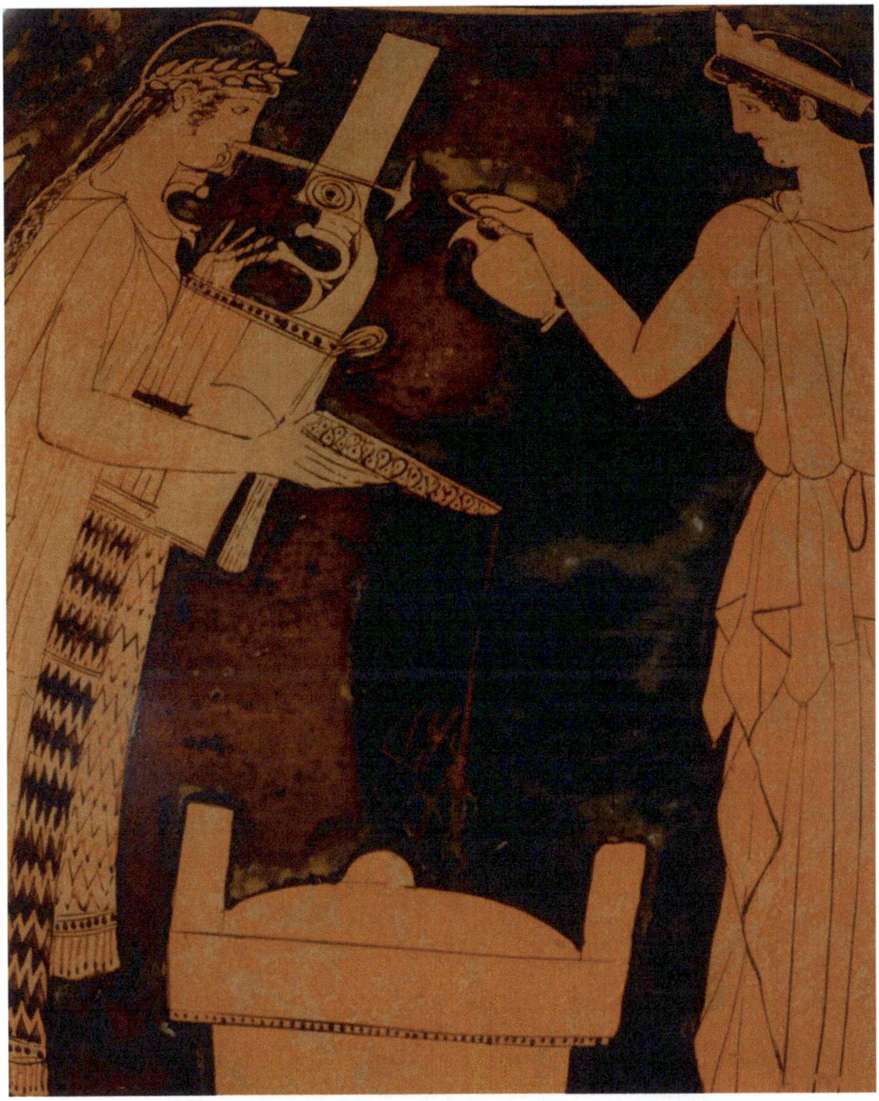

2.14. Detail. Attributed to an artist near the Chicago Painter, *Apollo and Artemis at an Altar* (side A), Attic red-figure *pelikē*, h. 41.9 cm, mid-fifth century BCE. New York, Metropolitan Museum of Art, 06.1021.191. Rogers Fund, 1906. Creative Commons CCO.

forms of the two gods are contrasted by the downward-sloping diagonal lines created by those elements that occupy the space between them. The crossbar of the *kithara*, the hand-strap on the instrument, the *phialē*, and the jug are all angled downwards. Cutting across these visual parallels is the body of the *kithara* itself, which moves upwards on a diagonal toward Artemis. The chiastic structure the instrument forms with the rest of the opposing diagonals draws the viewer's eye to it. Apollo and Artemis have thus been depicted as a series of interconnecting limbs and objects, an intricate pattern of movements that work together because they have been harmonized by the god's music. It is in this ordered movement and action, determined by the sounds emanating from the lyre, that Apollo's presence is visualized in the image, not only as the physical presence of the god himself, but rather within the tension between the participants' experience of hearing and then responding to musical sound.

That Apollo's auditory presence and the influence of his music may also be felt beyond the scene is suggested by the image on the reverse of the vase, where two female figures, who may be mortal women or perhaps even other divinities, stand next to each other (Fig. 2.15). The figure on the right lifts a jug

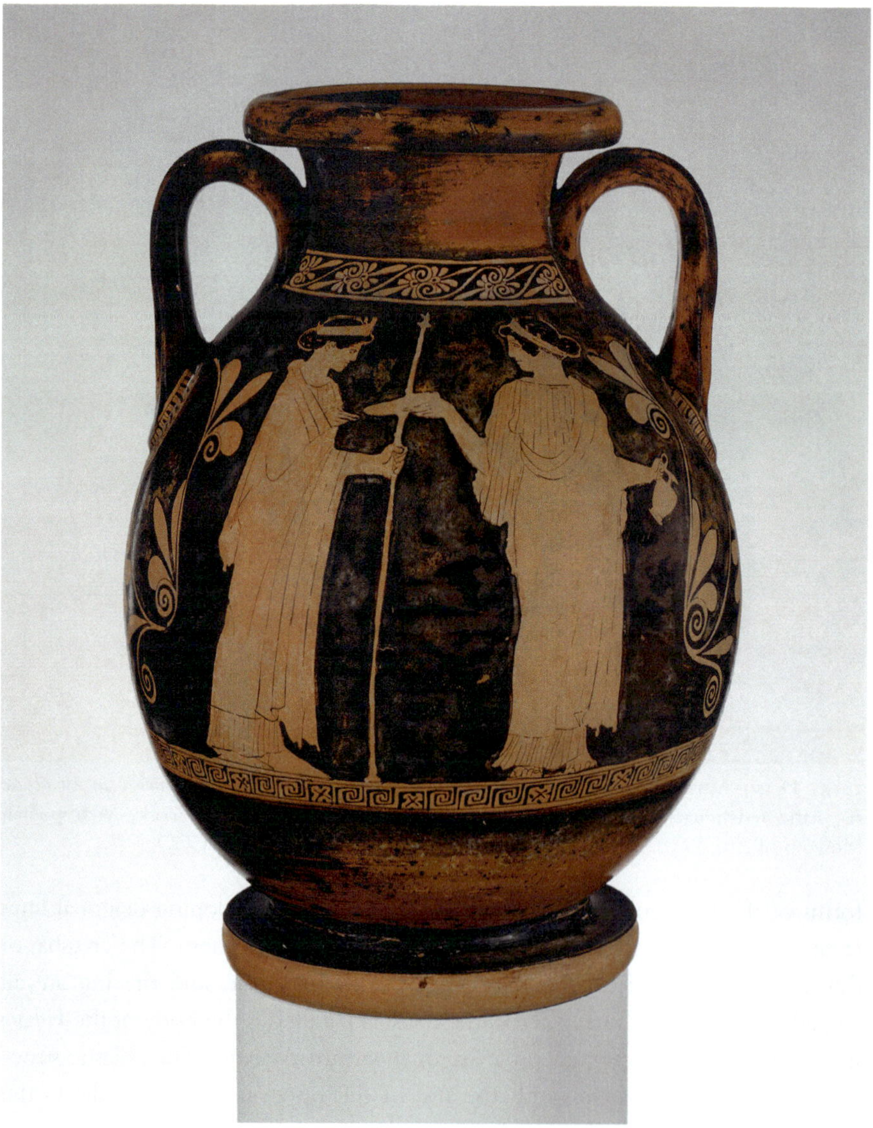

2.15. Attributed to an artist near the Chicago Painter, *Two Women* (side B), Attic red-figure *pelikē*, h. 41.9 cm, mid-fifth century BCE. New York, Metropolitan Museum of Art, 06.1021.191. Rogers Fund, 1906. © The Metropolitan Museum of Art.

in one hand while she holds out a *phialē* to her companion, who faces her and extends an arm, as if about to reach out and grasp the dish. The two figures are shown in the moments leading up to their libation, when they are still in the process of coming together and coordinating their actions. Although the scene features a different moment in their ritual, the image resonates with the representation on the other side of the vessel in that the compositions of the two images seem to have been carefully choreographed. It is not only the actions on each side that complement those found on the other, but the position of the female figures' bodies echo those of Apollo and Artemis. In drawing a visual connection between the two rituals, one mortal and one divine, the images thus suggest that the harmonized and rhythmic actions undertaken by Apollo, wherein the sounds of his music establish the rhythm to which the libation is poured, even extend outward to affect the actions of the women on the other side. As the music from his *kithara* moves around the vase, passing through the ornamental foliage but otherwise unencumbered by any other framing device, the women's positions and actions suggest that they hear his melody, feel its effect, and physically arrange themselves in harmony with each other and with the god who has influenced them.

THE ANCIENT AUDIENCE

By focusing on Apollo's music and the coordinating effect it has on the actions of the two gods, as well as on the actions of the female figures on the reverse, the images painted onto the sides of the Chicago Painter's jug reveal the magnitude of the god's musical abilities. Although we have considered the effect of Apollo's music on the other figures included in the painted image and the ancient viewer's role in activating the god's music, it remains to examine precisely how an ancient viewer might have engaged with the visual representation of Apollo's unique performance and how the context in which the external viewer encountered these images would have determined their interaction with the god and his musical libation. Above all, the musical Apollo painted onto the jug invites its viewers to enliven his performance through their own acts of looking at his performance and imaginatively hearing the sounds of the music. The viewer, possibly an elite, male symposiast, thus participates in the god's ritual through sight, acting almost as Apollo's other companion by animating the god's music and, in turn, being harmonized by the sounds of his lyre. Through the ancient viewer's sensory interaction with the image, whereby one's visual experience created the conditions to hear imaginatively the sounds of the music, Apollo's presence could emerge from the image, where it might be felt by the external viewer in a conflation of sight and sound. Perception and imagination, therefore, make it possible for the viewer to experience the presence of Apollo.

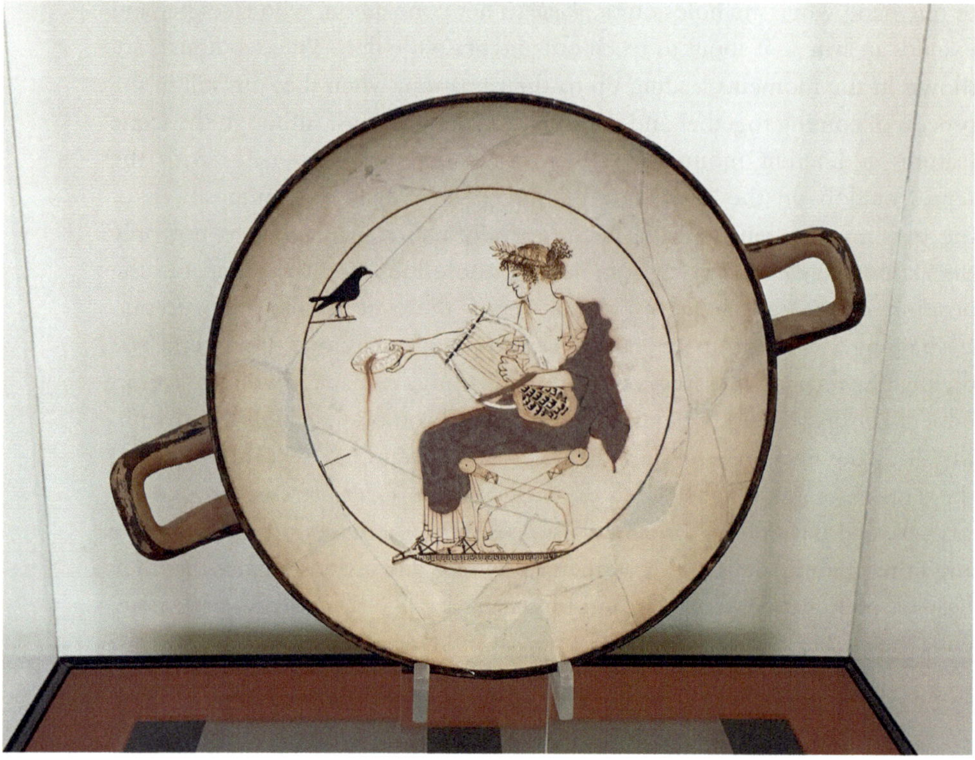

2.16. Possibly by the Pistoxenos Painter, *Apollo with lyre, phialē, and bird*, white-ground *kylix*, ceramic, d. 17.8 cm, *c.* 480–470 BCE. Delphi, Archaeological Museum, 8140. The rights of the depicted monuments belong to the Hellenic Ministry of Culture and Sports/Hellenic Organization of Cultural Resources Development (Law 4858/2021).

Another moment of a particularly powerful engagement with its ancient viewer is suggested by the white-ground scene painted on the tondo of a cup found at Delphi (Fig. 2.16).[79] The prominence of Apollo's activities immediately captures our attention: the god sits slightly off-center, faces the left, and extends a *phialē* with his right arm while his left holds a lyre and plucks its strings. He is wrapped in a dark *himation*, which draws a stark contrast with the white background, so that the viewer's eye is pulled to the seated god and the instrument he plays. The black slip used to create the dark pattern on the tortoise shell unifies the scene: black is repeated throughout the image, whether on the lyre's crossbar, the god's sandals, and the black bird, perhaps a black dove or a raven, who looks toward the god.[80] Having been drawn into the image by the god's striking appearance, the viewer's eye then travels to the lyre, which stands out against its dark background. From there, one's gaze moves up the strings and arms of the instrument to the crossbar, where it overlaps with the god's arm, and to the bird, whose gaze then redirects it back to Apollo. Our attention then follows Apollo's gaze, down his arm, through the lyre, toward the *phialē*, at which point the chiastic pattern breaks down, and the diagonal line abruptly turns and falls vertically to the bottom of the scene. Here, the pattern picks up again, as the eye may re-enter the scene through the upward diagonal line created by Apollo's foot and sandal, the black straps of which recommence the unity among visual elements in the scene.

Apollo is alone in this image, with no other companion present to help him perform his libation or his musical performance.[81] Instead, the god must perform the two actions by himself. The overlapping forms of the lyre and the god's arm that holds the *phialē* suggest a profound connection between the two instruments, so that within the composition, the source for Apollo's libation is the very music that he plays. Shown in the midst of performing his musical and ritual actions, Apollo's slow, quiet music fills the space around him and harmonizes his own actions. The small line on the bottom left of the scene, in line with the handles, further points to the relationship between music and libation here: so long as the libation remains suspended in the air and does not splash upon the earth, Apollo's music will continue to resound through the scene. The image suggests that with the end of the libation comes the end of Apollo's music, and with the end of his music, so too comes the end of the libation. Within this paused moment, Apollo's music forever swirls around the cup just as the red liquid moves around the *phialē* and falls toward the earth. It is through the material connection between the music and the libation, both continually in a state of being realized, that the image establishes Apollo as singular in his ability to undertake this particular musical ritual.

The most obvious context for this cup is the symposium, where, as with the other vases I have discussed, it would have been used for drinking wine or playing games. However, the white ground with which the vessel was decorated would have been too fragile to have been ever used.[82] Unable to sustain any contact with liquid,[83] the cup implicitly plays with the presence or absence of wine within it and, in so doing, invites the external viewer to understand Apollo's music in much the same way, since it similarly alternates between being visible in the image and unable to be heard by the viewer. Yet, Apollo is shown actively playing his lyre, having already plucked some of the instrument's strings and about to repeat the gesture. In depicting the god in the midst of both his musical and ritual action, the image encourages its viewers to imagine not just the completion of his simultaneous activities, but also to immerse themselves in the conflated sensory experience of witnessing both performances.

Although this particular cup was discovered in a tomb, where it was deposited as a funerary offering, the tomb's location is near Apollo's sanctuary at Delphi.[84] Such proximity invites us to consider further the relationship between the god's music, the libation he offers, the potential for similar white-ground vessels to be given as votive offerings, and the hymns that would have been performed by worshippers in Apollo's nearby sanctuary. There, the sounds of Apollo's *chelys* lyre could be imagined together with the performance of hymns for the god, so that the slow, punctuated notes infuse the viewer's perception of the image. Similarly, one might think of the sounds of the liquid rushing out of the god's *phialē*, perhaps recalling similar rituals undertaken by the god's human worshippers in the sanctuary. Thus, by relying upon the external viewer to contribute his or her own perception of the scene, the image establishes within the viewer's imagination the never-ending divine musical performance and the continual pouring of the libation.

Another vessel does, however, invoke the sympotic context in which it could have been used: a wine jug by the Altamura Painter similarly juxtaposes Apollo's two activities, but does so on a shape of vessel that is also included in its painted scene (Fig. 2.17).[85] Apollo and Artemis stand on either side of an altar and, as we have already seen, their postures mimic each other's. As Artemis extends her jug over the altar, Apollo reaches out with his *phialē*. No liquid has yet been poured, but the *kithara* and *phialē* have been layered in such a way that suggests that the instrument's strings, and by extension the music the god plays, cascade down the instrument's body and fall into Apollo's *phialē*. By layering musical and ritual instruments in this way, Apollo's music is presented as the offering the gods make in place of a libation. A similar effect is achieved by the other implements included in the image: the jug that Artemis holds overlaps with the fabric hanging from Apollo's *kithara*, so that the straight, vertical lines of the cloth reach down to the surface of the altar, mimicking the appearance of falling liquid.

The visual emphasis placed throughout this image on the careful coordination of music and libation explores how a sensory experience of seeing Apollo's music could bring about the god's manifestation, much like Callimachus would do later in his hymn for Apollo.[86] In foregrounding the music inherent to the god's libation, the image suggests that, for the ancient viewer, engaging with the god's performance could itself open a path to experiencing divine presence. Alternatively, each time wine was poured from the jug, its user recreates Artemis' actions, so that the scene could be reactivated not only by the visual and imaginative interaction with the representation of Apollo's music but also through using the vessel upon which the image was depicted. Within a symposium, where wine was first poured as a libation to the gods and was then ladled out of a mixing bowl and into jugs, which were then used to fill each symposiast's cup, the repetition of pouring liquid between image and reality lends an immediacy to the god's ritual. In this interplay between the materiality of liquid wine and the immateriality of divine musical sound, Apollo manifests among the elite male symposiasts who have been joined together in a harmonious group through their shared experience of the god's music.

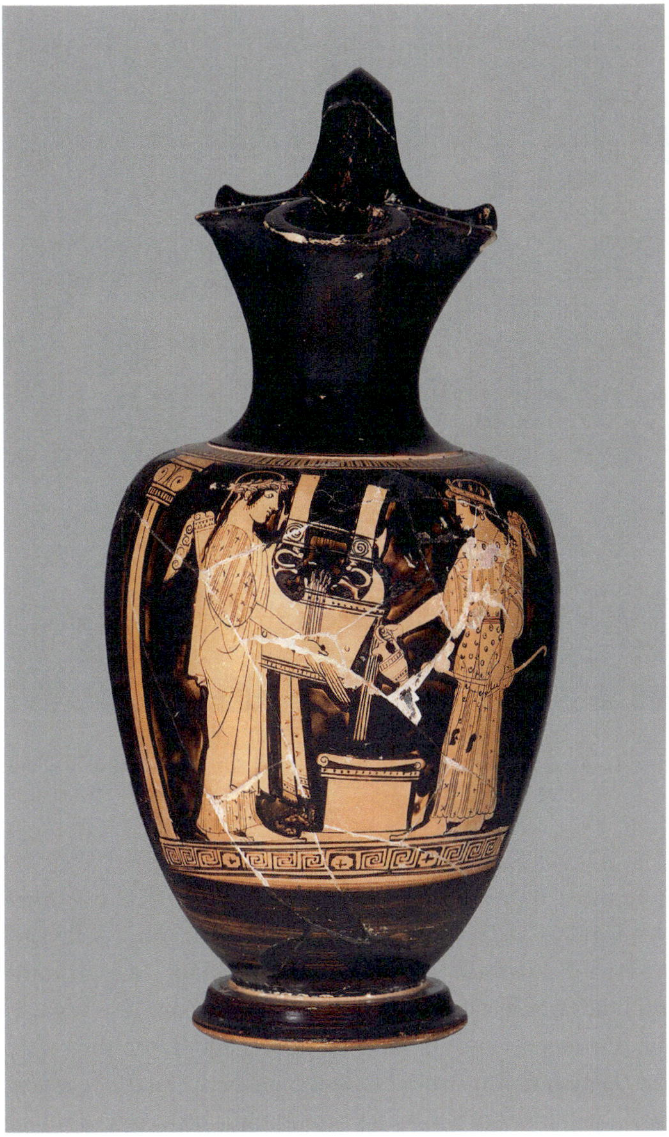

2.17. The Altamura Painter, *Apollo and Artemis at an Altar*, Attic red-figure *oinochoē*, ceramic, h. 34.8 cm, *c.* 465 BCE. Boston, Museum of Fine Arts, 97.370. Photograph © 2024 Museum of Fine Arts, Boston.

Musically coordinated actions and a deliberate visual echoing of the human context in which the vessel may once have been used are both especially relevant for the red-figure cup by the Painter of London E 80, the vessel with which I began this chapter (Figs. 2.1, 2.18). In addition to the tondo image where Apollo sits in front of an altar, playing his *kithara* and moments from pouring his libation, the images painted onto the exterior of the cup add to the vase's visual complexity by invoking its human viewers. On each side are three figures, two men with staffs and a woman, and although one image is too fragmentary to determine the nature

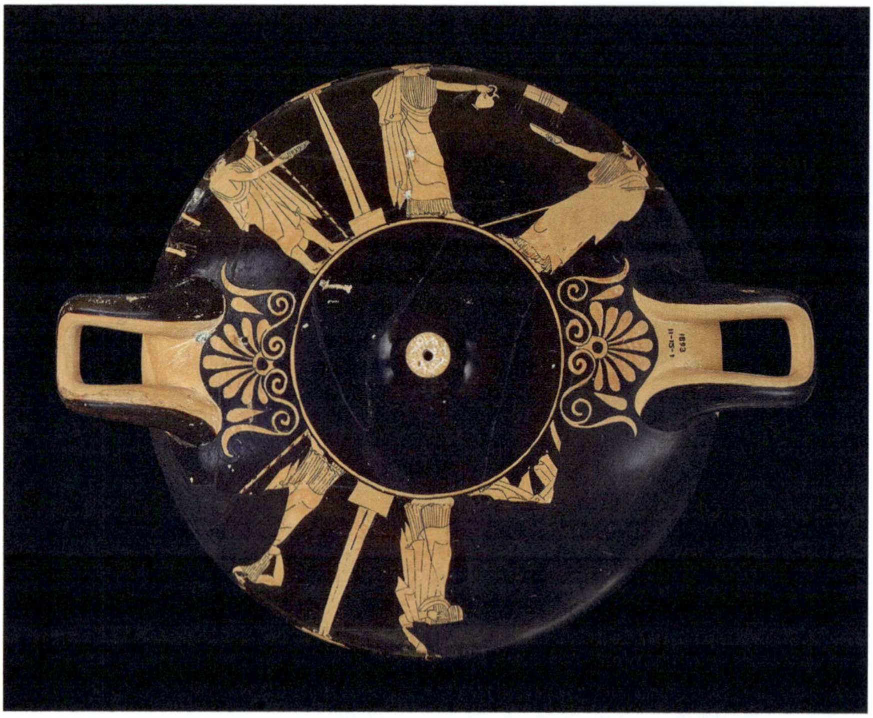

2.18. The Painter of London E 80, *Libation scene* (sides A, B), Attic red-figure *kylix*, ceramic, h. 8.89 cm, *c.* 480–470 BCE. London, British Museum, 1893,1115.1 (E80). © The Trustees of the British Museum.

of their actions, on the other they are engaged in ritual activity. The two men stand adjacent to the handles and face inwards, each leaning on a staff and extending a *phialē* toward the woman who stands in the center. She, in turn, faces to the right, and holds out her jug to one of her companions; the vessel is tilted slightly, as if she is moments away from pouring the liquid into the man's *phialē*. Completing the scene is an Ionic column positioned between the beardless youth and the woman, a pair of sandals hanging behind him, and a pair of rolled up tablets and a stylus in front of the older, bearded man. This scene of humans engaging in religious practice could potentially be located within a sanctuary, as is suggested by the column. As with the scene painted in the tondo, the visual resonances between the large curving folds of the three figures' drapery emphasize their connection to each other and their collective worship. They have come together for the performance of a ritual, one that unifies the many strata of Athenian society: the mature adults are connected with the young, and the men are joined by the woman, who performs the essential task of filling their *phialai*.

The two painted scenes echo each other, since each depicts those moments leading up to the libation. Yet there are important differences between the images. The exterior is characterized by expansive gestures as each figure's arm extends outwards into the negative space that separates the men and the woman from each other. The woman also broaches the empty space by taking a step to the right so that she may fill the older man's *phialē*, moving from the column that indicates sacred space toward the man leaning on his spear in the manner of an Athenian citizen. It is also an inherently silent image – no liquid drips or splashes as it is poured, no music accompanies the ritual, and the figures do not speak with each other. Instead, they communicate solely with their actions. Conversely, the tondo is filled with the god's music and the crackling of the fire that burns on the altar. Moreover, the multiplicity of figures on the exterior is contrasted with the sole god in the center, who alone produces the melody and performs the libation. Yet he still requires someone to fill his *phialē* with the liquid that he will offer at the altar. By striking the strings of his *kithara* and filling the space in the tondo with his slow, rhythmic music, the god's music may also expand upwards, following the line of his *kithara* and out onto the external scene. As his music breaks through the silence of the human scene, it moves directly to the woman, who is in line with the arms of the *kithara*, and whose attention Apollo has captured with his melody. Having been affected by the god's music and having been drawn into harmony with him, the woman on the exterior at once provides the liquid for her male companions' offering but also for the god who similarly extends his *phialē*.

For the viewer, who may have seen this image and used this cup in a symposium where he too could have been surrounded by instrumental music, lyrical songs, splashing wine, and the sight of his companions pouring their own libations to the gods, the distinction between the god's actions on the vase and the actions that occur in the external symposium might begin to blur together. In this way, the viewer not only acts as the individual who looks at the image and sees the god performing both music and ritual but, rather, the repetition of actions taken both in the painting and in the actual symposium would have blurred the distinction between the two spaces.[87] As a result, the viewer is much more than a member of Apollo's audience, but rather, in looking and imaginatively hearing, he becomes another figure within the scene, absorbed into the divinely coordinated actions as he aids Apollo in the completion of his musical and ritual performance.

With each image discussed in this chapter, Apollo's musical performance and his libation are presented as the unique purview of the god himself. His music is repeatedly shown affecting those around him, whether his immediate companions who help with his ritual, the mortal figures who are often depicted on the vessel's other side, or even the external viewers who encountered these scenes in sanctuaries or symposia. Each image within this small corpus thus comments on Apollo's divine nature, namely that his musical skill is unparalleled, that it has the ability to synchronize his actions with those of his companions, and that the god could potentially reveal himself to his human audience through the confluence of musical sound and ritual action.

Certain images, however, also point to Apollo's reliance on his human worshippers, who are needed to activate the god's actions in the images by imagining the musical and liquid sounds present within the scene. Upon encountering each image, the viewers could experience the presence of Apollo through multiple sensations, as they might see the painted vase, imagine the sounds of the *kithara* and falling liquid, and perhaps even sing their own spondaic hymns celebrating the god of music. In this interplay between visual image and imagined sound, and in one's own participation in animating the god's actions, the presence of Apollo could be physically experienced in a moment of coordinated musical and ritual rhythm and harmony.

NOTES

1 *BAPD* 210091; ARV^2 815.1; *Beazley Addenda* 143; *Beazley Addenda*^{2} 292; *LIMC* s.v. Apollon no. 457; Smith 1925: pl. 5; Bakalakis 1936: 64, fig. 7; Gaifman 2013: 51.
2 On libations being offered at altars, see Gaifman 2018a: 42–49.
3 Of the surviving red-figure vases listed on the Beazley Archive, 173 show Apollo with a *chelys* lyre and 128 show him with a *kithara*. Among this total group of just over 300 vases, only approximately 65 feature him both playing his lyre and pouring a libation. Though statistical analyses of surviving vase-paintings are never clear indications of production trends, that a significant number of vases depicting Apollo with a lyre and *phialē* survive suggests that it was a scene that was created numerous times by various artists.
4 Graf 1980; Lissarrague 1995b: 133–34; Simon 2004; Gaifman 2018a: 1–16.
5 To my knowledge, there only exist two examples where a musician plays an instrument while undertaking another task, both by the Berlin Painter. One is the name vase, where the satyr Orochares plays his *barbitos* and holds up a *kantharos* (*BAPD* 201809); the other is a fragmentary *amphora* of Panathenaic shape where Herakles holds a *kantharos* in his right hand while the left plays the *barbitos* (*BAPD* 41237).
6 For a full discussion of Pan's music-making, see Chapter 1.
7 I discuss Dionysos in Chapter 5.
8 The Berlin Painter, *Kitharoidos* (A), *Instructor* (B), Attic red-figure *amphora*, fired clay, h. 41.5 cm, *c.* 490 BCE. New York, Metropolitan Museum of Art, 56.171.38.
9 Maas and Snyder (1989: 55–57) provide the most detail on this particular mode of representing Apollo and establish that these scenes first appear at the beginning of the fifth century.
10 Noted by Power (2010: 134).
11 Mathiesen 1999: 247–48; Maas and Snyder 1989: 63–64.
12 For further discussion of left-handed plucking and right-handed picking, see especially Power 2010: 122–36.
13 We might think of, for instance, particularly impressive guitar solos that often occur during live musical performances.
14 I know of two other examples that feature left-handed playing, both by the Berlin Painter: *BAPD* 201809 and *BAPD* 41237. Moreover, as Power (2010: 134–36) notes, Asconius, in his commentary on Cicero's *Verrine Orations*, mentions a statue of a *kitharoidos* that also plays with the left hand (Asc. *Verr.* 2.1.53), though the statue he describes may alternatively depict Apollo.
15 In comparing these two types of images, I draw on Maas and Snyder's methodology, though with different results. Maas and Snyder 1989: 63–64.

16 In a 2014 performance, Stefan Hagel (2014) establishes that it is possible to play the *kithara* using only the left hand. For musical instruction on the lyre, see Hagel and Lynch 2015: 403–04; Laferrière 2023.

17 Painter of the Yale Oinochoe, *Judgement of Paris*, Attic red-figure *hydria*, ceramic, h. 33.02 cm, *c.* 470 BCE. London, British Museum, 1873,0820.353 (E178). *BAPD* 205649.

18 This last point, that the left hand might create different harmonic lengths, is controversial among scholars of ancient music, as it is unclear logistically or theoretically how this might work. Mathiesen (1999: 247–48) raises the possibility of harmonics being produced in such a manner, as does Stefan Hagel during his many performances on the *kithara* ("Ancient Greek Music on the *Kithara* and *Aulos*"), while Maas and Snyder (1989: 63), West (1981: 116), and Winnington-Ingram (1956: 183–86) all reject the possibility.

19 The Berlin Painter, *Apollo Entering Olympos* (A, B), Attic red-figure *stamnos*, ceramic, h. 29.21 cm, *c.* 490–460 BCE. London, British Museum, 1836,0224.8 (E444). *BAPD* 201968.

20 The Syracuse Painter, *Apollo with Lyre and Phiale*, Attic red-figure *hydria*, ceramic, h. 39 cm, *c.* 460 BCE. Basel, Antikenmuseum und Sammlung Ludwig, BS 476. *BAPD* 205841. Further examples of these articulations include a bell *krater* from Syracuse no. 45911 where the god's fingers are curled, (*ARV*[2] 1053.32) or a neck *amphora* in Providence (15.005) where Apollo's hand makes a fist (*ARV*[2] 653.1).

21 *BAPD* 207228; *ARV*[2] 623.73; Beazley 1925: 352.41; Lamb 1930: 1, 37, pl. 38.1–4;Robertson 1992: 171–72, fig. 81; Vassilika 1998: 56–57.

22 I thank Soffia Gunnarsdottir for her observations on Ganymede. For a possible identification of this figure as Ion acting as a temple attendant, see Shapiro 2009.

23 For the *phialē* as the distinctive vessel of the gods, see Veyne 1990. We might also consider a remarkable image on a cup by the Kodros Painter, where the gods have their own symposium and drink from *phialai* (London, British Museum, 1847,0909.6 (E82)). For more on the role of cupbearers on scenes of the symposium, see Topper 2013: 53–85.

24 Maas and Snyder 1989: 63–64; Mathiesen 1999: 247–48.

25 *BAPD* 15823; Mayo and Russell 1998: 52–53; Patton 2009: 64, 327.

26 Hurwit 1977.

27 Lambrinudakis et al. 1984; Maas and Snyder 1989: 55–57; Graf 2009: 33–51.

28 Patton 2009: 95, fig. 57.

29 On the specific handling of the *phialē* in a libation, see Gaifman 2018b.

30 Tanner (2006: 81–83) argues that Demeter's heavy-set torso and loose drapery, both of which evoke her matronly nature, help to identify her.

31 Johnston 2013: 370–401.

32 *BAPD* 207079; *ARV*[2] 611.32, 1661; Beazley 1925: 340.39; *Beazley Addenda* 131; *Beazley Addenda*[2] 268; Hölscher 1981: 22–24, fig.10, pls. 14.1–2, 15.1–6; Patton 2009: 88, fig. 52. On the Niobid Painter and his group, see Robertson 1992: 180–85.

33 Apollo and Artemis are joined by Leto, who also extends a libation dish towards her children, ready to participate in the ritual. A possible location for the scene is suggested by the addition of the column immediately behind the altar: this libation, performed by Apollo, Artemis, and Leto, takes place in a sanctuary, possibly dedicated to the Delian triad.

34 Patton (2009: 179) ascribes the initial appearance of the scenes to the uncertainty in Athens with respect to the Persians. She suggests that the disappearance of these scenes may be linked with the peace established with Persia from *c.* 449 BCE onwards.

35 Furtwängler (1881: 116–17) argued that the images of divine libations represent an attempt to depict the gods engaging in human activities. His central concept, *Übertragung*, refers to the transference of human ritual activity to the gods; in other words, in depicting gods pouring libations, the Greeks transferred to the gods their own social behaviors that involved drinking and dining. For a similar argument, see Schefold 1937. As Gaifman further notes, the theories on divine libations that arose after Furtwängler's 1881 article are, in many ways, responses to it. See, for instance, the work of Heinz Luschey (1893:

1026–27, 1030) and Walter Burkert (1979: 44; 1985: 72), who each argue that the *phialē* was a focalizing object within the interaction between human and divine, so that any communication took place from mortal to immortal hand. Within this framework, the *phialē* Apollo holds is emblematic of the relationship fostered between human worshipper and divine god, who each undertake this gesture as a means of connecting the two otherwise separate groups. For further discussion, see especially Gaifman 2018a: 118–20.

36 Simon 1953. For a full account of the critical response to Simon's work, see Patton 2009: 138–45; Gaifman 2013: 46–47; Gaifman 2018a: 120 n. 12 and 13.

37 Complicating the theories advanced by Furtwängler, Luschey, and Burkert is the work of Brigitte Eckstein-Wolf (1951). Though she similarly focuses her attention upon the *phialē*, she sees it not as a link between human and divine, but instead as a signifier of the gods' divinity. She argues that the *phialē* is responsible for pouring the libation, so that it assumes an essential role in mediating between human and divine, while the act of pouring a libation similarly becomes a connection between the two distinct groups. Paul Veyne (1990) similarly suggests that the *phialē* is a symbol of divine status since it is a vessel that belongs exclusively to the gods. More recently, Herbert Hoffmann (1997: 113–14) turned his attention again to the *phialē*, once again noting that it establishes a connection between men and gods because it is a ritually charged object that has been dedicated to the divine but is used by men and women in the context of ritual.

38 Largely in response to Simon's work, many theories have arisen, some of which argue that the figures in these images were intended to represent mortals dressed as gods (Nilsson 1957; Arafat 1990), that the images visualize the gods' relationship with the mortal men or women who venerated them (Himmelmann 1998), that all libations poured by the gods were intended for Gaia (Otto 1934; 1956, reprinted 1975: 82; Fuchs 1961: 167–81), or that the images served as divine prototypes for the related human action (Bakalakis 1967: 65–66; Mitropoulou 1975: 89–90).

39 Patton 2009; Gaifman 2018a.

40 For a full account of the historiography on divine libations, see Patton 2009: 121–60; Gaifman 2013: 46–49; Gaifman 2018a: 118–21.

41 Gaifman 2018a: 120–21.

42 Gaifman 2018a: 117–49.

43 *BAPD* 215310; *ARV*[2] 1156.10; *Beazley Addenda*[2] 337; *LIMC* s.v. Apollon no. 745; Patton 2009: 346 no. 204; Gaifman 2013: 44.

44 On the 's-curve' in Greek sculpture and its associations with Praxiteles, see Ridgway 1997: 261–67.

45 My thanks to Timothy Power for this observation.

46 On *harmonia*, see Chapter 3. See also Plato, *Kratylos*, 405c–d:

> With reference to music we have to understand that alpha often signifies "together" and here it denotes moving together in the heavens about the poles, as we call them, and harmony in song, which is called concord (*symphonia*); for, as the ingenious musicians and astronomers tell us, all these things move together by a kind of harmony (*harmonia*). And this god directs the *harmonia*, making them all move together, among both gods and men.

For more, see Frede 2010; Kurke 2013a; Kowalzig 2013: 186–94.

47 Rutherford 2004: 67–90. Though the paean was often performed for Apollo, there exist surviving examples of similar hymns sung for Dionysos. For more, see Rutherford 1993; Furley and Bremer 2001a: 121–29; 2001b: 52–84; Calame 2009; 2013.

48 *BAPD* 207308; *ARV*[2] 630.25; Pryce 1932: III Ic, pl. 61.2a; *LIMC* s.v. Apollon no. 676a; Patton 2009: 340, no. 157.

49 Beazley 1918: vi; Robertson 1992: 191–93.

50 Mortal *kithara* players, by contrast, are typically shown with short hair. Maas and Snyder 1989: 58; Mathiesen 1999: 259–60.

51 On the stages of sacrificial ritual, see Van Straten 1995: pre-kill: 13–102, post-kill: 15–60.
52 Gaifman 2017.
53 On the visual significance of the frame, see Derrida 1987: 37–82; Hurwit 1977; Platt and Squire 2017a.
54 *BAPD* 206343; *ARV*[2] 556.100; *Paralipomena* 387, 88; *Beazley Addenda*[2] 258; Beazley 1925: 103.38;. For more on the Pan Painter's style and his artistic development, see Smith 2006.
55 Smith 2006: 448–50.
56 For more on viewer absorption and theatricality, see Fried 1988: especially 107–60.
57 Neer 2002: 135–82.
58 Both Plato and Xenophon begin their symposia with libations (Pl. *Symp.* 176a; Xen. *Symp.* 2.1). The sixth-century BCE philosopher Xenophanes mentions pouring three libations at the beginning of a symposium (Ath. *Deipnosophistae* 11.462f). Other authors have elaborated upon the recipients of these offerings, with one scholiast specifying that the first libation went to Olympian Zeus, the second to Earth and the heroes, and the last to Zeus the Savior (scholiast ad Pindar, *Isthmian* 6.4, with further discussion in Tolles 1943; Lissarrague 1990b: 25–26; Gaifman 2018a: 66, 161 n.41 with previous bibliography). On the relationship between the symposium and religious ritual, see especially Hobden 2011.
59 Lissarrague 1990b: 3–18, 68–86, 123–39; Neer 2002: 9–26; Hobden 2013: 1–21.
60 *BAPD* 212276; *ARV*[2] 842.128; Beazley 1925: 264.35; Walters and Forsdyke 1930: III.Ic.8, pl. 61.2A–B; Patton 2009: 340 no. 156. For a similar scene, see the *hydria* by the Pan Painter in the M. H. de Young Memorial Museum in San Francisco, no. 707. Smith 1943: 36, pls. 15.2A–B,16.2; *ARV*[2] 555.97; *Paralipomena* 388; *Beazley Addenda*[2] 258.
61 For more on images of Athenian musical education, see Laferrière 2023.
62 The connection with the Athenian ephebes, the young men of the *polis*, may be seen on the reverse, where one such figure faces the right, as if witnessing the events that occur on the opposite side of the vase.
63 For a similar approach to the role music plays in drawing together human and divine, though within the context of epic performance, see Brouillet 2016: 398–99, 435–38; 2017.
64 As Karavites notes (1984: 60–70), *spondai/spendein* could also refer to a peace treaty, probably because of the libation poured to consecrate the agreement.
65 West 1982: 55.
66 West 1982: 55–56.
67 *PMG* 941. Translation adapted from West 1982: 55.
68 West 1982: 55.
69 Plato, *Leg.* 799b; Plut. [*De mus.*] 1134f–1135c. On *spondeion*, see Barker 1984: 157–58, 216–17, 22, 55–57, 300.
70 For more on changeable genres of poetry, see especially Ford 2011: 69–90.
71 Theoc., *Id.* 22.223. Translation adapted from Hopkinson 2015: 312–13.
72 *BAPD* 207333; *ARV*[2] 632; *Beazley Addenda*[2] 272; Picón, Mertens, et al. 2007: 113 no. 23, 429.
73 Callim. *Hymn 2*, 1–8. I have drawn on Peter Bing's evocative translation (Bing 1993: 183).
74 As pointed out by Williams 1978: 15; Platt 2011: 175–80. On the visual metaphor of a god emerging through a doorway, see McKay 1967; Weinreich 1968: 67–74; Santangelo 1972. The reader's breathless anticipation of a vision of the divine is suggested through the repeating aspirations that have been gathered together at the beginning. Bing 1993: 183–84. The natural world also lends its own soundscape to celebrate the god's arrival: the house and the laurel branch shake, the palm tree rustles, and the swan sings (Williams 1978: 16–17).
75 For another manipulation of the sigma in Greek poetry, see Lasos of Hermione's asigmatic compositions, that is, compositions in which no sigmas were used. According to tradition, when asked why he omitted this letter, he stresses that the hissing sound it made was not clear in tone, especially when contrasted with other syllables. It also produced a harsh

sound when accompanied by the *lyre*, the result of which creates a jarring effect. Porter 2010: 383–97; Gurd 2016: 98–114.

76 Callim. *Hymn 2*, 105–07. Bing 1993: 192.

77 Bing 1993: 186; Platt 2011: 180.

78 Gordon 1979; Vernant 1985a; 1985b; Tanner 2006: 106–08; Platt 2011: 119–22; Gaifman 2016; Elsner 2017: 457–71.

79 *BAPD* 5522; Konstantinou 1970; Mertens 1974: 106–08; Metzger 1977; *LIMC* s.v. Apollon no. 455; Bundrick 2005: 16; Patton 2009: 60, 326; Gaifman 2013.

80 Konstantinou (1970: 36) stipulates that the bird is a black dove, because of its inclusion in the description of Delphi in Euripides' *Ion*, 1196. Metzger (1977: 428), in a postscript to his article, references Christos Karouzos' interpretation that the bird is the raven that betrayed Koronis to Apollo, although Metzger has misgivings about simply applying a literary narrative onto a visual image. Schmidt (2002: 16), in his study of black birds in vase-painting, also argues that the bird is most likely a raven.

81 As Gaifman has noted (2013: 51), the image almost suggests that the god's *phialē* generates the liquid that the god offers. A similar depiction of Apollo may also be found on a red-figure oil container, a *lekythos*, by the Providence Painter, where Apollo is shown frontally and stretches his *kithara* out to the right and his *phialē* out to the left, to a companion who has not been included in the image (Boston, Museum of Fine Arts, 95.45; *ARV*[2] 640.74; Beazley 1925: 135.45; *Beazley Addenda*[2] 274; Maas and Snyder 1989: 78.)

82 Gaifman 2013: 50. The cup, therefore, was probably never seen inside a symposium.

83 Gaifman 2013: 50–51.

84 The vessel was discovered in a tomb at Delphi, where it seems to have been deposited in the middle of the fourth century BCE. A period of approximately 100 years thus separates its initial creation and deposition within the tomb; as such, the cup could have been displayed in a private home or perhaps displayed within the sanctuary to Apollo at Delphi. Konstantinou 1970: 27–29; Mertens 1974: 106.

85 *BAPD* 206887; *ARV*[2] 594.62; Beazley 1925: 336.36; Fairbanks and Chase 1948: 26; Maas and Snyder 1989: 71; Patton 2009: 82, 334 no. 113. According to the Boston Museum of Fine Arts online catalogue entry, Edward Perry Warren's records indicate that he bought the vessel in 1897, after it was found at Sounion. It is unclear, however, where at Sounion the vessel was uncovered.

86 Brouillet 2016: 398–99, 435–38; Brouillet 2017.

87 Hurwit 1977: 1–30; Derrida 1987: 56–58; Platt and Squire 2017a.

THREE

PAINTING WITH MUSIC

Of all the gods, Apollo is most often associated with music, so much so that in the *Theogony*, Hesiod presents him, together with the Muses, as the instigating force behind humanity's ability to create instrumental music and lyric song.[1] In the surviving visual material from Archaic and Classical Athens, Apollo's music is repeatedly shown to be powerfully affective, capable of bringing together the gods and even synchronizing their actions. In addition to those scenes that depict his coordinated music and ritual, Apollo's musical skill on the lyre is a prominent aspect of his representation across the surviving literary and visual sources, where it is presented as instilling social and even political harmony among both gods and men. His musical abilities often determine the nature of his relationship with his fellow gods, as can be seen in the *Homeric Hymn to Apollo* (201–03), where on Mount Olympos:

> . . . αὐτὰρ ὁ Φοῖβος Ἀπόλλων ἐγκιθαρίζει
> καλὰ καὶ ὕψι βιβάς, αἴγλη δέ μιν ἀμφι φαείνει
> μαρμαρυγαί τε ποδῶν καὶ ἐϋκλώστοιο χιτῶνος.
>
> . . . he, Phoibos Apollo, plays his lyre in the middle,
> stepping beautifully and high and radiance shines about him,
> and the flashing of his feet and his tunic of quality thread.[2]

In the hymn, his music is so beautiful and his performance so dazzling that he entices the other gods to dance and celebrate with him.

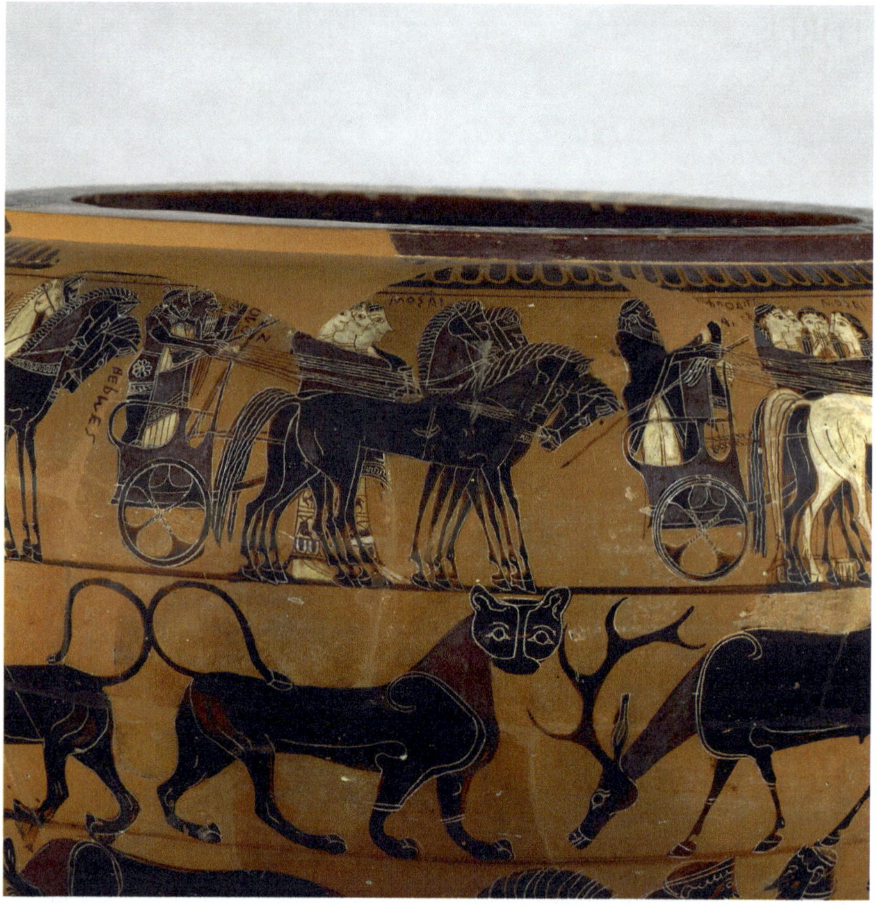

3.1. Detail of Apollo and Hermes. Sophilos, *The Wedding of Peleus and Thetis*, Attic black-figure *dinos*, h. 71 cm, *c.* 580–570 BCE. London, British Museum, 1971,1101.1. © The Trustees of the British Museum.

The skill with which Apollo plays his lyre as well as his role as a chorus leader contribute to a prevailing conception of Apollo as a masterful performer whose music had the ability to form bonds among his audience through their shared experience of listening to the sounds of his lyre. Indeed, we see this consequence of listening to Apollo's music at the end of book 1 of the *Iliad*, where it fosters peace and harmony among the gods (601–04). It is within this conception of the power of Apollo's music that we find him depicted on one of the most important early representations of Greek myth: the large mixing bowl painted and signed by the artist Sophilos, which features an early representation of Apollo as a musician (Fig. 3.1).[3]

The vessel is divided horizontally into a series of bands, each of which depicts a scene from myth or a sequence of animals. Of particular interest to us is the top register, which features the wedding of Peleus and Thetis, including the procession of the gods who have convened to celebrate the marriage.

Among the gods who approach is Apollo, who holds up his large *kithara* and strums on it with his *plektron* while Hermes drives the chariot. The only other divinities on the bowl who undertake an activity other than walking in the procession or driving a chariot are the Muses, who accompany Apollo's music with their singing; one Muse also holds up her panpipes to her mouth, adding her music to the sounds of Apollo's lyre.[4] The Muses and Apollo are thus singled out within the divine procession, drawing visual attention to the importance of music and song for this marriage celebration. There exists a crucial point of difference, however, between the two representations of music-making: Apollo stands in a chariot along with the other Olympian gods and plays a *kithara*, his profile performance placing his music at a distance from his viewers, while the central Muse's frontal face directly confronts the viewer's gaze.[5] The image thus suggests that divine music could, at any time, potentially have different intended audiences: while Apollo's music is directed to and intended to delight a divine audience and draw them together in celebration, the Muse's performance is directed to the human men and women who once looked at this scene.[6]

Leaving the particular texture of the Muses' performance for further discussion in Chapter 4, for now, what is clear from Sophilos' representation is that among all the gods, Apollo is clearly associated with the music of the lyre.[7] Throughout the Archaic and Classical periods, much of the corpus repeats the image of Apollo that we have already seen: Apollo holds the lyre up with his left arm, touches individual strings with his left hand, and draws the *plektron* across with his right hand, performing his music for the audience that has gathered. We also find suggestions in Archaic and Classical literature that Apollo's music could instill in his divine audience a sense of community and delight in music-making. The *Homeric Hymn to Apollo* offers a particularly evocative episode in which Apollo's music has a powerful effect on its audience. There, Apollo leaps up with his lyre to Mount Olympos where the other gods find his music irresistible, and "at once the immortals devote themselves to lyre music and song," αὐτίκα δ' ἀθανάτοισι μέλει κίθαρις καὶ ἀοιδή (188).[8] The Muses sing a hymn, while the Graces, the Seasons, Hebe, and Aphrodite dance with Harmonia, a personification of the aesthetically pleasing concord of diverse elements in both music and the visual arts.[9] Near the dancing women, Artemis raises her voice in song, distinguished from the other female deities by her status as Apollo's sister. Apollo, in this episode, acts as the catalyst for the songs the gods sing, the music they play, and the dances they perform.

Apollo, as the sources and images make clear, loved music, and in what follows I focus on the images that depict him actively engaging in his craft, in order to determine the specific visual characteristics that determined the representation of his music as well as the effect that it could have both on the other figures in the scene and on the external viewer. I begin by examining scenes of Apollo playing his lyre alone to isolate both the character of his music and its effect on his audience. I then position the scenes of Apollo's music-making within the broader context of the technical vocabulary used for discussing both visual and musical compositions, specifically with respect to three concepts: *rhythmos*, *symmetria*, and *harmonia*. I end by considering the ways in which the distinct character of Apollo's music, as it is represented in the surviving corpus, brings together potentially separated or even opposed groups of individuals, and how the musical harmony that he embodies could have had a similar effect on his human audience in sixth-century Athens. I argue that Apollo's powerfully affective music informs each scene's composition, whether it is through the physical position of the figures, who direct their attention to the god's music, or through the repetition of similar lines and forms among Apollo, his instrument, his audience, and the plants and animals that accompany him. It is these physical, material traces of divine, immaterial sound that make visible the unifying capacity of Apollo's music.

APOLLO THE MUSICIAN

Although it is unusual to find Apollo performing alone, I begin with a particularly powerful representation of the god, painted by the Berlin Painter onto the side of a water vessel.[10] In addition to its unusual subject matter, the scene brings together, in a single image, Apollo's quintessential characteristics (Fig. 3.2). Unencumbered by any framing device, the majority of the visual field is taken up by two large wings attached to a tripod. The wings are fully extended, caught in a moment of active flight as they propel the tripod forward. As the tripod floats through the air, the feet of the vessel skim the surface of the waves, below which fish and an octopus swim. Dolphins jump alongside, as if the tripod were a ship moving quickly through the sea. Atop the vessel, perched in the large bowl, is Apollo, with his feet dangling over one side. A quiver of arrows is strapped to his back, and in his left hand he holds out a *chelys* lyre, angled on a diagonal to the upper right, while his right hand holds a *plektron*, partially obscured by the tripod's handles.

By displaying objects commonly associated with Apollo, the image implicitly refers to the various mythological narratives associated with the god, each object acting as an index of the story in which it features. His bow and arrow, slung over his back, link him with Artemis, his divine twin with whom he shot the children of Niobe after they taunted Leto.[11] The tripod, conversely, draws a connection between the god, Delos, and Delphi, as well as with the oracle who sits in her tripod. Within the realm of myth, the vessel calls to mind the struggle between Herakles and Apollo over the Delphic tripod, elevating human competition to the divine stage. The tripod was also, however, a prize

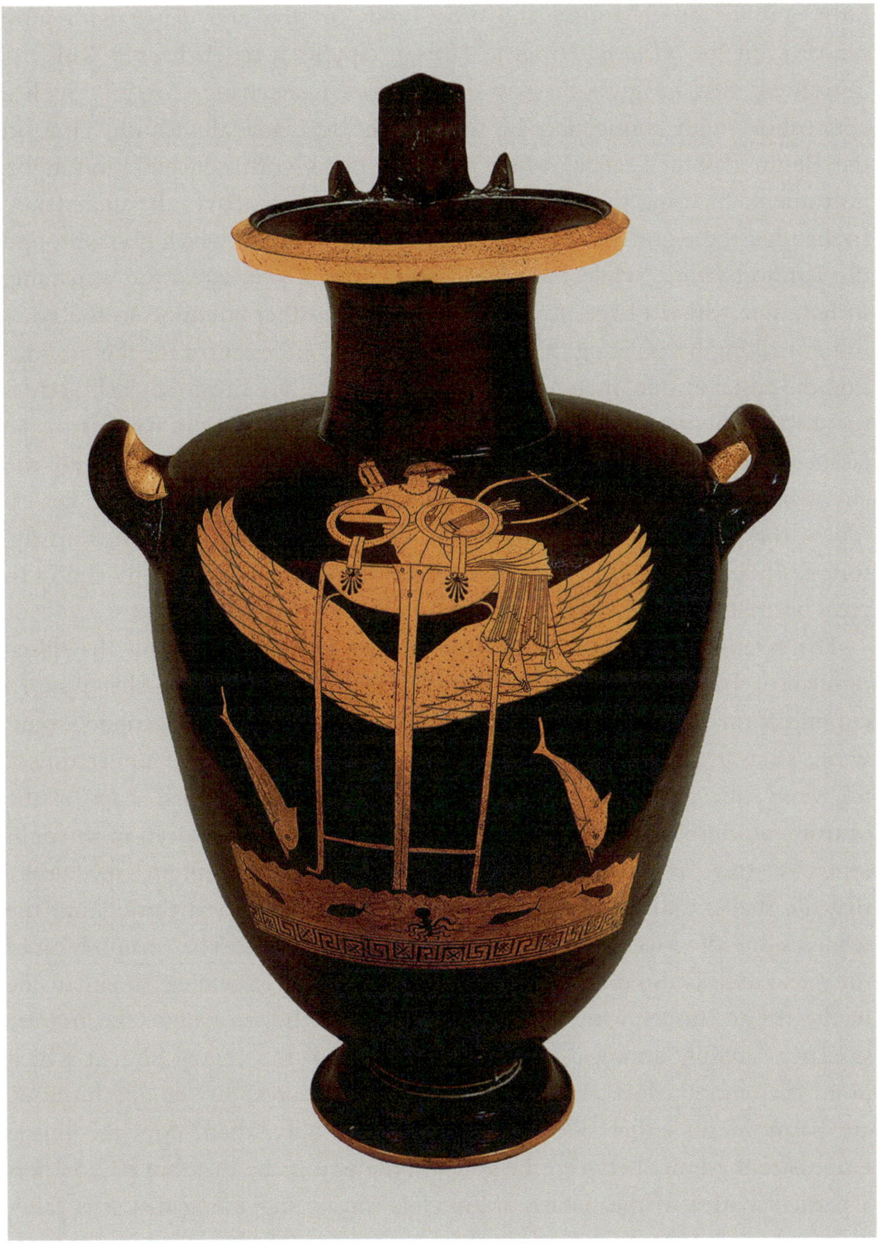

3.2. The Berlin Painter, *Apollo Hyperpontios*, Attic red-figure *hydria*, ceramic, h. 58.2 cm, *c.* 490–480 BCE. Vatican City, Museo Gregoriano Etrusco Vaticano, 16568. © Governorate of the Vatican City State – Directorate of the Vatican Museums.

in athletic competition, and thus has connotations of aristocratic physical skill and victory. The lyre, whose arms gracefully extend out to the right of the god, alludes to the particular relationship that existed between Apollo and this instrument: in the *Homeric Hymn to Apollo*, the god calls for it moments after his birth and his music entices the other gods to sing and dance with him; similarly, in the *Homeric Hymn to Hermes*, Apollo is so enchanted with the instrument that he gives his cows to Hermes in exchange for it.[12] Such a connection with music and his instrument is made abundantly clear in the Berlin Painter's scene, where the god stares with concentration at his instrument, focusing the viewer's attention upon the activity he undertakes. In the image, the god looks to his left hand, the thumb of which hooks around the leftmost string, while his other fingers stretch out across the remaining strings. The tripod's large, round handles draw further attention to the god's music-making by isolating the two activities that are essential for the production of music: in one opening, the majority of the lyre's tortoise-shell body is revealed to the viewer while, in the other, the god's arm and hand with the *plektron* stretch horizontally across, their linear form contrasting with the curving lines of the tripod and instrument. Layering the tripod's handles on top of the god's lyre, the arms of the instrument extend up both from the tortoise shell and from the large, round handle, so that the god seems almost to coax his melody from both the musical instrument and the tripod.

The relationship between the two objects is underscored by the visual resonances between the lines that make up their bodies. Parallel upward curving forms from the arm of the lyre are repeated for the tripod's right wing, as well as in the downward pointing palmettes on the upper rim of the vessel; the palmette, in turn, also reproduces the rounded shape of the instrument. Similarly, the folds of the god's robes are reproduced in the tight lines of feathers on the wings. The effect of these visual repetitions, specifically that the shapes and lines used to construct the image repeat throughout the scene, is one of visual unity among god, lyre, and tripod. The composition of the scene itself is also carefully balanced, with a wing extending on either side of the tripod, under which a dolphin jumps. In the sea below, the fish are similarly carefully arranged, two on either side of the central line, at which point the octopus floats. Even the god's two attributes, his lyre and his bow, are balanced on either side of his body. Not only, then, does the image emphasize the unity between the god and the objects he uses, but it also offers a particular idea of the nature of Apollo's music, suggesting that it is calm, balanced, and harmonious. It is this conception of the affective force of Apollo's music, where it could bring together gods, men, animals, and even plants, that we will see regularly explored in the surviving representations.

DIVINE SOUND AND VISUAL MUSIC

As with the evocative image painted onto the sides of the water vessel, on an earlier black-figure *amphora* we see a similar effort to draw out visually the connection that existed between Apollo and his music (Fig. 3.3).[13] Here, Apollo stands on the left, depicted in profile so the sweep and folds of his long drapery

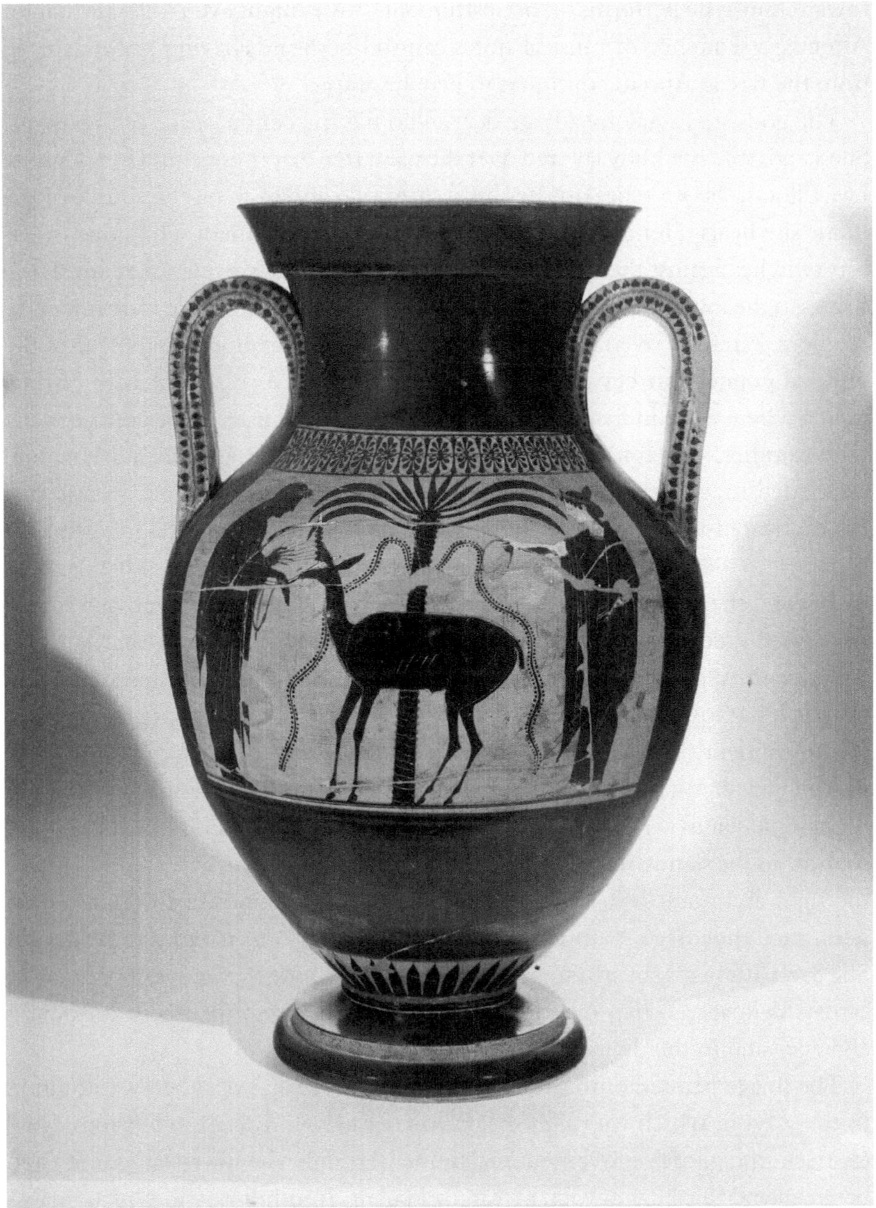

3.3. The Rycroft Painter, *Apollo and Artemis* (side A), Attic black-figure *amphora*, ceramic, h. 55.8 cm, *c.* 520–510 BCE. Oxford, Ashmolean Museum, 1965.118. © Ashmolean Museum, University of Oxford.

are highlighted. He holds out his *chelys* lyre in front of his torso, angling it in such a way that the strings are almost parallel to the ground. A cord that attaches the *plektron* to the body of the lyre hangs in a long curve, echoing the curving forms of the god's hanging drapery. Apollo grasps the *plektron* with his right hand and holds it just below the lyre, having drawn the tool across the strings. Artemis stands on the far side of the image, facing her brother and directing her attention toward him as he performs on his instrument.[14] We might even imagine that for Artemis, a sequence of musical notes can still be heard, having just emanated from the lyre as Apollo continues to play his music.

The gods are joined by a large deer, who fills the central space of the image. She stands still, her body layered over the palm tree that rises behind her. Despite her stillness, she stretches out her head to Apollo and his lyre, the source of the music she hears. Her nose touches the arm of the instrument while one of her ears twitches against the crossbar and the *kollops*, that is, the pegs that attach the strings to the instrument. In drawing visual attention to the subtle movements of the deer, carefully overlapping with lyre, the image explores the effect of the physical connection between god, music, and animal. By emphasizing those points where each individual or object overlaps or almost comes into contact with another, the image suggests that Apollo's music has been heard and responded to, so that here, it is the audible presence of the god's music that has captivated the deer's attention. We might even consider taking a similar approach to the outstretched branches and leaves of the palm tree, which extend far beyond the ridged trunk and pierce through the upper decorative frame.[15] As with the deer, the way the tree has been depicted suggests that it too is attentive to Apollo's music. The tree's leaves on the left side of the image seem to stretch out toward the lyre, the curving slope of its forms echoing the curve of the instrument's arms. The leaves are so large that they overlap with the instrument, so much so that the bottom leaf even touches the strings. Artemis, though she stands at a distance from Apollo, also seems to respond to the musical sounds. As she stands, listening to the music, the tree's leaves again stretch out to the right and point to her face, suggesting that the sounds of the music have permeated the image, so much so that Artemis both hears it and is moved by it. She even lifts her right arm to grasp a tendril of the vine that moves horizontally across the image, so that she too is connected to the other members of Apollo's audience and to the divine musician himself.

The image painted onto the Rycroft Painter's storage vessel draws attention to the ways in which we might begin to see the sounds of Apollo's music and to track the visual movement of music through the physical connection between and response of each pictorial element. Another way in which images may convey the presence of divine music is through written inscriptions, which, as we see in a scene of a divine procession (Fig. 3.4), track the progress of music as it emanates out from the lyre.[16] In this image, a female figure, possibly Artemis, stands in a chariot that is being pulled by four horses. They walk toward Apollo, who stands in front of the chariot. While he holds up a flower with his right hand, he holds a *chelys* lyre with his left hand. His fingers are spread out to touch the strings, while his thumb is hooked around the rightmost string, ready to pluck it and produce a musical note, or perhaps to add another sound to the music he has already created.

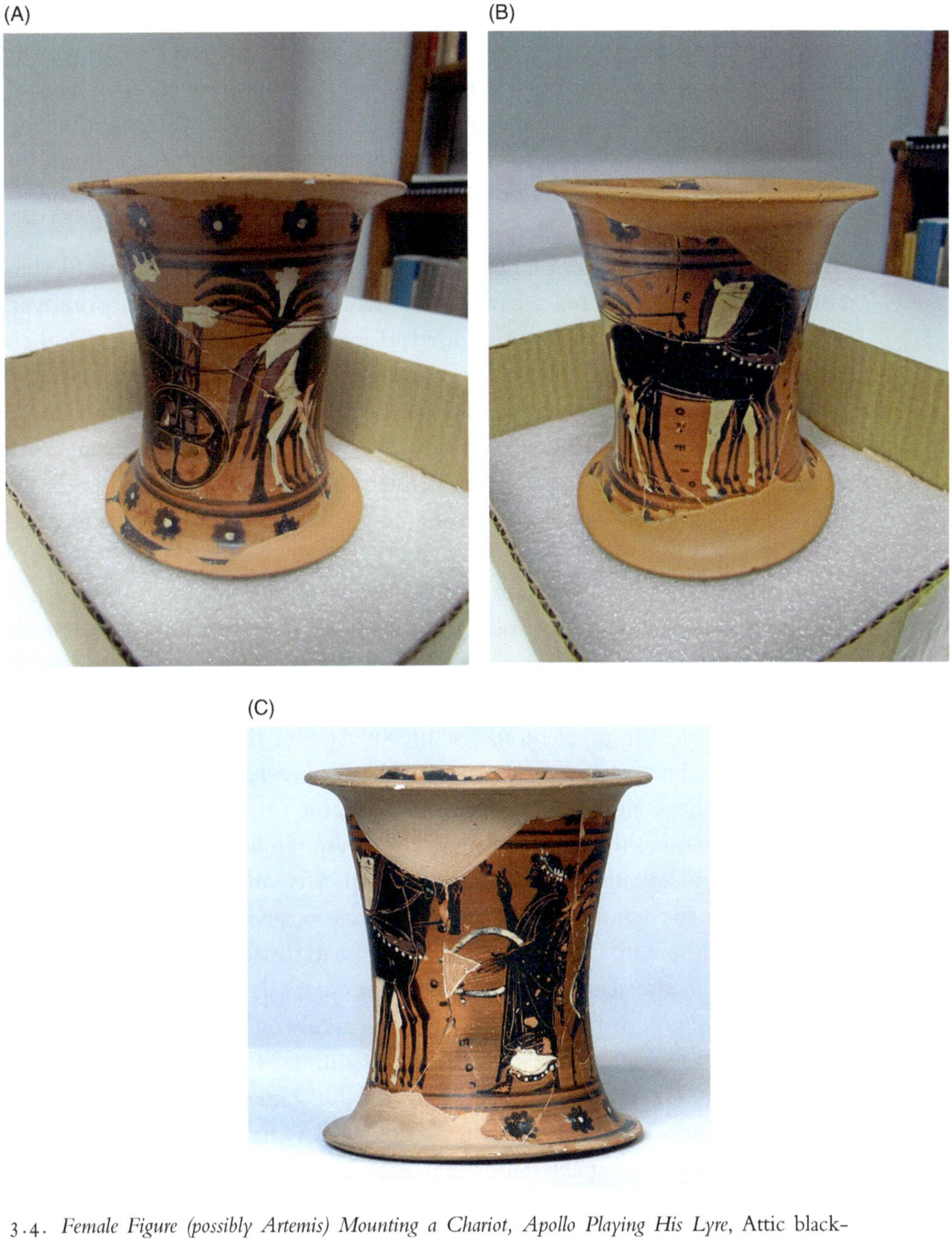

3.4. *Female Figure (possibly Artemis) Mounting a Chariot, Apollo Playing His Lyre*, Attic black-figure stand, ceramic, h. 13.4 cm, *c.* 525–500 BCE. Athens, Agora Museum, P9275. The rights of the depicted monuments belong to the Hellenic Ministry of Culture and Sports/Hellenic Organization of Cultural Resources Development (Law 4858/2021).

That we, as viewers, should imagine the scene to be filled with lyre music is suggested by the series of letters that the artist has included.[17] On the right, the letters Ο Ι Ε Ε Ο Γ cascade downwards from Apollo's instrument, emerging from the end of the lyre and then falling to the ground. Their downward descent is repeated by a similar pattern of letters, this time reading O P E I O, that are placed between the front and back legs of the horses. Above the horses' backs are three further letters, O I E, which are positioned in such a way that they continue the broad diagonal line of the letters that fall from the lyre. Although the letters do not form any comprehensible word, they should be distinguished from nonsense, or gibberish, inscriptions, insofar as they constitute actual letter forms.[18] There are also repetitions among the letter forms, so that, while no clear pattern emerges, the suggestion of a limited set of letters corresponding to a limited set of sounds may be further evoked. Moreover, some of the letters are closely positioned adjacent to Apollo's lyre, so that their placement implies that they emerge from the god's manipulation of the instrument's strings, and then spread out to fill the entire image with musical sound. Their inclusion, therefore, not only suggests the presence of Apollo's music in the image, but also renders visible the passage of musical sounds, for they trace the movement of music as it emerges from the strings of the lyre and passes into the rest of the scene.[19]

In many ways, the inclusion of the letters recalls the inscriptions on a number of Archaic statues or their accompanying bases that introduce a sonic element to their interaction with the viewer. A particularly compelling example for the use of writing to introduce sound into the viewing experience may be seen on the small bronze statue of Apollo, the so-called Mantiklos Apollo.[20] The inscription, written continuously in archaic Boiotian characters, runs in a U-shape along on the front of the statue's thighs as it asserts, in the statue's own voice, that Mantiklos gave it to Apollo as a gift.[21] Crucially, in addressing the god directly, the object itself acts on behalf of Mantiklos, ensuring that his actions will be properly reciprocated. The inscription thus infuses the statue with language and voice, so that, for any ancient viewer who encountered it, the statue is continually able to speak and convey the pious action that Mantiklos had undertaken.[22] By involving the viewer in its own exchange with Apollo, the statue makes the sounds of its carved voice visible to the reader. He or she, in turn, activates the statue and the force of the original dedication through his or her act of reading. In rendering aural speech through writing, the small figure makes its sonic voice visible, so that the "talking statue," as we might call it, freely communicates with its viewers. Similarly, the letters on the black-figure stand render visible Apollo's music, visually tracing the movement of sound throughout the scene, making it clear that the other figures in the scene hear Apollo's music and respond to it. The horses lift their legs and begin to walk forwards, the shape of their bent legs echoing the curving line of the letters that fall between their legs. Their heads also dip forward and bend back energetically, again picking up the movement of the letters around them. Their energy and forward movement, where they walk together with carefully coordinated steps, is thus visually tied to the musical sounds that originate with Apollo's lyre. A similar visual resonance exists between Apollo and the deer who stands to the right (Fig. 3.5), where she prances while lifting her head back. The animal, so clearly affected by the sounds she hears, dances beautifully behind the god, responding with her entire body to the musical performance underway. We need only think of the deer on the Rycroft Painter's *amphora*, or even the sea creatures on the Berlin Painter's water vessel, to see other instances of animals responding to Apollo's music. The shock of added white paint that delineates the fall of its chest further emphasizes the connection between its form and the white, curving arms of the lyre, underscoring the connection between the music and the animal's response. Not only, then, can the god's music affect other gods but, as this and the other images we have seen so far suggest, it can also profoundly influence the actions of animals.

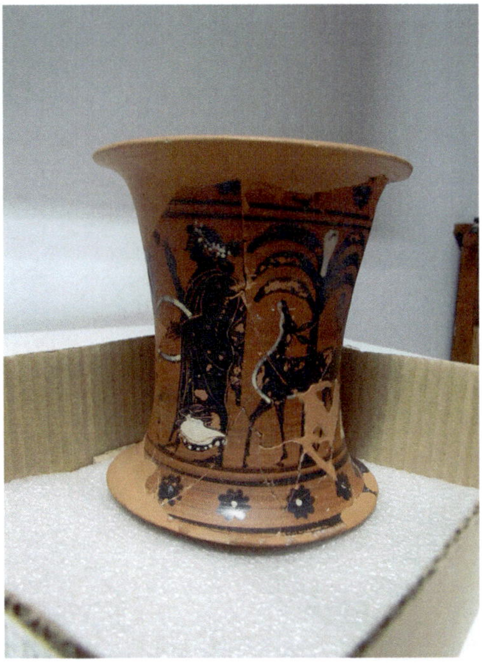

3.5. Detail. *Artemis Mounting a Chariot, Apollo Playing His Lyre*, Attic black-figure stand, ceramic, h. 13.4 cm, *c.* 525–500 BCE. Athens, Agora Museum, P9275. The rights of the depicted monuments belong to the Hellenic Ministry of Culture and Sports/Hellenic Organization of Cultural Resources Development (Law 4858/2021).

THEORIZING VISUAL MUSIC

Thus far, we have discussed Apollo's music within the confines of the images themselves, that is, by isolating various details in each representation that establish that Apollo plays his music, that his companions hear it, and that the sound of his performance has an effect upon his audience. In each instance, whether Apollo plays alone or for other gods and animals, what remains consistent is a visual emphasis on a restrained unity and ordered movements between Apollo and his instrument, as well as between Apollo and his audience. It is this visual resonance between the forms and lines that constitute the body of Apollo, his instrument, and his audience members that is particularly emphasized within the corpus of images depicting Apollo as a virtuoso *kitharoidos*.

If we consider our discussion of Apollo's music with the musical terminology that was beginning to be theorized and defined more carefully at this time, we find that there emerged a vocabulary with which to describe the various components of a melody and their corresponding effect. Building on the foundational work by J. J. Pollitt, I isolate three of these terms since they

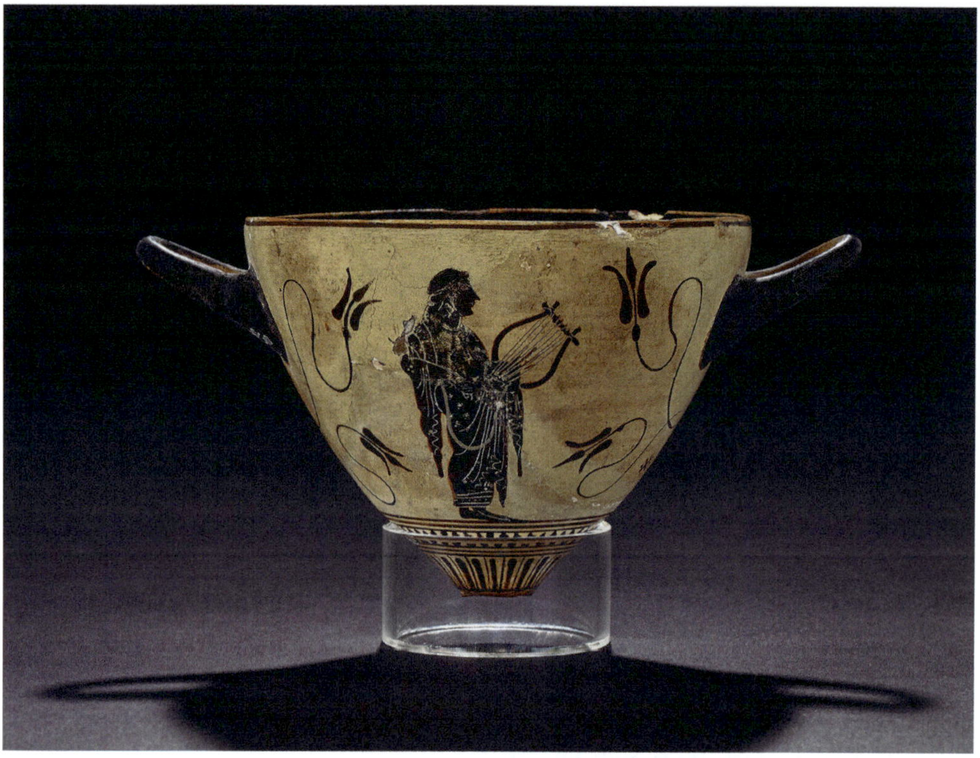

3.6. The Pistias Class, *Apollo Kitharoidos* (side A), Attic black-figure *mastos*, ceramic, h. 8.89 cm, *c.* 520–500 BCE. London, British Museum, 1882,1010.1 (B681). © The Trustees of the British Museum.

are the most immediately relevant to our discussion of how images might communicate the sounds of music: *rhythmos* (ῥυθμός), *symmetria* (συμμετρία), and *harmonia* (ἁρμονία).[23] Importantly, these concepts were also transferred to art criticism, so that the terminological language already invites a certain comparison between art and music.[24]

Let us begin our discussion with a small, black-figure *mastos*, that is, a pointed cup, which highlights Apollo's music by depicting him alone on one side, dressed in the elaborate performance costume of a *kitharoidos* (Fig. 3.6).[25] He holds out a *chelys* lyre, an instrument more typically used for young men's musical education since it was easier to play than the large, wooden *kithara* that professional musicians used for their public performances.[26] Regardless of his choice of instrument, the image nevertheless makes clear that the god plays his lyre: captured in the midst of his performance, the god's left hand stabilizes the instrument while his right hand holds a *plektron*, which he uses to pluck at the strings.[27] As with the other examples that we have seen thus far, Apollo's active musical performance suggests to the viewer that the sounds of his music fill the visual field. Indeed, the image even prompts us to wonder whether the flowers that bend and turn around the divine musician are perhaps intended to function not only as decoration, but rather act as further visual markers of the effects of Apollo's music, much as we saw on the Rycroft Painter's *amphora*, where the palm tree extended its leaves to touch the source of music. Here, the flowers' sinuous stems seem almost to move and pulse to the sound of Apollo's music, while the flower buds themselves echo the curving shape of the lyre that produces those sounds.[28]

Such visual resonances between instrument and flower or, as we have seen, between Apollo, his divine audience, or even the animals who accompany the musician, allow us to make general statements concerning the character of Apollo's music. We might say that there is something seductive about it, since it clearly affects those who hear it, or we might characterize it as lively and energetic, since it inspires its listening audience to move their bodies in response. However, we could also discuss the presence and effect of Apollo's music in terms of the *rhythmoi* that constitute the image's composition. *Rhythmos*, among the most challenging of the technical terms I address here, can be defined as the form or shape of each figure, animal, or object. In the course of the fifth and fourth centuries BCE, the term also took on the additional sense of repetition, so that it could refer to the configuration or proportion of the component parts of a scene or of a pattern painted onto a vase or sculpted into stone.[29] There seem to have been both artistic and musical implications to *rhythmos* in the earlier material – both art and music have discrete forms that are repeated throughout their respective compositions. Plato later elaborates upon the role that *rhythmos* played in music when he describes it as order within movement, so that it determines the order and pacing of notes within a composition.[30] The complexity of the term *rhythmos* has given way to various interpretations,[31] but what remains well established in the ancient material is its simultaneous use in discussions of the formal characteristics of both music and art.

Even though a more clearly defined understanding of *rhythmos* within music theory and art criticism developed after the *mastos* cup was created,[32] its earlier sense of denoting repeating forms helpfully gives us the vocabulary with which to describe how Apollo's music may be visible and how we may see the effect his music has on his audience. On the cup, as with other images that we have already encountered, similar visual forms make up the composition. For instance, the rounded shape of the lyre's arms is picked up by the cord attached to the *plektron*, so that the two objects are visually linked with each other beyond their obvious functional relationship. Moreover, the elaborate vegetation that surrounds Apollo resembles the shape of the god's lyre: the stalks of the flowers form curvilinear shapes similar to the rounded lines of the arms of the instrument and the sweep of the *plektron*'s ribbon, while the tops of the buds and central petal recall the upper portion of the instrument's arms and strings. Though these flowers are essentially decorative here, they transcend mere ornamentation in their visual resonances with Apollo and his instrument, and become visual echoes of the movement of Apollo's music through the

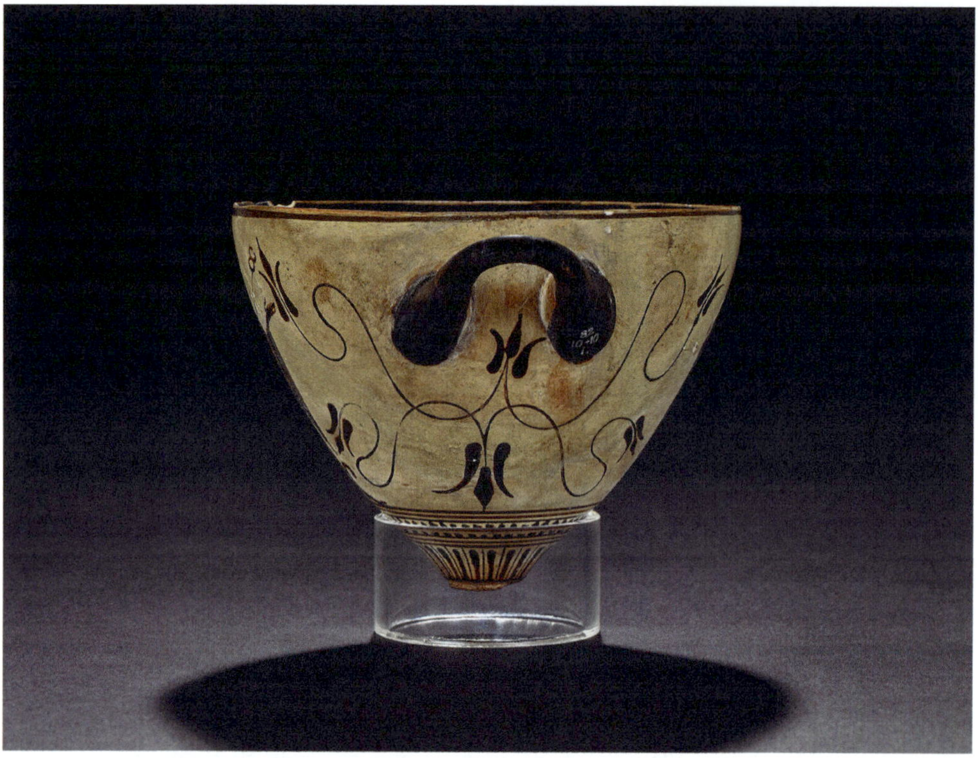

3.7. The Pistias Class, *Intertwined Flowers* (side view), Attic black-figure *mastos*, ceramic, h. 8.89 cm, *c.* 520–500 BCE. London, British Museum, 1882,1010.1 (B681). © The Trustees of the British Museum.

scene.[33] The flowering plants that surround him also spread around the sides of the vase, where under each handle they form arabesque patterns from their stalks and blossoms (Fig. 3.7). Although the effect of such visual resonances already suggests a relationship among the god, his music, and the surrounding landscape, it is also possible to discuss the repeating forms in the image within the context of a musico-visual *rhythmos*. The particular curving line of the lyre's arms could even be isolated as a defining *rhythmos* for the image, so that its repetition across the image acts almost as a visualization of Apollo's music, emanating outward from the lyre and Apollo to his surroundings.

In addition to the painted decoration, the pointed shape of the *mastos* cup, so named for its resemblance to the shape of a breast,[34] further amplifies the presence of Apollo's music, since the shape of the lyre and of the flowers mimic the shape of the vessel itself. Not only, then, do the elements within the composition demonstrate the effect that Apollo's music has upon them, but the material body of the vase itself is structured around curving lines that open up near the brim. Furthermore, the cup's pointed base, which cannot hold up the cup, required that the vessel be held at all times when it was full of liquid.[35] We can imagine, then, that as the cup moved within the drinker's grasp, when it was lifted to one's

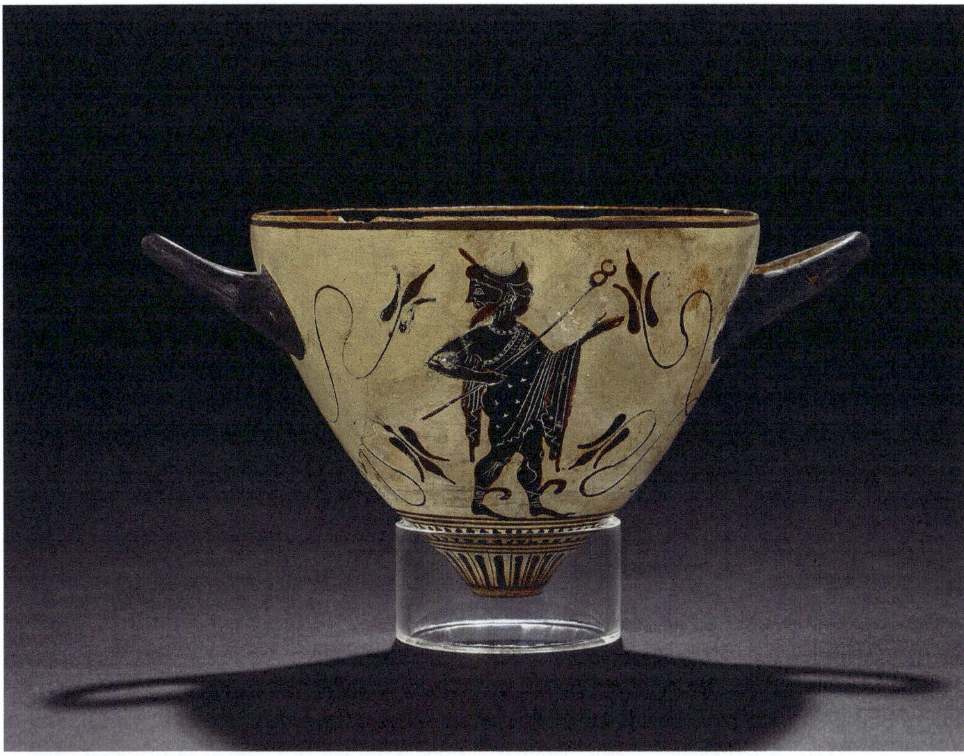

3.8. The Pistias Class, *Hermes* (side B), Attic black-figure *mastos*, ceramic, h. 8.89 cm, *c.* 520–500 BCE. London, British Museum, 1882,1010.1 (B681). © The Trustees of the British Museum.

mouth, or jostled as it was passed from person to person within a sympotic gathering, the painted vegetation would have appeared almost to move on the surface of the vase, dancing to the sound of Apollo's music.[36] Because of its unusual shape, the cup would rarely have been still or even been simply on display but, rather, it would have constantly been in motion as it was passed around or held up to one's mouth.[37] The physical movement that is intimately associated with the cup thus defines the ancient experience of the musical Apollo as he is represented here, where he appears to be continually in the process of actively creating the musical sounds that, in turn, animate the flowers that surround him. The inclusion of Hermes on the reverse, where he too is shown surrounded by the curvilinear dancing flowers, suggests that Apollo's music has fully infused the vase with its sounds (Fig. 3.8). Indeed, the messenger god has turned his head as if to listen to Apollo's music while with one hand he points to the space in front of him. Both gestures implicitly direct the viewer's attention back to Apollo, asking us, or the ancient viewer, to turn the cup around and around in our hands, animating the god's performance in the process.

Discussing a visual composition in terms of its *rhythmoi* can, as the *mastos* example has shown, helpfully isolate those formal elements of the scene that are drawn from the central musician or that repeating forms throughout the image. By determining the material presence of Apollo's music in this way, we can both characterize the kind of music the god creates and see the effect of the musical sounds on his audience. Let us turn to a red-figure storage vessel, by an artist who recalls the Bowdoin-Eye Painter, which depicts Apollo as a masterful *kithara* player, joined by Artemis and Leto (Fig. 3.9).[38] As with our previous example, here too can we discuss the *rhythmoi* that encompass the forms and structure of the composition. Apollo, identified by inscription and by his characteristic appearance, occupies a central position so that the viewer's eye easily falls upon the spectacle of his performance. The close connection the god has with his instrument is illustrated through the repetition of similar lines and shapes between the god's body and his *kithara*. Straight, vertical lines are replicated on the *kithara*'s frame and strings, on the fabric hanging from the instrument, and on Apollo's cascading drapery. The curvilinear forms that make up the attachment that holds together the arms and body of the instrument are repeated in Apollo's curly hair, in the swirl of drapery wrapped around his body, in the long curve of the *plektron*'s cord, and in the dappled decoration on the *kithara*'s suspended fabric. Unity between the god and his instrument, and by extension with the music he creates, is established through the repetition and layering of formal elements upon each other.

The visual forms, or the *rhythmoi*, that make up the figure of the performing Apollo and those of his audience draws them together in a shared experience of listening to the *kithara*'s music.[39] For instance, Apollo's gaze and the direction to which he points his *plektron* direct the viewer's attention to the right side of the painting, toward his sister Artemis. She holds up her skirt as if walking forward, having just finished turning to face her brother, whose music has physically arranged her body toward the divine melody. Leto has been similarly captivated and affected by Apollo's music, as is suggested through her physical position facing her son. The flower she holds also betrays the influence of the god's music: as she raises it behind Apollo's head, the plant extends back to her, twisting and turning as it approaches her face. In its sinuous form, we may perceive the effect of Apollo's music, in much the same way as on the *mastos*, where there exists a formal relationship between the god's lyre and the shape of the flowers. As a result, the curvilinear lines that predominate in this scene visually establish the figures' connection with Apollo's music. We can thus describe Artemis and Leto's physical reaction to his performance as the music working upon them to transform their *rhythmoi* until they are commensurate with Apollo's own.[40] In other words, Artemis and Leto, who hear Apollo's music, are understood visually as responding to the sounds of the lyre because of the *symmetria* of their *rhythmoi* with those of Apollo and his *kithara*. *Symmetria*, a fundamental concept in art criticism, music theory, and philosophy, may broadly be defined as the commensurability of the *rhythmoi* through which *symmetria* consists and is formed.[41] In other words, *symmetria* is

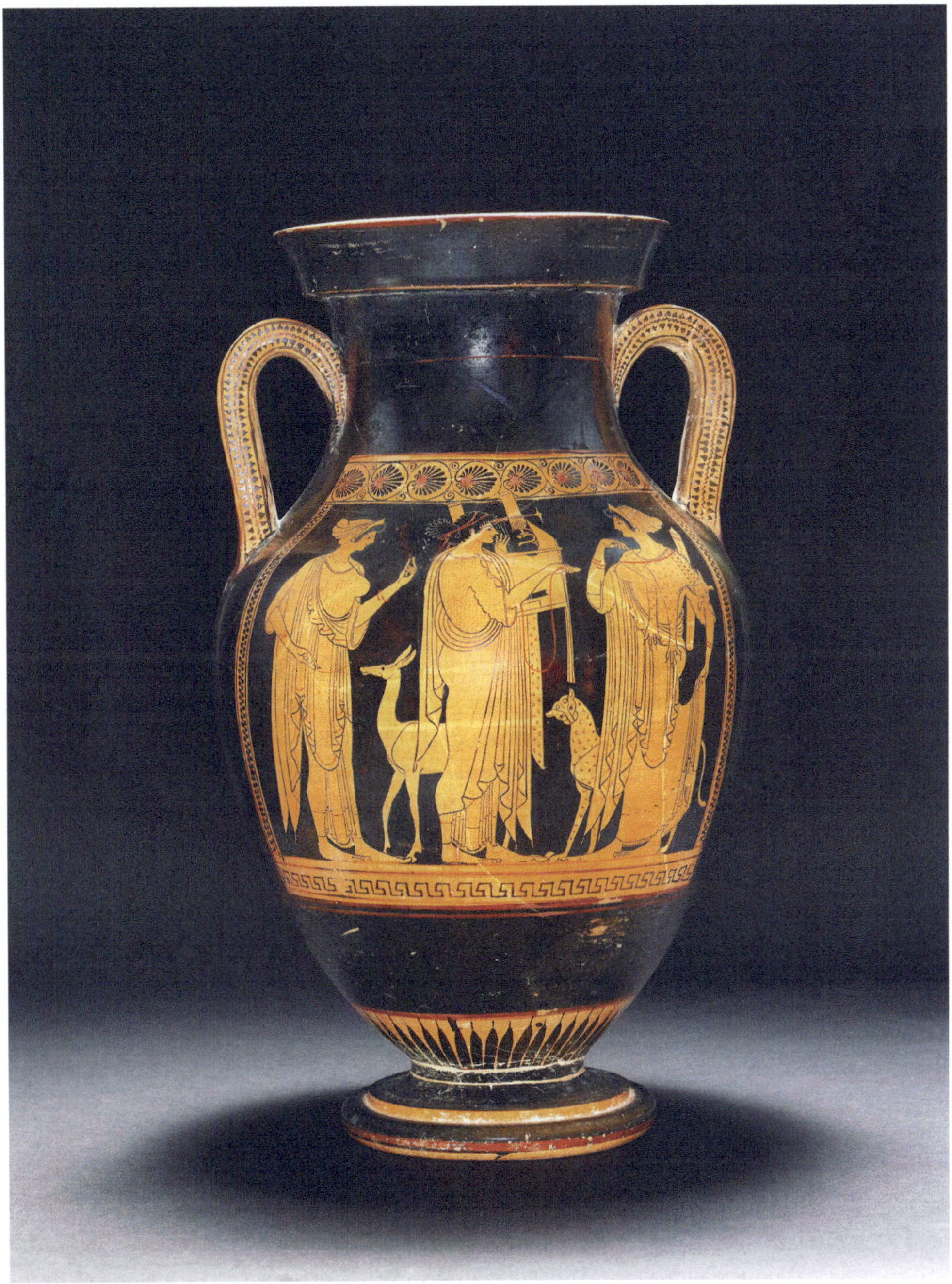

3.9. Recalls the Bowdoin-Eye Painter, *Apollo Kitharoidos, Artemis, and Leto* (side A), Attic red-figure *amphora* type A, ceramic, h. 71.12 cm, *c.* 520–500 BCE. London, British Museum 1843,1103.87 (E256). © The Trustees of the British Museum.

the measured proportionality of one *rhythmos* with respect to another. Moreover, as the *rhythmoi* are repeated across the surface of the vase in such a way that is balanced and appealing to the viewer, the pleasing effect created by their *symmetria* may also be described as their *eurhythmia*. We could thus describe the gods' visually connected bodies, where Artemis and Leto each face Apollo, as a visual expression of the *eurhythmia* inherent to Apollo's music.[42] The creation of art and the fundamental structure of music come together in their shared terminology, for just as Polykleitos laid out the correct, numerical proportions to which a sculpted body should conform, so too does Aristotle tell us that Pythagoras argued that numbers exist in a musical scale that in turn determines the form of all things.[43]

The *symmetria* of the Bowdoin-Eye Painter's composition further ensures the image's visual and musical *harmonia*, which may be characterized as the repetition of *symmetria* in a proportional unity, by which each form is shown to be balanced with the rest of the composition. As such, a visual unity, or a "fitting together," is established among the figures, so that the effect of the visual patterns is a composition unified through the lines and shapes used to create the forms themselves.[44] When Apollo actively plays his instrument, the visual representation of his musical performance thus brings together these three corresponding musical and visual elements, that is, *rhythmos*, *symmetria*, and *harmonia*. These theoretical concepts characterize the image as compositionally balanced and well structured, even as they also describe the quality of the god's music, that it too is melodically balanced and aesthetically pleasing. The image of Apollo's performance thus establishes that in playing his lyre and sharing the sounds of his music, the god cultivates balance and order among his audience and, in much the same way as he does in the *Homeric Hymn to Apollo*, he draws each figure, animal, and plant together into a musically determined *harmonia*. Even the shape of his instrument, with a larger base whose arms rise up in a gentle slanting curve, recalls the shape of the storage vessel upon which the image was painted, bringing the painted scene into a musical and visual harmony with the physical vase that bears the image. Crucially, the image offers this comment on the sounds and effect of Apollo's music in a visual medium, so that the *harmonia* inherent to the texture of his specific musical performance is understandable here through the visual representation of his music-making.

APOLLO, *HARMONIA*, AND THE GODS

Now that we have established a theoretical vocabulary with which to discuss the visual representation of Apollo's music and to determine the visual traces of his music's effect on its audience, we will examine scenes of Apollo playing his music for other divinities. Importantly, Apollo only performs for other gods, so that the corpus of images depicting Apollo Kitharoidos collectively explores how divine bodies respond to a corresponding divine music. We have already seen that Artemis is a frequent audience for Apollo's music, and we likely see her again on a black-figure *amphora* (Fig. 3.10). Here, Apollo stands in the center of

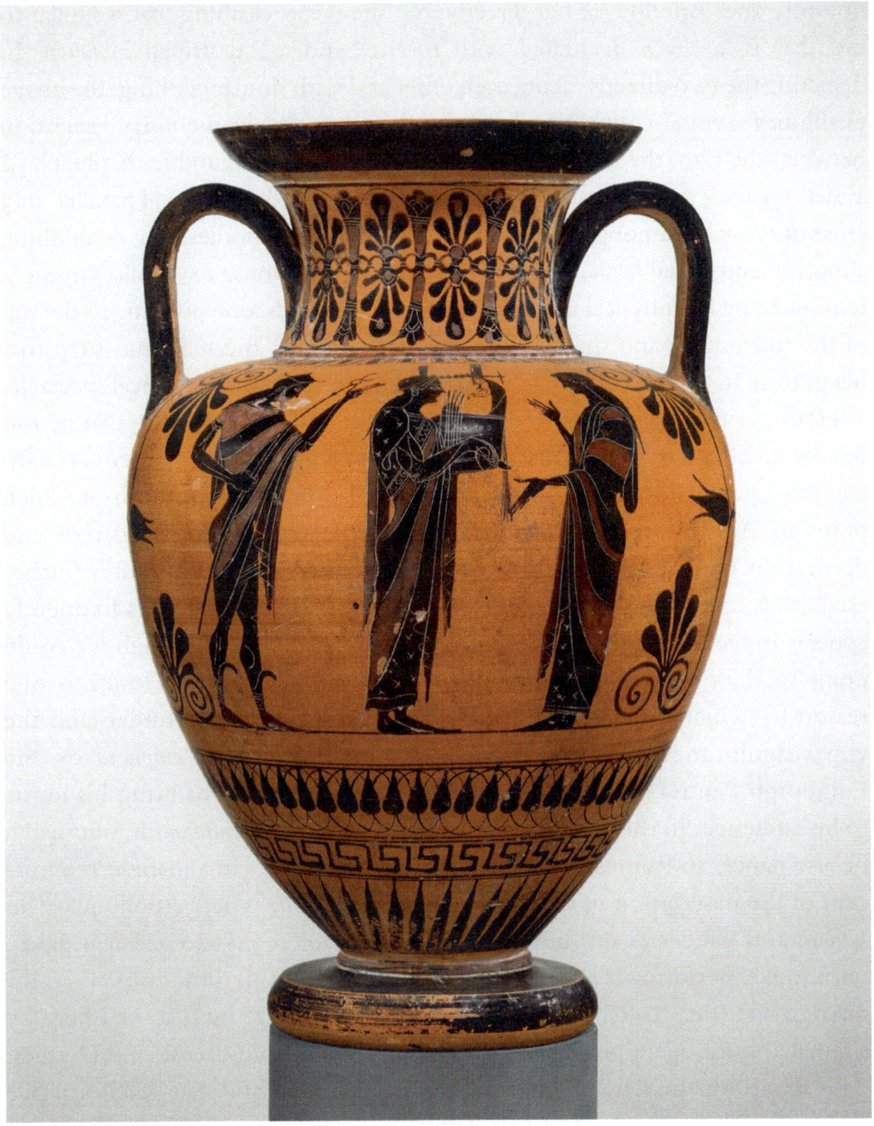

3.10. Attributed to an artist near Exekias, *Apollo Playing the Kithara between Hermes and Goddess* (side A), Attic black-figure neck *amphora*, ceramic, h. 40.3 cm, *c.* 530 BCE. New York, Metropolitan Museum of Art, 98.8.13. Gift of F. W. Rhinelander, 1898. Creative Commons CCO.

the image, unmoving except for his music-making. As with previous images that we have seen, the god is dressed in the robes of a professional *kitharoidos*, pointing to the virtuosity of his performance. Two other figures join him: in addition to Artemis, Hermes is also present. They each face inwards, directing their attention toward the musician.[45] Apollo is depicted with his right arm extended, having just struck the strings of his instrument with the *plektron*. Because of the god's position, he appears to perform primarily for Artemis, for not only does Apollo face her directly, but she wears clothing that is similar to his, that is, a *chitōn* decorated with rosettes and a red-striped *himation*. In depicting the two directly facing each other and with similar clothing, the image establishes a visual connection between them, so that in the visual repetition between the two, the image makes clear that she hears the music that he plays. Visual *rhythmoi* come together to suggest a corresponding musical parallel, or a sense of *symmetria* among the forms that constitute their bodies, thus establishing a musical and visual *harmonia* between them. Her response to Apollo's music is reinforced by her physical reaction: she raises her hands, one pointing to the top of the instrument and the other to the remainder of the red hand-strap that hangs from it, as if to draw the viewer's attention to Apollo's musical spectacle.

Hermes similarly directs his body to face the musician, hinting that he too has been affected by Apollo's music. His *kērykeion*, his messenger staff, extends upwards on a diagonal, parallel to his upraised arm, both of which point to Apollo and the *kithara*.[46] The similar repetition in pattern and decoration between his clothing and that of the other two figures further establishes him as a listening audience member. In fact, Hermes frequently appears in scenes where Apollo plays his instrument, and although we could point to their musical relationship in the *Homeric Hymn to Hermes* as one reason by which to explain his inclusion, it still remains to understand the visual significance of his presence. In one instance, an *amphora* by the Edinburgh Painter, Hermes works together with Apollo to bring his music to his audience. In this scene, Apollo similarly plays the *kithara* but, unusually, he also dances to its music, prancing forward on tiptoes in a manner reminiscent of the description in the *Homeric Hymn to Apollo* where Apollo plays his *kithara* and dances beautifully and high, ἐγκιθαρίζει | καλὰ καὶ ὕψι βιβάς, during his performance, with radiance shining from him, αἴγλη δέ μιν ἀμφιφαείωει (Fig. 3.11).[47] As with the previous image, he is joined here by a female figure, again probably Artemis, who stands to his right, and Hermes, who stands on the left. In front of Artemis grows a vine that reaches above and below the *kithara*, effectively framing the instrument within the composition. Hermes similarly draws attention to the music in the scene: with his left hand, he holds out his *kērykeion*, which reaches upwards, visually echoing the straight lines of the *kithara*'s strings, while his right hand points down to Apollo's dancing feet, as if acknowledging Apollo's physical reaction to the sounds of his own music. The vegetation is repeated on the other side of the vase, where Hermes appears again, though here he is accompanied by Dionysos, who holds the vine that curls down in front of the god and twists to grow back behind him.[48] Both gods actively stride forward as Hermes positions the *kērykeion* almost horizontally, as if directing Dionysos' movement within the image.

(A) (B)

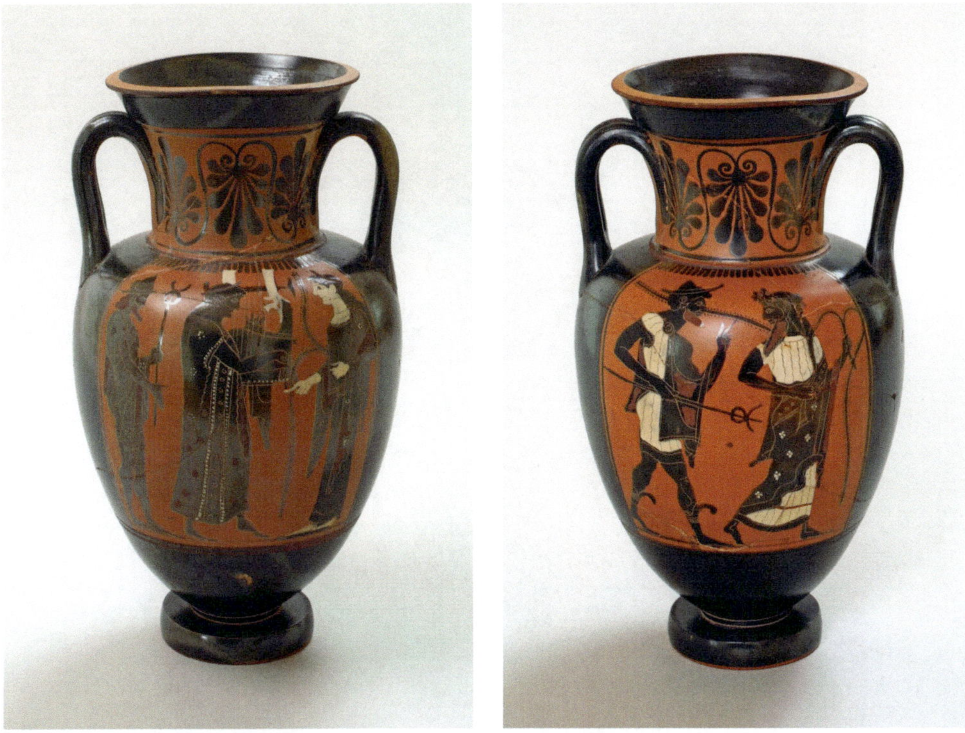

3.11. The Edinburgh Painter, *Apollo with Hermes and Female Figure (probably Artemis)* (side A), *Hermes and Dionysos* (side B), Attic black-figure neck *amphora*, ceramic, h. 28.5 cm, *c.* 515–500 BCE. Schwerin, Staatliches Museum, Inv. KG 726. Bpk Bildagentur/Staatliches Museum/Gabriele Bröcker/Art Resource, NY.

The two sides of the vase are thus visually connected by the vine, which repeats from side to side, suggesting that each scene is a continuous series of events. It is possible that Apollo's music both draws Artemis toward her brother and entices Hermes to appear; as Hermes was the inventor of the *chelys* lyre, the vase explores the close relationship the two male gods continue to share as lovers of lyre music. At the same time, the messenger god also begins to assemble a broader audience, which may account for his interaction with Dionysos on the reverse. Moreover, as if confirming that Dionysos can hear Apollo's music, even as the god moves forward, the vine he holds stretches out behind him, as if reaching out to the divine musician on the other side. Apollo's music thus acts as an instigating force that draws those who hear it toward the god, in order to join them together into a collective and harmonized audience.

Apollo and the sounds of his music are shown to affect his divine audience, gathering them together in their shared experience of listening to beautiful music. The inviting quality of Apollo's music, which has the power to convene the gods, seems to be exclusive to his musical performance. We see the

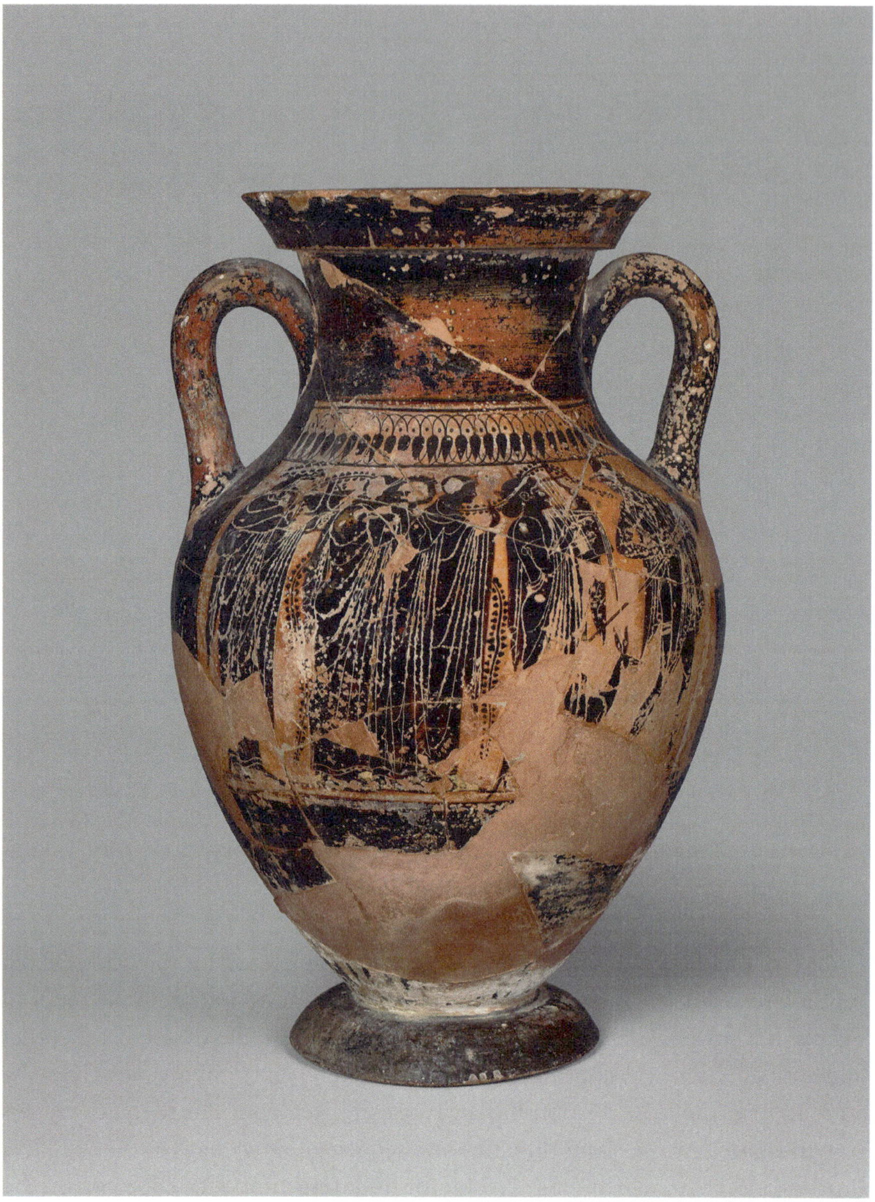

3.12. *Procession of Gods* (side A), Attic black-figure *amphora*, ceramic, h. 44.5 cm, *c.* 525–500 BCE. Paris, Musée du Louvre, F210. © RMN-Grand Palais/Art Resource, NY.

consequences of his ability to instill musical, visual, and even social *harmonia* on a black-figure *amphora*, where Apollo performs before a divine audience (Fig. 3.12).[49] Apollo is again paired closely with Hermes as he plays his *kithara*, so that the visual effect of linking his music with the messenger god suggests that the two work together to instigate the other gods' movements in the procession. Vines grow behind Hermes and Apollo, extending over the heads of all the gods, and cascade down between them. While the plant overlaps with the various divinities, it bends in its course so that it grows over Apollo's *kithara*. The overlapping bodies of plant, god, and instrument suggest that the *kithara* and the music that it produces may have inspired the plant's growth, nourishing it on divine music as it flourishes throughout the scene. Similarly, the visual link the plant establishes among the gods suggests that they too have been assembled through their response to Apollo's music. The repeating patterns across the image, where Apollo's drapery and the fabric hanging from the *kithara* are reminiscent of Dionysos' and the female figures' clothing, connect the entire group. As such, within this scene Apollo's music is shown joining the gods together into a collective whole, one single audience that is drawn together through their shared act of listening to Apollo's melody. We also see a similar response to his music exhibited by the deer who stands behind the musician, echoing other images that we have seen in asserting the profound effect that Apollo's music can have, not only on his fellow gods, but on the animals and plants that surround him. Together, the gods, creatures, and natural landscape exhibit a profound *harmonia*, brought together as the listening audience for Apollo's unmatched musical performance.

APOLLO AND THE BIRTH OF ATHENA

A further elaboration of Apollo's musical effect on the gods may be found in scenes depicting the birth of Athena. On a small subgroup of these images, Apollo stands to one side and actively plays his *kithara* as Athena emerges from Zeus' head.[50] Although the surviving Archaic vase-paintings present a very different account of the goddess' birth than is developed in the surviving literary accounts,[51] the images merit particular attention since the visual effect of Apollo's music has significance for the interpretation of the scenes and the broader Athenian context in which the vases were produced. Each scene is organized similarly: Zeus sits on a throne in the center while Athena either jumps up out of his head or stands on his lap. The central group is always surrounded by a community of gods,[52] the specific members of which seem to have been somewhat interchangeable.[53] Eileithyia, the daughter of Zeus and Hera,[54] is almost always present, whether as a single goddess or depicted in a group of two or three.[55] She typically stands in front of Zeus with her arms raised as she assists him with the birth. The other deities present may variously include Dionysos, Ares, Artemis, Apollo, Hephaistos, Poseidon, and Hermes. While the total number of examples featuring Apollo is quite small,[56] the choice to depict Apollo is significant within each image's composition.

A black-figure *amphora* by Group E displays a scene that is typical of the corpus: Zeus sits in the center and gives birth to Athena from his head, while two Eileithyiai and Ares stand to the right and Apollo Kitharoidos and Dionysos to the left (Fig. 3.13).[57] Despite the stable visual center where Zeus

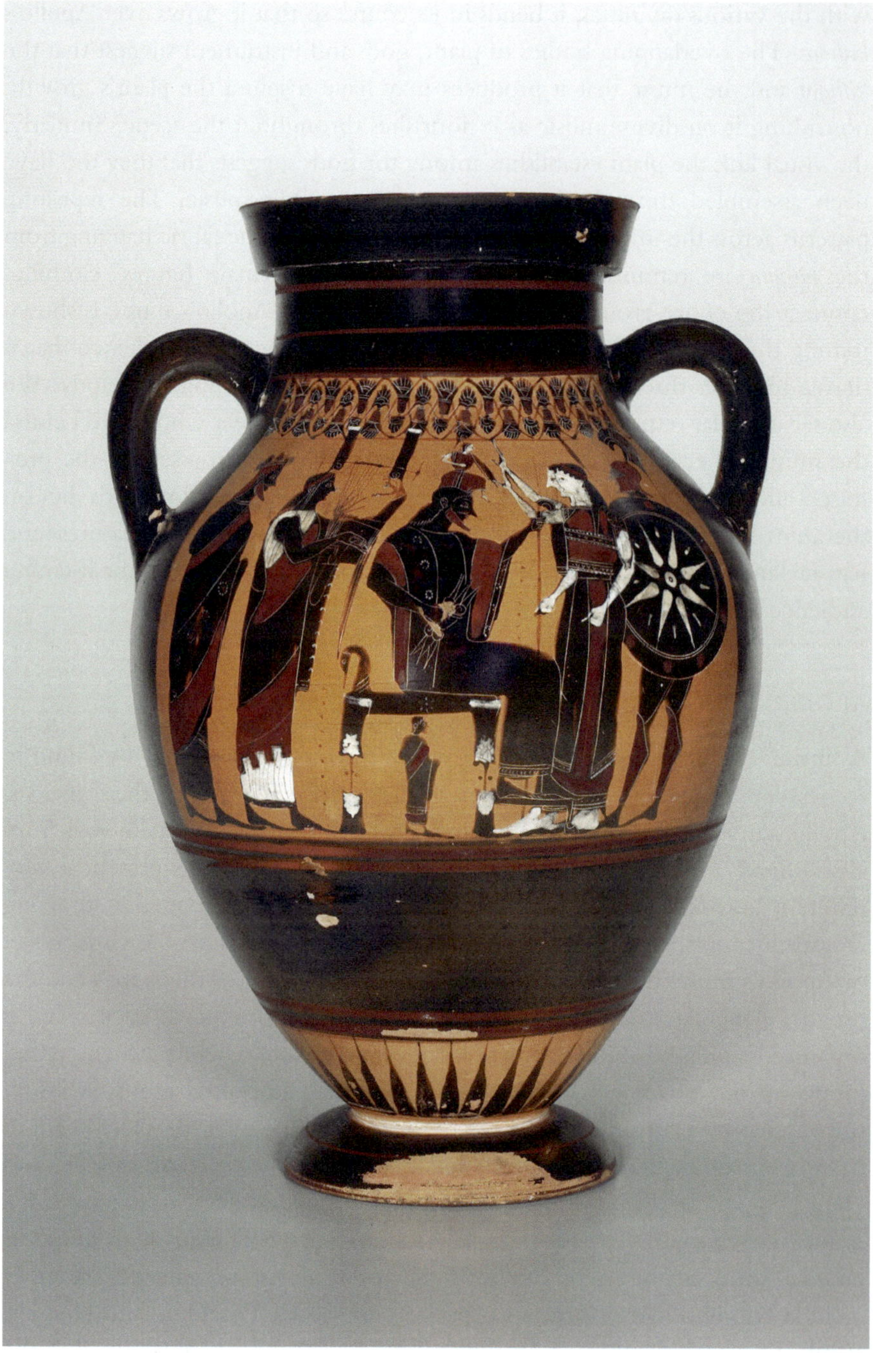

3.13. Attributed to an artist in Group E, *Birth of Athena* (side A), Attic red-figure *amphora*, ceramic, h. 40.9 cm, *c.* 540 BCE. New Haven, Yale University Art Gallery, 1983.22. Creative Commons CCO.

sits on his throne, the rest of the scene is filled with movement: the two Eileithyiai each raise a hand upwards; Ares is fully armed, suggesting that he could fight at any moment; at the center, Athena leaps up out of her father's head; and Apollo plays his *kithara*. The god is depicted in the midst of pulling the *plektron* across his instrument's strings, suggesting a flurry of musical sounds that emerge from the lyre. The decorative cloth that hangs from the *kithara* visually acts as a vertical extension of the god's instrument and melody. Similarly, the arms of the instrument encroach upon the upper decorative border of the scene, drawing the viewer's eye up from the *kithara*. In depicting the musician and his instrument in this way, the image suggests the sprawling nature of the god's music, which here travels outward from the instrument, filling the scene with sound. Zeus thus gives birth to Athena in conjunction with Apollo's performance, so that both goddess and music emerge into the divine world together. Moreover, as the arms of the instrument reach up and break through the frame, immediately beside them emerges the small figure of Athena, who also jumps up through the scene's decorative border.[58] Both music and goddess thus share a common visual characteristic, that they possess an expansive quality that cannot be restrained by the mere limitations of the image. In this way, the image draws attention to two essential elements of the scene – the goddess' birth and Apollo's music – and puts them on display for the audience of gods who have gathered. They, in turn, are joined together in the communal act of witnessing the coordinated musical performance and birth.

The transitional aspect present in many scenes of Athena's birth, where we see the goddess either at the moment of her birth or immediately following, is essential for understanding the significance of Apollo's music within the scene. In these scenes, Athena has not yet fully entered the divine world nor is she still contained with Zeus' body, but instead she occupies a liminal place between the state of being fully divine and having not yet acquired a fully defined form. While her parentage is nowhere in doubt, the images visually present the confirmation of her divine status by her fellow gods. In other words, expanding upon Jenny Strauss Clay's arguments about the *Homeric Hymns*, the newborn Athena requires acceptance by Zeus, who then confirms her divinity.[59] Thus, Zeus takes on increased visual importance within the image as he becomes associated with this task of making clear that the young Athena is fully divine. On our image of Athena's birth by Group E, we may see that Apollo's position as the visual counterpart to Eileithyia, each placed on either side of Zeus and Athena, points to their collective function within the painted narrative.[60] Their similar *rhythmoi* and complementary placement within the scene thus creates visual symmetry between the goddess of childbirth and the god of lyre music. Eileithyia stands facing Zeus, with her left arm by her side and her right raised up to Zeus' head. As the goddess lifts her hand, the image depicts a small Athena rising up, emerging from her father's head at Eileithyia's urging.[61] To the other side of Zeus, Apollo stands facing to the right, and instead of lifting his two arms, he lifts instead the arms, or the πήχεις, of his *kithara*. In this way, framing Athena's birth on either side are two "limbs," which belong either to the goddesses or to the instrument, each of which plays a crucial role in bringing Athena into the divine world and celebrating her birth.[62]

Eileithyia and Apollo are also paired in another representation of Athena's birth, in which they are physically connected through the small body of Athena, suggesting that each deity aids in her birth (Fig. 3.14).[63] Their shared

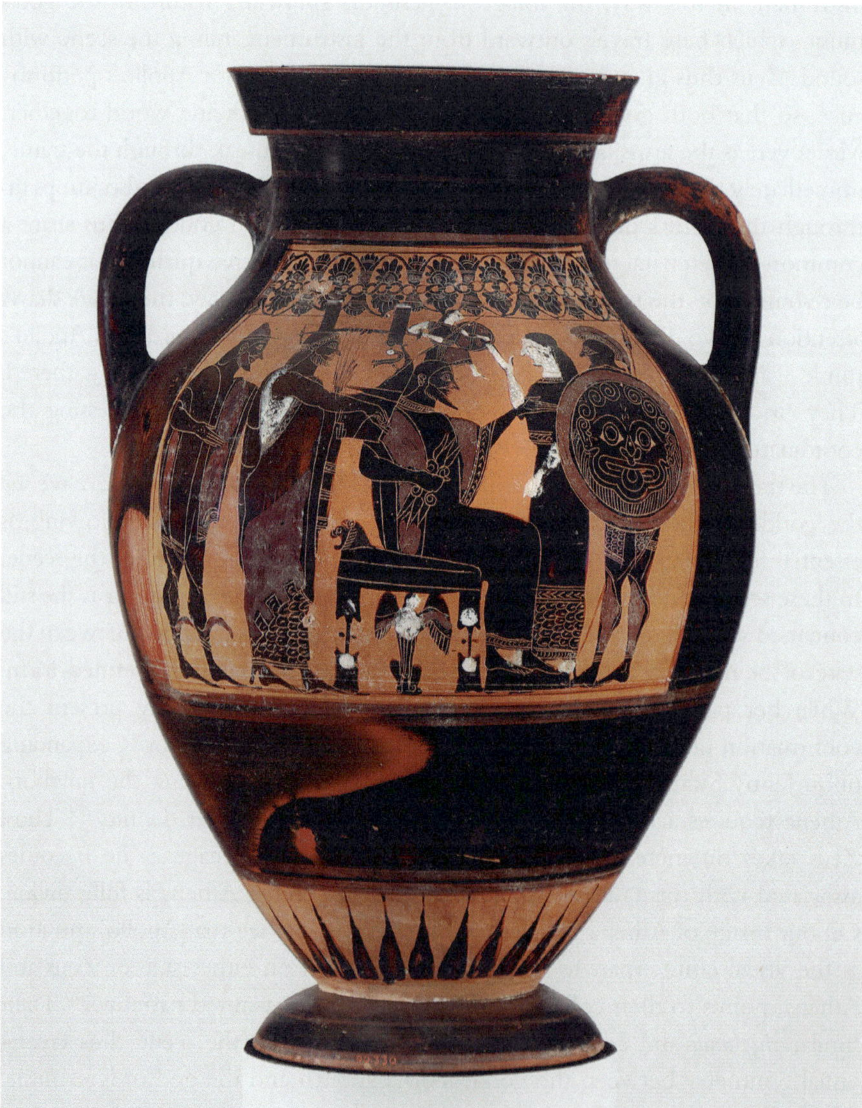

3.14. Group E, *Birth of Athena* (side A), Attic red-figure *amphora*, ceramic, h. 39.4 cm, *c.* 540 BCE. Boston, Museum of Fine Arts, 00.330. Photograph © 2024 Museum of Fine Arts, Boston.

role in bringing forth Athena is strengthened by formal elements that overlap: Eileithyia's upraised arm touches Zeus' hand and the small hand of Athena, while the body of Apollo's *kithara* reaches from Zeus' arm to his head. Moreover, the right arm of the instrument reaches up beside Athena's small form as the crossbar that extends horizontally connects Apollo's head with the young goddess' arm. Once again, Apollo actively plays his *kithara*, so that his *plektron*, which he has fully drawn across the instrument, now points at Zeus' thunderbolt. Visually, this gesture directs Apollo's music toward Zeus, so that as the god gives birth, his effort is accompanied by the melody. Having been born into a world that has been filled with Apollo's music, Athena immediately becomes a member of the divine audience, thereby securing her position as one of the Olympian gods. The visual relationship developed between Athena's birth and Apollo's music thus nuances the importance of the divine music within these images. By depicting Athena being born into a space filled with Apollo's music and being accepted among the other gods who are members of Apollo's audience, the images suggest that exposure to the divine melody, perhaps here in the form of a *paean*, could be another means by which to ascertain the goddess' divinity.

A final example, which is perhaps the closest rendition of Hesiod's literary account, allows us to nuance further the relationship between Apollo's music and Athena's birth, as well as with the broader Panhellenic, Olympian theology that Hesiod's myth advances (Fig. 3.15).[64] The scene is organized very much like the previous examples, with Zeus sitting on his throne in the center, accompanied by a group of gods.[65] Apollo once again stands immediately behind Zeus, his large *kithara* taking up a significant amount of the available visual space. Its arms stretch up and break through the frame, its upward movement mimicking Athena's own as she jumps up out of her father's head. Importantly, the presence of Apollo and his music is not discussed in the surviving literary accounts of the goddess' birth, and yet in this scene, his close proximity to Zeus suggests instead the crucial relationship between divine sound and divine birth. Moreover, Apollo's placement here reinforces his status as the non-threatening son of Zeus, as opposed to Athena, who ostensibly would have challenged Zeus' rule, had she been born a male child. Having Apollo play his music during Athena's birth thus acts as a visual reminder of their theological roles. The image also establishes the effect of Apollo's music: by drawing the gods together in a musical and visual unity, Apollo's music creates a sacred space, inhabited by other gods, into which Athena is immediately welcomed.

The human viewer who looks at this vase also witnesses Athena's birth, so that with each new occasion of seeing the image, Athena is miraculously reborn. With each rebirth, her bond with Zeus is renewed, so that both preside together over the political community of Athens, perhaps represented by the two young men beneath Zeus' throne. Indeed, one potential viewer for

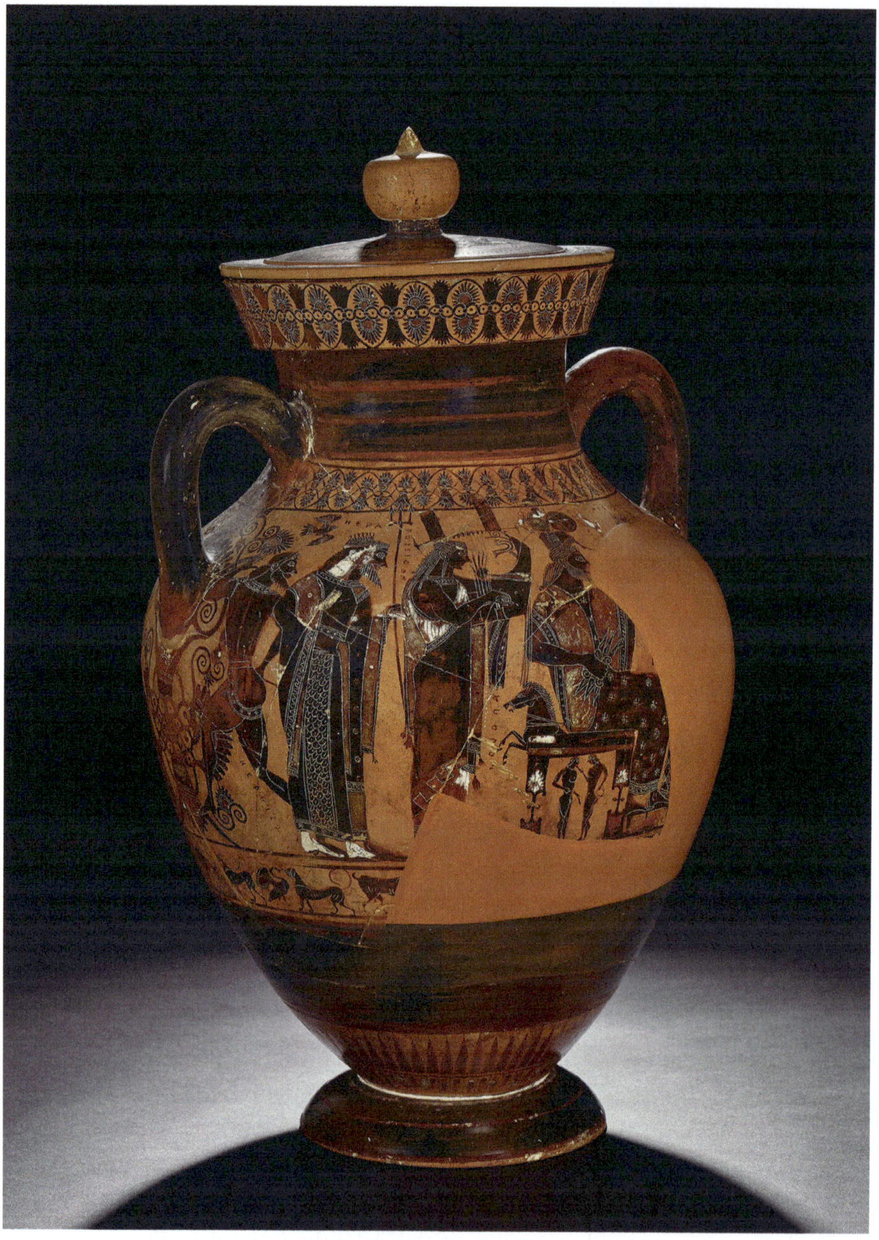

3.15. Group of London B147 (near Group E), *Birth of Athena* (side A), Attic black-figure *amphora*, ceramic, h. 47.6 cm, *c.* 560 BCE. London, British Museum, 1839,1109.1 (B147). © The Trustees of the British Museum.

this vase could well have been the elite male citizens who used this vessel during a symposium. If this was the case, then in repeatedly animating the goddess' birth and the divine music that accompanied it, the citizen men of Athens renewed both Athena's presence in the city and the importance of Apollo's music in establishing a musically infused sacred space. Music and rebirth, as well as the divine security and protection that they could ensure, are thus continually reaffirmed and promulgated by the elite, sympotic men who once visually experienced and imaginatively heard the sights and sounds of the goddess' birth. We find a similar blurring of music, poetry, and political harmony in Solon's surviving poems where, in fragments 4 and 36 in particular, the figure of the poet is presented as a heroic alternative to the martial heroes of epic poetry, wherein his poetic verse and the lyre music offer a separate route to civic unity and a harmonious political community that continually works toward balance and order among its population.[66] By convening to eat and drink, to pour libations together, to sing and play music, and to foster close relationships with each other, the symposiasts who looked at these scenes embodied the *harmonia* that Apollo's music also simultaneously fostered among the gods in the image. Within the intensely musical space of the symposium, human and divine bodies could come together through their shared experience of and bodily response to Apollo's music. As the collective audience for Apollo's music, then, the gods in the images and the men in the symposium together affirm Apollo's musically inspired *harmonia* and the ability of divine music to foster a lasting relationship with Athena as the patron deity for the city of Athens and, by extension, with Zeus.

EXPANSIVE MUSIC

Beyond the political connections established between Zeus, Athena, Apollo, and the Athenian *polis*, Apollo's presence in scenes of the birth of Athena also links the goddess and her city of Athens with the two geographical regions with which Apollo is associated, namely Delos and Delphi. The inclusion of the other gods within the images may also foster similar connections with important sanctuaries throughout Greece, such as Olympia, the major site most associated with Zeus. Thus, the vases that feature representations of Athena's birth visually link her with the network of Hellenic sanctuaries that celebrate the other gods present at her birth and, by extension, link Athens with the larger Hellenic assemblage of *poleis*. The effect of Apollo's music, then, is employed not only to legitimize Athena within the Olympian pantheon, but also to present the Athenians as a harmonious and unified political body that may contend with other Panhellenic *poleis*.

Bringing together the political and social world of Archaic and early Classical Athens with the musico-visual theoretical terms of *rhythmos*, *symmetria*, and *harmonia*, we can further explore the effect of divine music within the image and on the external ancient viewers. If we return to the water vessel by the Berlin Painter (Fig. 3.2), we may see a similar attempt to invoke particular locations: in tracking the god's journey from Delos to Delphi, the image visually associates Apollo with both places, recalling a similar relationship between the god, his music, and these sites as they are presented in the *Homeric Hymn to Apollo*. After recounting the god's birth, the hymn describes, in evocative language, how Apollo begins his journey.[67] Though he does not sit in a flying tripod as on the Berlin Painter's water vessel, he does play his lyre, producing beautiful music:

> εἶσι δὲ φορμίζων Λητοῦς ἐρικυδέος υἱὸς
> φόρμιγγι γλαφυρῇ πρὸς Πυθὼ πετρήεσσαν,
> ἄμβροτα εἵματ᾽ ἔχων τεθυωμένα· τοῖο δὲ φόρμιγξ
> χρυσέου ὑπὸ πλήκτρου καναχὴν ἔχει ἱμερόεσσαν.

> And playing his scooped-out lyre glorious Leto's son
> goes also to rocky Pytho, his divine garments scented,
> while his lyre under the golden *plektron*
> makes a delightful clangor.[68]

Apollo's journey is presented to the hymn's audience as a synesthetic experience, a confluence of sensory perceptions that characterizes divine movement and action.[69] Not only does the god play his lyre, itself evocatively described in language that recalls its creation in the *Homeric Hymn to Hermes*,[70] but his clothes are wonderfully scented, his music sounds delightfully while he moves, and his golden *plektron* sparkles and gleams in the sunlight. His journey is almost secondary to the spectacle of his performance and, in many ways, it is the astounding quality of his performance that ritually establishes the link between the two sites of his worship. That the hymn would itself have been conveyed through song further enhances the spectacle in its layering of human and divine musical sounds. And yet, the hymn also marks the distinction between the mortal singer's performance and the superlative, multisensory performance the god himself offers, for the god's music could only be physically heard by its audience through their experience of listening to the human musician's song. In other words, the ancient audience, going beyond the actual performance of the human musician, imaginatively creates the sounds of Apollo's music for themselves through the sung words the mortal poet supplies. Apollo's music, therefore, is perceived through the audience's multisensory encounter with the spectacle of the musician's performance and the sound of his song.[71]

This image of Apollo thus offers us the opportunity to consider how it may have once been regarded by an ancient viewer. In many ways, the painted image offers a powerful synesthetic experience of Apollo, similar to the multisensory traces suggested by the Homeric hymn. In its depiction of the god, the image invites us to imagine the reflective glint of the metallic tripod in the sun, the sounds and sparkle of wings flapping, the smell of the sea, the sounds of the lyre, the splashes of the sea creatures, the dolphins' skin that glistens in the sun, or even the sounds they create among themselves. Even more, the vessel, itself meant to hold water, could have contributed the sounds of water sloshing within it, adding a further layer of sound onto the powerfully evocative scene. By drawing visual attention to the connection between the dolphins' song and Apollo's music, the image recalls another moment in the *Homeric Hymn to Apollo*, where the god transformed himself into a dolphin in order to jump aboard the Cretan's ship (400). As the companions of Apollo, or even as the embodiment of the god, their presence here offers the possibility that their song is perhaps best understood as divine in some way, complementing the sounds of Apollo's music. The sensory elements the image evokes for its viewers contribute to their aesthetic appreciation of the scene, while, at the same time, it informs their experience of Apollo's divine presence as being materially bound up in the combination of these sensations. In both the Homeric hymn and the vase-painting, then, the viewer's experience of Apollo is rooted in the multisensory perception of the god. Moreover, by depicting the god's journey from Delos to Delphi, the image establishes a visual correlation between the two locations, one the site of his birth and the other the site of his oracular pronouncements. Apollo performing his music can thus act as the defining element of a composition, and can even carry overtones of contemporary political or social concerns. In showing the god actively playing his instrument, the image visually suggests to its viewers the presence of his music, so that the visual medium almost presupposes that the viewer could have recognized, imagined, and thus perceived the sonic features evoked by the image. This innovative mode of representation is not isolated to this singular image, but rather similarly creative and powerful scenes appear throughout the late Archaic and Classical periods, suggesting that this representational strategy was an essential component of Apollo's visual depiction.[72]

The image offers a number of possible interpretations for Apollo's striking representation, each of which draws on the socio-political context of early fifth-century Athens. If we were to focus on the particular instrument the god plays, the *chelys* lyre, we might, following Susanna Sarti and Sheramy Bundrick, suggest that its use here, rather than the *kithara*, points to a growing social emphasis on the importance of *mousikē* and *paideia* among the democratic elite in fifth-century Athens, when young men learned to play the instrument as part of their education.[73] Such musical training was necessary for their participation in the democratic institutions of the *polis*, where dithyrambic competitions required the participation of the men and boys of Attica.[74] In representing Apollo in the manner of an Athenian citizen, playing his *chelys* lyre as opposed to the professional musician's *kithara*, the image implicitly refers to the political unity that was achieved in 508/7 BCE and to the proper social cultivation of a younger generation of citizens.[75] Alternatively, we might instead focus on the implied connection between representations of Apollo Kitharoidos and the political landscape of sixth- and fifth-century Athens. Drawing on work by Alan Shapiro and Timothy Power, we could position the Berlin Painter's depiction of Apollo within a longer tradition of representing the god as a musician: as Shapiro notes, black-figure images of Apollo Kitharoidos increased in number under the Peisistratid tyrants and can be positioned within the context of the purification of Delos in 545–540 BCE and the increase in cult worship for Apollo in Athens.[76] Both Shapiro and Power also attribute the increased popularity of images of Apollo Kitharoidos with Peisistratos' potential introduction of musical contests into the Panathenaia, a move that would have included Apollo in the celebration of Athena, thus ensuring that Athens was another Hellenic "musico-poetic" center of worship for Apollo.[77] The image of Apollo as *kitharoidos* thus invokes a deliberate political symbolism, specific to Athens at this particular moment in its history. Such associations between Apollo and Athenian politics must have become particularly important in the years following the Persian Wars when, in 478 BCE the Delian League was founded; Athens was nominally at the head of this organization, which was based on Delos, Apollo's birthplace. The image may also implicitly point to an Athenian claim over Apollo's musical and oracular powers: since the god has been depicted in the typical clothing of the Athenian citizen youth, he is thus visually connected to the *polis* and its citizens. Within this framework, then, the god's music almost becomes a product that can be controlled and used by those who recognize its power.

One potential audience for this image could have been, again, the male symposiasts who were elite citizens of Athens. As Richard Neer has shown, there were many ideological forces at work within the symposium: in addition to the rituals performed throughout the evening, social and political relationships were constantly being renegotiated, reexamined, and reframed.[78] If we posit that at least some of the symposiasts were highly engaged viewers, then these elite men, both young and old, potentially experienced the vessels on which Apollo plays his *kithara* in a highly immersive way; we might even imagine that some of them physically manipulated the vases, turning the vases this way and that to see the entire scene. These active viewers could thus have had the evocative, synesthetic encounter with the Berlin Painter's vessel that I suggest above, at once seeing Apollo as he travels on a shiny tripod, smelling the salty sea, or hearing his music drift over the waves. These viewers may also have been very much aware of the political implications bound up with images of Apollo, so that through their multisensory encounter with the image of the musical god, they reinforced their role in upholding Athens' social and political efforts to establish itself as a focal point of worship for Apollo. Although Apollo is typically shown playing his music for the other gods who accompany him, there are nevertheless instances where the images display a clear awareness of their human Athenian viewers.

Returning to the Bowdoin-Eye Painter's *amphora* on which Apollo plays his lyre for Artemis and Leto (Fig. 3.9), I end this chapter by focusing on two further details in this scene that elaborate upon the effect that Apollo's music had on his audience. First, the arms of Apollo's *kithara* have been depicted in such a way that they break through the image's upper frame; we have already seen this in other images where Apollo performs, but here, they are the only visual element to do so. In representing Apollo's *kithara* traversing the formal limits of the composition, the image suggests, much as we saw with our tondo image in Chapter 2, that the god's music may similarly follow the lines of his instrument and move past the frame to enter into the space beyond the image.[79] Following the vertical line established by Apollo's lyre and its music takes us to the other side of the vase, where three young men exercise (Fig. 3.16). In the center, a youth prepares to throw his javelin. To the right is a boxer who is identified by inscription as Ladamas. The figure to the left is a discus thrower. He too is identified, so that we know his name is Phaullos; he is further described as *kalos*, a beautiful young man. Visual parallels occur between the scenes painted onto either side of the vase. In each, three figures are depicted, although the gods stand still while the young men move dynamically. The choice on each side as to which figures to identify by inscription also echoes the other: while Apollo, the central figure in his scene, is the only character who is identified, on the vessel's other image it is the two external athletes who receive further identification. In both scenes, the central figure's actions determine the positions of his two companions, who direct their attention back to the center of the scene. The large, swooping curves that constitute the body of Apollo similarly dominate the human sphere, showing off the athletes' rounded muscles as tight curls define their short hair. These coordinated resonances of *rhythmoi* and *symmetria* between the three male youths and the three gods are not a mere coincidence. Rather, I argue, we should discuss them with respect to Apollo's music, which has expanded beyond the divine scene and infuses both images with its sound. The young men, therefore, are not simply engaging in *gymnastikē*, that is, practicing the athletic feats that constituted one aspect of Athenian *paideia*, but, through their rhythmized movements, they display the influence of Apollo and his music in their bodies. The god thus encourages *harmonia* both among the gods who are shown listening to his performance and among the young men, who themselves embody the youthful appearance associated with Apollo and whose *rhythmoi* have been arranged in a balanced proportionality with respect to each other. Visual *harmonia*, in this instance, is established and upheld through the implied musical *harmonia* of Apollo's music, so that image and music work together to impart the presence of Apollo throughout each scene and around the surface of the vase.

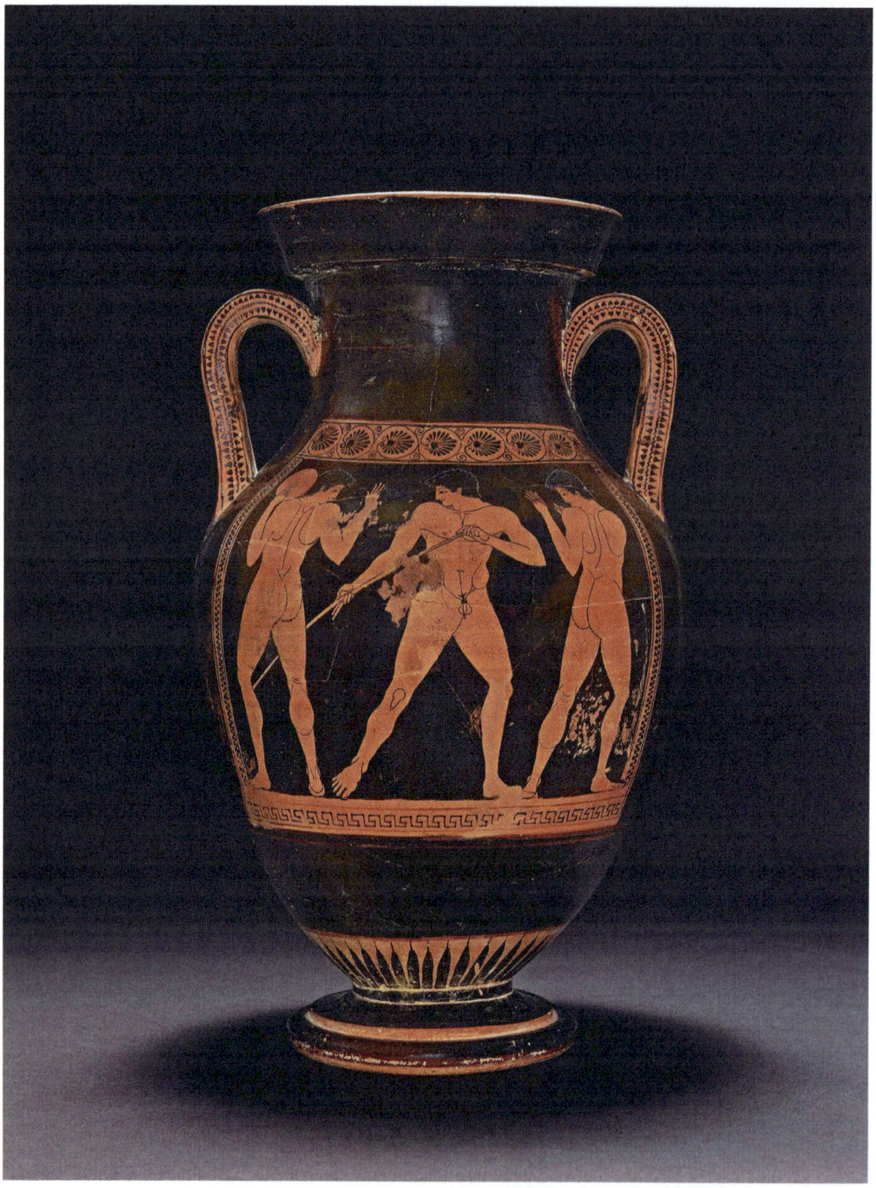

3.16. Recalls the Bowdoin-Eye Painter, *Three Athletes* (side B), Attic red-figure *amphora* type A, ceramic, h. 71.12 cm, *c.* 520–500 BCE. London, British Museum 1843,1103.87 (E256). © The Trustees of the British Museum.

The second detail that merits further attention in our discussion of the relationship between viewer and divine musician is the placement and representation of the animals within this and other scenes of Apollo's music-making (Fig. 3.17). We have already seen how animals regularly respond to the sounds of Apollo's music, whether it is a deer stepping toward the musician, a bird flying to him, or dolphins and sea creatures swimming alongside him. Here, in

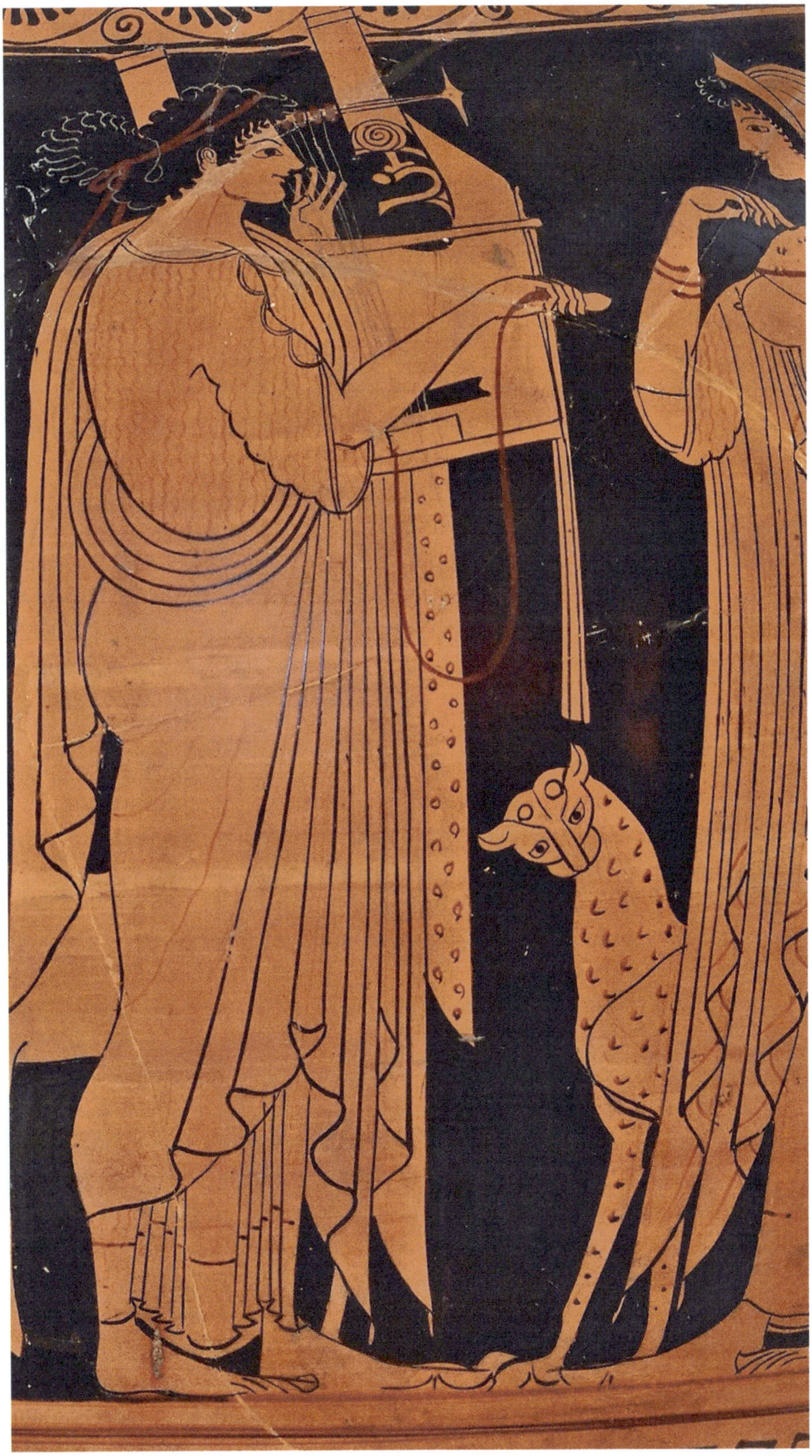

3.17. Detail of the panther. Recalls the Bowdoin-Eye Painter, *Apollo Kitharoidos, Artemis, and Leto* (side A), Attic red-figure *amphora* type A, ceramic, h. 71.12 cm, *c.* 520–500 BCE. London, British Museum 1843,1103.87 (E256). © The Trustees of the British Museum.

addition to the deer who visually connects Apollo with Leto, linking the musician with his audience, a panther also emerges from behind Artemis. It stands below the god's *plektron*, directly in line with the long sash hanging from the *kithara*. Aside from closely associating the two divine siblings within the organization of the composition, the panther's face also engages the external viewer through its frontal position. In breaking through the image's fourth wall, the animal stares directly out of the scene, piercing its surface with its gaze.[80] The animal confronts the external viewer, who, of course, must stare back, so that the two are caught in a moment of mutual acknowledgment.[81] Given the animal's close proximity to Apollo's *kithara*, which is also depicted frontally and which similarly challenges the surface of the painted image, the panther's gaze works together with Apollo's music to draw in the audience. Not only does the god's music drift over to the other side of the vase, where the three mortal athletes display its effects upon their bodies, but it also expands out beyond the frontal boundary of the image, where it may be seen and imaginatively heard by the external, human viewing audience. It is through the direct confrontation between panther, *kithara*, and viewer that the image invites its external audience to move past what is strictly visual, and instead to imagine the sounds of the music that Apollo plays. Immaterial sound, created and heard by the gods in a world that is inaccessible to human listeners, becomes materially present both in the image and for those external viewers who encountered this vessel.

For the mortal viewing audience, the visual and musical harmony that Apollo both embodies and cultivates must also have had an effect, not least since representations of Apollo Kitharoidos were found on numerous vases throughout the second half of the sixth century. For the most part, the scenes of Apollo Kitharoidos that I have discussed were painted onto *amphorai*, the storage vessels that held large quantities of liquid, such as olive oil or wine.[82] Importantly, this particular type of ceramic vessel was not only used in a sympotic context, but could be found throughout the house, sanctuary, tomb, or marketplace – it had no specific place of use, unlike the cups or mixing bowls that were used predominantly in the context of the symposium. The *amphora* is thus a vessel that is inherently flexible, so that it could have been used and seen in any number of locations and, importantly, by any number of people. By moving in this way, Apollo becomes physically present throughout the city, creating a culture of visuality specific to him as a divine musician who could establish musical *harmonia* in the bodies of whoever encountered his image.[83] Moreover, if the vases were seen outside of the symposium, then their viewing audience included not only the elite male symposiasts, but also potentially the general population of Athens. Both men and women alike could thus have encountered the image of Apollo Kitharoidos and have seen – and felt – the harmonizing effect of his music. The artistic choice to paint scenes of Apollo Kitharoidos onto the shape of the *amphora* may, therefore, have been deliberate, both for compositional decisions that required that Apollo and his melody be shown as particularly expansive and all-encompassing, and also for exposing the highest number of Athenians to the god's visual music.

Apollo's music and the effect it had on his audience is thus repeatedly made visible for his viewers, who, when confronted with the image of Apollo playing his lyre, were invited to see how the sounds of the god's music affects and draws together his fellow deities. By focusing our experience of Apollo's music to the visual realm, where we are invited to look closely at scenes of Apollo's performance, we are encouraged to see the sounds of his music as they manifest in the very composition of the image, in the relationship between musician and instrument, and in the positions of the figures. Each image also reaches out to its human audience, whose experience of listening-while-looking collectively activates Apollo's performance and, consequently, continually reaffirms the unifying character that is inherent to Apollo's music. In these scenes, Apollo's presence before his audience is established not just in the visual representations painted onto the side of vases, but rather he is experienced in the viewer's perception of the scene, in that moment of seeing the god's performance, imagining its sounds, and hearing the music. The images thus repeatedly suggest that it is, above all, through the conflation of sensory perceptions, where seeing is a kind of listening and where the viewers are invited to hear the sounds that they see on a physical, material object, that Apollo and the sounds of his music are revealed.

Moreover, the sheer number of images depicting Apollo Kitharoidos in the late Archaic period suggests that, at this time, there was a high value placed not only on musical culture generally, but on the god who, together with the Muses, gave humanity the gift of music. Images of Apollo as a masterful musician are therefore not only a symbol of political ideology at work but, rather, the scenes communicate visually one aspect of the god that was particularly important to the religious, social, and political aspects of Archaic and Classical Athens. Above all, the images point to a desire to be moved by music, to feel the music as a bodily experience, and to be joined together as a unified community in this musical experience. Earlier in the sixth century, Solon advanced much the same opinion of music and poetry in his surviving lyric fragments, where he argued that musical poetry has the ability to draw together disparate social groups and create a unified, harmonious polity.[84] Similarly, there is a rich tradition, going back to Terpander, of the kitharode as the social unifier *par excellence*, as he brings together fractious communities through an almost divine power of lyric music.[85] It is within this tradition that our images of Apollo Kitharoidos should be positioned, so that in looking and imaginatively listening to his music, the diverse citizen body living in Athens could be joined together into social harmony. Apollo, in other words, is the ultimate musician who, through his music, visually draws together gods, men, and the world in which they live.

NOTES

1 Hes. *Theog.* 93–95. This sentiment is repeated in *Hymn. Hom. Mous.* 25, 2–3.

2 *Hymn. Hom. Ap.* 201–03. Translation from West 2003: 86–87.

3 The artist signed the vase with *Sophilos megraphsen. BAPD* 350099; *Paralipomena* 19.16bis; *Beazley Addenda*[2] 10; Pedley 2012: 192–96; Moore 2016: 197–98, with previous bibliography.

4 Not even Dionysos is set apart from the other gods and instead he walks forward with the rest of the gods, holding up a grape vine. Conversely, on the François Vase, Dionysos carries a large *amphora* of wine. For the Muses depicted on the François Vase, see Chapter 4. On the vase more generally, see Shapiro, Iozzo, and Lezzi-Hafter 2013.

5 On the immediacy of the frontal gaze, see especially Frontisi-Ducroux 1995, 19f., 88, 90.

6 For more on the Muses' ability to impart musical inspiration, see Chapter 4.

7 Despite the rendition of Apollo as Kitharoidos painted here, scenes of Apollo as a lyre-player only begin to appear regularly in the second half of the sixth century, when he is consistently depicted in this guise on numerous surviving Athenian vases. On those representations of Apollo created between the *dinos* by Sophilos and the vases from the later sixth century, Apollo is shown more as a secondary figure within depictions of myth. Shapiro 1989: 53.

8 Translation adapted from West 2003. For a review of the problematic dating of the *Homeric Hymn to Apollo*, see Janko (1982: 99–132), who separates the hymn into two distinct sections, the first to Delian Apollo and the second to Pythian Apollo. West has argued that the Pythian hymn ought to be considered the oldest, although this argument is not widely accepted, as discussed by both Janko and Förstel. For more, see West 1975; Förstel 1979: 27 n. 14.

9 As I discuss further below, the most literal meaning of *harmonia* is 'a fitting together,' so derived from ἁρμόζω. It was used in this manner in Homer to describe the joining together of the planks and bolts of a ship. Hom. *Od.* 5.248, 5.361.

10 *BAPD* 201984; Beazley 1930: pls. 25, 26; *ARV*[2] 209.166; Young and Ashmole 1968: 150–54; Simon, Hirmer, and Hirmer 1981; Otto 1984; Paquette 1984: 163, L30; *LIMC* s.v. Apollon, no. 382; Kurtz 1989: 73–76, pl. 43.1; Buranelli and Sannibale 2003: 86, 116–17; Bundrick 2005: 143, fig. 84; Padgett 2017. The scene is unusual in Greek vase-painting, although not unique. As Beazley points out, the Berlin Painter seems to have been working from a preexisting model, given the similarity with an earlier black-figure neck *amphora* by the Ready Painter, currently in the Louvre (Cp 10619; *BAPD* 306550; *ABV* 685.8; Kurtz 1989: 73–74).

11 Hom. *Il.* 24.602–17. For a full account of the myth, see Gantz 1993: 536–40.

12 *Hymn. Hom. Ap.* 131, 186–206; *Hymn. Hom. Merc.* 496–502. Apollo was frequently depicted with his lyre on Attic vases. A search on the Beazley Archive revealed that of the 1758 surviving Athenian vases that feature Apollo, the god appears with a bow in 106 images, while he is shown with a *chelys* lyre in 363 and with a *kithara* in a further 725.

13 *BAPD* 301824; *ABV* 335.1; *Paralipomena* 148; *Beazley Addenda*[2] 91; Boardman 1974: fig. 226; Boardman 1975: 21, pls. 34.2–5, 35.1–2; Holmberg 1992: 13, fig. 1.

14 On spectator figures in Greek art, see, generally, Stansbury-O'Donnell 2006, with a working definition of spectator provided at 13, "For general purposes, we may define a spectator as a figure who observes the action of the nucleus but is not involved in it, or will not immediately be affected by it physically." I deviate somewhat from his definition, since,

I suggest, spectators of musical performances are regularly shown to be physically affected by the sounds they hear and often display these effects in their bodies. As such, they are necessarily involved in the actions depicted, though they themselves are not playing the instruments. On female spectators in particular, see 187–229 in the same volume.

15 The palm tree may refer to the tree on Delos upon which Leto leaned while giving birth to Apollo (*Hymn. Hom. Ap.* 117–19). For more on the inclusion of trees in vase-painting, see generally Dietrich 2010, and for further discussion on the role of objects or images acting as metaphors or indexes of sacred space, see Ferrari 2006.

16 Shear 1937: 179–80; Shear 1938: 342–44; Camp 1980: 9, fig. 14; Kahil 1984: no. 1210.

17 Shear (1937: 180) suggests that the letters are gibberish, although there may also be the possibility that this is an early attempt at indicating a basic musical notation, as Bélis (1984) argues with respect to an *epinetron* in Eleusis. Pöhlmann and West (2001: 8) suggest instead that this vessel depicts "an unsophisticated attempt to express the characteristic sound of the instrument." Yatromanolakis (2016) discusses other instances of painted inscriptions within the framework of a soundscape. For more on Greek musical notation, including its first appearance in the literary record, see West 1992: 254–76.

18 For more on gibberish, or nonsense, inscriptions generally, see Pappas 2012; Mayor, Colarusso, and Saunders 2014; Heesen 2016; Chiarini 2018.

19 For more on inscriptions and the sounds they evoke, see Porter 2010: 436–44; Yatromanolakis 2016.

20 Comstock and Vermeule 1971: no. 15; Vermeule and Comstock 1988: 118; Shakeshaft 2022, with previous bibliography.

21 The inscription reads: ΜΑΝΤΙΚΛΟΣΜΑΝΕΘΕΚΕϜΕΚΑΒΟΛΟΙΑΡΓΥΡΟΤΟΧΣΟΙΤΑΣΔΕΚΑ ΤΑΣΤΥΔΕΦΟΙΒΕΔΙΔΟΙΧΑΡΙϜΕΤΤΑΝΑΜΜΟΙ (Mantiklos donated me as a tithe to the far-shooter, the bearer of the silver bow. You Phoibos give something pleasing in return).

22 Day 2000.

23 Pollitt 1974.

24 Pollitt 1974: 14–23.

25 *BAPD* 352297; Walters, Forsdyke, and Smith 1893: no. B681; *Paralipomena* 309; *Beazley Addenda*[2] 144; Siebert 1990: 198B.

26 Unusually, a piece of decorated fabric, another feature of the *kitharoidos*' performance attire, hangs from the instrument, thereby elevating the smaller *chelys* lyre to the status of the more difficult and complicated *kithara*. For further discussion of the distinction between the *kithara* and *chelys* lyre, see Maas and Snyder 1989: 58–59; West 1992: 34–35.

27 For more on the role of the left hand while playing the lyre, including relevant bibliography, see Chapter 2.

28 Throughout the Pistias Class' surviving mastoid cups, there is a visual connection established between the figural scene – which is more often than not a musical one – and the decorative foliage that frames it. Shapes are regularly repeated between figures, objects, and plants, and the placement of the ornamental plants around the cup's body often suggests a connection between scene and decoration. The corpus as a whole also seems to play with visual representations of music and sound, as is clear with one particularly evocative example where a symposiast sits on a stool and plays his *chelys* lyre, while a stream of letters emerges from his mouth to suggest the sounds of his song. See Porter (2013: 22–25) for further analysis of this image, as well as *BAPD* 5153.

29 The term first appears among the lyric and elegiac poets of the seventh and sixth centuries. The earliest attested usage is in a fragment of Archilochus (frg. 67), in which he implores his heart to recognize the changeable nature of life (οἷος ῥυσμὸς ἀνθρώπους ἔχει). It acquired a sense of patterning already by the beginning of the fifth century, when Aeschylus (*Cho.* 783 ff.) describes the regular beat of a horse's strides as *rhythmos*. Pollitt 1974: 220–28.

30 Pl. *Leg.* 665a.

31 Much of the uncertainty can be traced to two competing etymologies for ῥυθμός: the first derives it from ῥέω, to flow, which suggests the idea of repetition and flow; the second sees it connected to ἐρύω, to draw or to protect. Pollitt 1974: 220–28.

32 Pollitt 1974: 220–21; Barker 1984: 225 n. 131, 229 n. 153.

33 On decorative plants on vase-painting, see Kéi 2015: 271–80; Kéi 2018; and generally on floral ornamentation, Kéi 2021.

34 This cup is of a mastoid shape, rather than a *mastos* proper since it lacks the pointed base and nipple. Coccagna 2014: 399–401.

35 Coccagna 2014: 408.

36 On the importance of touch and, by extension, hands, in fostering a crucial point of contact and engagement between viewer and object, see the discussion of embodied objects in Gaifman and Platt 2018, and especially 404–06; Gaifman 2018b: 446–51.

37 Coccagna 2014.

38 *BAPD* 201543; Walters 1927: III.IC.4, pl. 168, no. 3.2A–B; *ARV*[2] 168; *Paralipomena* 337; *Beazley Addenda*[2] 183.

39 On female spectators in particular, see Stansbury-O'Donnell 2006: 187–229; importantly, as I note above, I understand spectators to be involved in the image's main event through their experience of looking and listening to the music, and responding to it in turn. Following Stansbury-O'Donnell, however, with this and other scenes where the spectators are shown responding to the music, we may understand the inclusion of these figures as at once indicating the presence of music within the scene and as mediating the viewer's own response. On this topic, see also Grethlein 2016.

40 As Kowalzig (2013: 190) notes with respect to Plato's discussion of *rhythmos* and *choreia* in *Laws*, "*rhythmos* bears in itself a transformative element, an element of change, and of potential innovation."

41 Pollitt translates the word *symmetria* as 'commensurability,' and subsequent scholars have followed suit. On *symmetria*, see especially Pollitt 1974: 14–15; Gaifman 2017: 392.

42 I follow Pollitt's definition (1974: 177–80) of *eurhythmia* as "the quality of being well shaped, well formed," since he bases his argument on Xenophon's account (*Mem.* 3.10.10–12), which is the earliest surviving literary source that uses this term.

43 Arist. *Metaph.* 1090a23; Pollitt 1974: 14–18.

44 The most literal meaning of *harmonia* is 'a fitting together,' so derived from ἁρμόζω. It was used in this manner by Homer (*Od.* 5.248, 5.361) to describe the joining together of the planks and bolts of a ship. The term's meaning was later extended to refer to an aesthetically or spiritually pleasing concord of diverse elements. This innovation seems to have first arisen with the musicians, possibly due to the fact that the strings of a lyre had to be fitted together properly before tonal concord could be achieved, which then led to the identification of tonal concord with *harmonia*. Further discussion may be found in Pollitt 1974: 151–54; Mathiesen 1984; Barker 2007: especially 26, 29, 32–38, 45–48, 309–11. For a discussion of Apollo and *harmonia* in Attic vase-paintings, see Bundrick 2005: 140–50.

45 *BAPD* 310427; *ABV* 149; *Paralipomena* 62; *Beazley Addenda*[2] 42; Kossatz-Deissmann 1992: no. 6; Moore and von Bothmer 1976: 18, 19, 20, pl. 21.1–4.

46 He makes an unusual gesture with his upraised left hand, whereby he extends his index and middle finger straight ahead. Moore and von Bothmer 1976: 18, 19, 20, pl. 21.1–4. There is a similar gesture on three vases by the Andokides Painter: Berlin 2159 (*ARV*[2] 3.1; *Paralipomena* 320.1.); Louvre G1 (*ARV*[2] 3.2; 1971: 320.2.); and Boston 01.8037 (*ARV*[2] 4.7; 1971: 320.7).

47 *Hymn. Hom. Ap.* 202. This is an unusual depiction of the god who, in black-figure vases, is more commonly shown standing still while playing the *kithara*. *BAPD* 3273; Haspels 1936: 219.68; Kahil 1984: no. 1096, pl. 531; von Lücken 1972: 13–14, pls. 12.1–2, 13.1–4. I discuss dancing gods in more detail in Chapter 1.

48 For more on Dionysos and the vine, see Chapter 5, as well as Dietrich 2010: 69–79.

49 *BAPD* 10713; Gasparri 1986: 446; Queyrel 1992: no. 133, pl. 405; Pottier n.d.: III.He.15, pl. 25.4–5.

50 For more on representations of Athena in the sixth century, see especially Shapiro 1989.

51 The narrative of Athena's birth is first recounted in Hesiod's *Theogony* (886–900, 924–26, 929m–n), However, Hesiod provides little by way of surrounding details, so that his account does not elucidate the compositions of the Archaic vase-paintings. Subsequent surviving literary accounts fill in more detail, but are often conflicting in their treatment of the episode. Pindar (*Ol.* 7.35–38) writes that it was Hephaistos who helped Zeus give birth to Athena by cracking open Zeus' skull with his axe; from this cleft in his skull sprang Athena, screaming out a battle cry. Apollodoros (1.20) recounts a story similar to Pindar's, except he suggests that it was instead Prometheus who helped Zeus give birth. Importantly, in the three main literary accounts, there is little to no indication of who else was present at the birth, nor is there a sense of the other gods' reaction to the event. It is only in the Second Sophistic movement in imperial Rome where one finds reference to either of these details, where in Philostratus' *Imagines* (2.27) for example, the gods rejoice after Athena's birth. In the images, there is little visual indication for their setting, although Stansbury-O'Donnell (1999: 96–99) has convincingly pointed out that the presence of many gods establishes the context as one that is generally divine.

52 The strength of the relationship between Zeus and Athena is particularly developed in Solon's fourth poem. ἡμετέρη δὲ πόλις κατὰ μὲν Διὸς οὔποτ᾽ ὀλεῖται | αἶσαν καὶ μακάρων θεῶν φρένας ἀθανάτων· | τοίη γὰρ μεγάθυμος ἐπίσκοπος ὀβριμοπάτρη | Παλλὰς Ἀθηναίη χεῖρας ὕπερθεν ἔχει· "Our city will never be destroyed by a dispensation | from Zeus or the plans of the blessed immortal gods, | for truly a great-hearted guardian daughter of a mighty father | Pallas Athena holds her hands over it." Solon 4.1–4. Translation from Mittica 2015: 50, which was adapted from Lewis 2006: 148.

53 It also seems to have been a personal creative choice, as the selection of gods seems to be consistent within an artist's or group's oeuvre. So, for instance, many of the images in which Apollo Kitharoidos appears have been attributed to the workshop of Group E. Beazley 1986: 58; Stansbury-O'Donnell 1999: 96–99. For more on the representation of myth, and the distinction between pictorial narratives and descriptive scenes, see Giuliani 2013: especially 19–88.

54 According to Hes. *Theog.* 921–923.

55 In Homer (e.g. *Il.* 11.269.71), Eileithyia is referred to both in the singular and in the plural, much like the author does for the Muses (on this, see Chapter 4). Hes. *Theog.*, 921 and Pind. *Nem.* 7.1–5, by contrast, refer to her only as a single goddess. When she is depicted as two or three female figures, their bodies are layered one upon the other, as if indicating their nature as a singular plural. On the plurality of Eileithyia and of female pluralities generally, see Matheson 1984: 10–11; Nancy 1996: 1; Nancy 2000; Porter 2013.

56 Of the approximately seventy vases that make up the corpus, Apollo appears in fourteen examples. Eleven of the fourteen are the product of Beazley's Group E, a collection of painters active in the same workshop. As Beazley writes, these artists have been characterized as "a large and compact group which is very closely related to the work of Exekias, though earlier than the vases assigned to him." Beazley 1931–32: 3. On Group E generally, see Beazley 1931–32: 3–8; *ABV* 133–38; *Paralipomena* 54–57; *Beazley Addenda*^{2} 35–37.

57 *BAPD* 310306; *ABV* 135.46; Vermeule and von Bothmer 1959: 34041; Brommer 1961: 68, 75, no. 3; Matheson 1984: 811, fig. 45; 1988: 1213; Stansbury-O'Donnell 1999: 97, fig. 41; Matheson 2001: 63, fig. 51; Neils and Oakley 2003: 116, 207, no. 5; Neils and Oakley 2004: 13; Matheson 2016: 1, pls. 64–66.

58 Importantly, Ares' helmet and spear also break through the upper frame, indicating a connection between his martial abilities and Athena's.

59 Clay 2006: 10–16.

60 The connection between Eileithyia and Apollo may also be found in the *Homeric Hymn to Apollo* (127–32), where she helped Leto give birth. There are obvious similarities to the narrative of Athena's birth: both Apollo and Athena are children of Zeus; Leto and Zeus each had their own difficulties in giving birth and required some sort of external aid; and each child sprang up soon after his or her birth with a clear identity and set of attributes, Athena with her armor and Apollo with his bow and *kithara*.

61 Theirs is not exclusively a gesture of mere acclaim, as argued by Stansbury-O'Donnell, but they are shown here in their role as deities of childbirth, and as such are tasked with helping Zeus with this unusual birth. For further discussion, see Stansbury-O'Donnell 1999: 96–99; Matheson 2016: no. 1, pls. 64–66.

62 The word πῆχυς is used to describe the arms of the *chelys* lyre in *Hymn. Hom. Merc.* 50, but also it may also refer to human arms, such as at Hom. *Il.* 5.314, Hom. *Od.* 17.38, 23.240.

63 *BAPD* 310305; *ABV* 135.45; *Paralipomena* 55; *Beazley Addenda*[2] 36; Hoffman, von Bothmer, and Truitt 1973: 3–4, fig. 7, pl. 5.1–3; Maas and Snyder 1989: 47.

64 *BAPD* 310304; *ABV* 135.44; *Paralipomena* 55; *Beazley Addenda*[2] 36; Walters 1927: iii h.e. 3, pl. 24.1a–g; Kossatz-Deissmann 1988: no. 289; Siebert 1990: no. 682; Krauskopf 1994: no. 173; Felten 2009: no. 62; Schefold 1992: fig. 6; Marx 1993: 240, 242.

65 Underneath Zeus' chair, adorned with the bust of a horse that acts as a back rest, and legs decorated with white palmettes, stand two smaller men, who may represent the human race over which Zeus rules. Both are nude, and one holds a wreath in one hand while he reaches up to touch his companion's chin with the other. They may thus be indicative of the human practice of *gymnastikē*, which is juxtaposed here with Athena, who is completely dressed in her battle armor, with a shield, helmet, and spear. The purpose or function of the figures that occupy the space beneath Zeus' throne remains unclear in the broader context of black-figure vase-painting, since men, sphinxes, lions, or winged women may be shown here, with little variation in the rest of the scene.

66 Anhalt 1993: 114, 135–43.

67 The two locations are linked in the *Homeric Hymn to Apollo*, which, as has been well observed, is composed of two distinct hymns: one to the Delian Apollo, and a second to Pythian Apollo. Beazley suggested that the journey here is Apollo's initial one from Delos to Delphi. Kurtz and Beazley 1983: 73–74; Bundrick 2005: 140; Padgett 2017: 311.

68 *Hymn. Hom. Ap.* 182–185. Translation adapted from West 2003: 84–85.

69 On synesthesia in antiquity, see Porter 2010: 430–35; Butler and Purves 2013.

70 *Hymn. Hom. Merc.* 39–64.

71 That epiphanies could be multisensory, rather than merely visual, is explored more fully in Platt 2011; Petridou 2015.

72 Representations of Apollo playing music by himself not only occur in the late Archaic Period but proliferate into the Classical Period, appearing into the fourth century BCE. See, for instance, a cup that depicts Apollo playing the *chelys* lyre on the back of a griffin by the Painter of Vienna 202 (*BAPD* 231126, Vienna, Kunsthistorisches Museum, 202).

73 Sarti (1992) analyzes images of Apollo to determine the frequency with which he plays the *kithara* or the *chelys* lyre, arguing that the god plays the *kithara* in the Archaic period while, in the fifth century, he instead plays or holds the *chelys* lyre.

74 For more on the dithyramb, as well as its relationship with musical education, see Kowalzig and Wilson 2013a; Hagel and Lynch 2015; Laferrière 2023.

75 Bundrick 2005: 142–50.

76 The purification consisted of moving or removing the graves that were in sight of the temple to Apollo (Hdt. 1.64.2; Thuc. 3.104.1). In Athens, cult activity centered on the Pythion, dedicated by Peisistratos himself just south of the Olympieion (Hesychius s.v. ἐν Πυθίῳ χέσαι), the shrine of Apollo Delphinos (Paus. 1.19.1), the cave sanctuary of Apollo under the Acropolis, where Apollo and Kreousa conceived Ion, and the temple to Apollo Patroos in the agora. Shapiro 1989: 1–16, and especially 48–59; Power 2010: 440.

77 I borrow the phrase "musico-poetic" from Power 2010. As Shapiro (1989: 50–52) and Power (2010: 425–31) note, the Peisistratid involvement on Delos and investment in Apollo had two consequences: one, it strengthened the relationship between Athens and Ionia, since the Athenians were believed to be the ancestor of the Ionians; and two, it reinforced the importance of Apollo for Athenian religion through the repetition between the festival's musical contests for Apollo on Delos and the same contests for the Panathenaia in Athens. Power stipulates that Athens might even have been an important cultic alternative to Delphi. At this point in time, the Alkmaeonids were extremely influential at Delphi and the Peisistratids, as Power claims, contested Delphi's supremacy as the city most dear to Apollo on the Greek mainland, perhaps intending to make Athens into a rival site of oracular wisdom. Moreover, the Peisistratids seem to have deliberately avoided Delphi, and there is no record of the Peisistratids consulting its oracle. In this way, the Peisistratids may have undermined an important political connection that empowered the Alkmaeonids in Athens.

78 For more, see generally Neer 2002.

79 In conceptualizing how the god's music might move beyond the image, I draw from previous discussions on the role of the frame, such as Hurwit 1977: 1–30; Derrida 1987: 52–68; Platt and Squire 2017a; Marconi 2017; Gaifman 2017.

80 In discussing frontal faces, I draw especially upon Korshak 1987; Frontisi-Ducroux 1995; Mackay 2001; Mack 2002; Hedreen 2007; Hedreen 2017.

81 On the importance of the viewer's gaze for interpretations of Greek vase-paintings, see Grethlein 2016, and especially 85 nn. 3 and 4 for earlier scholarship on this topic in art-historical research more broadly. Generally, I follow Meyer Schapiro's argument (1973: 38ff.) that these frontal faces actively look at their viewers.

82 Lynch 2011: 147–66.

83 For an extended discussion of cultures of visuality, see Davis 2017, which expands upon Davis 2010.

84 See Solon's poems 4 and 36. Anhalt 1993: 1–9, 139. That Solon should be considered as a poet just as much as a politician is perhaps clear from Plato's *Timaeus* (21b), where Critias describes contests in which young boys recited the poems of well-known poets. Included among these is Solon, and he is described as a particularly popular option for the competitors to choose.

85 For further discussion, see Chapter 3 in Power 2010.

FOUR

DIVINE MUSIC IN CONTEXT

In addition to the immersive experience of divine music that was encouraged by fourth-century votive reliefs dedicated to Pan and the Nymphs, Archaic and Classical scenes of Apollo playing his lyre present a compelling argument for the ability of vase-paintings to make visible the sounds of the god's music. In these scenes of musical performance, I argued that the god's music coordinates his body and actions with those of his companions. Even more, the visual sounds of divine music could be synchronized with the ancient viewer's use of the vase upon which the image was painted; for perceptive and engaged viewers, upon looking at the visual representation of divine music, they too could have seen the musical sounds, imaginatively heard them, and responded with their own bodies, so that they might fall into harmony with the god and with their fellow audience members. We have also seen important differences between Apollo's music, with its inherent harmonizing capabilities, and Pan's music, which inspires Nymphs to dance and, in so doing, could provoke especially powerful multisensory ritual experiences for ancient worshippers. The Muses, as frequent companions of Apollo, also encourage a distinct kind of experience in their audience, one that is rooted in the particular kind of music that they played and that was associated with superlative skill in music and poetry.[1] After all, the proem of the *Theogony* establishes them as the source of the poem's inspiration: "From the Heliconian Muses let us begin to sing," Μουσάων Ἑλικωνιάδων ἀρχώμεθ' ἀείδειν, positioning the Muses first in the original Greek line.[2]

Moreover, as the only female divinities who are regularly shown playing music, their gender also inflects the musically determined relationship they develop with their ancient, typically male, audience and even with their fellow gods. For instance, we have already seen the Muses performing together with Apollo on Sophilos' vessel, discussed in Chapter 3 (Fig. 3.1), where they exhibit similar characteristics of *harmonia*.[3] The preliminary sketch found on a mixing bowl by the Clio Painter also visually establishes the Muses' connection with Apollo and, consequently, their shared interest in *harmonia* (Figs. 4.1 and 4.2).[4] Here, the artist divided the visual field into three, parallel rectangular spaces, each corresponding to the bodies of Apollo, Klio, and Terpsichore, who are identified through inscription.[5] While the line separating the two Muses was eventually painted over, the image retains the original symmetry

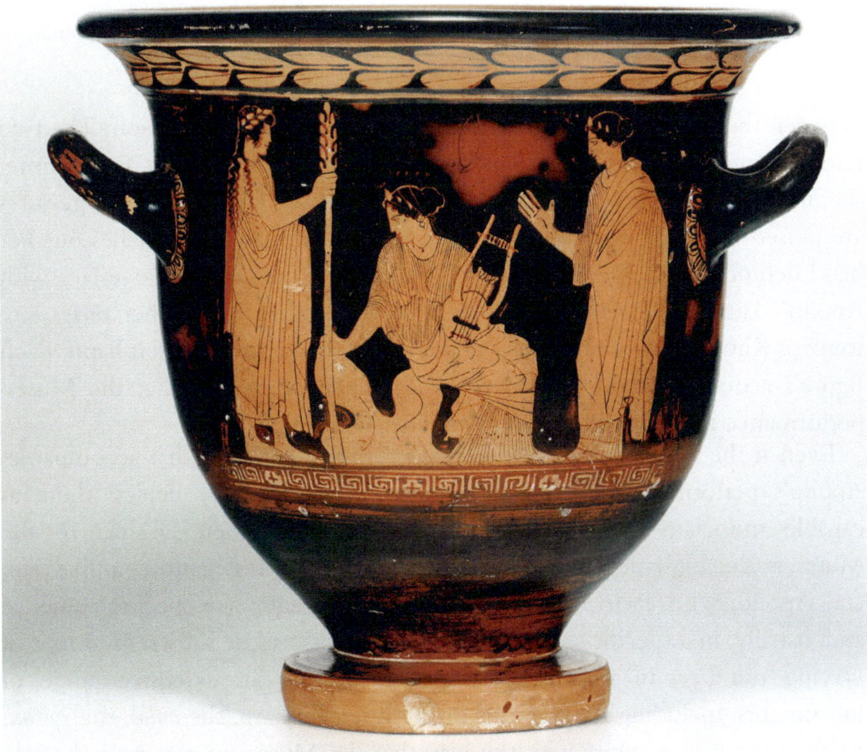

4.1. The Clio Painter, *Apollo with Terpsichore and Clio* (side A), Attic red-figure bell *kratēr*, ceramic, h. 31.2 cm, *c.* 450–415 BCE. Berlin, Antikensammlung, F2401. bpk Bildagentur/Antikensammlung/Johannes Laurentius/Art Resource, NY.

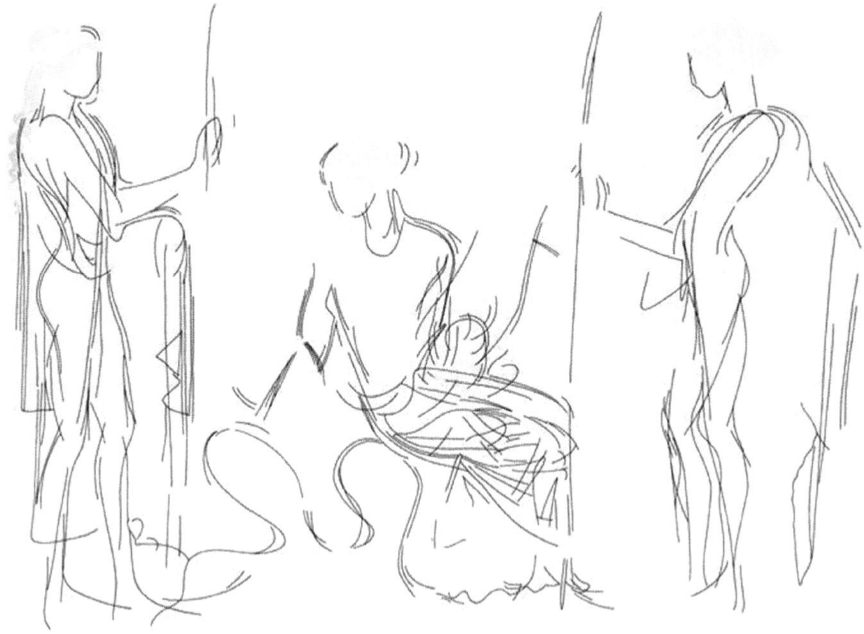

4.2. Underdrawing of the Attic red-figure bell *kratēr*. Drawing by Jörg Denkinger, Berlin.

between the figures, in order to maintain the balanced composition. The two standing forms of Apollo and Klio frame and enclose the seated Terpsichore; she, in turn, faces Klio, but turns her head to Apollo. Her actions and gestures are poised in equilibrium with each other. On one side, she reaches out her hand behind her, supporting her weight on a rock as her hand overlaps with Apollo's laurel staff. In front of her, she angles the arms of her *chelys* lyre towards Klio while she plucks the instrument's strings with her left hand. Each figure's actions thus mimic and respond to the other's, so that the Muses' performance is shown to be as harmonious as Apollo's.

Even if the Muses are occasionally shown as the chorus that accompanies Apollo's performance, the visual material also repeatedly depicts them as capable musicians who play their instruments together. Distinct to the Muses is the high degree of variability in their representation: unlike Pan and Apollo, who each play one type of instrument for a specific audience and, usually, in a specific space, the Muses may instead be shown in groups of varying number, in various settings, and playing an extensive range of instruments, including many forms of the lyre, the harp, the *aulos*, the *syrinx*, or even the *krotala*. Moreover, the way that the Muses are represented rarely makes their identity obvious unless identifying inscriptions are included. On the mixing bowl with which this chapter began, it is only clear who is Terpsichore or Klio based on the name written beside each figure; the inclusion of Apollo gives us a clue that they may be Muses, but offers little more to identify each goddess. This is yet another point of difference between the Muses and their male divine musician counterparts: Pan and Apollo are generally always identifiable, whether through their distinct form, such as Pan's hybrid appearance, or Apollo's *kitharoidos* costume and specific hairstyle. The Muses, however, defy clear identification: in those scenes where no inscriptions have been included, it is not clear whether the figures are even goddesses, or if they are simply human, female musicians. The lack of an established iconography for the goddesses throughout the Archaic and Classical periods thus lends a flexibility to images of female musicians, so that they may invoke a range of identities, be it a divine Muse, a citizen woman, or even a *hetaira*, the female entertainer hired for the symposium. It is this changeability inherent to the representation of the Muses, as well as their mysterious ability to impart creative inspiration to the men and women who encountered them, which made images of the goddesses and their musical performances so powerful for the ancient viewer.

Scenes of their musical performances are also depicted on an array of vases that were used in correspondingly diverse contexts – small cosmetic boxes in the home, drinking cups in the symposium, or even oil containers in the grave. Indeed, the contexts in which vases bearing representations of the Muses were used range widely, more so than for any other divine musician. Since the shape of each vessel's body suggests that it could have been used in specific contexts, we can also consider how ancient viewers engaged with the painted images in these spaces. Complicating this relationship between vase, image, and context is the inherent movability of vases: as we began to see already with images of Apollo, a single vase could have been seen, picked up, carried, and used in different places. Importantly, as the vase is handled, the representation of the Muse painted onto its sides becomes increasingly animated as she too moves between spaces, thus offering her viewers a particular experience of her musical performance that is tied to the space in which she appears to them. As I will show, much of the Muses' inspirational force in these scenes comes from the context in which they are encountered, so that the ancient experience of the Muses and the sounds of their music is intimately connected to the place in which their presence was felt. We need only recall Hesiod's account of his own encounter with the Muses, which he clearly positions on Mount Helicon, the home of the Muses.[6] Another poet, Archilochos, encountered the Muses on a country road, and because of the setting of this encounter, he believed they were human women returning from their work.[7] The location in which one experiences these goddesses is thus of paramount importance to our discussion, since it fundamentally determines how the Muses' music and inspiration is perceived. We might then consider the body of the Muse as one that is constantly adapting to her surroundings, even as she continues to play her music throughout all of these potential spaces. The Muse demands that her viewers experience her presence in such a way that is tied to the environment, so that any inspiration that they bestow is linked with that space; unlike the limited spaces in which images of the other musical gods might have once been seen, the broad range of contexts in which the Muse could have been encountered expands the range of possible effects that her music might have. It is precisely this relationship between the Muses' representation and the context in which the vase is used that sets them apart from the other musical gods.

Representations of the Muses thus offer an enticing opportunity to explore the importance of the ancient viewer's context for determining the character of his or her experience of divine music. Throughout this chapter, I show that when representations of the Muses are considered within their original contexts, the vases transform our understanding of the ancient experience of the Muses' divine music by making a powerful statement about the goddesses: since the Muses were divinities who were deliberately flexible in their appearance, their bodies could become visual forms capable of taking on multiple identities. By potentially encountering the Muses anywhere in daily life and, in so doing, being prompted to imaginatively hear their music, ancient viewers could gain access to the spark of creativity associated with the Muses.

SEEING THE MUSES

The difficult issue of the Muses' murky visual representation has largely determined the analysis of their depiction in the Archaic and Classical periods, so much so that attempts at identifying the Muses, establishing their individual iconographies, and relating their images to their respective spheres of influence have become a predominant approach for their study.[8] Such an undertaking, however, is only possible after the Classical period when, during the Hellenistic period, the Muses' iconography and areas of influence were more clearly established, in part by drawing on Hesiod's description in the *Theogony*. There, the poet describes the Muses as nine sisters, born from Zeus and Mnemosyne, or Memory; he goes on to list the Muses' names as Klio, Euterpe, Thaleia, Melpomene, Terpsichore, Erato, Polymnia, Ourania, and Kalliope.[9] In the surviving visual material from the Archaic and Classical periods, however, the Muses are notoriously difficult to identify: if they are not shown with Apollo or on Mount Helicon, they are only recognizable through identificatory inscriptions, since they lack any distinctive iconographic attributes in the Archaic and Classical periods.[10] Moreover, the very presence of such verbal markers itself indicates a problem of identification, as if the artists were trying to control the range of possible interpretations to which the images could be subjected.

An important exception to this general trend occurs on the François Vase, where, in the wedding procession of Peleus and Thetis, nine Muses are each

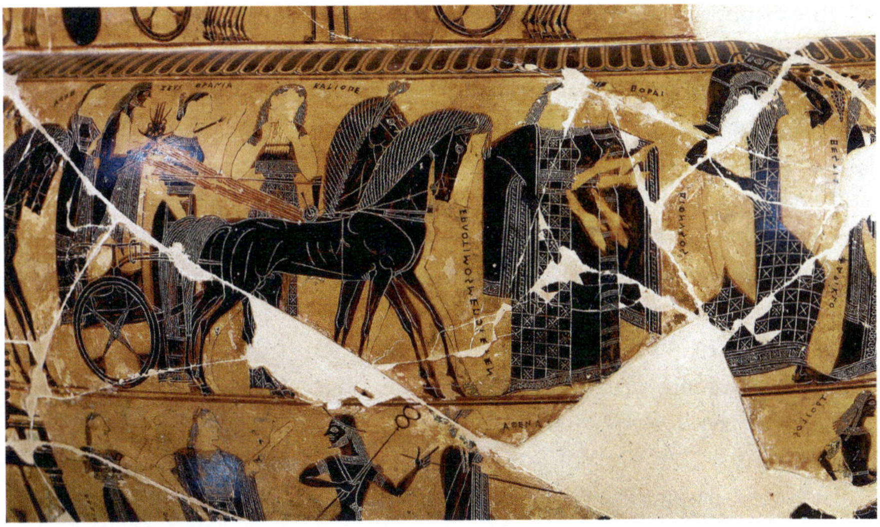

4.3. Detail of Kalliope. Signed by Kleitias (painter) and Ergotimas (potter), the so-called François Vase, *Wedding of Peleus and Thetis*, Attic black-figure volute *kratēr*, ceramic, h. 66 cm, *c.* 570–560 BCE. Florence, Museo Archeologico Etrusco, 4209. © Alinari Archives/Serge Domingie/Art Resource, NY.

identified by their Hesiodic names.[11] Superimposed behind the first chariot are two Muses: Kalliope, who faces the external viewer while she plays a *syrinx*, and Ourania, who raises her hand to draw the viewer's attention to Kalliope's musical performance (Fig. 4.3).[12] The other Muses, each of whom is labeled with her name, are divided into groups of three or four, working together as a divine musical chorus.[13] Within the scene, it is particularly Kalliope who captivates the viewer's attention. Of all the figures on the François Vase, only she and Dionysos are shown with a frontal gaze, so that they each stare directly out at the viewer.[14] Although Dionysos is one of the largest figures in the scene and the vase that he carries is the only object that extends beyond the upper limit of the frame, Kalliope is separated from him only by the Horai and the horses pulling Zeus' chariot. Together, she and Dionysos confront the external viewer, capturing his or her attention through the directness of their gaze. They also point to the defining elements of the scene, whether it is the wine that Dionysos brings that will be consumed during the celebration, or the music that pervades the scene and accompanies the procession and, presumably, the marriage celebration that will soon occur. Moreover, Kalliope's position in front of Zeus underscores her importance within the scene, for not only does she play her *syrinx* in front of the leader of the Olympians, but she also stands ahead of the majority of the gods in the procession.[15] As such, the image suggests that it is through her music and the song of the Muses' chorus more generally that the scene unfolds, so that its mythological narrative is conveyed through the Muses' performance. In much the same way,

Ourania's position directly adjacent to Zeus comments upon the gods' place within the cosmos that her name invokes, as well as the Muses' comprehensive knowledge of all events that have ever taken place in the history of the world. The François Vase thus presents the Muses and their music as foundational for the transmission of myth, as it is their inspiration and music that allows men and women to tell the stories of the gods. In this particular role, the visual representation of the Muses recalls Hesiod's *Theogony*, where the poet credits the Muses for imparting the inspiration for the poem's creation when he sings that "one time, they taught Hesiod a beautiful song . . . come then, let us begin from the Muses."[16] The poem, having been so inspired by the goddesses, thus unfolds, beginning first with a description of the Muses, their birth, their relationship with Zeus, and their role in the musical endeavors of men and women.

However, despite the prominent placement given to the goddesses on the François Vase and in Hesiod's *Theogony*, they are among the few surviving instances from the Archaic and Classical periods where the Hesiodic names are ascribed to the Muses.[17] More common instead in early visual representations and literary descriptions is an emphasis on the collective chorus that constitutes the Muses. The Homeric epics, for instance, refer to the divinities generically as *Mousa*, or "Muses," when the poet entreats them to "Tell me, then, Muse . . .," μοι ἔννεπε Μοῦσα . . .,[18] and when he describes the sounds of their music as "the antiphonal sweet sound of the Muses singing," Μουσάων θ' αἳ ἄειδον ἀμειβόμεναι ὀπὶ καλῇ.[19] Moving between a single Muse and multiple Muses, the Homeric description of the goddesses continues to confuse their identity: is there one Muse who inspires men's poetic language, or are there many Muses who undertake this work? Aside from a few singular exceptions, the number of Muses shown at any one time varies greatly, underscoring the inherently flexible nature of the goddesses.[20] On another early vase painted by Sophilos, which we encountered already in Chapter 3 (Fig. 3.1), eight female musicians are present at the wedding of Peleus and Thetis. They are simply labeled as "Mosai" (Fig. 4.4). The Muses are still shown as a chorus but without the individualization that is so pronounced on the uniquely decorated François Vase.

The multivalent flexibility of the Muses is thus already well established in the earliest surviving evidence. Indeed, if we turn to later Archaic and Classical depictions of the Muses, we may see that there is a similar range of representational strategies used for the goddesses, where they are shown in a variety of numbers, with different names, and without any distinguishing iconography that would identify them. The only point of consistency across their representation is the attention to their collective musical performances, but even here, the Muses regularly appear with very different instruments, playing, in various examples, an *aulos*, a *phorminx*, a *chelys* lyre, a *barbitos*, a harp, a *syrinx*, or

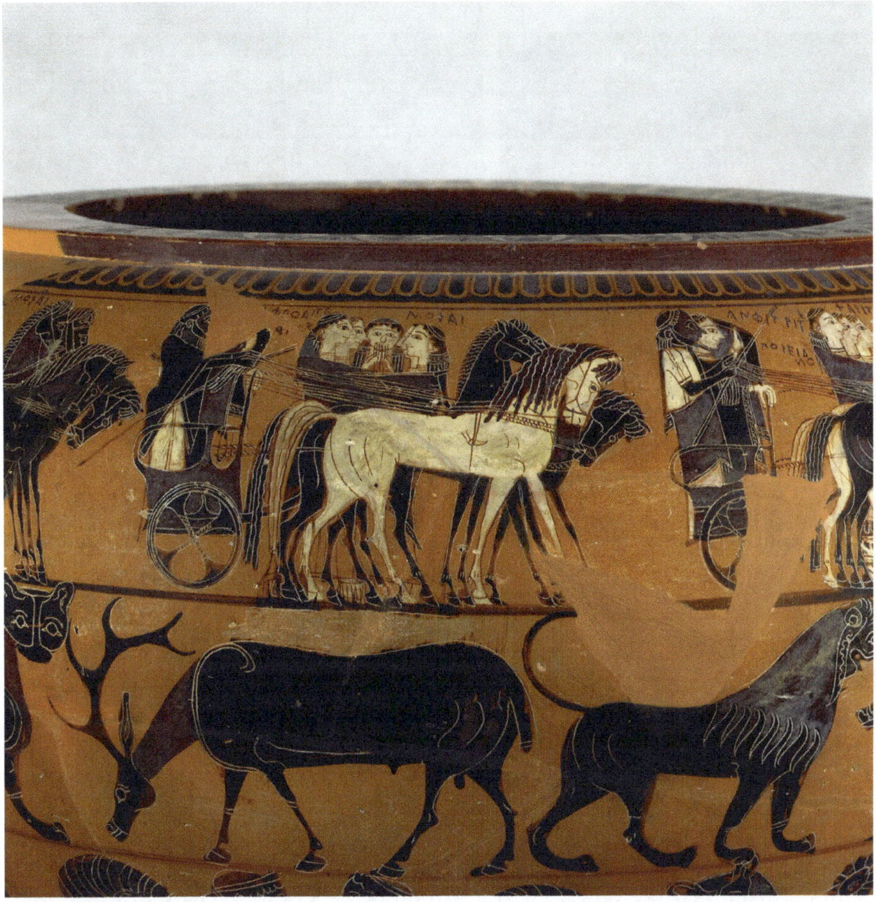

4.4. Detail of the top register. Sophilos, *The Wedding of Peleus and Thetis*, Attic black-figure *dinos*, ceramic, h. 71 cm, *c.* 580–570 BCE. London, British Museum, 1971,1101.1. © The Trustees of the British Museum.

even *krotala*. Such variability can be seen on a small, black-figure oil container that depicts female figures dancing, playing the *chelys* lyre and *krotala*, and singing, as is suggested by the small, black markings that emerge from their mouths and fall to the ground (Fig. 4.5).[21] Performing their music in front of Apollo, who plays his *kithara*, these figures would seem to be the Muses, especially given their association in literature with singing, which was their essential mode of communicating with mortal poets. The inclusion of the figures' *krotala* complicates their identification, however, since *krotala* are more commonly associated with ecstatic maenads in a Dionysian revel, who, as we will see in Chapter 5, play their instruments and dance under the influence of the god of wine. Yet Dionysos is not included in these scenes, nor are there other overt references to a Dionysian context within the image itself. Similarly, the specific type of vessel, a *lēkythos*, upon which the scene was painted, was meant to hold a small amount of oil, typically for funerary contexts, and thus it

(A) (B)

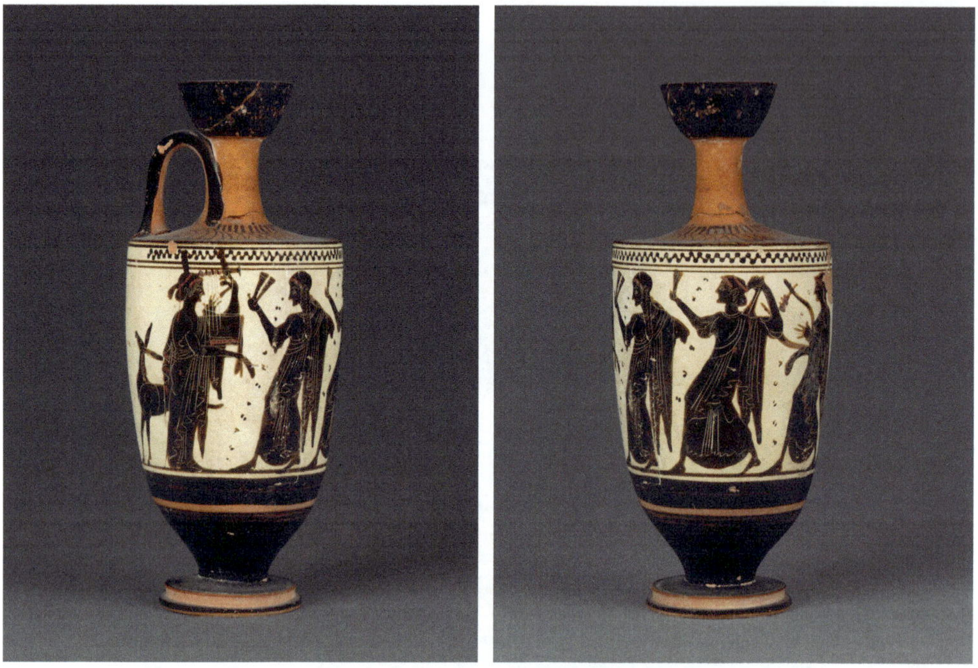

4.5. The Sappho Painter, *Apollo and Female Musicians*, Attic black-figure *lēkythos*, ceramic, h. 17.8 cm, *c.* 500 BCE. Paris, Musée du Louvre, MNB 910. Photo: Hervé Lewandowski. © RMN-Grand Palais/Art Resource, NY.

does not help to clarify the figures' identities here. As a grave good, this vessel could equally feature Muses, as the daughters of Memory, or Dionysos, who journeyed to the Underworld to retrieve his mother Semele. Moreover, even though the female figures play their *krotala* and wear ivy wreaths around their heads in the manner of maenads, they are here shown performing together, moving in similar patterns, almost as a chorus that supports Apollo's music. Their actions are harmonized between them, each figure lifting her arm and clacking the instrument together in unison before Apollo, who adds his own music to their performance. Given the lack of clarity regarding their identity, it remains unclear whether they are Muses or maenads.

The Muses are also often indistinguishable from human women who are shown engaging in music-making: both may be shown seated or standing together as a small group, giving all of their attention to their instruments. One such scene may be found on a water vessel, on which three female figures have gathered, two of whom hold instruments (Fig. 4.6).[22] Each figure is dressed beautifully, with her hair tied back, whether it is with a fabric covering called a *sakkos*, with fillets and a veil, or with a diadem. The central musician holds a *barbitos* and sits on a low chair positioned atop a large, two-tier stage; the top step is elaborately decorated with alternating black and red squares.[23] Her body

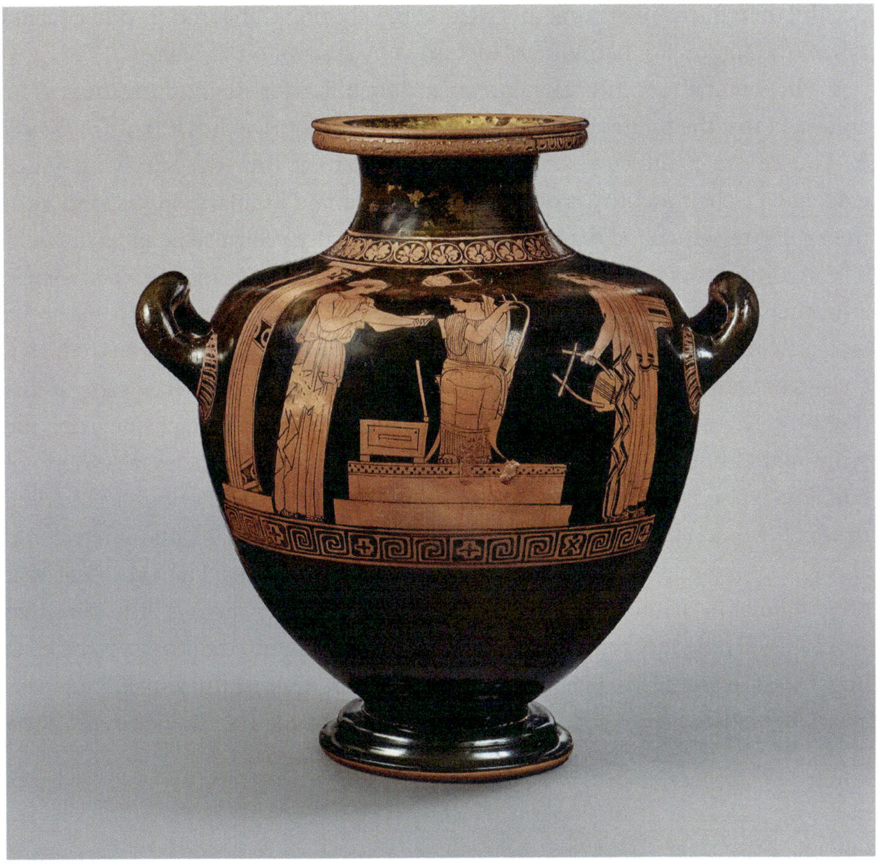

4.6. The Niobid Painter, *Female Musicians*, Attic red-figure *hydria*, ceramic, h. 28.8 cm, *c.* 460–450 BCE. Image courtesy of Sotheby's.

directly faces the frontal plane of the image, while she turns her head to the left side of the image, as if listening to the words spoken by her standing companion. This figure reads from the unfurled scroll that she has removed from the open box that sits next to the seated musician; given the context of the scene, it is possible that the scroll contains the poetic composition or perhaps even the musical notation that the musician will soon perform.[24] The third female figure in the scene stands to the right and carries a similar box in one hand and her *chelys* lyre in the other. Completing the scene is a *chelys* lyre that floats above the central figure's head, and a column that supports an open door.

Who are these three figures who have come together to play their instruments? They could perhaps be Sappho and her companions playing lyric poetry together.[25] Or they might be Athenian women, their clothing and activities marking them off as belonging to an elite social group while the central woman's elevated position establishes her as the leading member of the group.[26] Alternatively, they could be prostitutes in a brothel, where they receive musical instructions from the woman in charge.[27] Finally, the figures could be Muses playing their instruments together as a divine chorus, as they do in other scenes where the figures are definitively identified by inscription as Muses.[28]

Each potential identification presents difficulties for its interpretation. The argument that the figures are *hetairai* is challenging to prove, not least since *hetairai* in Greece are a difficult social group to isolate within the surviving visual evidence.[29] Their identity is only clear within certain sympotic scenes, and even then it can be difficult to determine the difference between a *pornē* and a *hetaira*.[30] The argument that the open door and architectural elements identify this scene as a brothel in some ways elides the important distinction between a *pornē* and a *hetaira*.[31] Since the women wear the clothing of Athenian female citizens, which is consistent with what is known of *hetairai*, their musical activities may suggest that the artist has shown a scene of *hetairai* practicing their craft, away from the symposium. Furthermore, the architectural structure resembles a variety of building-types, such as a domestic house, a temple, or another public building in which women have gathered to play their instruments. Its inclusion here could also simply indicate that the music practice occurs indoors. The argument that these figures are Muses is similarly difficult to prove, for there is little here that would readily identify the figures as divine. This ambiguity is not always the case, however. On a similar scene by the Peleus Painter, three of the female musicians are clearly labeled (Fig. 4.7):[32] Terpsichore stands to the left, Kalliope sits in the

(A)

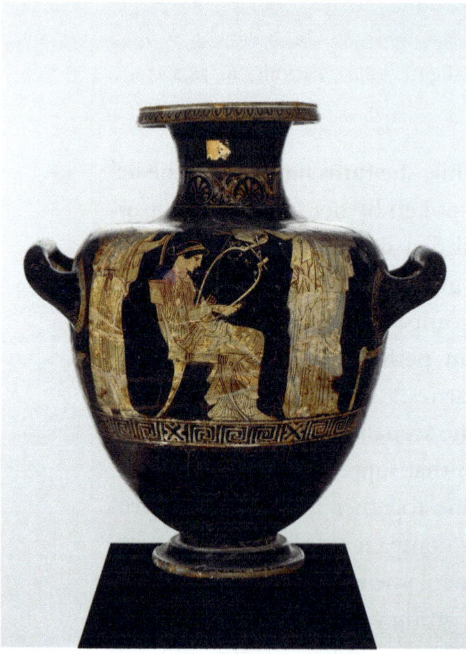

(B)

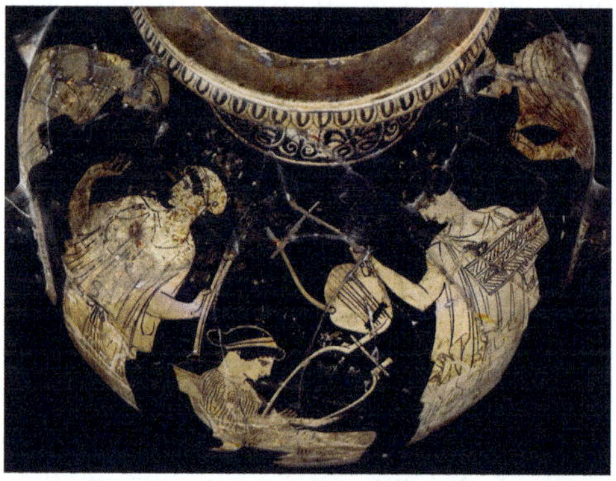

4.7. The Peleus Painter, in the Group of Polygnotos, *Muses with Instruments*, Attic red-figure *hydria*, ceramic, h. 34 cm, *c.* 440–420 BCE. Paris, Musée du Petit Palais, 308. Creative Commons CCO.

center, and Thaleia stands on the right. On the water vessel by the Niobid Painter, conversely, there are no inscriptions included, so that notwithstanding the visual resonances between the two scenes, where female figures have gathered together to play music, the figures' identities on the water vessel by the Niobid Painter necessarily remain unclear. The instruments the women carry do not help to clarify their identity, since they could be used by Athenian women, *hetairai*, Muses, or maenads. The *barbitos* that the central woman holds is often associated with Dionysian contexts, where it could be played by human *hetairai*, by maenads, or by Muses. It is also the instrument of choice for the elegiac and lyric poetry of the Archaic period. The *chelys* lyre held by the standing woman as well as the one that floats above the women's heads may be associated with Athenian *paideia*, in which young Athenian citizens would learn to play the relatively straightforward instrument.[33] The instrument is also used by the Muses on vases that bear inscriptions identifying the divinities, as well as by Apollo himself, who is often shown playing this instrument, especially in red-figure scenes.[34] In its subject matter, the scene is similar to others that definitively depict the Muses, so identified by inscription. Finally, the shape of the vessel offers little by way of clarification on this problem, since a water vessel could be used by both men and women alike and the subject matter that appears on this type of vessel is broad-ranging in scope.[35]

To answer our earlier question – who are these figures? – the image offers little by way of a conclusive response. They are divine Muses and, at the same time, human women, whether *hetairai* or citizen women within the home. The image keeps these identities open for the viewer, so that the music the image offered to its ancient viewers is divine, with the ability to inspire those who looked at it and heard its sound. At the same time, it is also music that is shown being performed by human women and encountered by an ancient audience throughout the home, city, and countryside. The images thus suggest that the Muses and their music are both fleeting and omnipresent, always ready to perform their music to their viewing audience.

ENCOUNTERING DIVINE MUSIC

The Muses are thus difficult to see and, even more, to hear and to experience.[36] Was it possible, then, for the ancient viewer to encounter the Muses through these images, to imaginatively hear their music, and to gain access to the inspiration they potentially offered? Did the location in which such inspired perception occurred matter to how a viewer might have experienced the image of the Muse? In the remainder of this chapter, let us take a mixing bowl by the Phiale Painter (Fig. 4.8) as our main example, in order to explore how the viewer's experience of the female figures depicted on it depends on the context in which the vessel is encountered, whether the

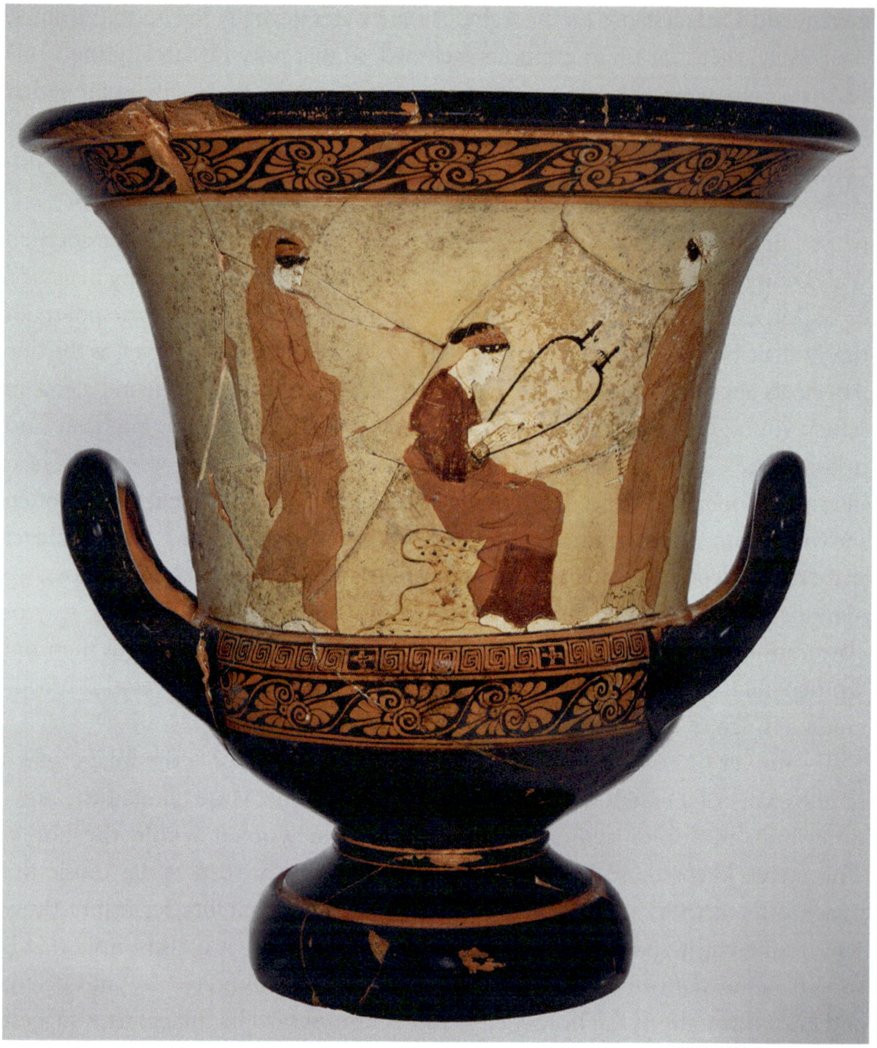

4.8. The Phiale Painter, *Three Muses* (side B), Attic white-ground *calyx kratēr*, ceramic, h. 32.8 cm, *c.* 440–435 BCE. Vatican City, Museo Gregoriano Etrusco Vaticano, 16586. © Governorate of the Vatican City State – Directorate of the Vatican Museums.

domestic space, the cemetery, the sanctuary, or the symposium.[37] For each space, I show the effect that the visual representation of the Muses' instrumental music performance has upon the external, viewing audience, that is, how one's particular perception of the Muses and the sounds of their music is affected by the correspondingly particular space in which this act of imaginative hearing occurs. In selecting the mixing bowl as my example, I do not claim that this particular vessel was used in each of these spaces, but, as a product of an Athenian craftsman, made within the context of an

Athenian visual culture, its painted imagery, its shape, and its corresponding intended function suggest that these contexts are all possible spaces in which it could have been seen and used. Above all, it offers us a helpful model with which to consider how closely intertwined the representations of the Muses are with the vase upon which they are painted, and, by extension, how this material relationship determines the goddesses' ability to engage with their ancient audience.

The scene on one side of the mixing bowl is composed around three female figures, two of whom stand on either side of a central figure, who sits on a gnarled rock. The lyre she holds, a *barbitos*, stands out dramatically against the background, its black body contrasting with the creamy white space behind it. We might imagine that the three figures depicted in this scene are surrounded by the ephemeral, musical sounds of the lyre, which are being actively created by the seated figure. She is not the only musician in this scene: her companion holds in her hand a *chelys* lyre, its shorter arms designed for and tuned to a higher register than the *barbitos* played by the central figure. Although she stands still with her lyre by her side, she seems almost ready to lift her instrument and blend its sounds with the musical performance already underway. A third figure stands to the left, wrapped in her drapery as she looks at her companions.

There is little by way of identifying markers that would clearly establish these figures as divine Muses. Although the bleak, rural setting filled with undulating rocks in which the musicians are depicted is often a feature of the Muses' representation,[38] without the inclusion of written inscriptions that identify the figures, it is difficult to identify conclusively the figures as divine Muses. It is precisely this ambiguity, or this flexibility, that the image offers to its viewers: the female figures here are not simply divine, nor are they simply human. Instead, the vase offers both identities to its viewers. Such multivalency will prove to have very different consequences for how the female figures interact with their viewing audiences in the various contexts in which this and other vessels were encountered.

MUSIC IN THE DOMESTIC SPHERE

The first context in which we might consider the image of the Muses is the domestic sphere, that is, the *oikos* and its surroundings.[39] At a formal level, the high quality and sophistication of the painted scene suggests that the vase is an expensive, luxury object that may even have been specifically commissioned by a wealthy family in Athens. Further hinting at the immense amount of labor the vase itself must have required is the symmetry of the vase's body and its carefully articulated foot, rim, and handles. Given the care that went into its manufacture and the expense that the purchase of this vessel probably involved, it could well have been intended to function as a display piece.[40] The image painted on the reverse further suggests its possible function as an object meant for display (Fig. 4.9). There, a mythological scene depicts a moment possibly inspired by Sophokles' satyr play, the *Dionysiskos*, where the messenger god Hermes delivers the infant god Dionysos to Silenus, the elderly satyr; the representation of this scene is unique among the surviving vase-paintings from Archaic and Classical Athens.[41] Hermes, who stands just left of center, holds his *kērykeion* while he hands the infant Dionysos, swaddled in brown cloth, to Silenos. Though the old satyr and the young god do not make eye contact, Hermes' *kērykeion* visually draws a link between the two as it bridges the negative space between them. Flanking the scene are two female figures, possibly the Nymphs on Mount Nysa who are said to have raised Dionysos, or maenads, the god's future companions in his ecstatic revel and dance.[42] One stands to Silenos' left and leans forward to touch the satyr's shoulder, while the other sits on the left, perched on a craggy rock decorated with ivy vines as she holds up her own vine. If this image does invoke a moment from the now-lost Sophoklean satyr play, it seems such a unique choice of subject matter that it may suggest that the individual who owned it was interested in displaying his wealth, social status, education, and involvement in the dramatic performances that occurred in the Athenian theater.[43]

Within this context, if we identify the female figures depicted on the mixing bowl as Muses, they, together with the vessel upon which they have been depicted, have been elevated to the status of expensive, luxury objects placed on display for visitors to look at and admire. Even more, though, with their continued exposure to the human gaze, their ability to impart creative inspiration may have been thought to be all the more present in daily life. In this way, the Muses' divine presence is kept continually available for those who live in the home. But beyond simply making the goddesses more accessible to their viewers, the flexibility inherent in the Muses' representation also encourages its viewers to attribute the imagined sounds of the divine musical performance to the actual music played and sung by the human women present in the home. After all, we should imagine that any Athenian home was regularly filled with the sounds of women singing in rhythmical patterns as they wove cloth on the loom.[44] Anthony Tuck has shown that songs could act as mnemonic devices that would help the weavers remember when to change the shed and where to pass the weft, essential steps that must be remembered when weaving an intricate pattern.[45] There is also much that is musical about the sounds of the loom itself, both in its structural similarities to a lyre, in that both consist of a wooden frame from which taut strings are suspended, but also in the sounds produced each time the shed is changed, the loom weights tap

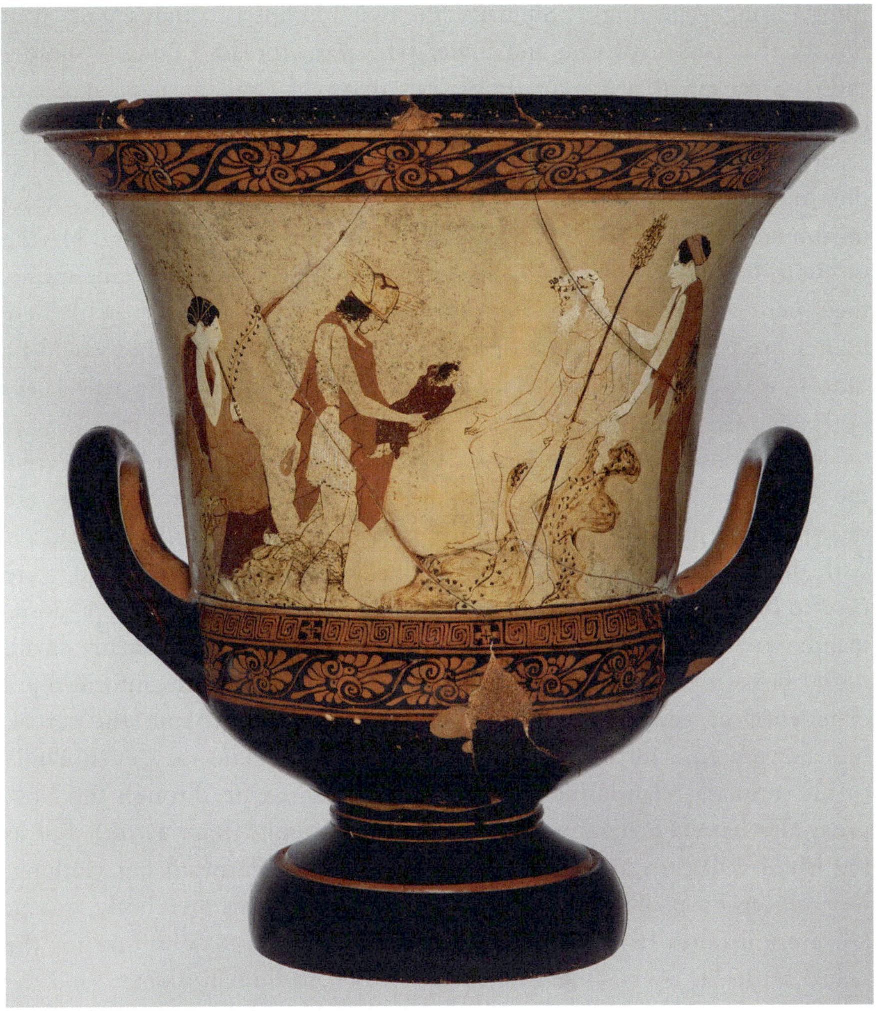

4.9. The Phiale Painter, *Hermes and the Infant Dionysos* (side A), Attic white-ground *calyx kratēr*, ceramic, h. 32.8 cm, *c*. 440–435 BCE. Vatican City, Museo Gregoriano Etrusco Vaticano, 16586. © Governorate of the Vatican City State – Directorate of the Vatican Museums.

against each other, or the warp is adjusted. The close association between the sounds of the loom and the home should not be underestimated; after all, Iphigenia, upon recalling her childhood, regrets that she will never be able to hear again its "beautifully sounding loom."[46] Moreover, the sounds of the loom and weaving certain patterns even seem to suggest a musical resonance with poetic meter.[47] As Marie-Louise Nosch notes, the metrical foot of an iamb (short – long) or a trochee (long – short) "recalls the tabby binding of weft threads going over and under the warp threads" (short – long, repeating).[48] Similarly, the twill binding is composed of "weft threads that pass over one and under two warp threads" (long – short – short), a pattern that evokes the dactyls that make up the basic meter of dactylic hexameter, the meter of epic poetry.[49] All of these sounds thus come together to establish the Greek home as intensely musical, whether the sounds are created by women singing, the loom shuttling, or an instrument being played. In encountering the three painted figures playing or about to play their lyres, in a space already filled with rhythmic music, their performance could seem to be actively underway. As such, these figures, painted onto the side of a vase, could be Muses, or they could be human women, who have come together to play music. The vase keeps both identities open for the viewer's interpretation.

Even for those instances where the figures are clearly intended to evoke the Muses, such as a scene on a round box from Athens where they are shown in the presence of Apollo, the very shape of the vessel associates it with the private, female space within the home, since these objects were used to hold cosmetics or jewelry (Fig. 4.10).[50] As objects that are predominantly associated with women in the domestic sphere, the many small, round boxes that feature representations of female musicians inform one's experience of gazing upon the painted images by evoking the actual, human women who once used the objects. This scene may even allude to the intimate relationship between husband and wife through the close proximity between standing Muse and seated Apollo (Fig. 4.10B). For as the Muse walks toward Apollo her body visible underneath her clothing, he positions his phallic lyre to extend outwards from his own body, so that the musical notes he plays for the Muse act almost as a substitute for the sexual act itself. By playing with divine Muse and human woman, and the particular ways each might interact with a male audience, this and other scenes of female music-making not only introduce the Muses to the domestic space, but they also implicate them in the tasks human women would have undertaken, so that both goddess and woman perform together. The Muses might thus have been present when women sang songs while they were weaving, the shuttling of the loom acting as a percussive rhythm for their melody, or they could have been the inspiration behind the sounds of a lyre that was played or the lines of poetry that were recited. In each case, the display of artistic creativity could be ascribed to the presence of the Muses, who are invoked and embodied by the women who move through the home. Let us not forget, too, that when the Muses appeared to the poet Archilochos, he initially believed that they were women returning from work; it was only when they had transformed his cow into a lyre that he knew, definitively, that he was mistaken about their identity.[51] The identity and representation of the

(A) (B)

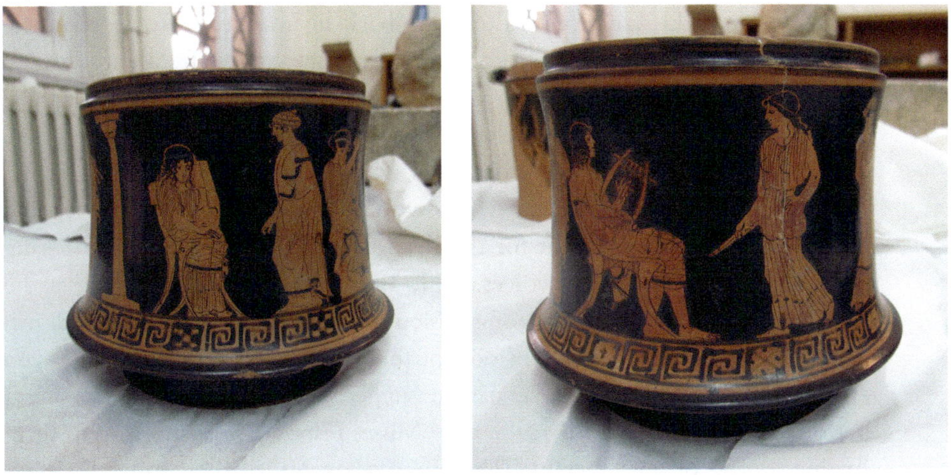

4.10. *Apollo and the Muses*, Attic red-figure *pyxis*, ceramic, h. 18.5 cm, *c.* 430 BCE. Athens, National Archaeological Museum, 1241. The rights of the depicted monuments belong to the Hellenic Ministry of Culture and Sports/Hellenic Organization of Cultural Resources Development (Law 4858/2021).

Muse are thus inherently flexible, so that she easily moves between appearing as a human woman, working at the loom, or as a divine goddess, singing and playing her instruments to her human worshippers.

MUSIC IN THE TOMB

Not only are representations of the Muses and female musicians common on those vessels associated with daily life, but they also often adorn the sides of vessels that were deposited as grave offerings in tombs. This was, in fact, a frequent occurrence for many of the vases discussed in this book: though their shape suggests one function, whether for drinking or preparing wine, at some point, either immediately after they were created in Athens or later after they had been used, their final destination was often a South Italian or Etruscan tomb.[52] The mixing bowl by the Phiale Painter is one such example. It was discovered in a tomb at Vulci, an Etruscan settlement in Italy, and its funerary context demands a different interpretative analysis for the ancient viewer's potential experience of and interaction with the female musicians painted onto the sides of the vessel.

The Muses, as daughters of Mnemosyne, hold a unique position within the Greek pantheon as bearers of knowledge of the past, a role that positions them outside of the human passage of time.[53] Their ability to sing of the past and future also links them, by extension, with the otherworldly associations developed on the other side of the vessel, namely through the inclusion of those gods who are linked with the Underworld. Dionysos, for instance, descended into the Underworld to bring back his mother, Semele, after she had been immolated by Zeus.[54] For his part, Hermes makes frequent journeys to the Underworld when he guides the souls of the dead to their final destination.[55] The Muses themselves, if we understand the female figures here as these goddesses, also have associations with funerary ritual and mourning. After all, in the *Odyssey*, it is the Muses who sing together as a chorus, leading the antiphonal *thrēnos* lament for the dead Achilles: "All nine Muses | sang lamentations in their lovely voices. | No one could keep from crying at the sound, | so moving was their song," Μοῦσαι δ' ἐννέα πᾶσαι ἀμειβόμεναι ὀπὶ καλῇι |· θρήνεον· ἔνθα κεν οὔ τιν' ἀδάκρυτόν γ' ἐνόησας | Ἀργείων· τοῖον γὰρ ἐπώρορε Μοῦσα λίγεια.[56] As the passage suggests, the lament the Muses sing is performed as a chorus, so that the nine Muses respond to each other in turn, singing a song of great beauty. The emotive quality of their song stirs their audience to great emotion, and ultimately proves to be capable of capturing the memory of the deceased hero.

The female musicians may further develop a relationship with the deceased with whom they were buried. It is possible that this vase was chosen to be a grave offering because one of the female figures was meant to represent the deceased, possibly the individual who stands to the left, dressed in such a way that recalls a mature, married woman. In this case, then, we might understand the scene as depicting two Muses playing, or about to play, their instruments before the deceased, whose memory will be preserved through the song the goddesses perform. If the three figures are all meant to represent Muses, the image may then suggest that the divine musicians have come together here as a chorus to perform a lament, perhaps one they will perform as an antiphonal call and response, similar to the *thrēnos* they sang for Achilles. However, whether one female figure represents the deceased or is instead another Muse makes little difference to our interpretation, because what is particularly significant here is that the figures infuse the funerary context with the sounds of music that is intended to preserve the memory of the deceased. Here, within the tomb, the female figures are shown continually singing of the human dead's *kleos*, the glory or fame he or she acquired in life. The memory of the deceased is thus captured in their melody, so that he or she becomes, as the poet Theognis writes, "like the subject of a song" that can be reperformed and reheard at any time.[57]

We may see a similar play between divine Muse and deceased human woman on a white-ground *lēkythos*, a funerary vessel intended to hold a small amount of oil, which was found in Athens in the tomb, ostensibly of a young girl (Fig. 4.11).[58] There are two figures in this scene: one, who sits on a rock, playing her lyre, and a second, who stands to the left and listens

(A) (B)

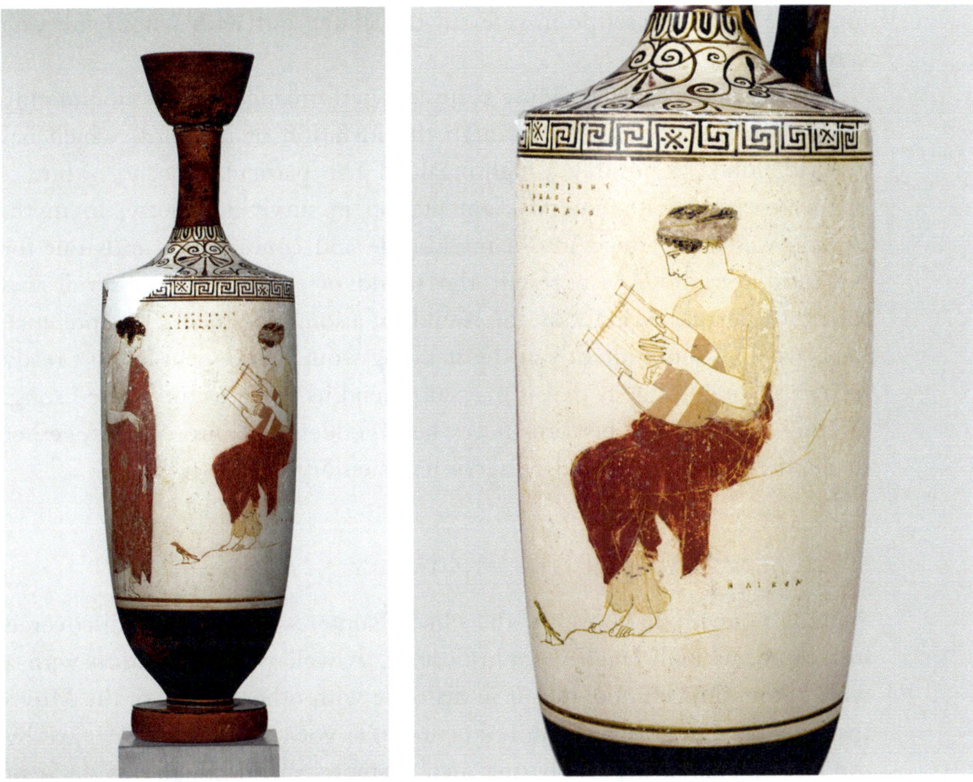

4.11. The Achilles Painter, *Muses on Mount Helicon*, Attic white-ground *lēkythos*, ceramic, h. 36.4 cm, *c.* 440 BCE. Munich, Antikensammlungen, S 80. Staatliche Antikensammlungen und Glyptothek München, photographs by Renate Kühling.

to the music. The setting in which the figures find themselves is identified through an inscription written on the rock: ΗΛΙΚΟΝ, that is, Mount Helicon, the home of the Muses.[59] The placement of the inscription suggests that the female figure who sits upon it may be a Muse, performing a song that commemorates the memory of the deceased little girl in whose tomb the vase was deposited. The identity of her companion is less clear: perhaps she is meant to represent the young girl, although here she is depicted as an adult, or perhaps she is another Muse who listens to her divine sister's music. Further underscoring the ambiguity in identities is the larger of the two inscriptions, positioned between the two female figures. It offers the viewer a name and a statement of beauty: Axiopeithes [son] of Alkimachos is beautiful, ΑΞΙΟΠΕΙΘΗΣ | ΚΑΛΟΣ | ΑΛΚΙΜΑΧΟ.[60] Given the masculine use of *kalos*, the individual to whom the inscription refers is clearly also male; the individual named cannot be either of the standing women, despite the inscription's placement adjacent to both figures, nor can the inscription refer to the young girl with whom the vase was interred.[61]

The importance of the Muse's musical performance in commemorating the deceased is emphasized through the inclusion of the bird, which has been identified as possibly a nightingale.[62] This particular species of bird is often associated with funerary lamentation in surviving poetry; in myth, Prokne was transformed into a nightingale and continuously calls out for her dead son, Itys. As a result, the sound of the nightingale's call was thought to evoke or embody the sounds of a song of lament.[63] Its presence here, where it looks intently at the standing woman and seems almost ready to start singing, suggests that it may soon lend its voice to the Muse's song, offering the viewer a performance where goddess and bird come together to mourn the deceased and preserve her memory for the future.

MUSICAL WORSHIP IN THE SANCTUARY

Although our mixing bowl by the Phiale Painter was ultimately discovered in a tomb, its high level of sophistication, as well as its fabrication with a white-ground technique, puts it in dialogue with other images of the Muses that may have been deposited in sanctuaries as votive offerings.[64] A *pyxis* by the Hesiod Painter is possibly one such example, and although this shape of vase is more typically associated with the domestic sphere, this particular object was discovered in Eretria, where it was probably discovered either in a tomb or in a sanctuary (Fig. 4.12).[65] Encircling the small box are six female figures, a solitary man, and a cow. Each female figure, with the exception of the one who stands next to the man and holds the cow's lead line, sits or stands while she holds or plays an instrument, whether a lyre, *aulos*, or *syrinx*.[66] By including such an array of musical instruments that are being played, the image evokes for its viewers the resonant sounds of the *aulos*, the shrill tones of the *syrinx*, and the cascading flow of notes emerging from the lyres. Although the musicians seem about to play their instruments together in tandem, each figure focuses on her own activity and takes little notice of the sole male figure who joins them. Initially thought to be Hesiod himself, given that the poet tells of his own encounter with the Muses on the slopes of Mount Helicon,[67] he may more plausibly be identified as the poet Archilochos, whose miraculous encounter with the Muses survives in the Mnesiepes inscription from Paros.[68] According to the inscription, when Archilochos was sent out into the field to collect the family cow to sell at market, he encountered a group of women. Thinking that they were returning from work, he began to tease them; returning his

(A)

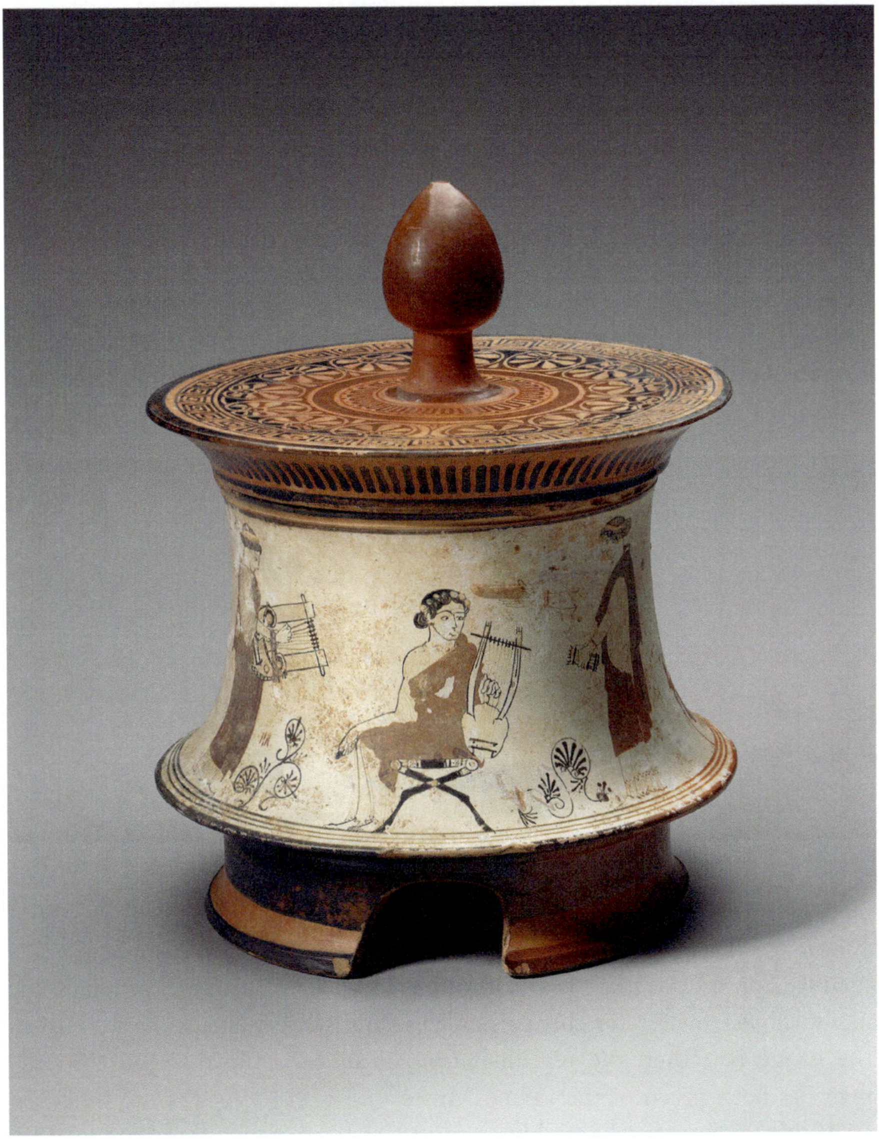

4.12. The Hesiod Painter, *Muses and Cowherd*, Attic white-ground *pyxis*, ceramic, h. 17.5 cm, *c.* 460–450 BCE. Boston, Museum of Fine Arts, 98.887. Digital rollout of the painted scene (B). Photograph © 2024 Museum of Fine Arts, Boston.

jests with their own, the women asked for how much he was selling his cow, and that they would give him an appropriate price. After he agreed, both the women and the cow disappeared, leaving behind a lyre. Disguised as human women, the Muses were only recognizable to Archilochos after their disappearance, relying upon the lyre left in their place to establish their

(B)

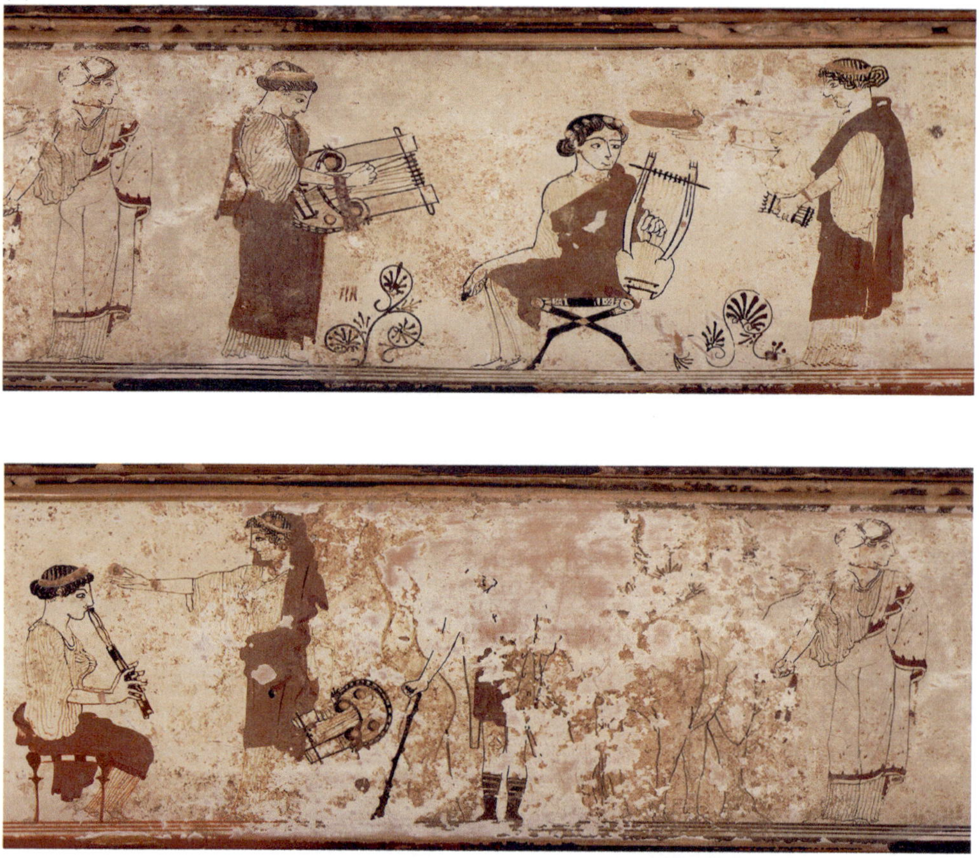

4.12. (*cont.*)

identity for the young man. Although the poetic narrative provides the likely subject matter for this particular scene, what seems truly at stake in the image is, rather, the representation of an exceptional vision a mortal man has been given of the divine Muses.

Within a framework of divine music and epiphany, there are various ways in which we might interpret this scene. For instance, the Muses could be understood as playing their music in front of their male audience, with all the figures having been positioned in the same rustic landscape, so that the man occupies the same space as the divine chorus. Yet, the lack of interaction between the Muses and the cowherd may be alternatively explained by isolating the two different spaces they each occupy. The Muses play their instruments in a divine space, where even the plants grow and twist in response to their music, the curvilinear shapes of the foliage echoing the shapes of the instruments themselves.[69] The cowherd, in turn, stands in the human world, listening to the music he hears but cannot see.

The Muses thus manifest as an auditory epiphany, making their presence known through the beautiful music he hears. The enticing, almost seductive, quality of their music is also emphasized: although the man's image is partially damaged, he stands completely still, leaning on his staff, seemingly unable to move as he listens to the sounds of the Muses' music.[70] The image further suggests that with each musical note the cowherd hears, the goddesses slowly appear before him, perhaps first as the musical sensation he experiences, then, later, as a visual manifestation. In considering how the cowherd might both see and hear the Muses' performance, we could even go so far to say that the man's sensory perception of the goddesses is blocked by the shape of the vase itself: despite the music he hears, his position on the vase relative to the goddesses suggests that he may never be able to see or hear all the Muses at once, since their bodies are blocked from his sight by the curvature of the vessel.[71]

Within a physical space that was itself sacred, such as a sanctuary, the Muses' musical epiphany could acquire further significance for the ancient viewer. As I mentioned above, this vessel was found in Eretria and though the archival records are unclear as to its precise find spot, it could either have been deposited – and later discovered – in a tomb or a sanctuary, perhaps even the area around the temple to Apollo Daphnephoros located there.[72] We have already seen how a funerary context might draw out particular aspects of the Muses' significance; similarly, if we were to tentatively position this round box within a sanctuary to Apollo, the sacred context could offer further layers of significance to the Muses' depiction. After all, since the Muses are often described as part of Apollo's chorus, a votive object depicting the Muses could have been considered to be an appropriate offering for the god. As gifts given to Apollo, the Muses thus become an integral component in the gift exchange between mortal dedicator and divine god, acting as a guarantee of the individual's devotion and the relationship he or she hoped to establish. For the human viewers of this vessel, who could have been worshippers who encountered it in a sanctuary, as they walked around the small box or perhaps even held it in their hands, would have had to rotate the vessel to take in the entire scene, turning its body to see and to hear the chorus of Muses.[73] Through this physical manipulation of the vessel, the Muses continually reveal and conceal themselves to their human audience, each figure appearing or disappearing depending on the vase's orientation. The Muses' manifestation is thus intimately bound up with the box's material body, which acts as the medium by which their musical performance is conveyed and their divine presence is experienced. Although not all of the Muses may have been visible at one time, their music nevertheless remains a constant presence in the viewer's perception of the scene, so that the goddesses are visually and musically joined together into a harmonious chorus by the viewer's very act of turning the vase.

Each external beholder thus becomes responsible for activating the Muses' revelation and, in turn, for receiving the poetic inspiration that their presence offered.

The Muses' divine music could also have been encountered at the same time as worshippers heard sacred music and hymnic songs emanating from the sanctuary space itself. Hymns and choral performances were regular features of sanctuaries, particularly during major festivals, when choral groups, often official *theōriai* who represented a specific *polis*, would sing hymns and perform dances for the gods.[74] During these religious events, as Power notes, the alternation of hymnic song and ritual silence "allowed the propitious voices of priests and singers to carry more clearly to the gods,"[75] making the hymn's invocation of the deity and the consequent possibility of an epiphany all the more powerful. We should imagine any Greek sanctuary as teeming with both musical and non-musical sounds; any experience of viewing the Muses on the box would have necessarily been punctuated by these other sounds. The hymns may even have begun with an invocation to the Muses. Such appeals to the goddesses to inspire one's song were common, and, as Brouillet notes with respect to book 2 of the *Iliad*, the invocation of the Muse allows for the presentification of the divine and connects the two temporalities at work, that is, the heroic action and the performance of epic.[76] Returning to the white-ground box, amplifying the blurred sensation of visual and auditory sound is the depiction of one instrument in particular, the *chelys* lyre held by a seated Muse. Shown frontally, the instrument confronts its external audience, demanding their visual and, implicitly, aural attention. The Muse who is shown holding the lyre in this unusual manner is clearly in the midst of performing: her left fingers are wrapped around the strings, while her right hand has just pulled the *plektron* across the instrument. Together with her companions who play the *aulos* and the *phorminx*, this Muse fills the scene with her music, and by drawing attention so dramatically to her instrument, she demands that her audience acknowledge and engage with her performance. If worshippers encountered this image of the Muses playing their instruments while they were surrounded by other external musical sounds, and even heard the goddesses being invoked in the hymnic lyrics, then their visual experience of the Muses could have been complicated and enhanced by their auditory perception of the actual musical sounds, in a similar way as I argued for the votive reliefs to Pan and the Nymphs. Within the sacred space of the sanctuary, human and divine music could blend together in the viewers' experience of the vessel, making it almost seem as if the viewers could hear the Muses' performance itself as they look at the painted image. In this moment of listening to the visual sounds of divine music, the viewers open themselves to the potential poetic inspiration that the Muses embody. In this way, the ancient viewers could themselves begin to compose songs that told the mythic stories of the past, both invoking and embodying the Muses through this act of poetic creation.

FROM SANCTUARY TO SYMPOSIUM

Created by the same painter as the small box by the Hesiod Painter is a shallow white-ground cup (Fig. 4.13).[77] While the cup's original context is similarly vague and could have similarly been deposited in a tomb or a sanctuary, its shape as a drinking cup further associates it with the symposium, the elite male drinking party during which, as I discussed previously, songs were performed, jokes were told, and intimate relationships were pursued. Thus, in addition to the layered identities placed upon the Muses in these representations, there is also a certain level of ambiguity between the contexts in which they may have appeared, so that they too become layered and inform the ancient viewer's perception of the object.[78]

The cup is stemless and its exterior is covered in black slip, which has the effect of focusing the viewer's attention upon the image painted within the tondo. There, a female figure is depicted against a plain, white background

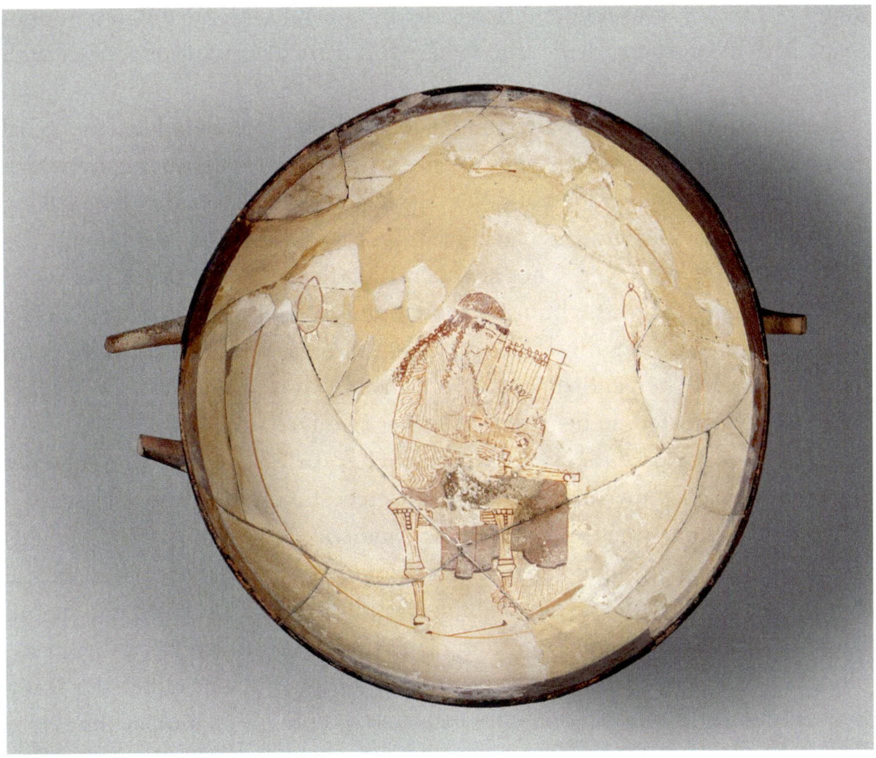

4.13. The Hesiod Painter, *Seated Muse Harmonizing Her Two Lyres*, Attic white-ground stemless *kylix*, ceramic, h. 3.7 cm, d. 15 cm, *c.* 470–460 BCE. Paris, Musée du Louvre, CA 482. Photo: Hervé Lewandowski. © RMN-Grand Palais/Art Resource, NY.

while she devotes her attention to her musical instrument. As with the female figures painted around the round box, given this cup's possible discovery in a sanctuary to Apollo, the female musician could potentially be identified as a Muse. Seated on a stool in the center of the image, she holds up a *phorminx* lyre as her thumb and index finger pluck one of its strings. At the same time, she rests another lyre on her lap and, with her right hand, pulls a string on the second instrument. The Muse is, unusually, shown tuning her two instruments, ensuring that the sounds they produce are in harmony with each other.[79]

That the Muse is depicted in the tondo of a drinking cup suggests that the goddess could have had an intimate encounter with her beholder, who may have seen the Muse emerge from the depths of the wine as he finished drinking. As the drinker's senses blur with each additional sip of wine, the Muse could slowly materialize as she gradually appears from within the dark liquid, displaying her musical skills to the symposiast in a moment of epiphany. Yet the white-ground with which the cup is decorated would never have been able to withstand contact with wine: both the white background and additional colors on this cup were added after the vessel was fired, so that the image would have been destroyed the moment it came into contact with the liquid.[80] The cup thus renders impossible the apparent intended function of its shape and, in so doing, denies the viewer this particular point of contact with the goddess.

Instead, as an image that always remained visible to its beholder, the visual representation of the Muse's performance itself becomes the means by which one might access the goddess and her music, so long as her audience is willing to enliven it. In depicting the technical preparation of the instruments, the image tantalizes its viewer, who, in anticipating the Muse's performance while potentially listening to the human-made sounds of hymnody in a sanctuary, is invited to imagine the music the goddess will soon create. The Muse is on display here for her audience: not only is she surrounded by the solitary musical notes created by her tuning, but her two lyres are delicately rendered, two wreaths hang on either side, pointing to her skill with music, and even her own body is carefully and elegantly depicted. Emerging from the creamy white background, the Muse offers her audience a glimpse into the sights and sounds of her world, where even those moments leading up to her musical performance are incomparably skillful, beautiful, and capable of inspiration. The Muse's creative inspiration, the image suggests, is not restricted to those who have the trained ability to create beautiful poems, but rather the Muse may choose to inspire anyone who pauses long enough to look at the image and imagine what beautiful sounds she will soon create with her equally beautiful lyres. The Muse could thus manifest before her human audience by moving between the material representation of her musical performance and the immaterial, imagined sound that existed within the viewer's perception of the scene.

Unlike the shallow cup, the Phiale Painter's mixing bowl with which we began our discussion of context (Figs. 4.7 and 4.8) could very well have been used during a symposium, for its shape positions it, even just theoretically, within any sympotic assemblage. Indeed, the mixing bowl was essential among sympotic vessels because it was the container in which water and wine were mixed together in preset ratios.[81] These ratios of water to wine were often the same ratios that figured into the tuning of musical instruments, so that there was a fundamental underlying musicality inherent to the mixture of wine itself.[82] Moreover, despite having been made in the fragile white-ground technique, here the yellow-white background as well as the added color were all applied before, rather than after, firing, as was the decoration along the top and bottom of the scene and the complete interior of the vase, which was covered in black slip (Fig. 4.14).[83] Every element of color on the vase is, therefore, extremely stable, and the surface could easily have withstood the wear and tear that came with extended use and contact with wine.[84] The presence of Dionysos and his maenads on one side of the vessel (Fig. 4.9) also directly relates to the primary activity within the symposium, allowing the god

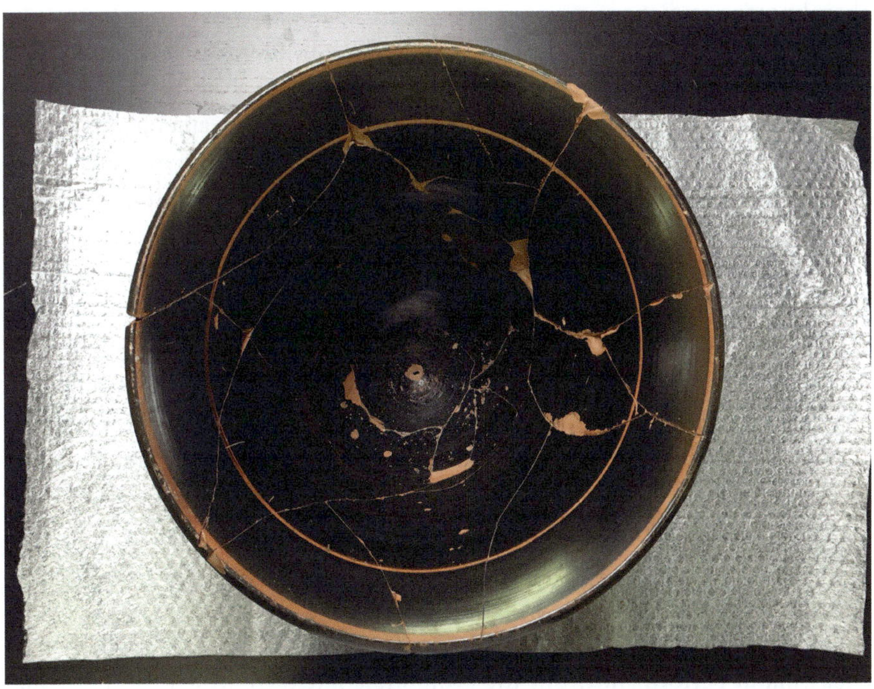

4.14. Detail of the interior. The Phiale Painter, *Hermes and the Infant Dionysos* (side A), *Three Muses* (side B), Attic white-ground *calyx kratēr*, ceramic, h. 32.8 cm, *c.* 440–435 BCE. Vatican City, Museo Gregoriano Etrusco Vaticano, 16586. Author's photograph. © Governorate of the Vatican City State – Directorate of the Vatican Museums.

of wine, even in his infant state, to preside over the mortal consumption of wine. The wine that is ladled out of the mixing bowl and consumed by the guests could seem to have originated from the god himself, since he is present on the vessel in which the mixture was produced. Similarly, the music performed by the female musicians on the vase's other side, who could represent Muses, flows around and out of the scene, moving together with the wine contained within the mixing bowl as it travels around the space of the symposium.

We may also see the metaphor of music flowing like wine in early fifth-century poetry. Pindar, in his sixth Olympian ode, describes the hero Aeneas as "a true messenger, a message stick of the fair-haired Muses, | a sweet mixing-bowl (γλυκὺςκρατήρ) of loudly-ringing songs (ἀγαφθέγκτων ἀοιδᾶν)."[85] In the poetic conflation of the distinct materialities of liquid wine and audible song, Pindar opens up the possibility for considering the ways in which the Muses' music may travel around the symposium, where it could be consumed in much the same way as the wine.[86] As the wine is shared among the guests, each individual not only partakes of Dionysos' presence, but he also opens himself up to the creative influence of the Muses. The material rendering of the musical performance thus bridges the gap between the representation of music and the actual, physical effect the goddesses' music could have upon their listening audience.

The Muses' depiction on vases that could have been used in the symposium inserts the goddesses into an otherwise human space, so that the Muse and the symposiast exist alongside one another. In considering how an engaged viewer might have responded to a representation of an otherwise remote Muse, consumed with her musical endeavors, a red-figure jug and its painted imagery offer one way by which we might understand the nature of the relationship between image, space, viewer, and goddess (Fig. 4.15).[87] Here, each Muse is labeled, conclusively establishing their respective identities: Ourania stands on the left, where she holds up a writing tablet that she may have taken from the box on the ground in front of her. Kalliope sits in the center, facing the right.[88] She holds what appears to be either a percussive instrument or a script and a short stick, perhaps intended to lead the performance of the third Muse, Melpomene, who faces her two companions and plays the pipes.[89] The image's symmetrical composition and the visual resonances between the figures suggest that the three goddesses have come together in harmony to play their instruments and listen to the music.

Insofar as the Muses are shown playing music, the image draws attention to their skillful performance, but the sympotic context in which the jug could have been used also includes the Muses within the human gathering.[90] In a symposium, this particular type of vase was typically filled with wine from the central mixing bowl and then was used to pour wine into each guest's

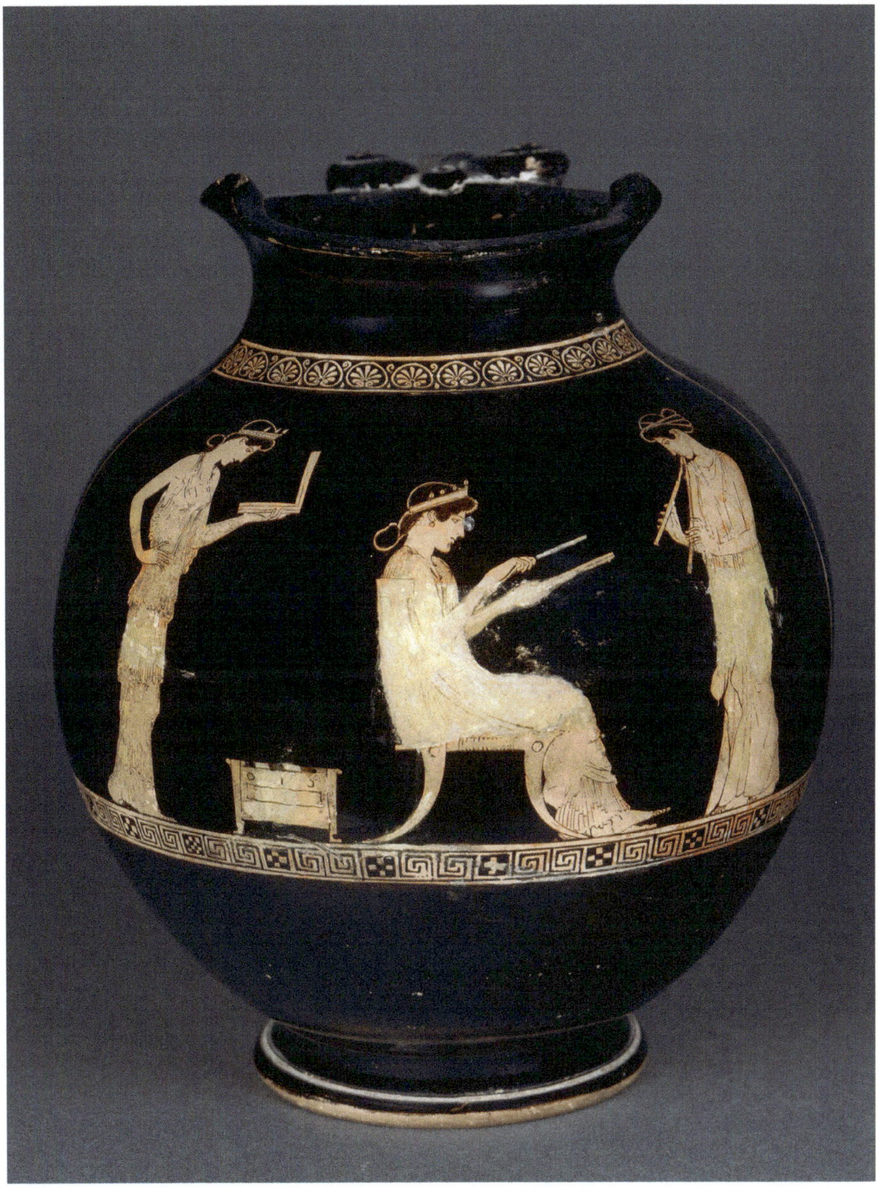

4.15. The Methyse Painter, *Three Muses (Ourania, Kalliope, and Melpomene)*, Attic red-figure *oinochoē*, ceramic, h. 21.4 cm, *c.* 455–440 BCE. Paris, Musée du Louvre, G 440. Photo: Hervé Lewandowski. © RMN-Grand Palais/Art Resource, NY.

individual cup. At any moment, then, the vessel physically travels throughout the room, as does the image painted upon it, so that the Muses and their music repeatedly approach and retreat from each symposiast. As the jug is tipped over to pour wine into each cup, the guest might perceive the Muses' movements becoming animated, making it almost appear that the vessel moves in time to the rhythm of the Muse's piped melody. The movement of the jug from guest to guest, accompanied by the Muse's *aulos* music, implicitly draws a comparison with the *skolion*, a sympotic game in which a laurel or myrtle branch was passed between guests once each had sung a few lines of poetry.[91] In positioning the Muses within this antiphonal structure, wherein they too are passed from individual to individual much like a call and response song, the vase suggests that their divine musical performance is an integral element for forging lasting social and political bonds. As with the other contexts we have examined, here too does the Muses' music blur with manmade music, so that the sounds present in the symposium, whether they are the *skolion* song sung by the guests, the sounds of the lyre or *aulos* played by the symposiasts, the music performed by the hired entertainers, or the music played by the Muses, seem to swirl and blend together, not unlike the liquids mixed in the bowls. This conflation of actual and imagined musical sounds thus makes audible the sounds of the Muses' music for their elite audience, further encouraging them to sing poetry, play music, and solidify their social bonds with each other through their shared musical activities.

Such a blurring of sensations is particularly suited to the symposium, not least since it was a space in which reality was easily suspended for the duration of an evening's festivities. In this fabricated world, guests had the opportunity to set aside their own identities and fashion new ones, or even adopt multiple personae throughout the evening. Through the poetry the guests recited, the music that they played, or the images that they saw on the cups and mixing bowls they used, men could transform themselves into the heroes and gods of Greek myth.[92] Indeed, the many images of the so-called Anakreontic dancers have been interpreted within precisely this framework, where the symposium offered its guests the opportunity to dress up in women's clothing and dance together.[93] Within the symposium, it is not simply representations of the Muses that are multivalent, but in this space anyone's identity becomes inherently fluid.[94]

As the men play with their identities through song and dance, they also transform the identities of the women present, that is, the *hetairai*, or hired entertainers, so that human and divine female companions come together before the symposiasts. In fact, it is within the transformative space of the symposium that images of the Muses become the most complex as the female musicians' identities shift and blur between divine goddess, human musician, and courtesan. We may see the layers of intricate play with identity in a tondo image painted by Makron (Fig. 4.16).[95] Here, one woman sits on a stool and plays her *aulos*, while a younger girl dances and plays her *krotala*, or castanets. The harmonious connection they have fostered between themselves as fellow musicians is developed through their interconnected gestures: their legs and feet overlap as the girl dances towards her companion, and as the pipes reach out to the right, so too does the dancing girl's arm extend to the left, just below the instrument.

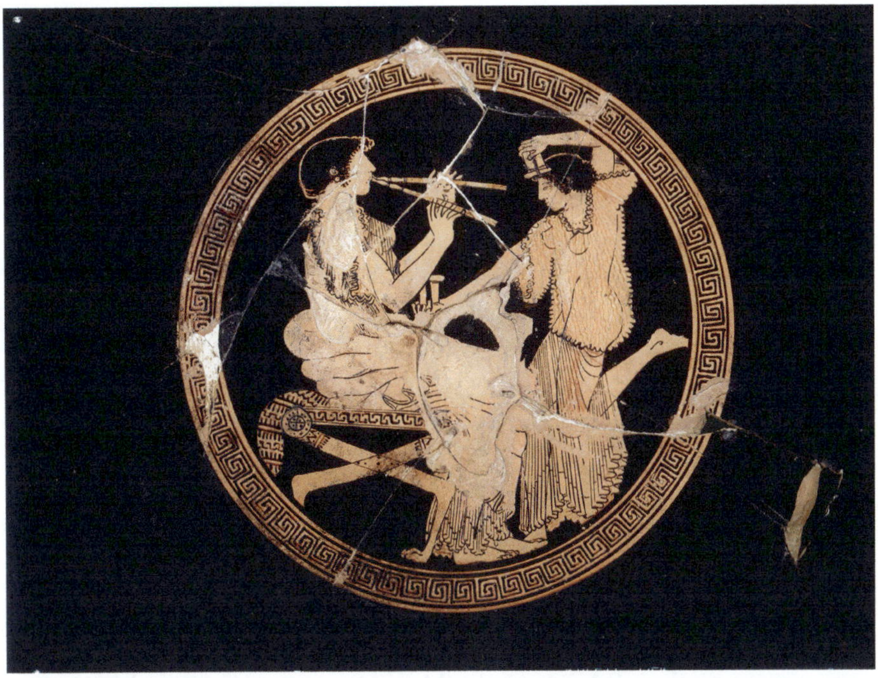

4.16. Makron, *Sympotic Scene* (tondo), Attic red-figure *kylix*, ceramic, h. 13 cm, *c.* 490–485 BCE. London, British Museum, 1867,0508.1063 (E61). © The Trustees of the British Museum.

The figures' multivalent identities are put on display in this image. On the one hand, the women's relatively transparent clothing and short hair suggest that they are probably courtesans. On the other hand, their close positions and musical connection with each other also suggests that they might also be intended to evoke the particular kind of symphonic music the Muses were often shown playing. For instance, the figure who sits on the stool and plays her *aulos* resembles depictions of other female musicians, such as one of the Muses featured on the white-ground round box we saw earlier; there, she similarly sits upright on a stool, facing to the right, with her instrument stretching out in front of her (Fig. 4.12). Although it is rare to find the Muses dancing in red-figure images, we might think back to the female figures on the *lēkythos* by the Sappho Painter (Fig. 4.5), where the figures also play their castanets while they dance, though the specific gestures that each figure performs differ between the two images. In each instance, however, the female figures dance while adding the sounds of their percussive instruments to the larger melody. On the *lēkythos*, the female dancers display a deep connection with the sounds of Apollo's music and respond to it with their own music, which, given their energetic dance, seems to have a lively and regular tempo, not unlike the girl's dance on the red-figure cup. Both female figures on the red-figure cup are similarly focused on their performance: the seated figure leans back, caught up in the creation of her music, while the young girl beside her looks down, absorbed in the music as she sways in time and kicks her feet to the rhythm. With their bodies overlapping and intertwined, the two women seem preoccupied by one another, each focused on making music while physically entangled with the other.

The dancing girl, whose embodied response to the music is so striking, further recalls representations of maenads, the mythical followers of Dionysos, who, in both black- and red-figure images, play the *krotala* and dance energetically together to the music. Moreover, the thin clothing worn by both women in the tondo image is similar to that worn by the Muses on a number of examples that I have discussed, including the white-ground round box (Fig. 4.12) or the stemless cup (Fig. 4.13), further blurring the distinction yet again between a mortal courtesan and a divine Muse. We might even compare these figures with the Dionysian maenads on a red-figure cup by Makron, discussed in further detail in Chapter 5 (Fig. 5.10), who similarly wear diaphanous clothing while they play instruments and dance. The visual record thus seems to deliberately blur together the visual appearances of Muses, maenads, and *hetairai* but, in doing so, it also creates an overlapping impression of their respective musical performances: the Muses may play calm and harmonious music, but so may human women, particularly when they are shown practicing their music together. At other times, the Muses may play wild, energetic music, as do maenads in Dionysiac frenzies and *hetairai* within the symposium. These images, then, encourage their viewers to imaginatively hear the sounds of divine music, even as they play with the kind of music that the viewers 'hear' and the specific musicians whom they see performing. In layering the female musicians' performances one atop the other, any identity, whether it is Muse, citizen wife, *hetaira*, or maenad, is available for the viewer to engage with and to listen to. By blurring the potential identities together, the images collectively suggest that there is something in the character of the Muses' music that is almost seductive, that it draws in its male audience in much the same way as could a woman in the home or in the symposium. The divine Muses are thus both available and remote, their music potentially offering a tantalizing glimpse into the stories of the past and future while, at the same time, giving their human audience the inspiration necessary to themselves compose lasting stories of myth and history.

We may see this fluid and ever-changing layering of identities even with the depiction of Sappho, the female lyric poet *par excellence*. As a female musician once described as being equal in skill to the Muses, as we hear from a quotation attributed to Plato, she similarly moves between identities in the visual material.[96] On the Brygos Painter's *kalathos*, a type of wine cooler, Sappho takes on the visual characteristics of a Muse, a *hetaira*, and a maenad (Fig. 4.17).[97] She stands almost facing the viewer, her *barbitos* lyre stretching out in front of her to

(A) (B)

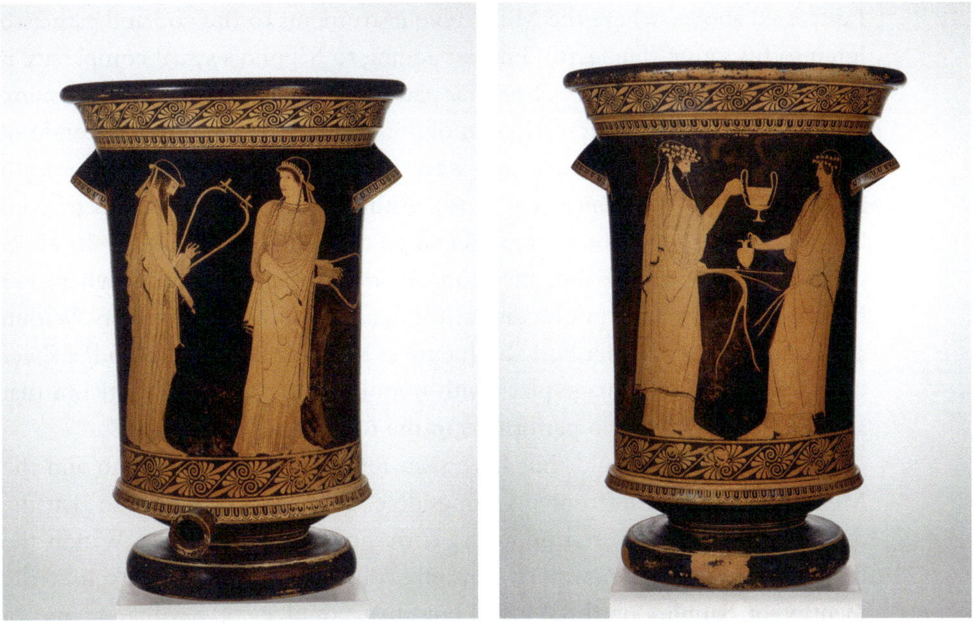

4.17. The Brygos Painter, *Sappho and Alkaios* (side A), *Dionysos and Female Devotee* (side B), Attic red-figure *kalathos*, h. 52 cm, *c.* 470 BCE. Munich, Antikensammlungen, 2416. Staatliche Antikensammlungen und Glyptothek München, photographs by Renate Kühling.

the right and her head turned back to the left to look at her companion. Beside her stands the poet Alkaios, who looks down at his lyre while he sings, a string of 'o's emerging from his mouth to indicate the sounds of his voice within the image.[98] The two poets are clearly in the middle of playing a musical composition: Sappho glances back at Alkaios, ensuring that their movements are harmonized as both pull a *plektron* across the strings of their lyres at the same time.

Though each figure is labeled, ascribing to them a specific, individual identity, their bodies encourage other visual comparisons. Alkaios bears a great resemblance to the figure of Dionysos who appears on the other side of the vase: both have long beards, their hair is pulled back, and each wears a long *himation* that has a dark border along its edges. Sappho, for her part, physically resembles the maenad who aids Dionysos in pouring a libation. This maenad is not the ecstatically dancing figure who so often appears with Dionysos, but rather she is calm and restrained as she holds out a jug to fill the god's cup. Her depiction is so unusual that it becomes increasingly unclear whether Sappho-as-Muse resembles the maenad, or whether the maenad has taken on elements of Sappho's almost divine representation. Sappho's depiction also evokes visual elements used for the Muses' representation. She plays the *barbitos*, as does the central figure on the Phiale Painter's mixing bowl (Fig. 4.8), and her deference to Alkaios recalls the Muses' interaction with Apollo on the other round box I discussed above, where the Muses give instruments to the god and gather to listen to his music (Fig. 4.10). Further adding to Sappho's visual complexity is her resemblance to images of *hetairai* playing instruments in the symposium. For instance, her clothing recalls that of the seated *aulos* player on the tondo of the cup we have just seen, who also wears a thin, diaphanous *chitōn* underneath her loosely draped *himation* (Fig. 4.16). Although such an outfit was perhaps best suited to a *hetaira*, for our representation of Sappho, it instead has the effect of visually drawing her into the erotic world of the symposium, where her body would have been put on display for her male and female viewers. Within a sympotic landscape, her body both entices her male audience with her sheer clothing even as her image plays with notions of female homoeroticism that are suggested by the two performers in the tondo image.

The symposiasts would thus have seen representations of Sappho and the Muses playing their instruments alongside courtesans performing, so that the divine activity was layered upon the corresponding mortal one. Within the flexible space of the symposium, not only could the *hetairai* have taken up the identity of Sappho or the Muses, but they could even have sung one of Sappho's poems or a song inspired by the Muses, using the ambiguity inherent to the representation of female musicians to blur, both visually and aurally, their identities. Through a visual conflation of Muse, maenad, *hetaira*, and the most famous female poet of antiquity, the entire scene draws together the otherwise improbable combination of serene Muses, who inspire beautiful music, and ecstatic maenads, who destabilize the harmonious chorus and potential inspiration offered by the Muses. Both identities were available for the courtesan to adopt and perform, and, at the same time, were presented to the male symposiasts as various ways by which they could identify the nearby female figures. The Muse thus could transform not only her body and the bodies of other women present in the symposium, but she also makes it possible for the male viewer to do the work of transforming the bodies of those who are around him.

HEARING THE MUSES

Each ceramic vessel discussed in this chapter comments on the effect the presence of the Muses could have had upon their human audience. In drawing their external viewers into the Muses' performance while, at the same time, projecting the Muses' song out into the human world, the vases give us a glimpse into the Athenian perception of these goddesses, where the flexibility in their representation allowed them to move across boundaries and between bodies. This ambiguity inherent to the Muses' representation is fundamentally tied to the context in which the images were once viewed.

In each scenario in which the Muses' representation may have appeared, whether a private home, a cemetery, a sanctuary, or a symposium, the figure of the Muse becomes one upon which multiple layers of identity could be placed, so that the Muses as a collective could potentially appear at any time and to anyone. As a result, the Muse was a pervasive presence in one's daily experience: she could be a wife in the home, a courtesan in the Athenian symposium, a maenad worshipping Dionysos, or the Muse herself. The Muses' visual flexibility was a crucial component of their identity, so that when a single image was seen in a different space, the goddesses could shift easily from one role to another.

In many ways, representations of the Muses both in antiquity and in later artistic traditions continue to evoke this accessible element in the Muses' depiction. What has thus remained consistent from antiquity onwards is a continued effort on the part of men and women to cultivate an encounter with these mysterious figures who offer inspired creativity to those who seek them out. Each vase thus stands as an example of the effort put forward by the Athenians to cultivate the presence of the Muses, to make it possible to experience an epiphany of these goddesses who are responsible for inspiring the very poems that recount the history of the Greeks. Above all, the images act as a point of contact between human men and women and their Muses, so that as the vases circulated throughout Athenian homes, sanctuaries, and cemeteries, the Muses became effectively omnipresent, always able to inspire their human viewers to create musical, poetic, and artistic feats of unparalleled skill.

NOTES

1 As West (1997: 170) notes, the Muses are a distinctly Greek conception: "The Muses are, so far as we know, purely Greek creatures." See also Maslov 2016: 414. For more on the absence of an Indo-European counterpart for the Muses, see West 2007: 94.

2 Hes. *Theog.* 1. Translation from Most 2007: 2–3.

3 Hesiod (*Theog.* 94–95) describes Apollo as responsible for leading the Muses' chorus and overseeing their musical activities.

4 *BAPD* 214508; *ARV*² 1080.1; *LIMC* s.v. Mousa, Mousai no. 48a; Schöne-Denkinger 2009: 44–46, fig. 18, pls. 40.1–3, 41.1–7, 76.1.

5 Schöne-Denkinger 2009: 45.

6 Hes. *Theog.* 22–23.

7 The story of Archilochos is preserved on the Mnesiepes inscription (*SEG* 15.517), discussed below.

8 See, for instance, Rystedt 1984: 89–91; Queyrel 1988; *LIMC* s.v. Mousa, Mousai, 657–81; Bélis 1992; Bundrick 2005: 51–54.

9 Hes. *Theog.* 1–103, especially 77–79. The names, if translated from the Greek, are: Fame-Spreading (Klio), Entertaining (Euterpe), Festive (Thaleia), Singing (Melpomene), Delighting in Dance (Terpsichore), Lovely (Erato), Rich in Hymns (Polyhymnia), Celestial (Ourania), and Beautiful Voice (Kalliope).

10 Also noted by Mojsik (2011: 7, 12–14) in relation to their description and appearance in literature. One should take care in not adhering too closely to Hesiod's description of the female deities and taking it as their canonical presentation, since it is not until the Hellenistic period that the names, number, and attributes of the Muses were represented and described with any degree of consistency. Murray 2004: 373–85; Bundrick 2005: 50–53; Murray 2014.

11 *BAPD* 300000; *ABV* 76.1, 682; *Paralipomena* 29; *Beazley Addenda*[2] 21; Shapiro, Iozzo, and Lezzi-Hafter 2013, with previous bibliography.

12 In the surviving visual material, the Muses are shown above all as instrumentalists, and not as singers, as is so often the case in poetry.

13 Immediately following are Thalia, Euterpe, Klio, and Melpomene, all identified by inscription; the final group consists of Polyhymnia, Erato, and Steisichore. Kleitias used Steisichore instead of the Hesiodic Terpsichore. Polyhymnia is here written as Polymnis. For the influence of the poet Steisichoros on the imagery of the François Vase, see Stewart 1983.

14 Carpenter 1986: 11. As noted throughout this volume, detailed work on frontal faces has been undertaken by Korshak 1987; Frontisi-Ducroux 1995; Mackay 2001; Mack 2002; Hedreen 2007; Hedreen 2017. I also follow Meyer Schapiro's argument (1973, 38f.) that these frontal faces actively look at their viewers.

15 For more on the role of the Muses' song in the *Theogony*, see Brockliss 2017–18.

16 Hes. *Theog.* 22, 36.

17 As noted above, one should take care, however, in not adhering too closely to Hesiod's description of the female divinities. Bundrick 2005: 50–53; Murray 2014. See also a small *pyxis* found in a grave dating to the late fifth century BCE, on which the nine Muses are depicted and labeled with Hesiodic names. Archibald et al. 2010–11: 38.

18 Hom. *Il.* 2.761; *Od.* 1.1.

19 Hom. *Il.* 1.604. Kirk 1985: 51; Porter 2013: 9; Maslov 2016: 415–17.

20 Nancy 1996; Nancy 2000; Porter 2013; Maslov 2016: 415–17.

21 BAPD 7974; *LIMC* s.v. Apollon no. 701a; Haspels 1936: 226.7, pl.32.2 A–B; Wegner 1949: 213; Zanker 1965: 57, no. 260; Queyrel 1985: 159. For more on representations of singing and on the presence of musical notes and sounds on vases, see Lissarrague 1990b: 123–39; Heesen 2016; Yatromanolakis 2016; Laferrière 2020.

22 *BAPD* 11020; Bérard 1989: 90–91; Voutira 1991: 77; Reeder 1995: 208–10, no. 45; Bundrick 2005: 92–93, fig. 57.

23 Bundrick (1998: 199–200) argues that the stepped platform, itself an iconographic element of musical performances, may have been taken from similar scenes of *mousikoi agones*.

24 Also suggested by Voutira 1991: 75; Reeder 1995: 209; Bundrick 2005: 92. Though Pöhlmann (1960: 83–84; 1976: 60–62) initially argued that the book rolls contained musical notation, he later amends his argument to suggest instead that the book rolls referred more generally to musical practice. Immerwahr, for his part, does not rule out the possibility of the rolls containing musical notation, but notes that neither is it clear that they do so nor that musical notation existed at this time. Immerwahr 1973: 146; Immerwahr 1964: 46.

25 For a similar scene, see the red-figure *hydria* by the Group of Polygnotos, currently in the National Archaeological Museum in Athens (*BAPD* 213777). For more on representations of Sappho, see Yatromanolakis 2007.

26 Bérard 1984: 86–87; Reeder 1995: 209.

27 Neils 2000: 225.

28 Rystedt (1984: 89–91) notes the related difficulty in determining that the women are *not* Muses.

29 Kurke 1997.

30 *Pornai* seem to have been women who were used merely for physical sexual release and thus were found primarily in brothels throughout Athens and Peiraeus. *Hetairai*, conversely,

were considered both as sexual partners and as entertainers who played music, engaged in riddles and storytelling, and danced in the *kōmos* revel. Davidson 1997: 73–78, 81–101; Kurke 1997; Kurke 1999: 175–218.

31 Neils (2000: 211–13) argues that the door marks the space as a brothel, whereas Bérard (1984: 86–87; 1989: 91), emphasizing the intimate character of the scene, states that it is the door to the house. These two very different interpretations for the same image underscore the visual ambiguity inherent to these scenes.

32 Although it was initially attributed to the Painter of the Petrograd Amazonomachy, Beazley instead attributes this vase to the Peleus Painter, stressing that it is close in style to the Hector Painter, and probably was made by the Group around Polygnotos. The most recent information within the Petit Palais agrees with this reattribution. The museum label suggests that the vessel came into contact with a funeral pyre, which accounts for its greyish color. *BAPD* 213520; *ARV*[2] 1040.22; *Beazley Addenda* 156; *Beazley Addenda*[2] 319; Maas and Snyder 1989: 136; Plaoutine 1941: 18, pl. 17.4–8.

33 Hagel and Lynch 2015; Laferrière 2023.

34 Sarti 1992; Bundrick 2005: 142–50.

35 As shown conclusively by Trinkl 2009. She stresses that water vessels, or *hydriai*, were used in a variety of contexts, whether domestic, ritual, or funerary, and moreover were used by both men and women. For instance, on the Parthenon frieze men are shown carrying these vases, whereas on fountain scenes, women fill them. Bundrick, conversely, argues that water vessels are particularly associated with female domestic space. As Lynch has pointed out, though water vessels belong in a sympotic assemblage, they have been infrequently found in Athenian deposits. Lynch interprets the dearth of archaeological support as evidence for the exportation or ritual dedication of painted water vessels. Lynch goes on to note that a metal vase could have been used but simply did not survive in the particular well upon which her study was based. She cautions that the surviving deposits should not be treated as exhaustive; for instance, though no mixing bowl was found in well J 2:4 (at the right height and deposit level), one cannot conclude that these vessels were not part of sympotic assemblages. Bundrick 2005: 94–95; Lynch 2011: 75–76, 78, 130–31; Bundrick 2012: 21–22; Lynch 2015: 232, 235.

36 That the Muses are deities whose presence is associated with sensory perception is also established by Brouillet in relation to epic poetry. After establishing that the Muses regularly invite conflated sensory experience in human poets, she continues by stating that "le mode d'être des Muses est celui de la présence" ("the Muses' mode of being is that of presence"). Brouillet 2016: 306. Translation by the author.

37 That scenes of the Muses should be considered within these various contexts, and particularly within the symposium, finds justification in the specific vase shapes upon which the images were painted. In addition to the *hydria*, scenes of the Muses, or women engaged in similar musical activities, may be found on *calyx*, bell, volute, and column *kratēres*, *kylikes*, *pelikēs*, *amphorai*, *lēkythoi*, *skyphoi*, *pyxides*, *oinochoai*, and *stamnoi*. *BAPD* 214232; *ABV*[2] 1017.54, 1678; *Paralipomena* 440; *Beazley Addenda* 154; *Beazley Addenda*[2] 315; *LIMC* s.v. Mousa, Mousai no. 12; Oakley 1990: no. 54 with previous bibliography; Bundrick 2005: 59; Cohen 2006: 232–34; Dietrich 2010: 474–73; Lissarrague 2013: 219.

38 Dietrich 2010: 462–75.

39 On the division of space within the *oikos*, and women's movements in the urban sphere more generally, see Nevett 1994; Nevett 1995; Goldberg 1999; Nevett 1999: 39–50; Antonaccio 2000; Nevett 2011.

40 Though there is little evidence for vases having been used in this way, there is also little evidence to suggest that they were not used as symbols of status. Rather, it simply means that little evidence has survived for the use and presentation of luxury items within private spaces.

41 The scene may even have been initially represented on a lost panel painting, which could have been on display in a public space within Athens, so that owning a reproduction of the famous painting that in turn reproduces a dramatic scene created by the famous playwright Sophokles, becomes a further statement regarding one's cultural and educational achievements. Mertens 2006: 233. Oakley (1990: 33) argues instead that while the painting and drawing styles appear to derive from panel painting, the subject matter was taken from Sophokles' satyr play. Though such arguments have rarely been made regarding Athenian vases due to a lack of evidence, and are more commonly made in regards to Pompeian wall paintings, where clear assemblages and notions of 'collecting' seem to be more clear, that does not necessarily imply that similar aspirations were not cultivated in fifth-century Athens.

42 Mertens (2006: 233) notes the similarity in rustic setting between the two sides, suggesting that the Muses may be on Mount Helicon while Dionysos and the Nymphs are on Mount Nysa. Bundrick (2005: 58) argues that the scene of the Muses is only symbolically related to that of Dionysos, so that the Muses should be understood not as the actual teachers of the infant god but rather as symbolic of the ideal education in *mousikē*. Van Keuren (1998: 19), by contrast, argues that the Muses here are Dionysos' actual teachers.

43 Oakley 1990: 32–33; Bundrick 2005: 57.

44 As Nevett (1994: 107–09; 1995: 368–74) has shown, women worked in areas throughout the home, including the outside courtyard. On the potential soundscape of the ancient Greek house, see Harrington 2015; on the Roman house, see Öhrman 2018 and 2020.

45 Tuck 2006.

46 Eur. *IT* 208–25. On childhood weaving, the so-called tortoise game, and lullabies, see Karanika 2014: 165–77. For more on the general domestic acoustic environment, see Nosch 2014: 95.

47 I draw on Öhrman 2018.

48 Nosch 2014: 94.

49 Nosch 2014: 94.

50 Roberts 1978.

51 This is the account preserved on the third-century BCE Mnesiepes inscription, *SEG* 15.517. Karanika 2014: 111–13.

52 On the use of Greek vases in tombs, see Bundrick 2015; Bundrick 2019. The economic aspect of the vase trade is treated in Langridge-Noti 2015. The diverse audiences who may have encountered Greek vases are treated by two papers, written as responses to each other: Marconi 2004; Osborne 2004.

53 Mojsik 2013: 80, 84.

54 Hes. *Theog.* 940–42; *Hymn. Hom. Bacch.* 1–5, 17–18; Pind. *Ol.* 2.22–27.

55 He is first represented as Psychopompos in Book 24 of the Odyssey.

56 *Od.* 24.60–62. Text from West 2017: 489, with additional notes, and translation by Wilson 2018: 509. Within the context of lamentation, there existed two particular genres of commemoration: the *goös* lament, spoken by both women and men who had a particularly personal and unique relationship with the deceased, and the *thrēnos*, a lament that was typically sung by hired musicians. Alexiou 2002: 102–04; Tsagalis 2004: 2–8; González 2019: 25–31.

57 Thgn. 237–54. For more on the relationship between music and memory, see Bundrick 2021. For another approach, see Tsingarida (2012: 51, 56), who has recently suggested that within funerary contexts, representations of the Muses should be understood in relation to Apollo and oracular pronouncements, since the Muses are linked specifically with Orpheus and Mousaios, both famous seers and poets.

58 *BAPD* 213977; *ARV*^{2} 997.155; *Paralipomena* 438; *Beazley Addenda* 152; *Beazley Addenda*^{2} 312; Maas and Snyder 1989: 158; Robertson 1992: 201; *LIMC* s.v. Mousa, Mousai no. 6; Oakley 1997: 65, pl. 2; Steiner 2002: 359, fig. 10a; Oakley 2004: 96–97; Bundrick 2005: 27, 58; Kunze-Götte 2010: 61–64, figs. 22, 23, drawing 11.2, pls. 33.1–3, 34.1–4, 35.2.

59 Hes. *Theog.* 1; Beazley 1938: 16; Oakley 1997: 65, no. 209.

60 Written in *stoichēdon* letters, where the capital letter forms are aligned both horizontally and vertically, the name itself has been inscribed in a manner that was old fashioned for the 440s BCE in Athens, wherein only the name and patronymic are included, rather than the name, patronymic, and demotic. Shapiro connects this with the Periklean Citizenship laws of 451/450 BCE. As Bundrick points out, the style of inscription also recalls fifth century public inscriptions in Athens. For more, see Shapiro 1987: 108, 111–14; Bundrick 2005: 212, n. 54.

61 Oakley (2004: 96–97) states that it provides a male counterpart to the female figures represented, underscoring the message of *oikos*. See Bundrick (2005: 58, 212 n. 54) for further discussion. For more on the relationship between inscriptions and devotional practices, see Gaifman 2008.

62 Black birds also may appear alongside Apollo, particularly in black-figure scenes, perhaps alluding to the mutual interest between god and bird in creating beautiful music. See also Chapter 3, where I discuss the relationship between animals and Apollo's music.

63 See Bundrick 2021 for more on the significance of the nightingale with respect to this scene. On the lamenting nightingale more broadly, see Weiss 2017: 253–63, with earlier bibliography.

64 As Mertens (1977: 108) and Wehgartner (1983: 76–78) each note, white-ground vases were often dedicated in sanctuaries or deposited in tombs. For an extensive study on Archaic and Classical ceramics, including white-ground, that were deposited in sanctuaries, see Gunnarsdottir 2023.

65 The information on its findspot is taken from Edward Perry Warren's records. *BAPD* 209554; *ARV*[2] 774.1; *Paralipomena* 416; *Beazley Addenda* 141; *Beazley Addenda*[2] 287; Maas and Snyder 1989: 102, 57; Bélis 1992: 58; *LIMC* s.v. Mousa, Mousai no. 77; Clay 2004: 14–16, 55–57; Bundrick 2005: 43, fig. 27; Dietrich 2010: 468–69.

66 The larger lyre with a rounded soundbox held by two standing figures is the *phorminx*, an early type of lyre often associated with the performance of epic poetry. Maas and Snyder 1989: 139–45, 56–59.

67 This vessel is the name vase for the Hesiod Painter, whose name was based on the scene shown here.

68 Clay 2004: 14–16, 55–57; Karanika 2014: 111–13. Clay, mistakenly I believe, identifies the seated figure playing the *chelys* lyre as male, and more specifically, as Archilochos himself. Clay compares the seated musician with the Apollo Kitharoidos type, such as is depicted on the tondo of a cup in Delphi (8140). However, the specific manner in which Apollo Kitharoidos is depicted is reserved for his representation alone; the iconography is not used for any other figure, human or divine. Moreover, the seated figure is clearly female, and if one were to identify any figure as Archilochos, it would more plausibly be the standing male figure.

69 Dietrich (2010: 468) rightly identifies such plants as "Phantasiegewächse," noting that their form, as they are represented on fifth-century vases, bear little resemblance to actual, living plants.

70 His cow is also controlled by one Muse, who ensures that her audience remains captivated with little distraction.

71 For my discussion of depictions of a mythical landscape and the viewer's sightlines, I draw upon Dietrich 2010.

72 Wehgartner 1983: 148. Though she suggests that the *pyxis* could also have been deposited in a Sanctuary to the Muses, no sanctuary sacred to these goddesses has thus far been found. Alternatively, the vessel may have been discovered in an Eretrian grave. Following Gunnarsdottir (2023), there is evidence for the dedication of white-ground vessels in both sacred and funerary spaces.

73 I draw here on the notion of the embodied object, that is, "a physical, spatially situated entity which invites interaction with other bodies" (Gaifman and Platt 2018: 404).

My discussion also owes much to recent work on viewer interaction, particularly as it has been articulated with respect to epigrams. Meyer 2005; Männlein-Robert 2007; Tueller 2008; Day 2010: 1–75.

74 Rutherford 2004; Power 2018: 16–17.

75 Power 2018: 17.

76 "l'appel à la Muse permet . . . la présentification de l'instance divine et fait se rejoindre les deux temporalités" ("the call to the Muse allows for the presentification of her divine presence and allows for the two moments in time to be joined together"). Brouillet 2016: 306–07 and, more generally, 301–14. Translation by the author.

77 *BAPD* 209555; *ARV*[2] 774.2; *Paralipomena* 416; *Beazley Addenda*[2] 287; Pottier 1895: 39–56; Wehgartner 1983: 72, no. 84, 96; Bélis 1992; *LIMC* s.v. Mousa, Mousai no. 1; Robertson 1992: 179. The cup was found with another white-ground cup, also by the same painter (Paris, Musée du Louvre, CA 483). The original context for both vessels is unclear: the Louvre online catalogue states that they were found at Eretria, while Beazley notes that it possibly had an Attic context.

78 Also established in Grethlein 2017: 191–248.

79 As shown conclusively by Bélis 1992.

80 Gaifman conclusively demonstrated this point with respect to a cup found at Delphi (8140), which was also made in the white-ground technique and is too fragile to have withstood contact with liquid. Gaifman 2018a: 48; 2013: 50. On the fragility of white-ground cups generally, see Griffiths 1986: 59; Wehgartner 1983: 168–70; Mertens 1977: 91–108, 222.

81 For more on the importance of the *kratēr* within a symposium, see Lissarrague 1990a.

82 Lissarrague 1990b: 19–46.

83 Mertens 2006: 233–34.

84 Mertens 2006: 233–34. Although the mixing bowl was discovered in a tomb in Vulci, that does not preclude its use in an Athenian symposium prior to its exportation. Moreover, even if it was immediately exported after its creation, the shape itself is enough to associate it, even if just symbolically, with the space of the symposium.

85 Pind. *Ol.* 6.90–91. ἐσσὶ γὰρ ἄγγελος ὀρθός | ἠυκόμων σκυτάλα Μοι | σᾶν, γλυκὺς κρατὴρ ἀγαφθέγκτων ἀοιδᾶν· Translation from Athanassaki 2022: 185–86. The message stick (σκυτάλα) was used in Sparta, where writing material was wound around the stick, inscribed, and cut into a strip. Only with a duplicate stick could the strip be correctly wound to reveal the message.

86 For more on Pindar, material objects, and chorality, see generally Kurke and Neer 2019.

87 *BAPD* 207346; *ARV*[2] 633.11; *Beazley Addenda* 133; *Beazley Addenda*[2] 272; Couve 1895: 102–03; *LIMC* s.v. Mousa, Mousai no. 13; Kaufman-Samara 1997: 286. On the complex relationship between vase-painting, seeing, and the symposium, see especially Grethlein 2017: 191–248.

88 Couve 1895: 102.

89 Although there is no ancient evidence for the practice of conducting or directing a performance, the specific position of the Muse's staff could indicate that she, at the very least, may lead her companion's performance.

90 Lynch 2011: 75–76.

91 On the use of myrtle or laurel to mark the song's progression, see Ar. *Nub.* 1364; Plut. *Quaest. conv.* 1.1.5; scholiast to Ar. *Vesp.* 1222, 1239; *Souda* s.v. *skolion*; Phot. s.v. *skolion*. On *skolia* more generally, see Reitzenstein 1893, reprinted in 1970; Rösler 1980: 94–95; Vetta 1983a: xxxiii–xxxiv; Vetta 1983b; Bowie 1986; Nagy 1990: 107; Neer 2002: 13–14. For surviving representations of *skolia* within the symposium, see Neer 2002: 219–20, n. 42.

92 Greenblatt 1980; Foucault 1985: 72–77; Neer 2002: 14–15; Grethlein 2017: 191–248.

93 On Anacreontic dancers, see Frontisi-Ducroux and Lissarrague 1983; Price 1990: 133–75; Delavaud-Roux 1995; Ladianou 2005.

94 Davidson 1997: 44; Neer 2002: 17–18.

95 *BAPD* 204827; *ARV*[2] 468.145, 482, 1654; *Beazley Addenda* 120; *Beazley Addenda*[2] 245; Robertson 1992: 101; Williams 1993: 49–51, pls. 50a–b, 51a–b; Kunisch 1997: 29–30, 32, 44–45, 67; Robson 2013: 267.

96 Preserved in the Greek Anthology is a quotation attributed to Plato, in which the philosopher says "Some say the Muses are nine but how carelessly! Look at the tenth, Sappho from Lesbos," Ἐννέα τὰς Μούσας φασίν τινες· ὡς ὀλιγώρως· | ἠνίδε καὶ Σαπφὼ Λεσβόθεν ἡ δεκάτη (IX.506). Translation by Paton 1917: 280–81. On the representation of Sappho, see generally Yatromanolakis 2007.

97 *BAPD* 204129 with a complete bibliography; *ARV*[2] 385.228, 1649; *Paralipomena* 367; *Beazley Addenda* 113; *Beazley Addenda*[2] 228; Wegner 1973: no. 37D; Paquette 1984: 177; Robertson 1992: 100; Yatromanolakis 2007: 74–75.

98 The two poets are identified through inscriptions located to the right of each of their heads: ΑΛΚΑΙΟΣ and ΣΑΦΟ. Yatromanolakis discusses other instances of painted inscriptions within the framework of a soundscape (2016, and especially 21–42). For a brief discussion of the inclusion of letters specifically within musical and sympotic scenes, see Lissarrague 1990b: 123–39.

FIVE

RESPONDING TO DIVINE MUSIC

The sounds of Pan's music could inspire embodied dance, Apollo's music could harmonize his mortal and divine audience, and the Muses' visual ambiguity allowed the goddesses to take on the bodies of human women throughout Athens and, in so doing, to promulgate their inspirational music throughout the ancient city. Images of Dionysos, by contrast, offer a very different type of divine music to the ancient viewer, one that is rooted in active and passive music-making, listening, and responding. In a paean composed by Philodamos of Skarpheia, Dionysos' journey to Mount Olympos is punctuated by the radical musical transformation he enacts on the Muses:

> [Ἔ]ν[θεν ἀ]π' ὀλβίας χθονὸς
> Θεσ[σαλίας] ἔκελσας ἄσ-
> τη τέμενός τ' Ὀλύμπι[ον
> Πιερ]ίαν τε κλειτάν
>   – Εὐοῖ ὧ ἰὸ Βάκχ', [ὦ ἰὲ Παι]αν –
> Μοῦσαι δ' αὐτίκα παρθένοι
> κ[ισσῶι] στεψάμεναι κύκλωι σε πᾶσαι
> μ[έλψαν] . . .
>
> From that blessed country you came
> to the cities of Thessaly,
> to the sacred domain of Olympos
> and famous Pieria
>   *– ehoi, o io Bakchos, o ie Paian–*

and straightaway did the chaste Muses
crown themselves with ivy;
[and] they all sang and danced around you . . .[1]

Having encountered Dionysos, the Muses immediately wind ivy vines around their heads and begin to sing and dance around the god. With these short lines of poetry, Philodamos communicates a profound statement about the god: Dionysos not only manipulates or incites the emotions and actions of his human followers, as we see in Euripides' *Bacchai*, but he can also generate similar reactions in the gods themselves by exposing them to the force of his presence. After all, he is even capable of transforming the Muses into maenads,[2] subverting their musical skills and inspiration into a different character of performance that is more reminiscent of that enacted by his followers. Despite the music and dance he has inspired, what is striking in this episode is that Dionysos does not participate in the celebration. Rather, he stands still in the center of the dance, as if observing the performance that is underway all around him.

The relationship Dionysos has with music and the ways he encourages others to engage with music differ significantly from the musicality associated with other divine musicians: unlike Apollo and the Muses, Dionysos rarely undertakes his own music-making. For a god who is regularly shown and described as being surrounded by music and dance, the paucity of scenes that depict the god actively playing an instrument is both striking and puzzling. Yet, on one of the few surviving scenes in which Dionysos does perform on an instrument, he displays a profound engagement with and absorption into his own musical performance (Fig. 5.1).[3] Painted in the center of a drinking cup, Dionysos stands slightly off center, wearing an elaborately decorated costume that focuses the viewer's attention on his performance. He holds a large *barbitos* by his side, where it seems almost to emerge from his body, filling the space in front of him with its undulating arms. Having just pulled the *plektron* across the instrument's strings, Dionysos tilts his head back and opens his mouth, adding the sounds of his singing to the deep, resonant sounds of the lyre. Although the *barbitos* is not a particularly loud instrument, the low timbre and wavering quality of its sound carries easily through the air. With this image, then, we are invited to imagine that instrumental music and vocal song fully infuse the space around the musician.

Accompanying Dionysos are two satyrs, each of whom dances energetically with arms raised and legs splayed, moving in tandem with the music's rhythm. Each also holds *krotala*, percussion instruments that would have added a distinct, rhythmic 'clack' to the music emerging from the stringed instrument. One of the satyrs holds up his *krotala* near the arms of the *barbitos*, visually linking the god's music with his own; in turn, Dionysos' *plektron* points directly at the dancing satyr, drawing out the connection between the two musicians.[4]

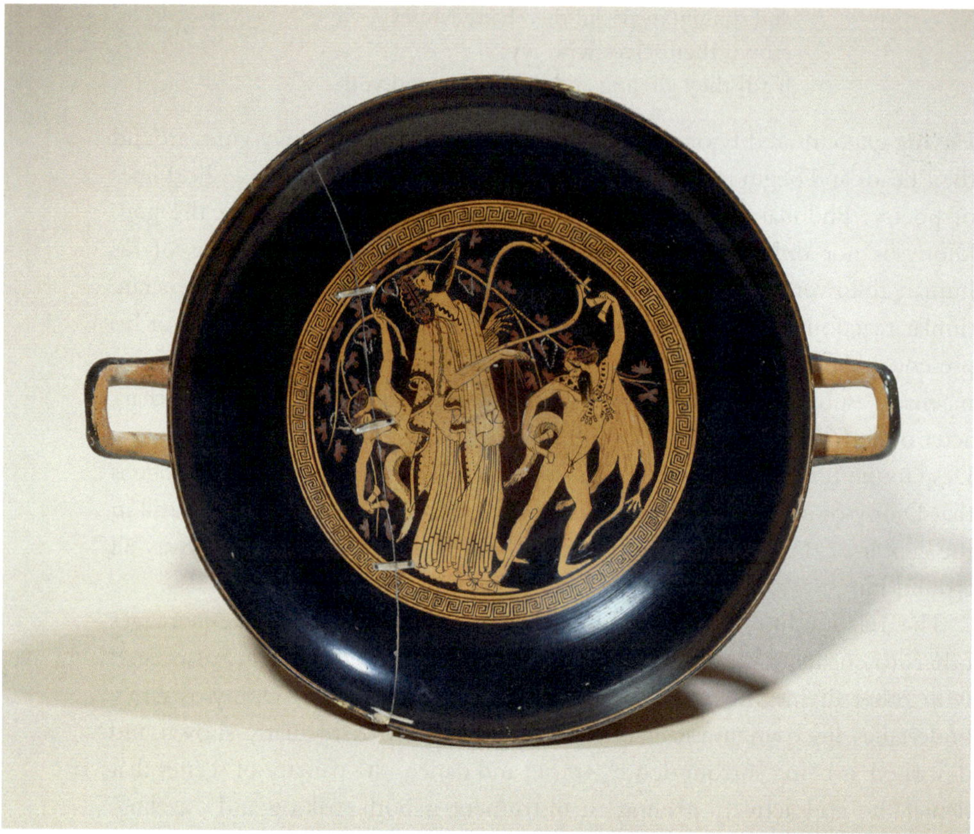

5.1. The Brygos Painter, *Dionysos Playing a Barbitos* (tondo), Attic red-figure *kylix*, ceramic, h. 12.1 cm, d. 30 cm, *c.* 480 BCE. Paris, Cabinet des Médailles, 576. © Bibliothèque nationale de France.

The other satyr, who also plays *krotala*, holds a large vine in his upstretched hand, where it is positioned in such a way that the ivy leaves gracefully bend and twist, enveloping each figure under its curvilinear arc. As Dionysos throws back his head in song, he leans into the vine, so that it appears, much as we have already seen with Apollo, that the god's music has caused the plant to flourish and surround the figures. The 'v' shape formed by the god's body and the outstretched body of the *barbitos* draws the viewer's attention to the point at which god and instrument intersect, visually connecting Dionysos with the resounding music, as well as with the profoundly moving effect his music could exert upon anyone who might listen to it.[5]

Yet, despite the passion Dionysos gives to his performance on this image and the close association in the literary record between Dionysos, song, dance, and theatrical performance, it is rare to find the god playing his own music. More typical, instead, is the representation of Dionysos as a remote observer, where he watches and listens to the performances undertaken by his followers, who play the *aulos*, various types of lyres, or *krotala* while they dance to the music they have created.[6] In considering the significance of Dionysos' relationship with music, we must thus reckon with the role he fills with respect to music-making generally, since he is routinely shown acting as the audience for a musical performance. Above all, within the framework of divine music, Dionysos acts not as the musician, but rather as the inspiration, or even the instigating force, behind the lively performance styles, energetic music, and elaborate acrobatic dances.

François Lissarrague addresses this puzzling absence of a musical Dionysos, noting that although Dionysos rarely picks up an instrument, the satyrs who accompany him are shown to be extremely competent musicians and dancers whose performances indicate the importance of music for Dionysos.[7] In her work on Dionysos' music-making, Sheramy Bundrick explores how the images of Dionysos might evoke an *ēthos* specific to the god, focusing in particular on the ecstatic elements of the god's worship.[8] More broadly, representations of Dionysos and his revels have received a great deal of attention, particularly with respect to how the scenes are constructed, what their relationship is to mythic narratives, and in what contexts the vases were seen and used.[9] With each of these approaches, by incorporating Dionysian myth and ritual into the analyses, the scenes are convincingly positioned within their ancient context to draw out the multivalent interpretations the images offered their viewers.[10] Another important facet of Dionysian imagery is the inclusion of satyrs; these figures too have been much studied, and important conclusions have been advanced concerning their relationship with mythological narratives, rituals for Dionysos, and satyr plays.[11]

In this chapter, I build upon these earlier studies in order to explore Dionysos' specific relationship with music, not least since it is so distinct among the type of music performed by the other gods. Working between the god's representation in musical scenes, his visual association with satyr and maenad musicians and dancers, and the spaces in which ancient viewers would have most probably encountered the vase-paintings, I examine how Dionysos acts in the presence of music, how he responds to the musicians and dancers, and how he himself eventually comes to participate in the musical and danced performance that he has inspired. I begin with scenes in which Dionysos stands or sits still while another musician, typically a satyr, plays music for him, arguing that though the god is unmoving, he has nevertheless inspired his followers' musical activities. Dionysos' influence becomes most obvious in those scenes which display otherwise transgressive behavior, whether it is a satyr who wears the clothing of a citizen while he plays a *kithara*, or maenads who dance while they rip apart Pentheus. He is also able to determine how his fellow gods react, often transforming their actions into the energetic and wild musical modality that characterizes the music of Dionysos' followers. I end by considering those scenes where Dionysos himself begins to respond physically to the music and dance exhibited by his followers, arguing that Dionysos, as a dancer, thus both moves his followers to music and is himself moved by the music he has inspired in them.

DIVINE MUSICAL INSPIRATION

Dionysos is often shown as a passive spectator for the music and dance undertaken by his satyrs and maenads.[12] He is thus both the god who watches over the theatrical performances conducted for him,[13] as well as the god who watches over the power dynamics in symposia, where the intoxicated participants look at others performing ecstatically around them. We see this particular conception of Dionysos as an observer on a black-figure storage vessel by the Euphiletos Painter (Fig. 5.2).[14] Here, Dionysos sits in the center of the scene, gazing intently at his companions while he holds a drinking cup, a *kantharos*, in one hand and a grape vine in the other. Positioned in front and behind the god are two satyrs, one of whom plays the *aulos* while the other plays a *barbitos*.[15] Each kneels before the god, their limbs overlapping with his, while their instruments also intersect with his body. The series of overlapping and touching forms underscores the fundamental connection that exists between musician and audience, between the creation of music and the effect that it may have both on the individual who created it and on those who listen to it. Layered behind the instruments are the tendrils of grape vines and even bunches of grapes, making it clear for whom this musical performance is intended.

The relationship between the satyr musicians and the god as audience is further deepened by the music's clear directionality: not only do the satyrs perform for the god, but their instruments are each directed toward Dionysos, projecting the sounds of their music to him, the sole spectator of their performance. On the god's right, one of the satyr's *auloi* is directed to Dionysos' face, while the other points to his chest, hinting at the melody's ability to affect its audience, both physically and emotionally.[16] Behind the god, the satyr's *barbitos* is pointed upwards, intersecting with the god's back as it points again to Dionysos' head. The god is thus shown being serenaded with the low, resonant sounds of the *barbitos* and the continuous piped notes emerging from the *aulos*, and, in turn, as he leans toward the source of music and the grape vine twists and turns across the scene, both god and plant appear to respond to the music's influence.

Yet this representation, in which Dionysos is shown enjoying and responding to the satyrs' music, is complicated by the question of musical authority. Is the viewer meant to understand the satyrs as musically autonomous, deciding to perform for the god in their own personal musical style and by their own decision? Or did Dionysos, as the god of wine, the theater, and wild

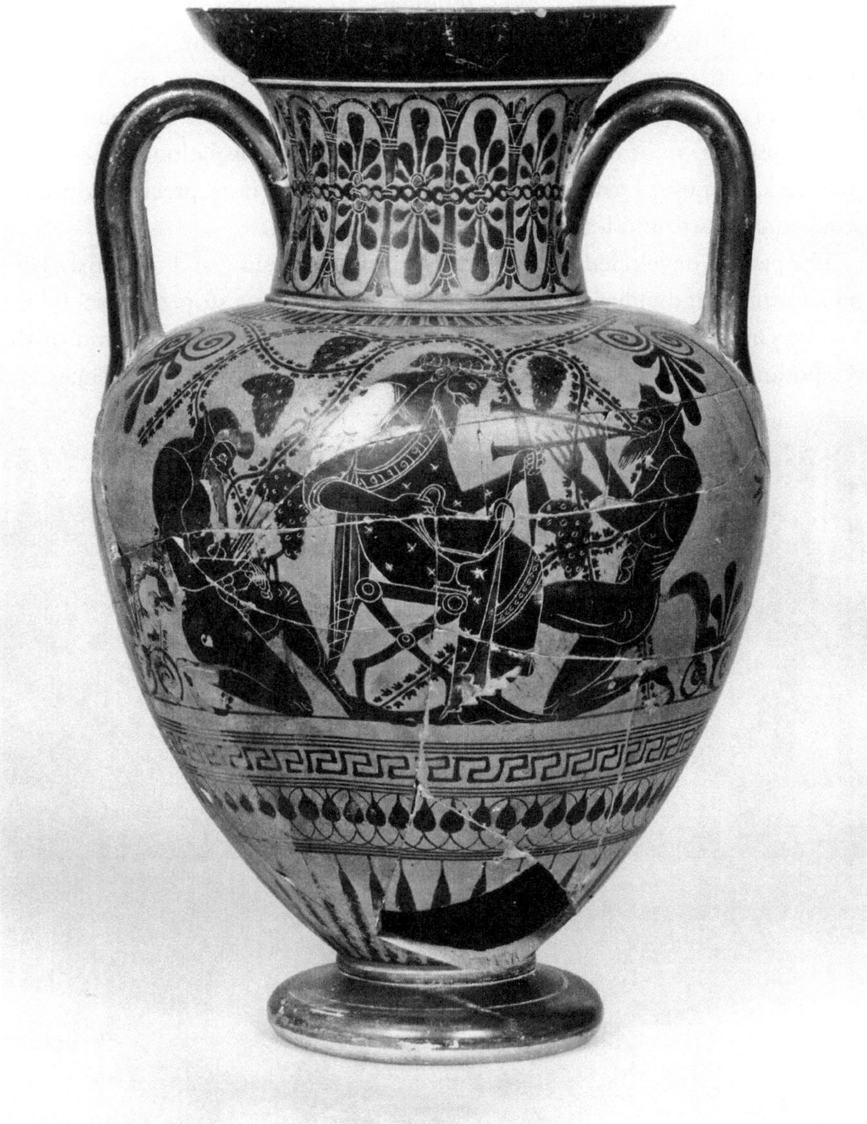

5.2. The Euphiletos Painter, *Dionysos Seated on a Stool, Listening to the Satyrs' Musical Performance* (side A), Attic black-figure neck *amphora*, ceramic, h. 39.7 cm, *c.* 520–510 BCE. Copenhagen, Thorvaldsen's Museum, H572. Photographer: Lennart Larsen. © Thorvaldsen's Museum. Creative Commons CCO.

revels, prompt their musical performance through his own divine vitality? Could the god be at once a spectator for a performance and yet also be responsible for having inspired that performance?

The sheer number of images in which Dionysos remains stationary while other figures play music and dance around him suggests that he should be understood as being in some way responsible for prompting the revel. Although the most obvious source of inspiration may be the group's consumption of wine, so that the god's followers are intoxicated with Dionysos' presence and thus act in such a way that is pleasing to him, it still does not explain the affective distance the god displays toward the music that surrounds him. Moreover, merely attributing the musical activities of his followers to their consumption of wine does not offer a satisfying explanation for Dionysos' own lack of musical activity, nor does it make clear how precisely drinking wine correlates to musical activity, beyond all others.

The parallel developed between the similar effect music and wine may have on a group of individuals is particularly highlighted on a storage vessel by the Mastos Group and the Affecter (Figs. 5.3 and 5.4).[17] Here, the world of the symposium is brought together with wine, viniculture, music, dance, and

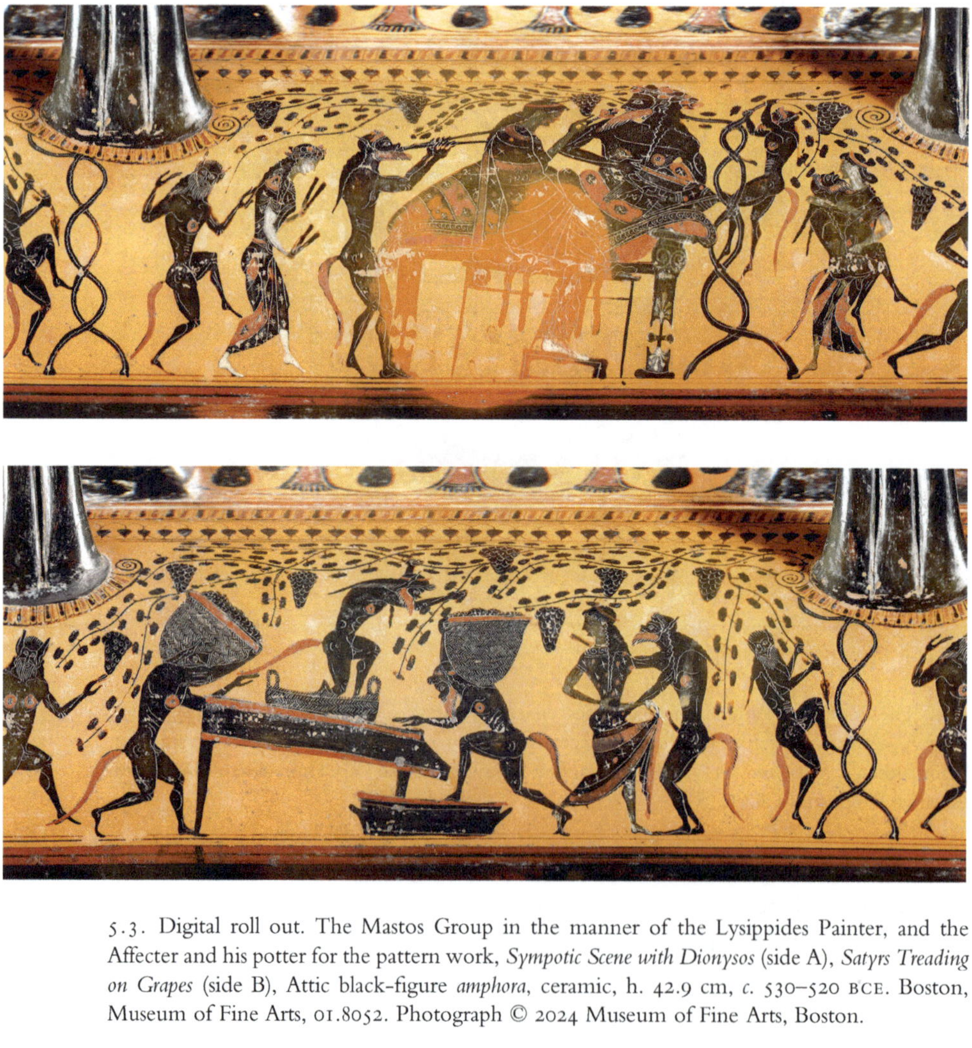

5.3. Digital roll out. The Mastos Group in the manner of the Lysippides Painter, and the Affecter and his potter for the pattern work, *Sympotic Scene with Dionysos* (side A), *Satyrs Treading on Grapes* (side B), Attic black-figure *amphora*, ceramic, h. 42.9 cm, *c.* 530–520 BCE. Boston, Museum of Fine Arts, 01.8052. Photograph © 2024 Museum of Fine Arts, Boston.

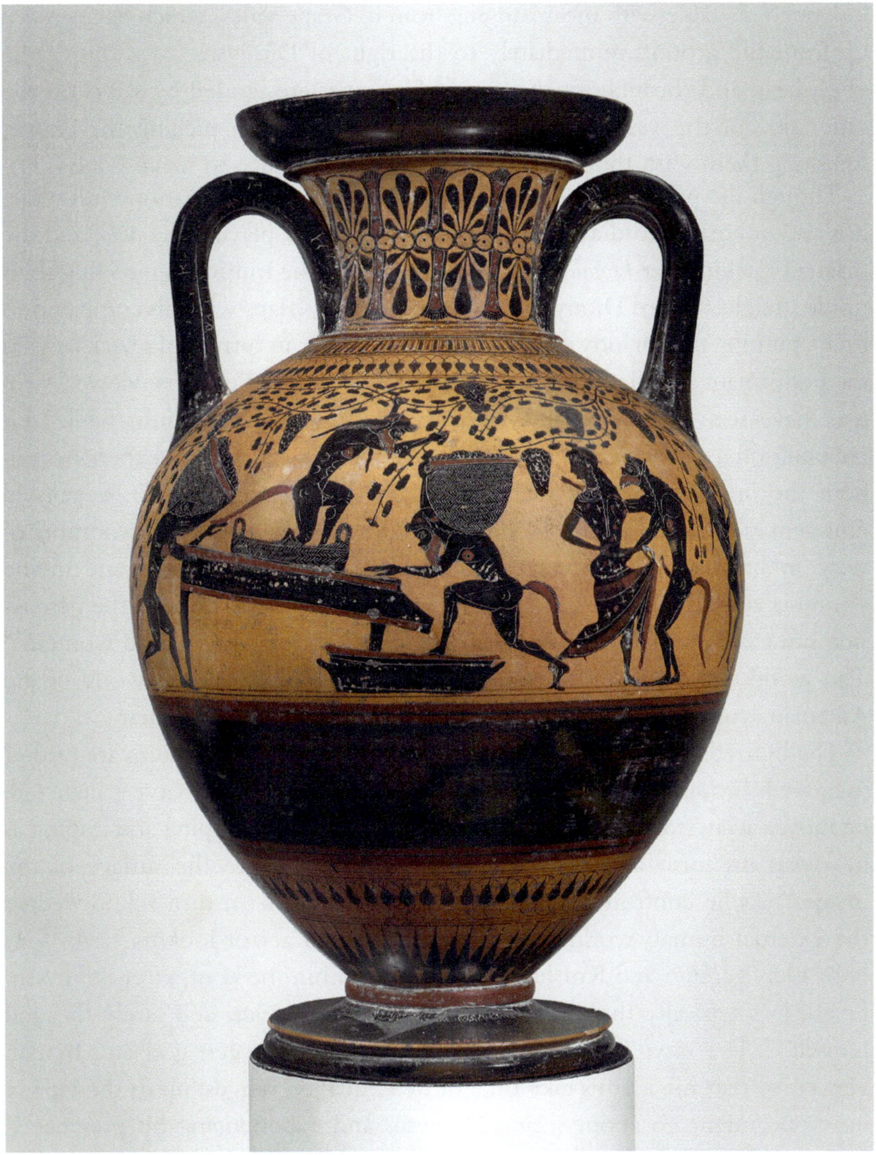

5.4. The Mastos Group in the manner of the Lysippides Painter, and the Affecter and his potter for the pattern work, *Satyrs Treading on Grapes* (side B), Attic black-figure *amphora*, ceramic, h. 42.9 cm, *c.* 530–520 BCE. Boston, Museum of Fine Arts, 01.8052. Photograph © 2024 Museum of Fine Arts, Boston.

ecstatic revels. Dionysos once again is depicted as a spectator, removed from the main action of the scene; at the same time, his large size within the composition suggests that he is responsible for instigating all the movement in the scene by instilling his erratic and chaotic vitality in the bodies of the satyrs and maenads.[18] He reclines, bare-chested, on a couch, accompanied by a female figure. He holds a cup delicately by one handle, while set up in front of his couch is a table with meat hanging from it. Grape vines, which have grown up from the ground immediately to the right of Dionysos, twist above the god's head and throughout the scene. The vines are tended by satyrs on the other side of the vase, where they are kept busy with picking the grapes, squishing them with their feet, and collecting their juice to make wine.

Though the painted scene clearly explores Dionysos' association with wine, it is also important to draw our attention to the satyr playing the *aulos* and the maenad clacking her *krotala*. Once again, we find the musicians directing their music straight toward Dionysos: the satyr's *aulos* overlaps with his companion's body, pushing the melody past her to the god, who, in turn, looks back toward the performance while he reclines on his couch. For the external viewer, who may have seen this vessel in a similarly music-filled symposium while also reclining on a couch with his companions, the parallel sensory experiences in both the image and the actual symposium could have blurred the painted representation with reality. Here, in addition to the mimetic invocation of wine in human and divine spaces, the sounds of both human and divine symposia could potentially include the music of the *aulos* and lyre, the percussion noise of *krotala*, and the sounds and sights of dancing men and women.[19] The world depicted on the vase could thus easily slip into the world of the Athenian symposium, creating a shared sensoryscape between them.[20]

The blurred boundaries between image and external symposium are further suggested through the particular manner in which a dancing satyr is depicted: he moves away from Dionysos toward the grape vines, hopping and leaping as he twists his torso and head, so that they directly face the surface of the image.[21] As he confronts the viewer with his stare, he in turn acknowledges the external human world through the reciprocal act of looking back.[22] As both Isler-Kerényi and Korshak have noted, within the context of Dionysian revels, it is typically the satyr who addresses the viewer, and rarely the god himself.[23] The satyr thus acts as an intermediary between god and human viewer, so that his actions take on a didactic quality, suggesting to the viewer how one might go about seeing Dionysos and experiencing his presence.[24] In this moment of connected and interlocked gazes between satyr and man, wherein both hear, see, and even taste the same things, Dionysos' presence flows from image to human world, filling the symposium and the guests with his presence and inviting them to join in his musical and danced celebration.

The relative distance Dionysos exhibits with respect to the musical activities of his followers is particularly pronounced on a mixing bowl attributed to Lydos. Here, the return of Hephaistos to Mount Olympos is depicted within a more general Dionysian revel,[25] in which satyrs and maenads play music, dance, and drink (Fig. 5.5).[26] On one side, Hephaistos sits atop a donkey, while satyrs and maenads dance energetically alongside with raised arms and bent knees. The satyrs also hold out bunches of grapes and one bears a wineskin slung over his

(A) (B)

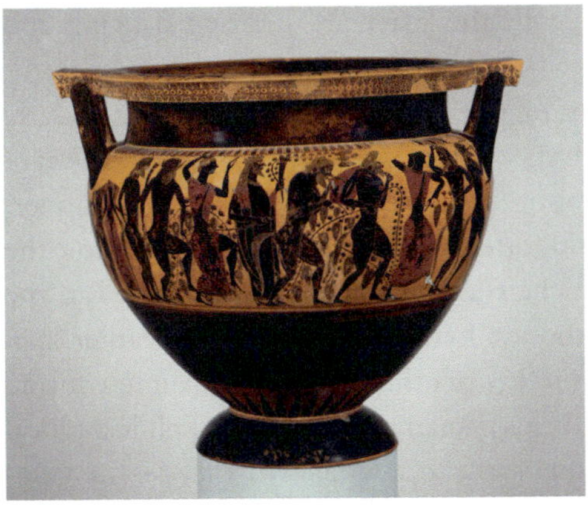

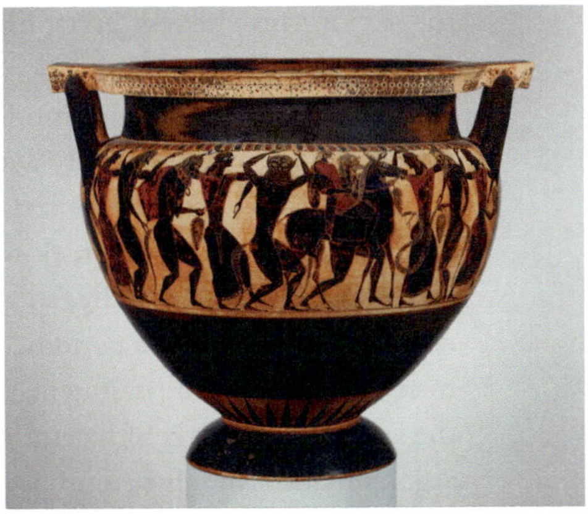

5.5. Lydos, *Dionysian Revel* (side A), the *Return of Hephaistos* (side B), Attic black-figure *kratēr*, ceramic, h. 56.4 cm, *c.* 550 BCE. New York, Metropolitan Museum of Art, 31.11.11. Fletcher Fund, 1931. Creative Commons CCO.

back, reinforcing the effect that Dionysos has had on their movements. The source of music to which the figures dance may be found on the opposite side, where a satyr, perhaps leading the procession as he walks to the right, plays the *aulos*. Satyrs and maenads follow, each enthusiastically dancing with arms and legs raised to the energetic and lively music they hear.

Dionysos, however, is still amidst the chaos; his only action is to raise his drinking horn. He stands in the center of the image, an unmoving figure juxtaposed against the frenetic movement of the satyrs' and maenads' danced procession. Yet despite his immobility, visually he functions as the stable center around which all the other action occurs, so that his stillness anchors the satyrs' and maenads' movements within a clearly defined space. The image also suggests that the grape vine, which grows and flourishes throughout the image, emerges from the god's drinking horn and stretches out across the surface of the vase. As the vine expands, it moves behind and around the dancing figures, drawing in and uniting the figures under the influence of Dionysos and the music he has inspired.

Many of the visual features in this image are relatively common in scenes of Dionysian revels, which are shown filled with wine, eroticism, and ecstatic dance. However, Dionysos' inaction within the otherwise active scene remains puzzling. Indeed, the unmoving quality inherent to Dionysos' depiction in these images is so pronounced that it has been often remarked upon, with Alan Shapiro, in particular, noting that "only Dionysos himself is still, unmoved by the music and dance around him."[27] This is very much the description of the god that we find in Euripides' *Bacchai*, where the chorus, during the *parodos*, offers the audience an elaborate picture of the effect the god's presence has on them, claiming that αὐτικα γᾶ πᾶσα χορεύσει, "all the land shall dance" (114) when he is nearby. Indeed, throughout the tragedy Dionysos stands apart from the action, his stillness juxtaposed with the maenads' frenzied dancing and violence.

One explanation for this mode of representation may find its roots in early Greek philosophy, specifically with respect to ideas concerning the formation of the cosmos that were advanced among the Presocratics. These philosophers traveled throughout the Greek world, often moving between Asia Minor, the Greek mainland, and Sicily, so that their ideas were broadly discussed in the middle and late Archaic periods. Although Lydos' vase was created earlier than many of our surviving fragments, a number of other scenes were painted during the late sixth and early fifth centuries, a particularly vibrant time of philosophical argumentation and discussion. It is impossible to ascertain whether certain vase-painters were in touch with the work of contemporaneous philosophers, but we may nevertheless see in the surviving representations certain visual features or structures of thought and conception of the world that also appear in Presocratic thinking and Athenian tragedy.[28] Specifically, I want to draw attention to one line of thought that argues for an unmoving force that determines all action within the cosmos. Anticipating Aristotle's theory of the prime mover, we find in a number of surviving fragments the articulation of a similar idea. Xenophanes, for instance, argues that a single god "sees as a whole, thinks as a whole, and hears as a whole"[29] and that it is "without effort [that] he shakes all things by the thought of his mind... He always remains in one place, without moving not at all."[30] We may also see in Aeschylus' *Suppliants* a similar sentiment when the chorus sings that "everything gods do is done without toil: | he sits still (ἥμενος), and nevertheless somehow | carries out his will (ἐξέπραξεν) directly | from his holy abode."[31] Building upon Richard Seaford's argument that Aeschylus incorporated aspects of Presocratic philosophy in his dramas,[32] I suggest that the particular way in which Dionysos is depicted in these scenes may draw from similar ideas that were circulating among the Athenian elite at the time. If considered within the conception of a divine force who is capable of moving those around him with only his mind, the unmoveability that Dionysos exhibits in the scene painted by the Mastos Group and the Affecter (Figs. 5.3 and 5.4), for instance, gains more clarity. Here, Dionysos is not merely a passive spectator but, rather, he sits still and generates the movement around him, so that satyrs diligently work at making wine, others play the *aulos*, and still others dance with maenads. Images of Dionysos thus invite us to reflect on the relationship between the musician's music and the listening audience, where it is not simply that one affects the other, but rather, under the watchful eye of Dionysos, it is the interaction and blending of the two groups that makes these images of performance so powerful. The figure of Dionysos, as he is shown in the images, thus creates the world around him in a way that both reflects those aspects which are particularly associated with him in cult and that offers this world to all those who encounter it. It is within this expanded understanding of Dionysos' inactive action that the satyr depicted under the handle becomes particularly crucial. Depicted with a frontal face, he confronts the viewers in an act of mutual recognition, inviting them to enter the scene and to feel the force of Dionysos working upon them, so that they too may join in the revel.

Moreover, visual representations of a Dionysian world of music would have been layered upon the sights and sounds of actual drinking and reveling that may have occurred in the same space where the majority of vases were designed to have been used. Just as the satyrs and maenads are depicted consuming wine, feeling its effect in their bodies, playing or listening to music, and dancing to its rhythm, so too within the space of the symposium would the male guests and female entertainers have engaged in similar activities.[33] Although the visual continuum between image and symposium has been much discussed,[34] it is also worth drawing attention to the effect that the visual suggestion of ecstatic music inspired by the god of wine would have played within the dynamic established among symposiast and image.[35] If we look again at the storage vessel by the Mastos Group and the Affecter (Figs. 5.3 and 5.4), we can imagine that a symposiast would have not only encountered the god of wine as he himself reclined, consumed wine, and felt its effect upon his body, but he would also have seen a satyr playing the *aulos* while other satyrs and maenads danced in response to the music. Within the physical space of the symposium, where music would also have been performed on the lyre or the *aulos* and where one's intoxication would have steadily increased throughout the evening,[36] the ambiguity between the visual representation and one's haptic and auditory experience of the symposium could have blurred and fused together, so that there may have been little distinction perceived between the divine and mythical realm depicted on the vase and the actual space in which the Archaic symposium took place.

CHALLENGING ORDER

I have argued that Dionysos is depicted in these scenes in a way that is reminiscent of the Presocratic conception of cosmic movement and stability, yet he is also capable of acting upon and eliciting change in those who surround him. The transformative effect he has upon his followers varies dramatically, in one instance invoking a harmony otherwise associated with Apollo while, in another, a chaotic revel. Indeed, the vast range of musical responses Dionysos offers recalls in many ways the cosmic movement between the forces of Love and Strife that Empedokles describes: just as the elements in the cosmos mix and unmix according to the waxing and waning influences of Love and Strife, so too we can think of the unmoving influence that Dionysos

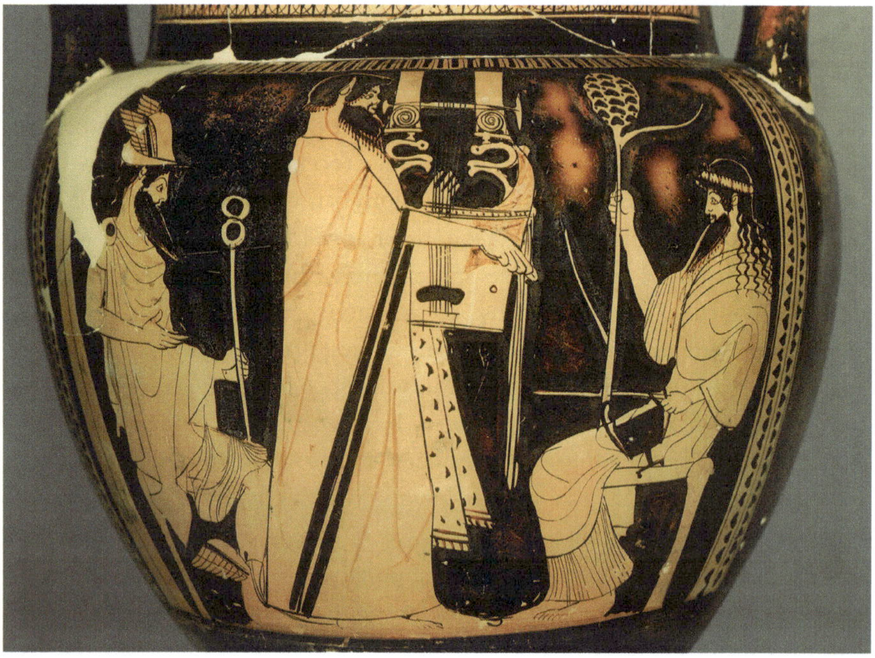

5.6. Circle of the Pan Painter, *Music Concert* (side A), Attic red-figure column *kratēr*, ceramic, h. 39.7 cm, *c.* 460 BCE. Ferrara, Museo Nazionale di Spina, 4110. © akg-images/André Held.

exerts at times encouraging a harmonious musical mode, while at other times it offers a devolving, chaotic music that tears apart social fabric.[37]

A red-figure mixing bowl by an artist in the circle of the Pan Painter explores this aspect of Dionysos' influence within the context of a musical performance, in which a satyr, possibly Silenos, plays his instrument for Hermes and Dionysos (Fig. 5.6).[38] The two gods sit on opposite sides of the image, each holding their typical iconographic attributes: Hermes with his *kērykeion*, winged sandals, and hat, and Dionysos with his *thyrsos* and drinking cup depicted in silhouette. The location of their encounter is hinted at by a column that rises behind Hermes, suggesting that they sit in sacred space, perhaps a sanctuary or even Mount Olympos.[39] Between them stands the object of their attention: Silenos, who plays an enormous concert *kithara* while he, surprisingly, wears a full-length *chitōn* and *himation*, the costume of an agonistic performer.[40] The instrument, over life-size, is beautifully adorned with a long piece of decorated cloth hanging from its body. Its intricately carved arms extend directly upwards as Silenos plucks the strings with his *plektron*. Were it not for his distinct facial appearance, the satyr could almost have been identified as Apollo himself, especially given the absence of his satyr tail, the choice of clothing that is typically worn only by Apollo or a human *kitharoidos*, the large instrument, and the composition's balanced symmetry.[41] Although Apollo is typically associated with this type of music, Dionysos' prominent placement in the scene, directly facing the musician, suggests that he has inspired the satyr to adopt a new musicality through his own proximity to the musician. The image almost suggests that through the changed experience of playing a different kind of music, one more akin to performances during religious festivals, the satyr could even become a skilled musician capable of creating music that might instill a musical and social harmony in a similar way to Apollo's performances.

The image on the other side of the mixing bowl further underscores Dionysos' connection with the urban, civic life of Athenian citizens. In this scene, three young, beardless Athenian men gather together, each dressed as a citizen with long drapery while holding a walking stick. Dionysos' sphere of influence, and the specific manner of his influence, is shown not simply as a negative reversal of Apolline harmony, that is, a Nietzschean duality of wild otherness in the face of urbane civility, but rather the image suggests that the god plays a fundamental role in the rearing and nurturing of the Athenian youth. It is above all within the context of the theater, where musical competitions and dramatic performances were undertaken, that Dionysos' involvement in the city is especially pronounced.[42] During the City Dionysia, dithyrambs were performed by ten choruses of fifty men (*andres*) and ten choruses of fifty boys (*paides*); competing on the opening day of the contests, citizens pitted their musical, vocal, and danced performances against each other.[43] Dithyrambic choruses thus especially highlighted Dionysos' significance for the ritual and civic life of Athens, when he became symbolically responsible for the continual performance of Athenian identity and belonging.[44] Beyond the importance of the theater and its associated Dionysian rituals for promoting civic and political ideology, Eric Csapo, Barbara Kowalzig, Peter Wilson, and Salvatore Lavecchia have each shown that the dithyramb, which originated as a ritual hymn for Dionysos, could be further conceived as a musical manifestation of Dionysos' divine presence.[45] The myths conveyed through these songs often seem to have narrated the story of Dionysos' birth; the surviving fragments of Pindar's second dithyramb convey this myth through the use of powerful language that evokes the overwhelming multisensory experience of Dionysos' presence.[46] Not only is his birth accompanied by music, whether the buzzing of tambourines or the ringing of castanets (9–10), but the Naiads also groan loudly as they shriek ecstatically (12–13). Other fragments also use evocative language to play with the word dithyramb, in order to establish Dithyrambos as another name for Dionysos.[47] Within the City Dionysia, when dithyrambs were performed by the citizens of Athens, the choruses repeatedly invoked Dionysos through his name Dithyrambos. Each performance, therefore, sang Dionysos into a musical epiphany, so that he was made manifest both through the collective singing by the choruses and through the shared audience experience of hearing and feeling his presence.[48]

(A)

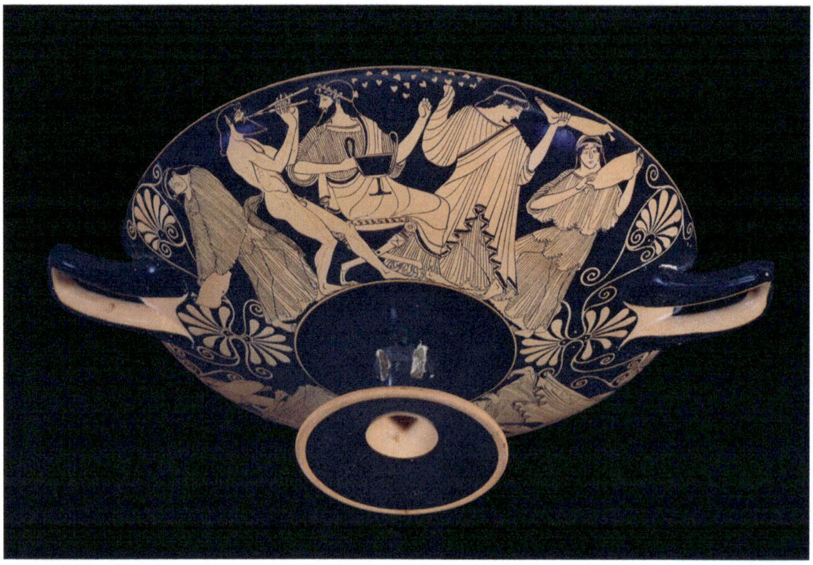

(B)

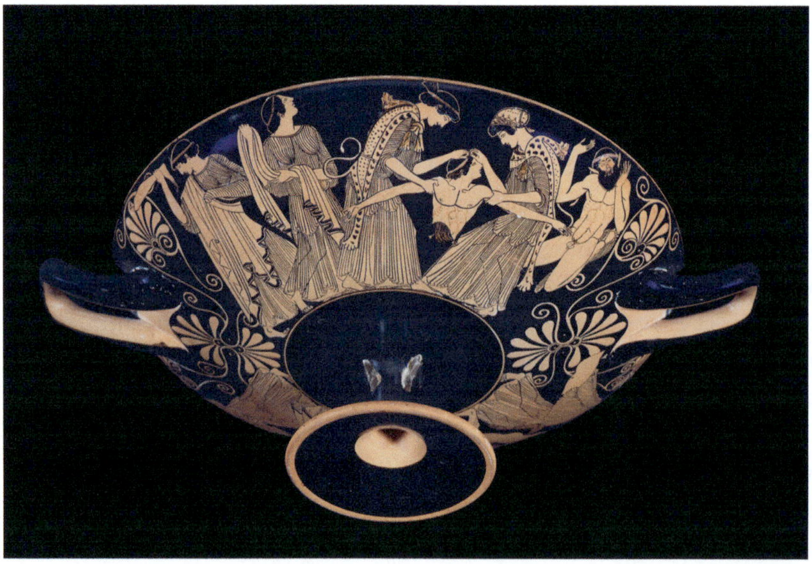

5.7. Douris, *Death of Pentheus* (exterior), Attic red-figure *kylix*, ceramic, h. 12.7 cm, c. 480 BCE. Fort Worth, Kimbell Art Museum, AP 2000.02. © Kimbell Art Museum, Fort Worth, Texas.

Dionysos was not always depicted, however, as a god who fostered civic unity through his musical influence. Instead, a cup by Douris points to the disastrous consequences that could arise from being moved by Dionysos (Fig. 5.7).[49] As we have seen before, here again Dionysos is positioned as a stable center for the music and chaos that swirls around him. He sits on a chair holding his drinking cup, his elaborate drapery falling around his body as he turns to look back at a satyr, who plays the *aulos* behind him. The satyr's arms and legs overlap with Dionysos' body, while the instrument almost extends to touch the god's face; performer and audience, mover and moved, are thus shown to be inextricably connected. As Dionysos sedately listens to the music, he betrays little reaction to the performance other than to hold up his ivy vine, which begins to grow up and over the maenads' and satyr's heads. The other figures in the scene powerfully respond to Dionysos' presence and the music he has inspired: maenads dance expansively around the satyr musician and the god, their drapery flowing out behind them as they move almost frantically to the music. Each maenad, however, does more than simply dance: she also holds a dismembered body part. The maenad directly to the right of Dionysos brandishes a foot and lower leg above her head. The limb's placement and the maenad's actions mimic those of Dionysos, who similarly raises his ivy vine above his head, so that the maenad responds to the satyr's music in a manner determined by the god's own reaction. Two other maenads dance at the far left and right, each holding a thigh, one extending it behind her as she dances forward and the other lifting it to her face, cradling it as though it were a prized possession. Both maenads, consumed with their dance, direct their faces toward the external viewer, confronting their audience with their ecstatic state and demanding that the viewer feel the presence of the *aulos* music and Dionysos' reaction to it, and then join them in their revel.

The potentially dangerous consequences of coming into contact with Dionysos are made clear throughout the scene, both in the threat of death on this side of the vessel, where the maenads have torn their victim apart, and even more dramatically on the other side, where two maenads hold the torso of a man, his bottom half already gone as they prepare to tear off his arms and head.[50] Around the image's dramatic center, two more maenads dance, one holding a foot and leg while the other swings her drapery around, both responding to the music with their macabre dance. A lone satyr appears on the right, hopping on one leg while he throws up his arms, dancing to the *aulos* music. He looks out through the surface of the image with his mouth ajar, seemingly frightened of the maenads' actions that unfold beside him. Although the scene probably depicts the death of Pentheus, it does so in a markedly different manner from Euripides' *Bacchai*. Instead of simply suggesting that the female figures' actions are divinely inspired in response to Pentheus' hubris against Dionysos, the image painted onto the vase instead anchors Dionysos' agency in the music he inspires, focalizing the maenads' ecstatic state in the particular kind of music that they hear. It is precisely Dionysos' ability to instill this powerful and transformative musicality in those near him that this scene explores, suggesting that the god's presence is made visible through the reactions of his followers, who here play music and dance with revelrous – and violent – abandon.

Similarly, a mixing bowl by the Curti Painter highlights the role of music in one's experience of Dionysos and the dangers associated with slighting the god (Fig. 5.8).[51] Despite the murderous scene on one side, Dionysos is once again

(A) (B)

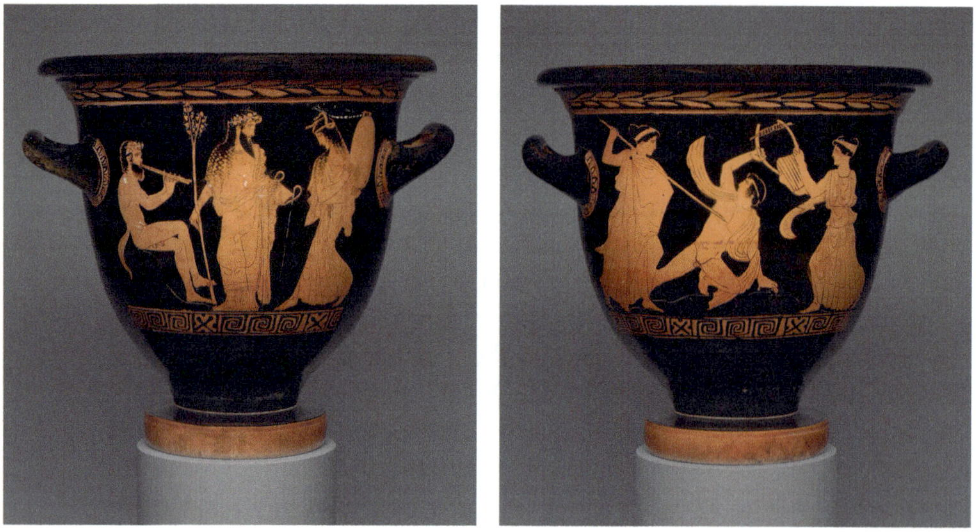

5.8. The Curti Painter, *Dionysos with Satyr and Maenad* (side A), *Death of Orpheus* (side B), Attic red-figure bell *kratēr*, ceramic, h. 30 cm, *c.* 440–430 BCE. Cambridge, MA, Harvard Art Museums/Arthur M. Sackler Museum, Bequest of David M. Robinson, 1960.343. Photo © President and Fellows of Harvard College.

presented here as a spectator to his followers' musical performance, much as he is later described in Euripides' *Bacchai*. He listens to a satyr playing the *aulos* while he watches a maenad dancing and playing the tambourine. Prompted by the maenad's dance, we are invited to imagine the sounds of the continuous music emitted by the *aulos*, punctuated by the regular beating of the tambourine. Amplifying the maenad's response to the music are the two snakes wrapped around her head, which seem to sway together with her, so that both animal and woman move together to the music. As he observes the performance, Dionysos holds up a staff of ivy. The vertical line it creates draws the viewer's eye up to the vegetation that forms the upper border of the image. The decorative plant wraps around the vase, and its regular, rhythmic progression, upheld by the beating percussion instrument, draws the eye around to the other side of the vase. This lateral movement is further facilitated by the lack of framing device on the sides of the scene, so that both images could be understood as occupying a continuous place in the visual field. The reverse side depicts a man, most likely Orpheus, who is falling down, lyre flung above his head.[52] Two women attack him, one pulling at his lyre and the other stabbing him with a spear.[53]

The continuity of the visual field from one side to the other makes it possible for us to speculate that the women who accompany Orpheus have been affected by Dionysos' presence because they can hear the music that the satyr and the maenad perform. Although the musical performance is clearly intended for Dionysos, the boundless image allows the sound of the music to spread around the surface of the vase, infusing both sides with the continuous buzzing sound

(A)

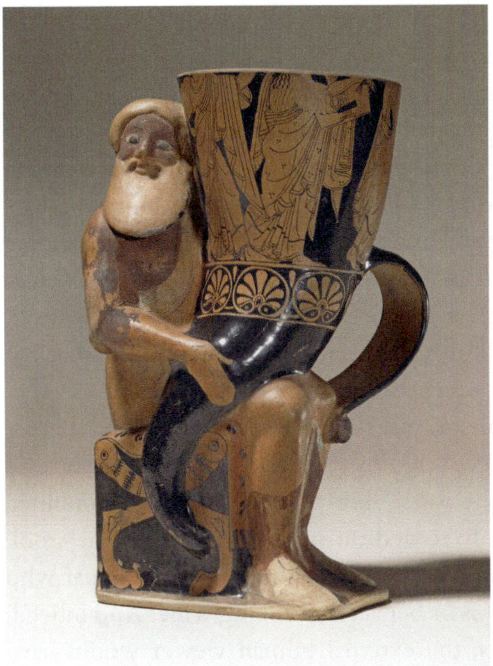

(B)

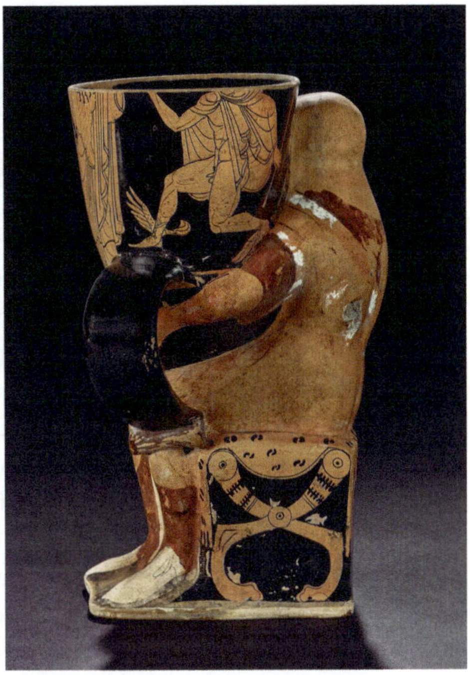

5.9. In the manner of the Kachrylion Potter, *Dionysos Holding a Rhyton, on which Apollo Plays His Kithara while Aphrodite, Artemis, and Hermes Dance*, Attic red-figure figurine and *rhyton*, ceramic, h. 24.13 cm, *c.* 500–480 BCE. London, British Museum, 1873,0820.267 (E785). © The Trustees of the British Museum.

from the *aulos* and percussive beat from the tambourine. In this way, Dionysos' presence moves easily around the vessel, drawing in the women on the reverse into his unpredictable and chaotic world through the hypnotic and rhythmic quality of the music. And, having been thus captivated by Dionysos, the women are shown to be fully under the influence of the god, and in this state of ecstasy, they attack Orpheus, the mortal musician of great renown.

Dionysos' ability to affect the actions of his companions is a recurring theme throughout the textual accounts, as we may see in Euripides' *Bacchai*, where Dionysos dramatically determines the actions of those who surround him. But it is also a prevalent mode of representing the god: not only is he shown to be capable of affecting both men and women, as well as his satyr and maenad followers but, like Apollo, he also can affect the *rhythmoi* of his fellow gods. A particularly evocative object, a drinking horn, or *rhyton*, held by a three-dimensional figurine, explores this relationship between Dionysos and the other gods (Fig. 5.9).[54] On the vase, the gods dance together in a procession. To the right of the handle, closest to the seated figure's left shoulder, is Hermes, who strides energetically forward.[55] His *chlamys* billows out behind him while the wings on his sandals stretch forward, as if indicating the speed with which he is travelling. He holds out his *kērykeion* behind him, directing the viewer's gaze past the handle, around the side of the vessel as if to indicate the group's unified movements around the surface of the vase. Immediately adjacent to the handle on the other side is Artemis, who, unusually, plays the *krotala* as she dances to the right, adding a rhythmic clacking sound to the gods' dance.[56] She follows her brother Apollo, who wears a decorated *himation* reminiscent of the costume worn by mortal *kithara* players. He also strides energetically forward, walking in rhythm to the music that he plays on his large *kithara*, which he angles dramatically back toward his face while he pulls the *plektron* across the strings, providing the music for the lively dance.[57] In front of Apollo dances Aphrodite, who holds a small swan, depicted in silhouette, in her right hand. As she moves forward, across the space of the handle, she lifts her left hand and seems to look back at Apollo, the source of the music to which she moves.

Holding the *rhyton* is a three-dimensional figure of the bearded and mature Dionysos, who sits on a low stool covered by a panther skin as he wraps his hands around the lower body of the vase.[58] His protective gesture combined with the stability of his form, firmly rooted on the square base of the stool, creates the impression that the god balances the vase for the individual who might fill it with wine, facilitating his or her act of drinking wine. And indeed, in consuming the vessel's contents, the external human viewer would have been introduced into a world in which Dionysos' presence has completely determined the actions of his companions. In this way, the viewer, or rather the user of this vessel, becomes a fellow participant in the gods' revel. Although wine is the means by which Dionysos entices the human viewer into his revel here, the vase suggests that it is through music that the divine participants maintain their bond with each other, dancing as a collective group, asserting through their movements their devotion to Dionysos. The god's power over his divine companions has been so effective that even Apollo's otherwise restrained, harmonious, and balanced musicality has been transformed into an energetic performance, accompanied by an equally frenetic divine revel, which almost appears to risk unsettling the balance of the cup. The other gods on the vase also exhibit uncharacteristic behavior. Artemis now appears more akin to a maenad, clacking her *krotala* and dancing energetically to the rhythmic and fast-paced music. Aphrodite, with her bird, is an unexpected companion to this revel, perhaps hinting at the erotic overtones present in the symposium where this vessel could have been used or, at the very least, could have been seen. Within the symposium, two activities associated with Dionysos, that is, music-making and drinking, are performed and consumed by the symposiasts, whether through listening to the music performed by the hired entertainers or taking up the *aulos* or lyre themselves, or by passing around the *rhyton*, each guest drinking from it. The presence of Dionysos is thus taken into the body of each symposiast, so that he might feel the disruptive nature of the god in the wine that he consumes, disorienting his senses, or in the music that he listens to, filling his mind with its music. In this way,

(A)

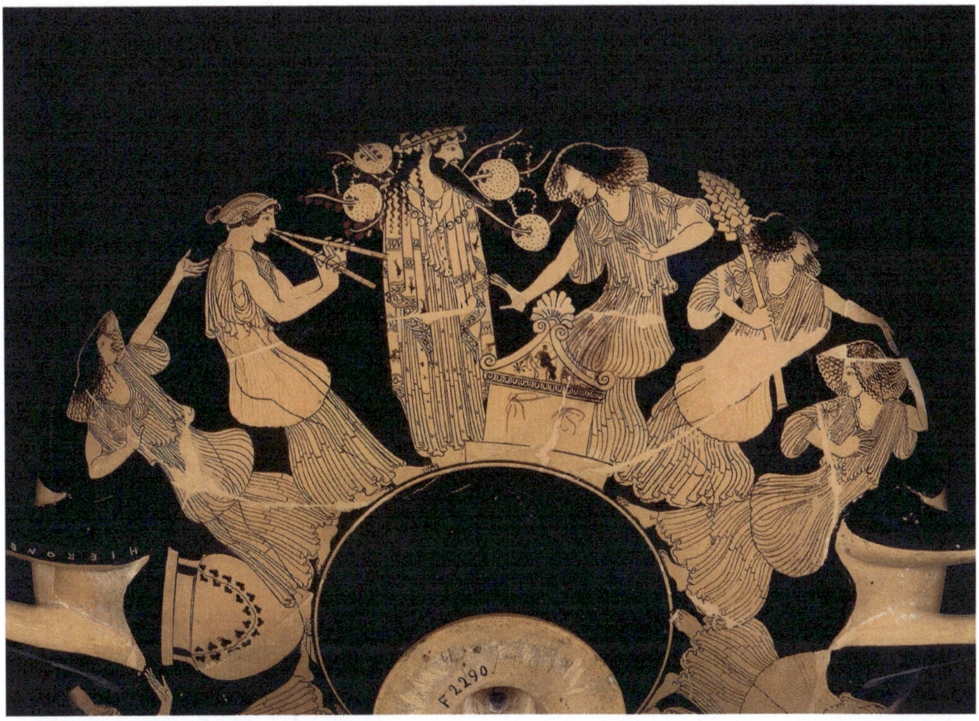

(B)

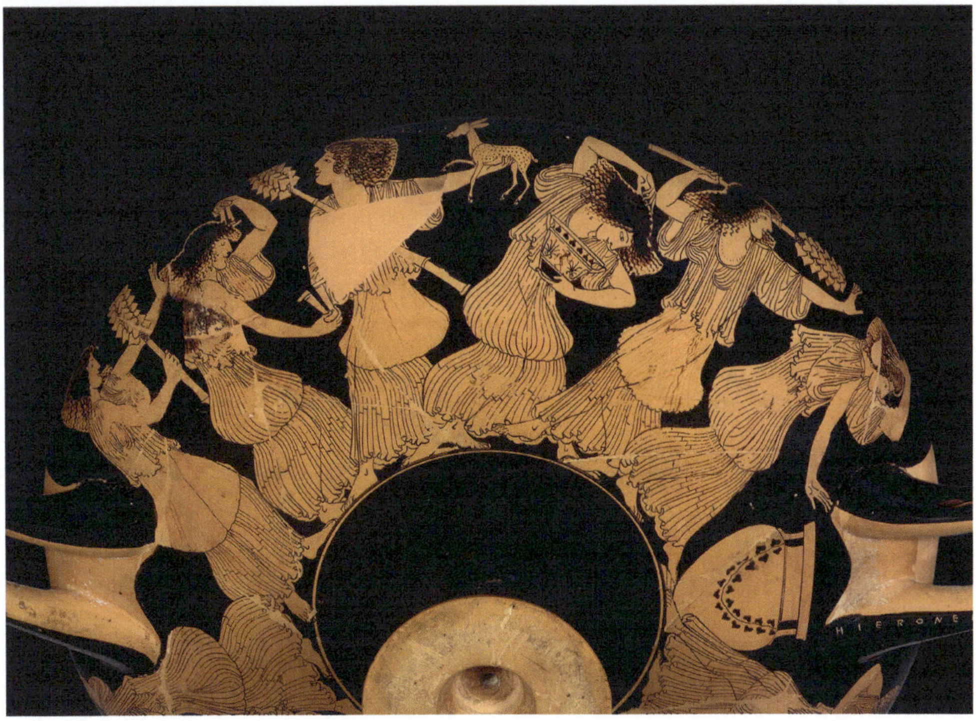

5.10. Makron, *Dionysian Revel* (sides A, B), Attic red-figure *kylix*, ceramic, h. 12.3 cm, d. 33 cm, *c.* 480 BCE. Berlin, Antikensammlung, F2290. bpk Bildagentur/Antikensammlung/Johannes Laurentius/Art Resource, NY.

Dionysos is able to pulse through each physical body present in the room. Just as he stabilizes the *rhyton*, holding it steady while the divine revel swirls energetically around it, so too does he guide the symposiasts into an embodied experience of the divine, drawing them into his world through the music he inspires and the wine that he represents.

BREAKING BOUNDARIES

We may see the fullest extent of Dionysos' influence upon both his mythical followers and his human viewers on a cup by Makron (Fig. 5.10).[59] The god is represented yet again as a static figure but, unlike the previous examples, here he is little more than a mask and drapery adorning a pole. Dionysos stands just left of center, slightly behind an altar on which is painted a figure in silhouette, seated and holding a staff. The god's body overlaps with the altar, suggesting that it may even be sacred to Dionysos himself and that the figure in silhouette may be a representation of the god. If this is the case, then Dionysos is doubly present in this scene, both as a recipient of cult and as a spectator to the musical and danced performance that occurs around him.[60] Immediately adjacent to the god a maenad plays the *aulos*, providing the music to which her companions dance in an energetic and ecstatic manner. Her instrument reaches out to touch Dionysos' drapery, once again suggesting that the god, who here lacks a body and any capacity for physical movement, has nevertheless moved the musician, animating her actions and creating her music. In response to the divinely generated music, the other figures twist and turn, losing themselves to the melody as they dip their heads, throw their arms up, and dance together. The revel continues on the other side, where one maenad plays the *krotala*, establishing a percussive rhythm to which both the *aulos* player and the dancers keep time as they move together. As they dance, the maenads brandish their *thyrsoi*, accentuating their wide-ranging movements. One maenad just left of center also holds a small deer up in her hand, which, together with the blood splattered on the altar on the opposite side, hints at the culmination of the danced ritual they are in the process of enacting.[61]

The inclusion of two vases on this side amplifies the visual traces of Dionysos' musical presence.[62] The first, a mixing bowl depicted underneath one handle, offers the more straightforward interpretation of the two: it introduces the presence of wine, even though none of the maenads actively partake of it. The vessel's prominent placement in the scene, moreover, marks the wine, and by extension the god Dionysos, as responsible for inspiring the musical celebration as the maenads dance in front of it, their toes overlapping and touching in front of its body. It draws further attention to itself and the presumed importance of wine within this Dionysian scene through its plain, red surface, broken only by a garland of ivy that has been draped around it, a point of visual contrast with the frenetic sequence of lines that makes up the rest of the scene.

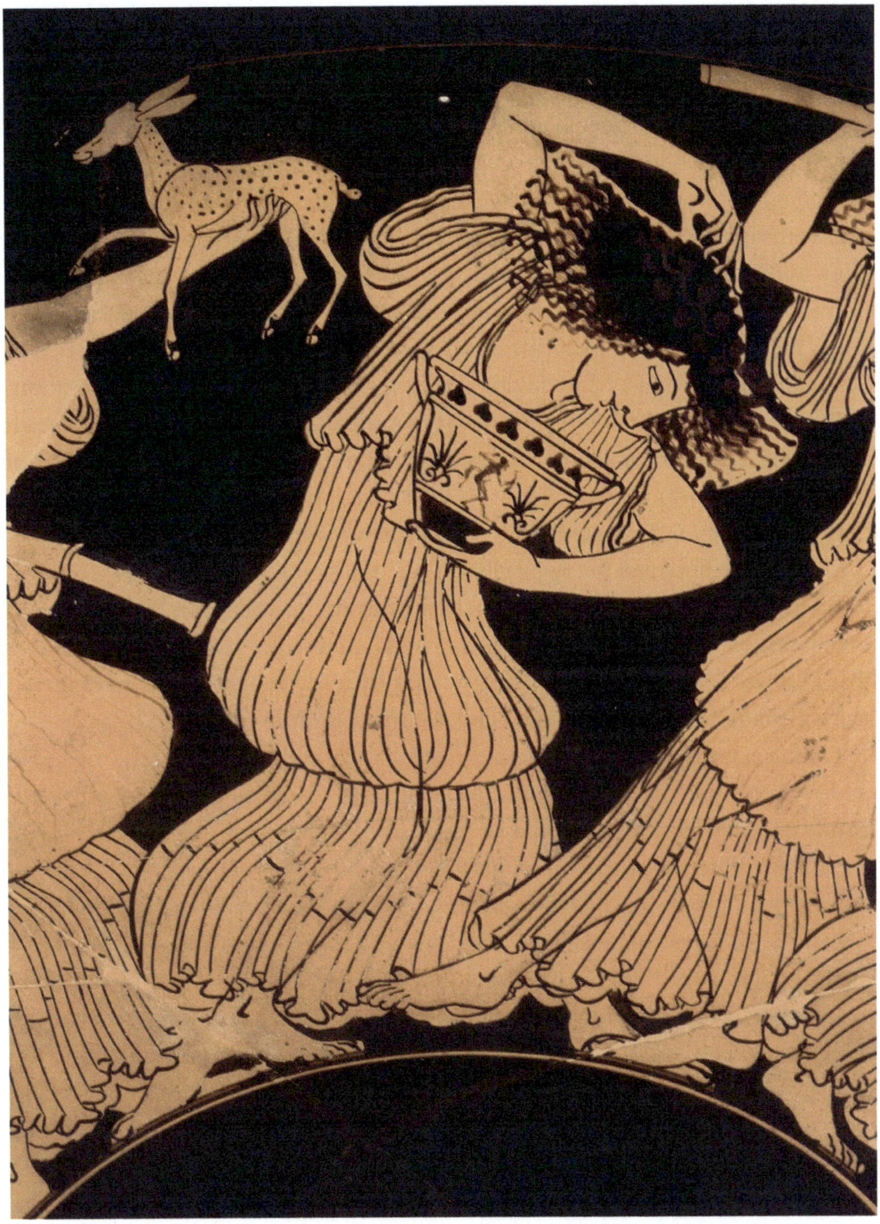

5.11. Detail of a maenad. Makron, *Dionysian Revel* (side B), Attic red-figure *kylix*, ceramic, h. 12.3 cm, d. 33 cm, *c.* 480 BCE. Berlin, Antikensammlung, F2290. bpk Bildagentur/ Antikensammlung/Johannes Laurentius/Art Resource, NY.

The second vase included within the image offers a further level of complexity, for not only does the *skyphos* feature its own black-figure painted decoration, but it is also held by a maenad as she dances exuberantly. Painted onto the cup, below a border of plant motifs and interspersed between two palmettes, is a satyr, who extends one leg forward while bending the other, his hands raised in the air above his head (Fig. 5.11). He is clearly dancing, moving his body to music he hears.

On a basic, thematic level, the subject matter of the embedded vase represents a continuation of the scene painted onto the cup, in that each displays the destabilizing, wild effect Dionysos could have upon his followers. However, there exists a further layer of significance between the two, for the maenad who holds up the cup has positioned her body in a remarkably similar way to the satyr, with one leg extending forward, one arm raised up in the air, and head tilted downwards. A play with reality seems to be at work here. Not only does the painted image of the satyr mimic the danced pose of the maenad – or perhaps the maenad's body mimics the satyr's – but the music to which they both dance may even be the same, performed by the maenads on their *krotala* and *auloi* around the surface of the cup. The two figures thus do not simply replicate each other's bodily positions but, rather, they dance the same steps to the same music, their connection to each other established through their shared embodied response to the presence of Dionysos. This mimetic layering of painted image with painted image, whereby both bodies respond kinesthetically in similar ways to each other, thus collapses the distinction between the two layers of representation. Both are shown at once to be images painted onto vases, whether onto the physical vase or the painted one, while at the same time they each give tangible voice to the powerful effect that Dionysos could have on his followers, physically moving them into altered states through the wine consumed and the music heard.

For the external viewer, or indeed the actual user, of this cup, he or she too could interact with the maenad and her dancing satyr companion. In collapsing the boundary between the maenad and the painted imagery on the vase she holds, the image painted onto the cup offers the same immersive experience to whoever holds it, manipulates it, and drinks from it. As with the mixing bowl, the cup as a vase-shape is overwhelmingly associated with the symposium and was specifically used to drink wine. These cups, then, full of wine, could be passed among the guests, circulating throughout the room, moving the presence of Dionysos together with them. The physical manipulation of the vessel is thus presented as being partially responsible for blurring the distinction between the external viewer and the painted imagery. Not only do the scenes show Dionysos and his mythical followers under the effects of wine and music, but they invite their human viewers, when positioned in a similar context and participating in similar activities, to give themselves completely over to the experience, to put aside their identities and lose themselves in the music and wine. By moving the cup and in so doing subsequently animating the maenads' wild dance, the beholder, much like the painted maenad and the satyr, begins to take on the characteristics of the painted scene. Or, rather, the two scenes begin to move closer together, resembling each other as they each draw out the presence of Dionysos, who in turn works through the vase's material body to interact with its user. The cup thus suggests that it is in this moment of shedding individual identity and subsuming oneself within the collective group of symposiasts that one may enter into the world of Dionysos and experience the god's presence as an embodied experience of divine music and wine.

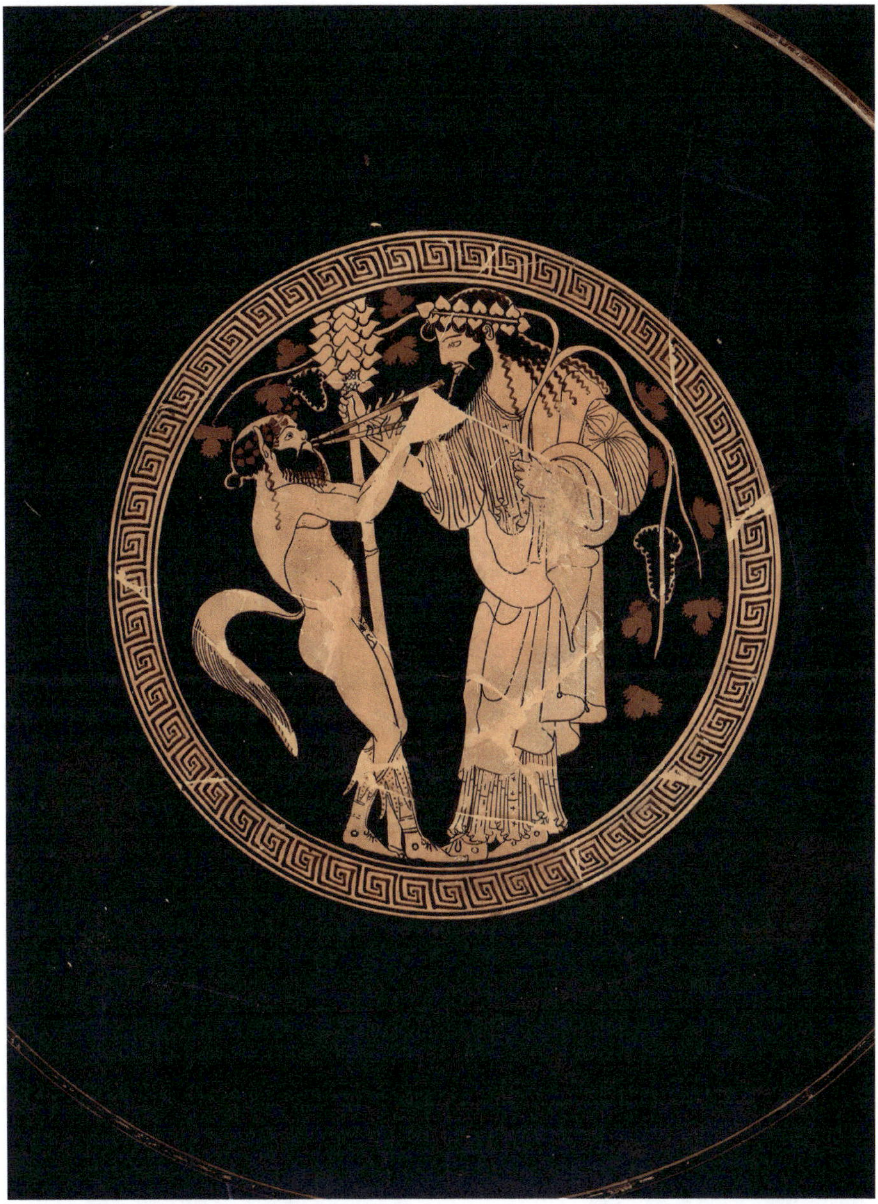

5.12. Makron, *Dionysos Listening to a Satyr Play the Aulos* (tondo), Attic red-figure *kylix*, ceramic, h. 12.3 cm, d. 33 cm, *c.* 480 BCE. Berlin, Antikensammlung, F2290. bpk Bildagentur/Antikensammlung/Johannes Laurentius/Art Resource, NY.

DIONYSOS THE DANCER

Unlike the exterior image on Makron's cup, where the partially anthropomorphic god cannot move, in the tondo of the same cup he is depicted both as a fully embodied experience and as an active, external force that generates music (Fig. 5.12). Here, Dionysos and a satyr step toward each other, while their feet, covered in similar boots, overlap in the bottom center of the tondo.

As the satyr leans back, he directs his *aulos* up to the god's face, so that the far end of one pipe almost reaches Dionysos' mouth. Though it is the satyr who actually plays the instrument, the intimate relationship between it and Dionysos suggests that he is at once the source of inspiration and the individual for whom the performance has been undertaken. The overlapping gesture between god and musician, where Dionysos' *thyrsos* is layered with the instrument, underscores the association between Dionysos and the satyr's music. Similarly, the expansive reach of the vine, which arches upwards, mimicking the rounded curve of the satyr musician's tail, before wrapping around the two figures, demonstrates the effect both the music and the god's presence have on those who hear the music or feel his divine presence.[63] We are now presented with a different conception of Dionysos, where he is not simply the static, immobile god whom we have encountered previously, both on the exterior of this cup and on other vases. Rather, here he has begun to move, to step forward, to engage with the performance that he has caused.

What, then, does it mean for our interpretation of Dionysos as an unmoving source of inspiration when he begins to move, to participate in the very actions that he has inspired? In other words, what happens when the unmoving source of movement begins to respond to his own influence? Dionysos' ability to generate musicality in his followers and to participate actively in the music and dance that he has inspired may be seen on an image painted around the sides of a storage vessel (Fig. 5.13).[64] On one side, a satyr playing the *aulos* leads a procession, using his music to guide the other figures and to determine the rhythm of their dance.

(A) (B)

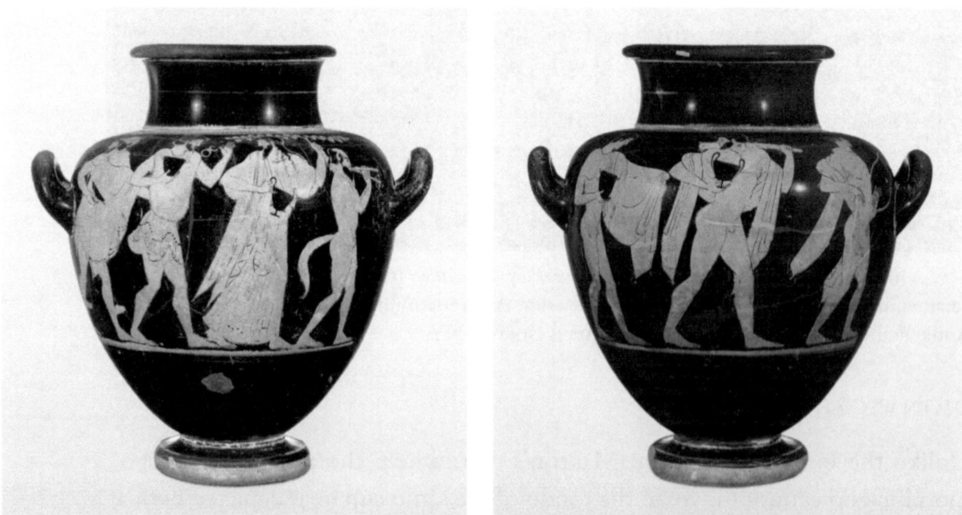

5.13. The Tyszkiewicz Painter, *Kōmos Revel* (sides A, B), Attic red-figure *stamnos*, ceramic, h. 37.5 cm, *c.* 480–470 BCE. Malibu, The J. Paul Getty Museum, Villa Collection, Gift of Stefan Hornak, 83.AE.326. Available through Getty Open Content.

As with the other images we have seen, the satyr's close proximity to Dionysos, who follows him, suggests that the god is ultimately his source of musical inspiration, so that the creation of music brings Dionysos' immaterial divine presence into the world. It is particularly significant that the satyr plays an *aulos*, since it requires the musician to fill the instrument with his breath. The sound it generates is created by his physical body, which produces, holds, and emits the breath that ultimately becomes music. Having been inspired by the god to play the instrument, the satyr also breathes Dionysos' influence into the world through his musical performance. Dionysian presence thus manifests in the image as musical sound, but also as breath itself, a tangible yet immaterial marker here of the god's presence that affects all those who come into contact with it.

The god similarly exerts his influence over the other figures who take part in the procession. As he walks forward, almost dancing to the music he has created, he looks back to his companions and lifts an ivy branch above his head. Its tendrils extend to cover the other figures, linking them all in a single, unified action. Among his companions is Herakles, who energetically walks behind, lifting one hand to acknowledge Dionysos while the other holds up a *skyphos*, the large cup depicted in silhouette. Together with the shallow cup that Hermes holds, the three gods are visually united by their drinking vessels. Beyond the repeating black used to depict the cups, the figures' similar positions create a consistent visual rhythm across the surface of the image. Each god or satyr steps forward, creating a staccato pattern with each individual's extended legs. Each also has one bent arm while the other extends outwards in front of him; the only exception is the satyr who leads the group, and his unique bodily position marks him off as distinct within the procession, where he fulfills the crucial role of providing the enticing music that draws in the other participants. Finally, each figure's head faces in alternating directions: the satyr stares resolutely ahead, leading the procession with his music and with his gaze, while Dionysos looks back to Herakles, who in turn looks to Dionysos. Following this pattern, Hermes looks behind him, but since he is the last figure on this side of the image, he must look through the vacuum of space created by the handle to the other side of the vase. He thus acts as a visual cue to the viewer to turn the vase, to understand the two images as continuous in theme, space, and time.

The scene that Hermes looks onto consists of three male figures, all nude except for a loosely draped piece of fabric around their shoulders. Given his line of sight, Hermes directs his attention to the leader of this second group, a beardless youth who plays a *chelys* lyre while walking forward at a rapid pace, his swinging drapery suggesting the pace and tempo of the group's movements and of the music he plays. The focus that Hermes directs toward another source of music, ostensibly beyond the visual space that constitutes his own scene, emphasizes the ability of Dionysos' musical inspiration to bring disparate individuals together. Following the *chelys* player is Herakles; in contrast to the other side, here he is depicted as mostly nude. He carries the same large cup that Dionysos typically carries, while he also bears his club on one shoulder. The final figure is another beardless youth, who holds a large cup in one hand while the other holds out a piece of fabric, as if using the movement of the drapery to accentuate his dance.

That the two scenes are not simply continuations of a single procession is made clear by the repetition of Herakles across the two sides. Yet, the image suggests that the events are, nevertheless, continuous with each other: Hermes hears the youth's *chelys* lyre, just as the mortal youths must hear the satyr's *aulos*, which follows them in their revel. When in the company of the youths, Herakles takes on elements of Dionysos' appearance: he holds a *kantharos*, a type of drinking cup typically held by Dionysos, though he grasps it here by its base, much as he does with his *skyphos* on the reverse, whereas Dionysos typically holds it by a handle. Herakles' position on the second side evokes that of Dionysos, a comparison further emphasized by the two objects they carry, the god with the vine and the hero with the knotty club. Herakles also stands out on this side as the only bearded figure, which may have been intended to recall or evoke Dionysos' appearance on the other side. The Dionysian characteristics that Herakles embodies suggest the active presence of Dionysos, even though the god himself has not been physically depicted. Moreover, Herakles' presence on both sides of the vase invites the viewer to turn the vessel around and see the hero on either side. By animating the vessel itself, the viewer is thus presented with an image of an extended Dionysian procession, one where Dionysos dances among his fellow gods, heroes, and satyrs, and another where he is implicitly present among the young men who drink his wine, perform his energetic and wild music, and dance together in procession. The god thus moves across the boundaries separating the mythic from the human. Herakles in many ways bridges this divide, since he was initially a mortal man, then a hero, and finally an immortal god. In embodying Dionysos in the company of the young men, the hero channels the god's presence: through his movement, Dionysos not only influences those in the image with him, but his active dance expands the effect his presence has, so that the figures around the vase listen to the same music and drink the same wine.

Dionysos dances even more exuberantly on the exterior of a cup by the Briseis Painter, where he actively responds to the music that he has inspired (Fig. 5.14).[65] The revelers fill the scene with curvilinear, sweeping lines that amplify the quality and degree of movement exhibited by each figure. Prominently filling the central visual field is Dionysos, who balances precariously on one foot as he tips forward, holding out a curling snake that extends behind him and an ivy branch that reaches in front. He moves rapidly, his drapery flowing out behind him as he dances to the fast-paced *aulos*-music played by the satyr who follows him. In addition to an *aulos*-playing satyr on each side, two maenads and another satyr accompany the god, each figure

(A)

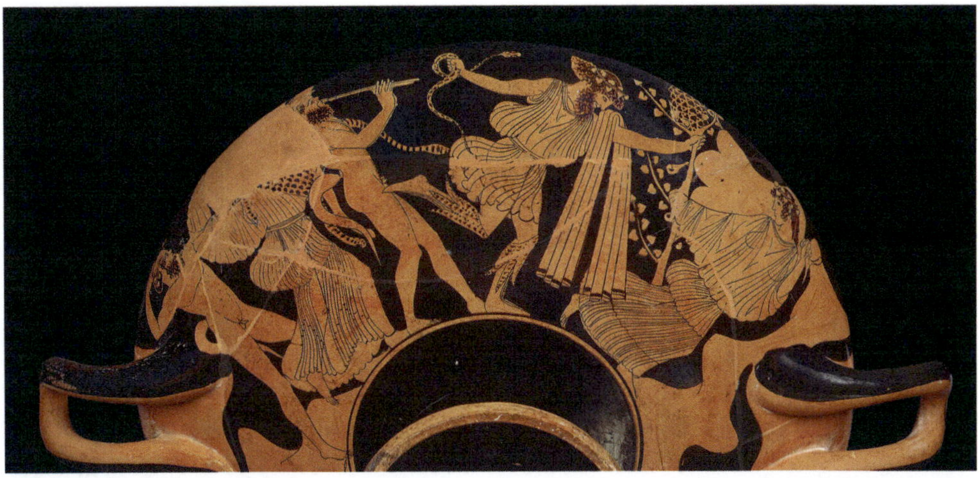

(B)

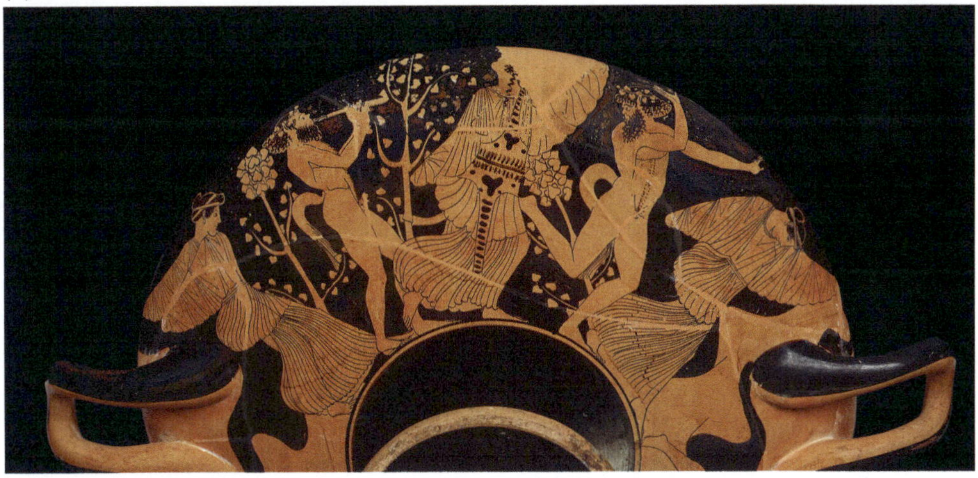

5.14. The Briseis Painter, *Dionysian Revel* (sides A, B), Attic red-figure *kylix*, ceramic, h. 12.7 cm, *c.* 485–480 BCE. London, British Museum, 1843,1103.54 (E75). © The Trustees of the British Museum.

dancing similarly exuberantly.[66] The other side of the cup displays a similar scene, as a satyr plays the *aulos* while another satyr and maenads dance, limbs raised as the figures sway and jump across the visual field.

Across both sides of the cup, Dionysos in particular stands out, not just for the acrobatic dance he performs, but also for the visual space given to his body, which has been carefully surrounded by a black background. The space afforded him in the scene is distinct as the other revelers overlap with each other, and are surrounded by plants, *thyrsoi*, and large rocks. As a result of this compositional choice, Dionysos acts as the swirling focal point from which the revel unfolds: he is at once the source of inspiration for the music the satyrs play, one of whom overlaps with the god's outstretched dancing feet, while he is also the embodiment of the ecstatic response his presence demands. In other words, the music played by the satyrs is so powerful and inherently affective that it even draws in the god himself, who, paradoxically, is then consumed by the very music that he inspires and that draws together his followers.

For the external viewer who could have encountered this cup in a symposium, the full extent of the transgressive and ecstatic states associated with Dionysos could similarly manifest through one's exposure to music, song, and dance that pervaded the symposium. In drinking wine from this cup, the symposiasts or *hetairai* physically consumed the god's presence and thus opened themselves up to the destabilizing and wild energy Dionysos and his followers exhibit in the image. Similarly, by listening to music played on the *aulos*, particularly in a blurred, intoxicated state, the symposiasts or *hetairai* might have imagined that they listen to the same music as does the god. The image offers its viewers the opportunity to share, both imaginatively and potentially also actually, the same sensory experience as Dionysos, where both man and god hear the same sounds, respond the same way, dance the same steps. The image thus suggests that Dionysos draws his followers in through a fully embodied experience of the god, where his surprisingly active movements are reflective of the musical movement and abandon that he has inspired in those who surround him.

The ability Dionysos has to inspire his followers to play and dance to music and to react to his own creative inspiration may also project beyond the pictorial frame to interact with the viewer. If we look at another revel (Fig. 5.15), Dionysos, satyrs, and maenads dance to the sound of the *aulos* being played by a satyr.[67] Dionysos is, once again, depicted in the center where he holds a *kantharos* by his side and an ivy vine above his head. He dances to the right while glancing over his shoulder to a maenad who dances with the *thyrsos* and snake. Further maenads dance, encircling the vase with their swirling bodies as they move together to the music. They hold up their *thyrsoi*, so that we might imagine the air rushing between the small petals of the pine cone creating a distinct hollow, rustling noise that amplified the dancers' movements. That the maenads are completely subsumed into the music is made clear by two figures on the reverse, who frame the *aulos*-playing satyr. The satyr's central position mimics that of Dionysos on the other side, a visual repetition that suggests that he has been moved by Dionysos to play his instrument. We may see the powerful force of his music in the responses the two maenads have to the sounds of his music. Unlike the figures directly adjacent to Dionysos, these two maenads throw their heads back, lost in a moment of complete musical immersion as they sing and dance enthusiastically. The outward direction of their movements, away from the source of instrumental music, suggests the expansive nature of the satyr's music, which quickly flows throughout the scene, captivating all those present with its rhythm.

(A)

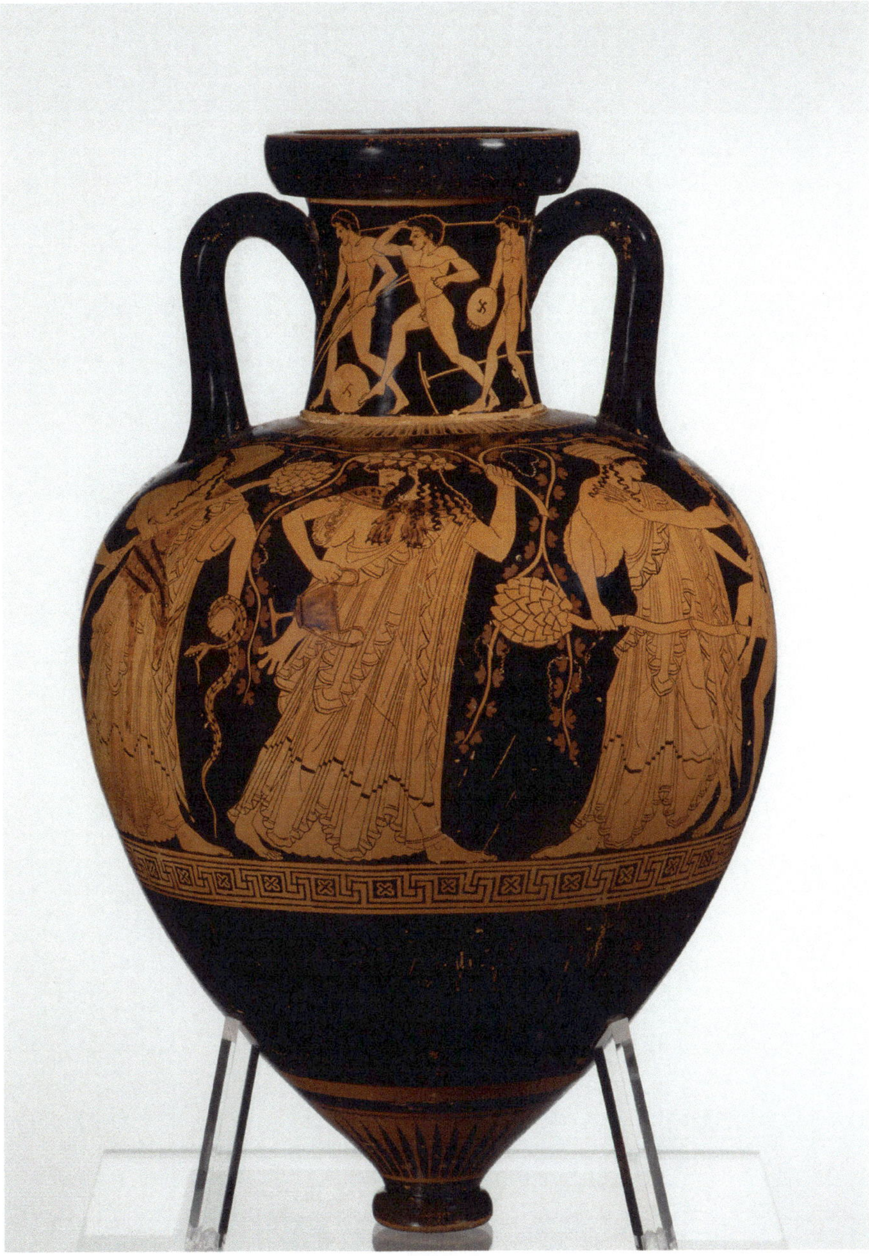

5.15. The Kleophrades Painter, *Dionysian Revel* (sides A, B), Attic red-figure pointed *amphora*, ceramic, h. 56 cm, *c.* 500 BCE. Munich, Antikensammlungen, 2344. Staatliche Antikensammlungen und Glyptothek München, photographs by Renate Kühling.

Despite rarely picking up an instrument to play it himself, there is nevertheless something inherently direct about the kind of music that Dionysos offers. Unlike Apollo's performances, where he harmonizes his audience through his music, or the Muses, who offer embodied inspiration through the viewer's

(B)

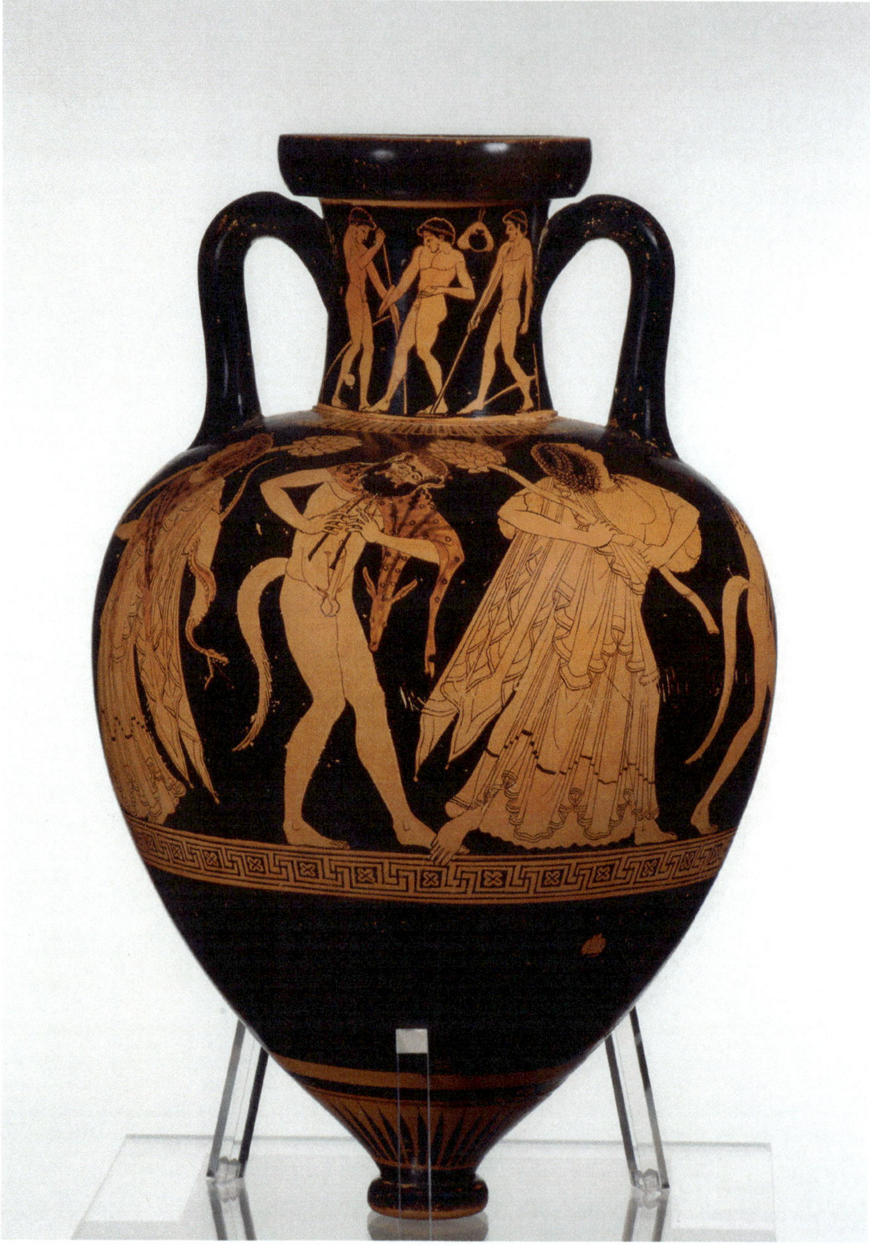

5.15. (*cont.*)

engagement with their pervasive music, or even Pan, who inspires immersive choral dance, Dionysos instead surrounds himself with lively music that in turn elicits energetic, almost ecstatic, dancing. The god thus exhibits the extremes of musical performance: he either stands still, listening to the wild music he has inspired, or he is himself wild and ecstatic as he dances. The effect of his musical inspiration becomes apparent not only in how members of his audience respond to his own music-making, but also in how they respond to his presence through their own musical performance. Satyrs could play the *kithara*, dress in performance attire, create similar music to Apollo's, and elicit a similarly harmonized response. They could also play a range of musical instruments, which reminds us of the Muses' virtuosity on a similar number of instruments, though, of course, with very different results for their audience. They also seem to play upbeat, lively music, prompting an energetic dance that defies the typical restraint we see with scenes of *choreia*, which further marks the Dionysian-inspired musical revel as distinct from the Nymphs' danced response to Pan's music. Above all, when Dionysos is shown involving himself in the musical processions that he has brought about, the images suggest the boundless nature of his music, which stretches everywhere and is heard by everyone. It even, as we saw in Philodamos' paean or in Euripides' *Bacchai*, can affect and transform everyone, human and divine, including the very god who inspired its creation.

Even the formal limits of the image can be pierced by Dionysian-inspired music. Much as we saw on the vessel by the Mastos Group and the Affecter (Figs. 5.3 and 5.4), here too on the *amphora* the satyr's face is shown frontally, so that he stares through the surface of the image to look directly at the viewer.[68] This visual point of contact between musician and audience member suggests that the satyr plays his instrument not only for the benefit of his companions, but that he also plays it for the external viewer, who, in looking at the satyr musician, could imaginatively hear the music (Fig. 5.16). Moreover, the satyr's music is so powerful in its ability to transcend the boundary between image and reality that he begins to push a maenad out into the external world. As she sings along to his melody, lost to the music, the satyr nudges her foot outwards, past the decorative framing border and into the external viewer's world.[69] As a result, the image suggests that as the maenad moves out from the image toward the viewer, he or she in turn is absorbed into the scene, becoming a fellow dancer in the revel. Dionysos, as the source of music-making in this scene, thus provokes a specific kind of music in his followers, but when he himself participates in that music, his presence has a destabilizing effect on the boundaries between image and reality.

If Dionysian influence may extend beyond the image painted onto the vase, we must also consider the context in which the image could have been seen and used. The inclusion of young nude male athletes around the neck of the vase (Fig. 5.17) suggests one intended audience for this image, that is, the young citizen men of Athens who could have participated in symposia where they may have seen this and other similar vases, drunk the wine that was stored in it, and listened to the *aulos* music that filled the room as wine cups were passed and songs exchanged.[70] Positioned within this space, we might imagine Dionysos manifesting for the symposiasts not only through the effects of the

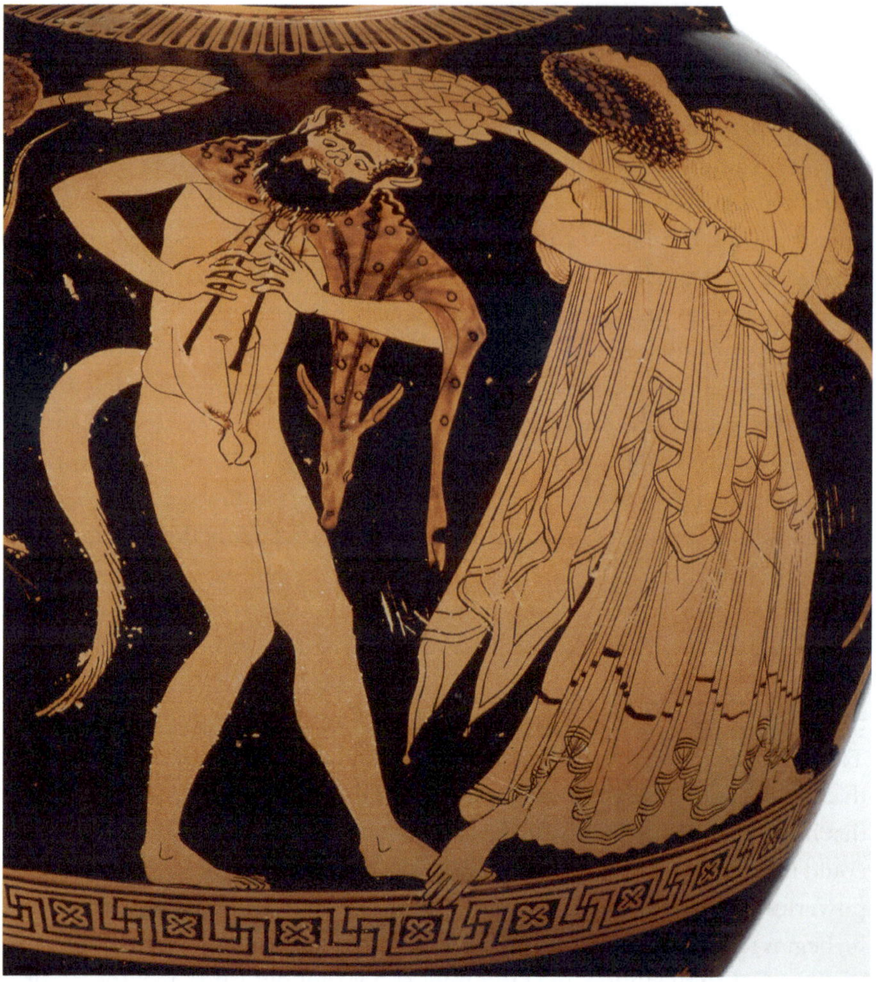

5.16. Detail of a satyr. The Kleophrades Painter, *Dionysian Revel* (sides A, B), Attic red-figure pointed *amphora*, ceramic, h. 56 cm, *c.* 500 BCE. Munich, Antikensammlungen, 2344. Staatliche Antikensammlungen und Glyptothek München, photographs by Renate Kühling.

wine that each guest consumed, but also though the conflation of sensory experiences one underwent in the symposium, where the sounds of music and song, the smell and taste of wine, and the bodily sensation of dance were all experienced together. By inviting its viewers to undergo similar sensations to the satyrs and maenads in the scene, the image draws in its viewers to a world where Dionysos directly affects them by provoking in them a specific range of sensations. In presenting the effect Dionysos has on his followers, the vase hints at the real power behind the god: not only can he draw men, mythological beings, and even gods away from other forms of divine music, but through the shared sensory experience of music and intoxication, Dionysos makes it possible to lose oneself to these sensations and, consequently, join in the revel.

(A) (B)

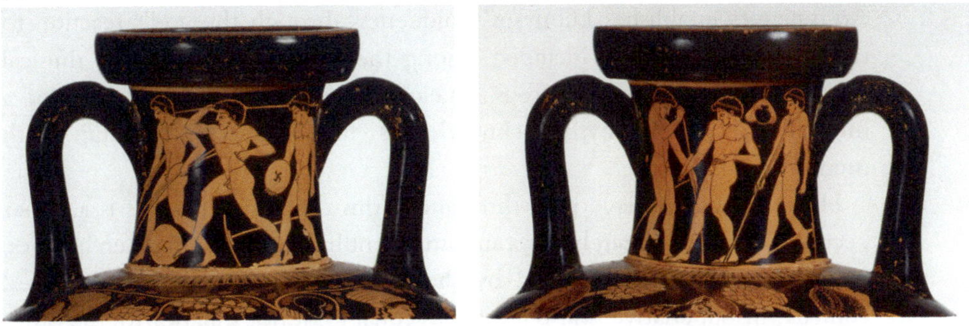

5.17. Detail of the neck. The Kleophrades Painter, *Dionysian Revel* (sides A, B), Attic red-figure pointed *amphora*, ceramic, h. 56 cm, *c.* 500 BCE. Munich, Antikensammlungen, 2344. Staatliche Antikensammlungen und Glyptothek München, photographs by Renate Kühling.

EMBODYING DIONYSOS

In the comedy *Frogs*, Aristophanes presents a rare example of Dionysos participating in a musical performance. During his journey to the Underworld, Dionysos must cross a lake in Charon's ferry. As the boat slowly makes its way across, Dionysos, disguised as Herakles, is confronted by a chorus of frogs, who attract his attention with their persistent refrain "*Brekekekex koax koax*."[71] Their croaking echoes over the still water as they recount how they used to sing a beautiful and harmonic hymn for Dionysos, "let's voice a cry together | with the pipes (σύναυλος), our own euphonious | song (εὔγηρυν ἐμὰν ἀοιδάν) –*koax koax* – that we once sounded for the Nysean son | of Zeus, Dionysos . . ."[72] They also mock Dionysos' lack of appreciation for their song, singing that the other musical gods all had professed their love of the frogs' musical abilities.[73] According to the frogs, "the Muses skillful on the fine lyre cherish us, | and hornfoot Pan, who plays the tuneful reeds, | and Apollo the lyre-player delights in us too, | in thanks for the stalks that I grow | in the lake water, as girding for his lyre."[74] In positioning Dionysos against the other musical gods, the frogs establish him as distinct from his peers, both in his relationship with music generally and in his lack of appreciation of the frogs' musicality.

Dionysos displays his versatility as a musician in his response, with which he attempts to defeat the frogs in a musical contest, engaging in a sort of call and response between god and animal. Taunting them, he replies that "you won't beat me either, | never, for if need be I'll bellow all the livelong day, until | I vanquish you at *koax*." Taking over their refrain, he ultimately wins the struggle, beating the frogs with their own song as he shouts "*brekekekex koax koax*" at them until, at last, he exclaims that "I knew I'd put a stop to that *koax* of yours!"[75] He thus emerges victorious in the musical contest, a victory that points to his own skill in music, his appreciation of sung dialogue in the theater, and the presiding role the god was thought to have taken with respect to the symposium in Archaic and Classical Athens. Above all, Aristophanes establishes Dionysos' uniqueness through the god's reaction to the frogs: though he is included among the frogs' song about the musical gods, in dismissing the frogs' melody and challenging them to a musical contest, Dionysos acknowledges his distinct relationship with musical performance.

However, as we have seen throughout this chapter, Dionysos is a rather peculiar musician: he rarely plays an instrument himself, though when he does, whether on the scene created by the Brygos Painter or in Aristophanes' comedy, his superlative skill is posited as equal to, if not superior to, the other gods. The choice, therefore, to depict him more frequently as an observer of music must have some theological ramifications inherent to him as a god. Above all, it is by inspiring those around him to perform acts of great musical and dancing skill that the god's affinity for a specific kind of music becomes apparent. Unlike Pan's piped music that inspires the Nymphs' choral dance, Apollo's harmonious performances, or the Muses' ability to inspire through their variable appearances and musical performances, Dionysos immerses all those near him, be they satyrs, maenads, or gods, in his ecstatic music. His divine presence in these scenes is repeatedly shown in the surviving visual material through the musical responses that others exhibit. His ability to foster musicality in others is thus unquestionably a display of the god's particular musicality, as distinct to him as the other gods' performances.

There is also something very physical, almost visceral, about the texture of his particular music. It is not simply that Dionysos generates music-making in his followers, but it is the physical absorption into the music that is so striking. Maenads on Makron's cup dance with abandon, a satyr on Kleophrades' vessel plays such seductive music that he both pushes a maenad out of the scene while he also confronts his viewers and draws us into the revel. Even Dionysos loses himself to his music: he dances in processions, he tips off balance while precariously holding snakes, he rips animals in two. The viewer, too, is implicated in Dionysos' music as we are confronted by the frontal faces of satyrs, who stare out of the scene as if looking directly at us. It seems significant that Dionysos himself never looks out of the image in these musical scenes, but rather he works through his satyrs and maenads, using them to draw us into the world he has moved so profoundly. We are asked to react as they react, or as Dionysos himself eventually begins to react. We are invited to be so moved by his influence that we too take up our instruments to play them, that we begin to dance, limbs flying this way and that as we lose ourselves to the music. It is this moment of abandon, of feeling lost in a musical melody that these images suggest is akin to experiencing the presence of Dionysos. He is there in that visceral and embodied reaction, where we physically express what we hear.

Crucially, the vases I have discussed in this chapter are sympotic in character; that is, their shape associates them with the symposium, so that regardless of their eventual findspot, they can all be considered within a context filled with wine, music, song, and dancing. Much as we saw in the previous chapters where the visual effect of Pan's, Apollo's, or the Muses' music depended upon the context in which they were seen, the images of Dionysos and his musical retinue engage with the Athenian viewer, who probably saw the scenes in a symposium, where they were handled or used for drinking while symposiasts played music, sang songs, and danced, all under the influence of Dionysos. The god thus becomes doubly present in the symposium, where he not only acts upon those who physically drink in the wine that he embodies, but he also affects those who lose themselves to the music they hear, who sing in response to the piping of the *aulos*. When positioned within the symposium, human efforts toward music-making are juxtaposed with scenes of satyrs playing, such on the vessel by the Mastos Group and the Affecter (Figs. 5.3 and 5.4), or with the image on Makron's cup where maenads play music and dance together (Fig. 5.10). Collectively, the images suggest that though Dionysos does not actively play an instrument, it is nevertheless a direct result of his influence that men, women, satyrs, maenads, and even other gods are moved to music. And this music, the images caution, is the kind that makes all who hear it lose themselves to it, so great is its effect on its listening audience.

Beyond the symposium, the theater is another locus of Dionysian-inspired music. Even though few of our surviving images were used or were physically present in the theater, not only did it offer its audience a clear link between Dionysos and the performances held there, it was also a profoundly immersive space, where, again, one could lose oneself to the narratives unfolding in the orchestra. Although much has already been written on the triangulation of ritual, music, and affective performances, as well as on the Athenian theater more generally, I conclude this chapter by considering one particularly evocative scene of music that incorporates aspects of the theater, the symposium, and veneration of Dionysos, since it displays the effect that Dionysos was believed to have on those who open themselves up to him.

Side A on the Pronomos Vase has received much attention in scholarship, not least for its plausible representation of a satyr drama.[76] Here, men dressed in loin cloths with tails and satyr masks stand or dance around a central scene in which an aulete, labeled as the famous musician Pronomos, performs. In the top center of the scene recline Dionysos and a female companion, as if observing the performance that is just, or will soon be, underway. As important as Side A is for enhancing our understanding of satyr drama, it is Side B to which I wish to turn (Fig. 5.18). This particular image of music-making is at once a continuation of the opposite side but also clearly a distinct moment in time. Here, however, we do not find men dressed as satyrs, but

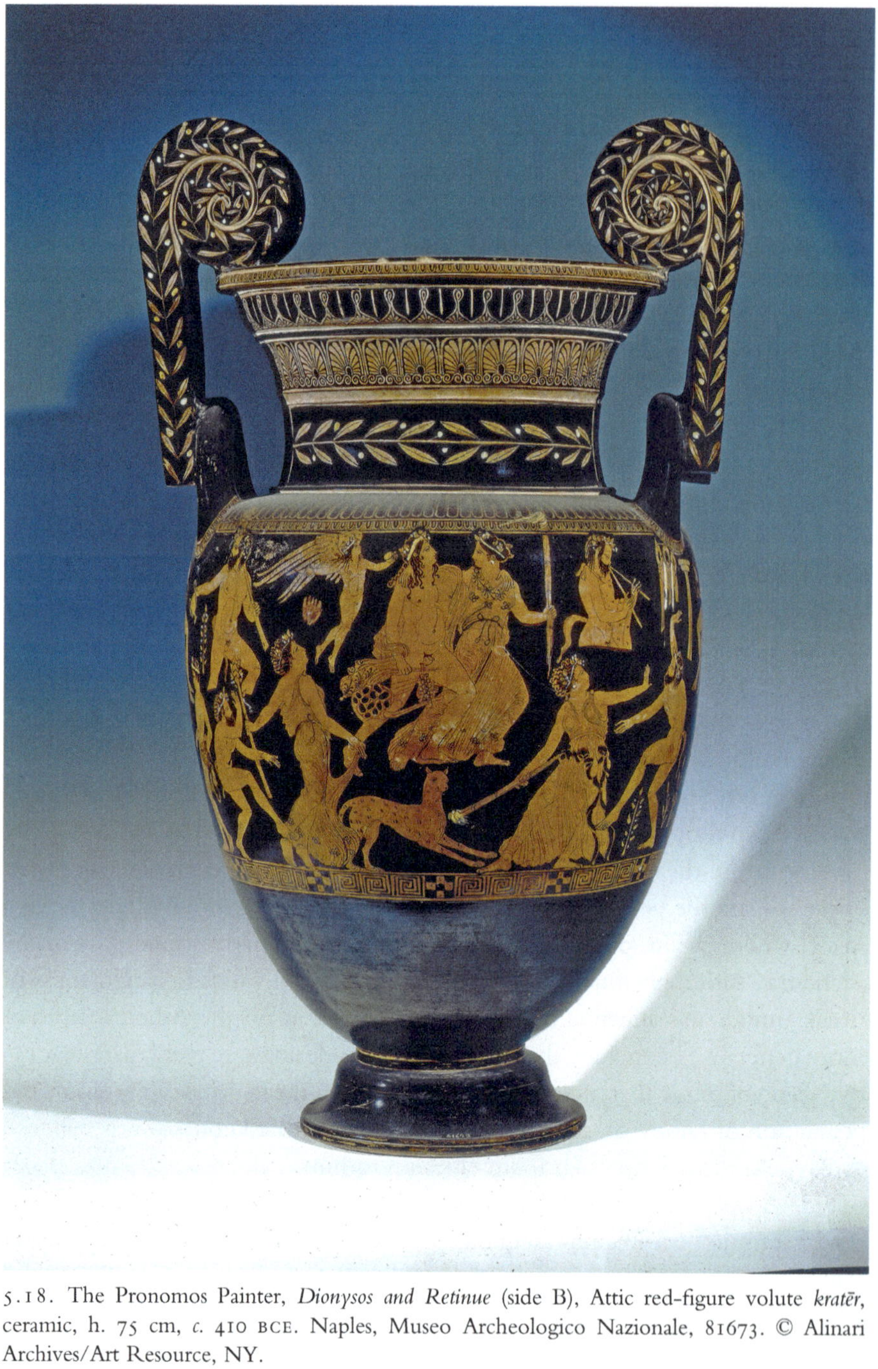

5.18. The Pronomos Painter, *Dionysos and Retinue* (side B), Attic red-figure volute *kratēr*, ceramic, h. 75 cm, *c.* 410 BCE. Naples, Museo Archeologico Nazionale, 81673. © Alinari Archives/Art Resource, NY.

rather the satyrs themselves, who play the pipes, hold out drinking vessels, and dance acrobatically to the lively music. Two maenads accompany them, one of whom is positioned on the right and appears to be dancing an intricate duet with a satyr, as indicated by the similar position of their limbs. The other maenad, depicted on the left, also dances. Despite her relative isolation as she dances alone,[77] her three-quarter position is striking, as she appears to step into the image, moving from our space, the space of the viewer, into the image itself. Importantly, as the other figures in the scene are preoccupied with their respective actions, whether it is to play the *aulos*, to drink, or to dance, she instead gives all of her attention to Dionysos. The god, for his part, moves swiftly in the center, his destination unclear, as he hangs onto a female companion and holds a *chelys* lyre by his side. Given its composition, the image suggests not only that Dionysos has inspired this scene of musical and danced reveling, but that his movement here, where he draws his followers with him wherever he goes, has inspired the maenad's movements. Caught up in the music that the god has inspired, she loses herself to its melody and, with her entire body, dances her way toward him. We might think of the performances that took place in the theater, or indeed on the reverse side of this vessel, in much the same way. Through the performance of music and dance, created as part of ritual worship for the god, the human audience at once gives itself over to the experience of listening, playing, and moving one's body, even as the collective, creative experience of making music or dancing brought forth the presence of Dionysos within each individual's own body. And so, in this way, Dionysos becomes the source of inspiration for the audience's musical actions, even as he himself is moved by it through the group's own embodied experiences of divine presence.

NOTES

1 Philodamos of Skarpheia, *Paean to Dionysos*, v. 53–60. Translation adapted from Furley and Bremer 2001a: 122; Furley and Bremer 2001b: 52–84.

2 Furley and Bremer 2001b: 72–73. I use the term 'maenad' throughout this chapter to refer to the female figures that are included in Dionysian scenes. The precise identity of these female figures is often difficult to determine and they may be variously identified in scholarship as either maenads or nymphs. For more on maenads, see Rapp 1872; Lawler 1927; Philippart 1930; Dodds 1940; Coche de la Ferté 1951; Edwards 1960; McNally 1978; Bremmer 1984; *LIMC* s.v. Mousa, Mousai 673–76; Hedreen 1994; Isler-Kerényi 2015: 5–8.

3 *BAPD* 203913 with complete bibliography; *ARV*[2] 371.14, 1649; *Paralipomena* 365, 67; *Beazley Addenda*[2] 225; Paquette 1984: 51, A38; Gasparri 1986: no. 465; Lissarrague 1990b: 138–39; Carpenter 1997: pl. 34a–b; Bundrick 2005: 107–09; Simon 2009: no. 70; Lissarrague 2013: 154; Osborne 2014: 44–46.

4 For more on danced responses to music, see Chapter 1.

5 Although Bélis (1988: 10, 23–25) argues that the *aulos* is primarily used in Dionysian revels, it is by no means the exclusive instrument found in Dionysian scenes; as Bundrick notes (2005: 106), one may find the *barbitos*, as here, the *krotala*, the *tympanon*, and even the *kithara*. Similarly, Jacquet-Rimassa (1999) notes the use of a variety of instruments – string, wind, and percussive – in the symposium. Though he restricts his study to vases created between 440–300 BCE, the broad range of instruments that were included in sympotic scenes would suggest that no single instrument was preferred above all others within a sympotic, and therefore a generally Dionysian, context.

6 Otto 1965: 143–44.
7 Lissarrague 2013: 149–73.
8 Bundrick (2005: 106–08) develops upon previous scholarship, especially Otto and Lawler's respective treatments of Dionysos, mania, and music (Lawler 1964: 74–76; Otto 1965: 133–44).
9 Thomas Carpenter (1986: xv–xvi) focuses on the development of Archaic imagery, arguing that the majority of black-figure scenes are primarily non-narrative in character and are related to the sympotic context in which the vessels were predominantly used. His subsequent volume on fifth-century images (Carpenter 1997: 1) examines Dionysian myths, exploring how they were depicted and what relationship they had with contemporaneous ritual, literature, and society. Cornelia Isler-Kerényi (2007: 1–4, 214–15; 2015: 1–15) similarly focuses on Archaic and Classical images featuring Dionysos, in order to bring together narratives of Dionysos with an iconographical approach and an awareness of the compositional possibilities specific to each vase.
10 See especially Isler-Kerényi 2015: 7– 8, 237–39.
11 Hedreen 1992: especially 1–9 for an overview of his methodology. The importance of myth for the study of Dionysos cannot be underestimated. Moreover, as Simon notes, often the distinction in cult between the separate facets of Dionysos' personality expressed itself in terms of geography, that is, from where the god was said to have come. Simon 1969: 279–89; Simon 1983: 89–104. See also Isler-Kerényi's 2004 work on sixth-century images of satyrs as well as Lissarrague's extensive work on the topic, as seen, for example, in 1990c: 53–82 and generally 2003.
12 On the various types of dance movements exhibited in the visual material by maenads and satyrs, see Delavaud-Roux 1988: 37–51.
13 As Sourvinou-Inwood notes (1994; 2003: 67–100), a statue of Dionysos was brought into the theater during the City Dionysia, where it watched the dramatic performances. There was also a seat reserved for the priest of Dionysos, further reinforcing the god's presence. See also Goldhill 1990: 98–100; Parker 2005: 317–18.
14 *BAPD* 301700; *ABV* 322.14; *Paralipomena* 143; *Beazley Addenda*^{2} 87; Melander 2000: 22–23, fig. 4, pls. 363–69; Lissarrague 2013: 153, fig. 26.
15 The *barbitos* depicted here is a rare version of the instrument, wherein the arms are elongated with an undulating form. Maas and Snyder 1989: 124–25; Lissarrague 2013: 153–54.
16 Though working later in the fourth century BCE, Aristotle provides a good indication of the effect music and performance could have on the audience. See, in particular, Arist. *Pol.* 8.5, 7; *Rh.* 2.1.2–3. Similarly, Plato, in book 8 of the *Laws*, values certain types of music over others because of the effect they had on their audience. See also Porter 2010: 99–102.
17 *BAPD* 302258; *ABV* 259.26, 42.35, 57; *Paralipomena* 110, 14; *Beazley Addenda*^{2} 67; Hoffman, von Bothmer, and Truitt 1973: 24, fig. 22, pl. 24.1–4; Korshak 1987: 84, fig. 6; Hedreen 1992: pl. 16; Isler-Kerényi 2007: figs. 83–85.
18 Otto 1965: 133–42; Seaford 2006: 32–34; Bierl 2012: 2–3; Kowalzig and Wilson 2013b: 10–11; Lavecchia 2013: 59–60.
19 Lissarrague 1990b: 22–36, 87–90, 102–03, 23–30; Murray 1990: 6–7; Hamdorf 1990; Jacquet-Rimassa 1999; Bundrick 2005: 80–92; Goldman 2015.
20 On the significance of sensoryscapes in Greek ritual, see Laferrière 2019b.
21 On frontal facing satyrs, see in particular Greifenhagen 1929: 69–74; Carpenter 1986: 96–97; Korshak 1987: 5–7; Frontisi-Ducroux 1995; Hedreen 1992: 17–18; Lissarrague 2013: 149–56; Hedreen 2017: 155.
22 On the viewer's interaction with frontal faces, see Schapiro 1973: 37–49; Frontisi-Ducroux 1995: 19–21; Hedreen 2017: 158–59, 175–77, 181–83.
23 Korshak 1987: 5–11, 44, 45–51; Isler-Kerényi 2004: 43.
24 As a particularly evocative example of a didactic moment in vase-painting, see a black-figure *amphora* by the Affecter, on which a satyr looks at the viewer and points to Dionysos,

who stands beside him (Orvieto, Museo Civico, 240; *ABV* 246.73; *Beazley Addenda*[2] 63; Isler-Kerényi 2004: 43).

25 Carpenter 1986: 13; Shapiro 1989: 90; Isler-Kerényi 2004: 20–21; Seaford 2006: 30–32; Isler-Kerényi 2007: 80, 89–92, 97–98. For further discussion of depicting myth in the visual arts, see generally Shapiro 1994.

26 *BAPD* 310151 with full bibliography; *ABV* 108.5, 684; *Paralipomena* 43; *Beazley Addenda*[2] 29; Korshak 1987: 83; Shapiro 1989: 90–91; Isler-Kerényi 2004: 51–56; Picón, Mertens, et al. 2007: 84, no. 86; Moore 2010; Heinemann 2016: 264–66.

27 Shapiro 1989: 91.

28 Seaford 2013: 17.

29 Xenophanes, DK 21B24. Translation adapted from McKirahan 1994: 62.

30 Xenophanes, DK 21B25–26; Porter 2010: 163–65. Translation by McKirahan 1994: 62.

31 Aesch. *Supp.* 100–103. I follow Sommerstein's recent translation (2008).

32 Specifically, Richard Seaford (2013: 17) has argued that "certain basic structures are shared by tragedy and presocratic cosmology."

33 For more on male–female interaction within the symposium, see Chapter 4. On the relationship between Dionysos and intoxication, see Osborne 2014.

34 See, for example, Simonides *PMG* 647 in Ath., 2.40a.: "Simonides claimed that wine and music originated together." Lissarrague 1990b: 139; Neer 2002: 1–4; Bundrick 2005: 106; Osborne 2014.

35 Importantly, Bundrick (2005: 106–16) situates the vases within the symposium, although her discussion does not address the interaction between image and external viewer.

36 As Osborne (2014: 40) has convincingly argued, "to see Greek sympotic pottery through the eyes of its users we must look at it through inebriated eyes."

37 For more on Empedokles' theory of cosmogony, see Porter 2010: 153–57.

38 *BAPD* 31648; Arias 1963: 15, pl. 36.4–5; Lezzi-Hafter and Zindel 1991: 51, 70, no. 35; Lissarrague 2013: 157, fig. 30.

39 Arias 1963: 15.

40 On satyrs playing the *kithara*, see Castaldo 2000: 111–22. For more on satyrs wearing clothing, see Lissarrague 2013: 204–10; Heinemann 2016: 387–99.

41 For more on *kitharoidia*, see Chapter 3 and, more generally, Power 2010.

42 Much work has been done on the relationship between Dionysos and the theater. Particularly relevant arguments include: Simon 1983: 89–104; Henrichs 1990; Winkler and Zeitlin 1990; Sourvinou-Inwood 1994; Csapo 2003; Seaford 2006: 26–48; Kowalzig 2007a; Bierl 2012; Kowalzig and Wilson 2013b.

43 Kowalzig and Wilson 2013a; Hagel and Lynch 2015: 403; Laferrière 2023.

44 Kowalzig and Wilson 2013b.

45 Csapo 2003: 69–78, 90–95; Kowalzig 2007a: 226, 229–31; Kowalzig and Wilson 2013b: 9–11; Lavecchia 2013: 59–60.

46 Pind. frg. 70b, 8–18.

47 For a fuller discussion, see Kowalzig and Wilson 2013b: 9–11.

48 Kowalzig 2007a: 229–30; Kowalzig and Wilson 2013b: 9–11; Lavecchia 2013: 59–60, 69. For the relationship among Dionysos, *choroi*, and circular dances, see D'Angour 1997; Kowalzig and Wilson 2013b: 9–11.

49 *BAPD* 11686 with full bibliography; Shapiro 1994: 174–75; Buitron-Oliver 1995: 80, no. 121, pl. 73; Neer 2002: 60; Weaver 2009: 24–25; Lissarrague 2013: 169; Isler-Kerényi 2015: 59. The image clearly draws upon the same myth that Euripides' invoked in *Bacchai*, where Dionysos instills in a group of women a desire to rip apart Pentheus. Importantly, however, this cup was painted around 480 BCE, whereas Euripides' tragedy was only performed in 405. Weaver (2009) analyses the visual representations of Pentheus' death created prior to the *Bacchai*. For a cautionary statement against assuming the primacy of Dionysos in the *Bacchai* when considering the role of Dionysos within the city of Athens, see Henrichs 1990: 257–58.

50 Otto 1965: 133–42; Bundrick 2005: 109–11; Seaford 2006: 32–34, 41–44.

51 *BAPD* 213539; *ARV*[2] 1042.2; *Beazley Addenda*[2] 320; Robinson and Freeman 1937: 33–34, pls. 46.1A–C, 47.1; Matheson 1995: 134; Carpenter 1997: pl. 30B.

52 Otto 1965: 131, 133–42; Bundrick 2005: 118–19.

53 There exist two competing myths concerning the death of Orpheus: one, that Thracian women killed him because he had forsaken women following his failure to rescue Eurydice (Phanocles in Stob. 4.20.47; Verg. *G.* 4.520ff.; Paus. 9.30.5); and two, that maenads ripped him apart because he worshipped the sun, and Apollo by extension, more than any other god, including Dionysos (Pseudo-Eratosth. *Katasterismoi* 24 p. 29 Olivieri). Both of these versions seem plausibly the subject of the image: though the women do not the wear animal skins that maenads are often depicted wearing, neither does the woman who plays the tambourine and dances for Dionysos on the other side. Furthermore, they are not clearly recognizable as Thracian. They thus seem to have been represented as generic women who enact violence upon Orpheus.

54 *BAPD* 7870; Walters 1928: III i c, 7, pl. 37 1a–d; Cohen 2006: no. 77 with previous bibliography. The upper portion of the *rhyton* was thrown on a wheel and then attached to the sinuous bottom half that is held by the seated figure. The top lip was cut off all around the top of the vase, so that the heads of the painted figures have disappeared. The figures may still be identified, however, given the inclusion of attributes and inscriptions that label each figure. Removing the top rim of the cup may have been an ancient repair to fix a chipped lip.

55 The god is identified by an inscription, [Ε]ρμης. He is shown in a slightly adapted *Knielauf* position. On the history of the *Knielauf* as a visual mode of representation that can be particularly associated with running Gorgons, see Schmidt 1909: 250–91, 370–97; Weingarten 1985: 179–80; Carter 1987: 360–61.

56 Artemis is identified by a retrograde inscription, which reads Αρ]τεμις.

57 He is also identified by inscription: Ἀπόλλων.

58 Known as a plastic or molded vase, this particular category of vessels is presented in combination with a three-dimensional sculptural element. For more on plastic vases, see Lissarrague 1990b: 47–59; Lissarrague 1995a; True 2006.

59 *BAPD* 204730 with complete bibliography; *ARV*[2] 462.48, 81, 1654; *Paralipomena* 377; *Beazley Addenda* 120; *Beazley Addenda*[2] 244; Carpenter 1997: pls. 20B, 21; Lissarrague 1990b: 100–102; Isler-Kerényi 2015: 126, fig. 69; Heinemann 2016: 129, 493, fig. 69. For more on representations featuring masks of Dionysos, see Frontisi-Ducroux 1991; Peirce 1998.

60 As noted by Lissarrague 1990b: 100–102.

61 Otto 1965: 133–42. Though, importantly, the vases in no way suggest that ripping apart a deer was a ritual practiced by mortal worshippers of Dionysos.

62 For more on painted vases on vases, see Neils 2004; Venit 2006.

63 Otto 1965: 133–42.

64 *BAPD* 5344; Wolf 1993: figs. 136–38; Lissarrague 2013: 230.

65 *BAPD* 204401; *ARV*[2] 406.2; *Paralipomena* 371; *Beazley Addenda* 115; *Beazley Addenda*[2] 232; Hartwig 1893: pls. 42.2, 43; Lawler 1964: 64, fig. 24, 65; Williams 1993: 66–68, fig.12D, pls. 74.A–B, 75.A–B; Carpenter 1997: pl. 10A.

66 The maenads wear the unusual 'wing sleeve,' which is often included when they are shown dancing. Schöne 1987: 152–56.

67 *BAPD* 201659 with complete bibliography; *ARV*[2] 182.6, 1632; *Paralipomena* 340; *Beazley Addenda* 115; *Beazley Addenda*[2] 186; Lullies 1956: 26–27, pls. 199.1–2, 200.1–2, 01.1–2, 02.1–2, 03.1–2, 04.1–3; Lawler 1964: 62, 64–65; Beazley 1974: 14; Korshak 1987: 124; Schöne 1987: 148, pls. 22–23; Carpenter 1997: pl. 33A; Lissarrague 2013: 152; Heinemann 2016: 136, 175.

68 Detailed work on frontal faces has been undertaken by Korshak 1987; Frontisi-Ducroux 1995; Mackay 2001; Mack 2002; Hedreen 2007; Hedreen 2017. I also follow Meyer Schapiro's argument (1973, 38f.) that these frontal faces actively look at their viewers.

69 On frames in vase-painting, see especially Hurwit 1977: 5–15; Platt and Squire 2017a; Marconi 2017.

70 Lissarrague 1990a: 206; Lissarrague 1990b: 19–36; Neer 2002: 9–26; Osborne 2014: 40–41, 45–46.

71 Nooter 2019: 204–06.

72 Ar. *Ran.* 209–17. Translation lightly adapted from Henderson 2002: 52–53.

73 Ar. *Ran.* 228–35.

74 As Nooter (2019: 205) notes, the frogs "root their musical value in the material of the marshes." See also Porter (2010: 262–75) on the issue of aesthetic materiality in the comedy. Translation lightly adapted from Henderson 2002: 54–55.

75 Ar. *Ran.* 263–68. Translation from Henderson 2002: 58–59.

76 See, with earlier bibliography, *BAPD* 217500; Taplin and Wyles 2010.

77 On solo dancers in Greek literature, see Olsen 2020.

CONCLUSION

Experiencing Divine Music

Moving between the poetic ekphrasis of a Greek vase and a felt desire to hear the sounds of the ancient music depicted on the vessel, Keats offers his readers the enigmatic sentiment that

> Heard melodies are sweet, but those unheard
> Are sweeter; therefore, ye soft pipes, play on;
> Not to the sensual ear, but, more endear'd,
> Pipe to the spirit ditties of no tone . . .[1]

There is clearly a paradox at work here: how can sounds that are unheard, that are silent, be more pleasing to the ear than those that can be heard? In invoking this tension between the sounds of music and its corresponding visual representation, Keats points to the role of the imagination in the aesthetic experience of ancient Greek vase-painting. Images of musical performances are sweeter precisely because they cannot be heard. The audience must instead imagine the sounds, creating an infinite variety of melodic possibilities that emanate from the image. Permanently captured in a state of continued poetic performance, the pipes play on, repeatedly offering to the viewer the opportunity to imagine the acoustic sounds that fill the visual scene.

In his poem, Keats powerfully evokes the enticing range of sensory experiences offered by ancient art. Throughout this book, I have shown how ancient images offer similar experiences to us, in each instance evocatively communicating the beauty, power, and seductive effect of the gods' music. By isolating our experience of divine musicians to the visual realm, where we are invited to look closely at scenes of divine musical performance, we are encouraged to see the sounds as they manifest throughout the composition, in the relationship between musician and instrument, and in the positions of the other figures. Music fills these otherwise silent images, and in each instance, it proves to be a powerful force in determining not only how each divine musician is depicted, but also showing how its effect upon the other figures and the ancient viewers was visualized and provoked. Again and again, in both textual and visual evidence, it is this wonderous and tantalizing quality that is associated with divine music. Pan's *syrinx* music encourages the Nymphs' choral dance. Apollo is so profoundly moved by the lyre that he takes up the instrument and plays it beautifully, even enticing the gods to sing and dance. The Muses inspire the songs of mortal poets and accompany divine celebrations with their music. And Dionysos provokes a frenetic musical energy in his followers. Consistent, then, across the ancient evidence is the gods' shared ability to offer their audience a profoundly moving experience of their music.

Each image also reaches out to its human audience, whose experience of listening-while-looking collectively activates Pan's piped tunes, Apollo's performance on the lyre, a Muse's on the *aulos*, or Dionysos' revel. Consequently, the human response these images offer continually reaffirms the superlative character of divine music, whether it is the harmonizing effect of Apollo's song or the embodied encounter with Dionysos' presence. In these scenes, the gods' presence before their audience is established not just in the visual representation painted onto the side of a vase or carved into a shallow stone, but rather the gods' music is experienced within the viewers' perception of the scene, in that moment of seeing the performance, imagining its sounds, and hearing the music. The images thus repeatedly suggest that it is, above all, through the conflation of sensory perceptions, where seeing is a kind of listening and where the viewers are invited to hear the sounds that they see on a physical, material object, that the gods and the sounds of their music are fully revealed.

We have also encountered the consistent impulse for the gods' music to expand beyond the image itself, repeatedly pushing at the boundaries of their representation, as if visually embodying the expansive and compelling qualities associated with the sounds of divinely created music. Pan himself sits upon the rocky frame, at once enclosing the dancing Nymphs with his melody while also sending his music out into the larger cave for their worshippers to hear. The arms of Apollo's lyre are so often shown pushing through the scene's upper frame, even as his musical and ritual actions are coordinated with those of his human worshippers. The Muses' very identity becomes malleable, so that they and their music may appear at any time and place in the Athenian city. Finally, Dionysos' influence upon his satyrs and their musical performance also pushes the sounds of their instruments beyond the frame, so that their music blends in with the music performed within the symposium.

By allowing the god's music to expand beyond the limits of the visual image, each representation allows the music performed by the divine musician to move beyond the image and into the context in which the vase was used or the relief was set up. The human viewers, who looked upon a scene of Apollo with his lyre or Pan with his pipes, were thus offered the opportunity to become a member of the audience. As such, mortal men and women could become fellow spectators as they watched the divine performance and, consequently, imaginatively generated the sound of the music produced by the specific instrument the god is depicted playing. By looking at the deity's performance, seeing the effect that his or her music has on the divine audience, and then imaginatively hearing the god's performance, men and women could more fully experience divine presence as a conflation of sensory perceptions.

The space in which the images were encountered played a crucial role in one's engagement with the gods, as it could exaggerate or amplify one's interaction with divine music. Pan's music becomes all the more powerful when seen within a cave, precisely because the repetition between the sculpted and real cave brings the two spaces together, creating a continuum between the world of the divine and that of mankind. Similarly, the effect Dionysos has upon his satyrs and maenads is more poignant when the scenes of musical and danced revelry were encountered within the symposium, where the human audience also drank wine, played music, danced, and sang poetry. The repetitions between the context in which the images were seen and the individual god's musical performance helped blur the distinction between image and reality, so that the viewer could fully perceive and engage with the gods, and, consequently, experience divine presence as a bodily response to the representation of the god's music.

Beyond the powerful effect that divine music could have on its audience, the vases and reliefs that bear these scenes also communicate something profound about their human audience. Not only did the images offer their viewers the chance to experience a multisensory epiphany, but through the human experience of participating in the gods' musical performances, the images also established deep and lasting bonds among their viewers through the shared act of seeing, hearing, and worshipping the divine.

NOTE

1 John Keats, *Ode on a Grecian Urn*, 11–14.

BIBLIOGRAPHY

Alexiou, M. (2002). *The Ritual Lament in Greek Tradition*. Revised by Dimitrios Yatromanolakis and Panagiotis Roilos. 2nd ed. Lanham.

Allen, T. W., W. R. Halliday, and E. E. Sikes, eds. (1936). *The Homeric Hymns 2*. Oxford.

Anhalt, E. K. (1993). *Solon the Singer: Politics and Poetics*. Greek Studies: Interdisciplinary Approaches. Lanham.

Antonaccio, C. M. (2000). "Architecture and Behavior: Building Gender into Greek Houses." *CW* 93: 517–33.

Arafat, K. W. (1990). *Classical Zeus: A Study in Art and Literature*. Oxford Monographs on Classical Archaeology. Oxford.

Archibald, Z., C. Morgan, B. Cavanagh, A. Dunn, R. Pitt, D. Stewart, J. Bennet, and M. Stamatopoulou. (2010–11). "Archaeology in Greece 2010–2011." *AR* 57: 1–108.

Arias, P. E. (1963). *Ferrara, Museo Nazionale I*. Corpus Vasorum Antiquorum. Italy 37. Mainz.

Arnott, W. G., ed. and trans. (1979). *Menander. Aspis. Georgos. Dis Exapaton. Dyskolos. Encheiridion. Epitrepontes*. Loeb Classical Library 132. Cambridge, MA.

Bakalakis, G. (1936). "Un torse archaïque d'Apollon citharède à Délos." *BCH* 60: 59–65.

(1967). *Ἀνασκαφὴ Στρύμης. Ἀριστοτέλιον Πανεπιστήμιον Θεσσαλονίκησ, Ἐπιστημονικὴ ἐπετηρις Φιλοσοφικῆς σχολῆς*. Thessaloniki.

Baldwin, A. (1903). "The Cave at Vari. V. Coins." *AJA* 7, no. 3: 335–37.

Barker, A., ed. (1984). *Greek Musical Writings: I, The Musician and His Art*, Cambridge Readings in the Literature of Music. Cambridge.

(1989). *Greek Musical Writings: II, Harmonic and Acoustic Theory*. Cambridge Readings in the Literature of Music. Cambridge.

(2007). *The Science of Harmonics in Classical Greece*. Cambridge.

Bassett, S. E. (1903). "The Cave at Vari. VI. The Terra-Cotta Lamps." *AJA* 7, no. 3: 338–49.

Bathrellou, E. (2012). "Menander's Epitrepontes and the Festival of the Tauropolia." *ClAnt* 31, no. 2: 151–92.

Beazley, J. D. (1918). *Attic Red-Figured Vases in American Museums*. Cambridge, MA.

(1925). *Attische Vasenmaler des rotfiguren Stils*. Tübingen.

(1930). *Der Berliner Maler*. Forschungen zur antiken Keramik. Berlin-Wilmersdorf.

(1931–32). "Groups of Mid-Sixth-Century Black-Figure." *BSA* 32: 1–22.

(1938). *Attic White Lekythoi: William Henry Charlton Memorial Lecture*. London.

(1956). *Attic Black-Figure Vase-Painters*. Oxford.

(1963). *Attic Red-Figure Vase-Painters*. 2nd ed. Oxford.

(1971). *Paralipomena: Additions to Attic Black-Figure Vase-Painters and to Attic Red-Figure Vase-Painters*. 2nd ed. Oxford.

(1974). *The Kleophrades Painter*. Mainz.

(1986). *The Development of Attic Black-Figure: Sather Classical Lectures*. Revised ed. Vol. 24. Berkeley, Los Angeles, and London.

Becker, R.-M. (1977). *Formen attischer Peliken von der Pionier-Gruppe bis zum Beginn der Frühklassik*. Böblingen.

Bélis, A. (1984). "Un nouveau document musical." *BCH* 108, no. 1: 99–109.

(1988). "Musique et transe dans le cortège dionysiaque." In *Transe et Théâtre: Actes de la Table Ronde Internationale, Montpellier, 3–5 mars 1988*, edited by Paulette Ghiron-Bistagne. Cahiers du GITA, 9–29. Montpellier.

(1992). "À propos de la coupe CA 482 du Louvre." *BCH* 116: 53–59.

Bennett, J. (2010. *Vibrant Matter: A Political Ecology of Things*. Durham, NC.

Bérard, C. (1984). "L'ordre des femmes." In *La cité des images: religion et société en Grèce antique*, edited by Claude Bérard, 85–103. Paris.

(1989). "The Order of Women." In *A City of Images: Iconography and Society in Ancient Greece*, edited by Claude Bérard et al., 89–99. Princeton.

Betts, E. (2017a). "Introduction: Senses of Empire." In *Senses of the Empire: Multisensory Approaches to Roman Culture*, edited by Eleanor Betts, 1–12. London.

(2017b). "Afterword: Towards a Methodology for Roman Sensory Studies." In *Senses of the Empire: Multisensory Approaches to Roman Culture*, edited by Eleanor Betts, 193–99. London.

Bicknell, J. (2009). *Why Music Moves Us*. New York.

Bielfeldt, R., ed. (2014). *Ding und Mensch in der Antike: Gegenwart und Vergegenwärtigung*. Akademiekonferenzen, 16. Heidelberg.

Bierl, A. (2012). "Dionysos' Epiphany in Performance: The God of Ecstatic Cry, Noise, Song, Music, and Choral Dance." *Electra* 2: 1–12.

Bing, P. (1993). "Impersonation of Voice in Callimachus' Hymn to Apollo." *TAPA* 123: 181–98.

Birchler Emery, P., B. Bottini, C. Courtois, and F. van der Wielen. (1996). *La musique et la danse dans l'antiquité: regards sur les collections du Musée d'art et d'histoire de Genève*. Geneva.

Blümel, C. (1971). "Die Acheloosmaske aus Marathon und das Weihrelief mit Acheloos und Göttermersammlung aus Megara." *AA* 85: 185–94.

Boardman, J. (1974). *Athenian Black-Figure Vases: A Handbook*. London.

(1975). *Oxford, Ashmolean Museum III*. Corpus Vasorum Antiquorum. Great Britain 14. Oxford.

(1995). *Greek Sculpture: The Late Classical Period and Sculpture in Colonies and Overseas*. London.

Borgeaud, P. (1988). *The Cult of Pan in Ancient Greece*. Chicago.

Bowie, E. (1986). "Early Greek Elegy, Symposium, and Public Festival." *JHS* 106: 13–35.

Bradley, M., ed. (2015). *Smell and the Ancient Senses*. Abingdon and New York.

Bremmer, J. N. (1984). "Greek Maenadism Reconsidered." *ZPE* 55: 267–86.

Brockliss, W. (2017–2018). "Olympian Sound in the Theogony and the Catalogue of Women: Sweet Music and Disorderly Noise." *CJ* 113, no. 2: 129–49.

Brommer, F. (1938). "Panbilder des Fünften Jahrhunderts." *AA* 53: 376–81.

(1949). "Pan im 5. und 4. Jahrhundert v. Chr." *MarbJb* 15: 5–42.

(1956). "s. v. Pan." In *RE, Supplement*, vol. 8.

(1961). "Die Geburt der Athena auf der Reliefamphora in Tenos." *JRGZM* 8: 66–83.

Brouillet, M. (2016). "Des chants en partage: l'épopée homérique comme expérience religieuse." PhD dissertation, École des Hautes Études en Sciences Sociales.

(2017). "*Thambos* et *kharis*: constructions sensorielles et éxperiences du divin dans les épopées homériques." *Mythos* 11: 83–93.

Brown, P. G. M. (1993). "Love and Marriage in Greek New Comedy." *CQ* 43, no. 1: 189–205.

Budelmann, F., and P. LeVen. (2014). "Timotheus' Poetics of Blending: A Cognitive Approach to the Language of the New Music." *CP* 109: 191–210.

Budelmann, F., and T. Power. (2015). "Another Look at Female Choruses in Classical Athens." *ClAnt* 34, no. 2: 252–295.

Buitron-Oliver, D. (1995). *Douris: A Master-Painter of Athenian Red-Figure Vases*.

Forschungen zur antiken Keramik. Vol. 11 Reihe, Kerameus, Mainz.

Bundrick, S. (1998). "Expressions of Harmony: Representations of Female Musicians in Fifth-Century Athenian Vase Painting." PhD Dissertation, Emory University.

(2005). *Music and Image in Classical Athens.* Cambridge.

(2012). "Housewives, *Hetairai*, and the Ambiguity of Genre in Attic Vase Painting." *Phoenix* 66, nos. 1–2: 11–35.

(2015). "Athenian Eye Cups in Context." *AJA* 119, no. 3: 295–341.

(2019). *Athens, Etruria, and the Many Lives of Greek Figured Pottery.* Madison, WI.

(2021). "Music as Mnema on Athenian White Ground Lekythoi." In *Music and Memory in the Ancient Greek and Roman Worlds*, edited by Lauren Curtis and Naomi A. Weiss, 287–310.

Buranelli, F., and M. Sannibale. (2003). *Vaticano: Museo gregoriano etrusco.* Milan.

Burkert, W. (1979). *Structure and History in Greek Mythology and Ritual.* Berkeley.

(1985). *Greek Religion.* Cambridge, MA.

Burn, L., and R. Glynn. (1983). *Beazley Addenda: Additional References to ABV, ARV^2 and Paralipomena.* Oxford.

Butler, S., and A. Purves, eds. (2013). *Synaesthesia and the Ancient Senses.* Senses in Antiquity. Durham.

Butler, S., and S. Nooter, eds. (2019). *Sound and the Ancient Senses.* Abingdon and New York.

Calame, C. (2001). *Choruses of Young Women in Ancient Greece: Their Morphology, Religious Role, and Social Functions.* Translated by Derek Collins and Janice Orion. New and revised ed. Oxford.

(2009). "Apollo in Delphi and in Delos: Poetic Performances between Paean and Dithyramb." In *Apolline Politics and Poetics*, edited by Lucia Athanassaki, R. P. Martin, and J. F. Miller, 169–98. Athens.

(2013). "'Rien pour Dionysos?' Le dithyrambe comme forme poétique entre Apollon et Dionysos." In *Redefining Dionysos*, edited by Alberto Bernabé et al., 82–99. Berlin.

Camp, J. M. (1977). "The Water Supply of Ancient Athens from 3000 to 86 BC." PhD Dissertation, Princeton University.

(1980). *Gods and Heroes in the Athenian Agora.* Excavations of the Athenian Agora. Vol. 19. Athens and Princeton.

Carpenter, T. H. T. Mannack, and M. Mendonça. (1989). *Beazley Addenda: Additional References to ABV, ARV2, & Paralipomena.* 2nd ed. Oxford.

Carpenter, T. H. (1986). *Dionysian Imagery in Archaic Greek Art: Its Development in Black-Figure Vase Painting.* Oxford.

(1997). *Dionysian Imagery in Fifth-Century Athens.* Oxford.

Carter, J. B. (1987). "The Masks of Ortheia." *AJA* 91, no. 3: 355–83.

Casson, S. (1912). *Catalogue of the Acropolis Museum.* Vol. 2. Cambridge.

Castaldo, D. (2000). *Il pantheon musicale: iconografia nella ceramica Attica tra VI e IV secolo.* Ravenna.

Chandler, R. (1776). *Travels in Greece, or, An account of a Tour Made at the Expense of the Society of Dilettanti.* Oxford.

Chiarini, S. (2018). *The So-called Nonsense Inscriptions on Ancient Greek Vases: Between Paideia and Paidiá.* Leiden.

Clay, D. (2004). *Archilochos Heros: The Cult of Poets in the Greek Polis.* Center for Hellenic Studies. Cambridge, MA and London.

Clay, J. S. (2006). *The Politics of Olympus: Form and Meaning in the Major Homeric Hymns.* 2nd ed. London.

Coccagna, H. A. (2014). "Manipulating Mastoi: The Female Breast in the Sympotic Setting." In Amalia Avramidou and Denise Demetriou, eds., *Approaching the Ancient Artifact: Representation, Narrative, and Function*, 399–411. Berlin.

Coche de la Ferté, E. (1951). "Les ménades et le contenu réel des représentations de scènes bachiques autour de l'idole de Dionysos." *RA* 38: 12–23.

Cohen, B., ed. (2006). *The Colors of Clay: Special Techniques in Athenian Vases*. Los Angeles.

Comstock, M., and C. Vermeule. (1971). *Greek, Etruscan, and Roman Bronzes in the Museum of Fine Arts, Boston*. Boston.

Connor, W. R. (1988). "Seized by the Nymphs: Nympholepsy and Symbolic Expression in Classical Greece." *ClAnt* 7, no. 2: 155–89.

Couve, L. (1895). "Vases attiques à figures rouges." *BCH* 19: 94–108.

Creese, D., and P. Destrée, eds. (forthcoming). *The Beauties of Song: Aesthetic Appreciations of Music in the Greek and Roman World*. Cambridge.

Csapo, E. (2003). "The Dolphins of Dionysus." In *Poetry, Theory, Praxis: The Social Life of Myth, Word and Image in Ancient Greece. Essays in Honour of William J. Slater*, edited by Eric Csapo and M. C. Miller, 69–98. Oxford.

Curd, P. (2013). "The Divine and the Thinkable: Toward an Account of the Intelligible Cosmos." *Rhizomata* 1, no. 2: 217–47.

(2019). "Presocratic Accounts of Perception and Cognition." In *Philosophy of Mind in Antiquity: The History of the Philosophy of Mind*, edited by J. E. Sisko, 44–63. London and New York.

Curtis, L., and N. A. Weiss, eds. (2021). *Music and Memory in the Ancient Greek and Roman Worlds*. Cambridge.

D'Angour, A. (1997). "How the Dithyramb Got Its Shape." *CQ* 47, no. 2: 331–51.

(2006). "The New Music: So What's New?". In *Rethinking Revolutions through Ancient Greece*, edited by Simon Goldhill and Robin Osborne, 264–83. Cambridge.

(2007). "The Sound of *Mousikē*: Reflections on Aural Change in Ancient Greece." In *Debating the Athenian Cultural Revolution: Art, Literature, Philosophy, and Politics, 430–380 bc*, edited by Robin Osborne, 288–300. Cambridge.

(2015). "Sense and Sensation in Music." In *A Companion to Ancient Aesthetics*, edited by Pierre Destrée and Penelope Murray, 188–203. Malden, MA.

(2019). "Hearing Ancient Sounds through Modern Ears." In *Sound and the Ancient Senses*, edited by Shane Butler and Sarah Nooter, 31–43. Abingdon and New York.

Davidson, J. N. (1997). *Courtesans and Fishcakes: The Consuming Passions of Classical Athens*. London.

Davis, W. (2010). *A General Theory of Visual Culture*. Princeton.

(2017). *Visuality and Virtuality: Images and Pictures from Prehistory to Perspective*. Princeton.

Day, J., ed. (2013). *Making Senses of the Past: Toward a Sensory Archaeology*. Carbondale.

Day, J. (1994). "Interactive Offerings: Early Greek Dedicatory Epigrams and Ritual." *HSCP* 96: 37–74.

(2000). "Epigram and Reader: Generic Force as (Re-)Activation of Ritual." In *Matrices of Genre: Authors, Canons, and Society*, edited by Mary Depew and Dirk Obbink, 37–58. Cambridge, MA.

(2010). *Archaic Greek Epigram and Dedication: Representation and Reperformance*. Cambridge and New York.

Delavaud-Roux, M. (1988). "Danse et transe: la danse au service du culte de Dionysos dans l'antiquité grecque." In *Transe et Théâtre: Actes de la Table Ronde Internationale, Montpellier, 3–5 mars 1988*, edited by Paulette Ghiron-Bistagne. Cahiers du GITA, 31–53. Montpellier.

(1995). "L'énigme des danseurs barbus au parasol et les vases "des Lénéennes"." *Revue Archéologique, n.s.* 2: 227–63.

Demargne, P. (1984). "Athena." In *LIMC*, 955–1044. Zurich and Munich.

Derrida, J. (1987). *The Truth in Painting*. Translated by Geoff Bennington and Ian McLeod. Chicago and London.

Dietrich, N. (2010). *Figur ohne Raum? Bäume und Felsen in der attischen Vasenmalerei des 6. und 5. Jahrhunderts v. Chr.* Berlin.

Dietrich, N., and M. Squire, eds. (2018). *Ornament and Figure in Graeco-Roman Art: Rethinking Visual Ontologies in Classical Antiquity*. Berlin and Boston.

Diggle, J., ed. (1981). *Euripidis Fabulae*. Vol. 2. Oxford.
Dodds, E. R. (1940). "Maenadism in the Bacchae." *HTR* 33, no. 3: 155–76.
Donohue, A. A. (1997). "The Greek Images of the Gods: Consideration on Terminology and Methodology." *Hephaistos* 15: 31–45.
Dunham, M. E. (1903). "The Cave at Vari. II. Inscriptions." *AJA* 7, no. 3: 289–300.
Eckstein-Wolf, B. (1951). "Zur Darstellung spendender Götter." *MdI IV*: 39–75.
Edelmann, M. (1999). *Menschen auf griechischen Weihreliefs*. Quellen und Forschungen zur antiken Welt. Munich.
Edwards, C. M. (1985)."Greek Votive Reliefs to Pan and the Nymphs." PhD Dissertation, Institute of Fine Arts, New York University.
Edwards, M. W. (1960). "Representations of Maenads on Archaic Red-Figure Vases." *JHS* 80: 78–87.
Eitrem, S. (1906). "Der homerische *Hymnus an Hermes*." *Philologus* 65: 248–82.
Elsner, J. (1996). "Image and Ritual: Reflections on the Religious Appreciation of Classical Art." *CQ* 46: 515–31.
(2007). *Roman Eyes: Visuality and Subjectivity in Art and Text*. Princeton and Oxford.
(2017). "Visual Ontologies: Style, Archaism and Framing in the Construction of the Sacred in the Western Tradition." In *The Frame in Classical Art: A Cultural History*, edited by Verity Platt and Michael Squire, 457–99. Cambridge.
Emlyn-Jones, C., and W. Preddy, eds. and trans. (2017). *Plato. Plato I. Euthyphro, Apology, Crito, Phaedo, Phaedrus*. Loeb Classical Library 36. Cambridge, MA.
Fahlander, F., and A. Kjellström, eds. (2010). *Making Sense of Things: Archaeologies of Sensory Perception*. Stockholm.
Fairbanks, A., and G. H. Chase. (1948). *Greek Gods and Heroes: As Represented in the Classical Collections of the Museum*. Boston.
Felten, W. (2009). "Zeus." In *LIMC*, 495–535. Dusseldorf.
Ferrari, G. (2006). "Architectural Space as Metaphor in the Greek Sanctuary." In *The Artful Mind: Cognitive Science and the Riddle of Human Creativity*, edited by Mark Turner, 225–42. Oxford.
Feubel, R. (1935). "Die attischen Nymphenreliefs und ihre Vorbilder." Heidelberg.
Ford, A. (2011). *Aristotle as Poet: The Song for Hermias and Its Contexts*. Oxford.
Förstel, K. (1979). *Untersuchungen zum homerischen Apollonhymnos*. Bochum.
Foster, S. L. (2008). "Movement's Contagion: The Kinesthetic Impact of Performance." *The Cambridge Companion to Performance Studies*, edited by T. C. Davis, 46–59. Cambridge.
(2011). *Choreographing Empathy: Kinesthesia in Performance*. London and New York.
Foucault, M. (1985). *History of Sexuality. Vol. 2: The Use of Pleasure*. Translated by Robert Hurley. New York.
Frede, D. (2010). "Puppets On Strings: Moral Psychology in Laws Books 1 and 2." In *Plato's Laws: A Critical Guide*, edited by Christian Bobonich, 108–26. Cambridge.
Fried, M. (1988). *Absorption and Theatricality: Painting and Beholder in the Age of Diderot*. Chicago.
Frontisi-Ducroux, F. (1991). *Le dieu-masque, une figure du Dionysos d'Athènes*. Paris and Rome.
(1995). *Du masque au visage: aspects de l'identité en Grèce ancienne*. Paris.
Frontisi-Ducroux, F., and F. Lissarrague. (1983). "D.e l'ambiguité .à l'ambivalence: un parcours dionsiaque." *Annali dell'Istituto universitario orientale di Napoli. Seminario di studi del mondo classico. Sezione di archeologia e storia antica* V: 11–32.
Fuchs, W. (1959). "Die Vorbilder der neuattischen Reliefs." *JdI* Suppl. 20.
(1961). "Ein attisches Weihrelief im Vatikan." *MdI, Römische Abteilung* 68: 167–81.
(1962). "Attischen Nymphenreliefs." *AM* 77: 242–49.
Furley, W. D., and J. M. Bremer. (2001a). *Greek Hymns: Selected Cult Songs from the Archaic to the Hellenistic Period. Vol. 1: The Texts in Translation*, Tübingen.

(2001b). *Greek Hymns: Selected Cult Songs from the Archaic to the Hellenistic Period. Vol. 2: Greek Texts and Commentary*, Tübingen.

Furtwängler, A. (1878). "Die Chariten der Akropolis." *MdI, Athenische Abteilung* 3: 181–202.

(1881). "Zwei Theongefässe aus Athen."*MdI, Athenische Abteilung* 6: 106–18.

Furtwängler, A., K. Reichhold, and F. Hauser. (1904–1932). *Griechische Vasenmalerei: Auswahl hervorragender Vasenbilder*. Munich.

Gaifman, M. (2008). "Visualized Rituals and Dedicatory Inscriptions on Votive Offerings to the Nymphs." *Opuscula: Annual of the Swedish Institute at Athens and Rome* 1: 85–103.

(2013). "Timelessness, Fluidity, and Apollo's Libation." *RES: Anthropology and Aesthetics* 63/64: 39–52.

(2016). "Theologies of Statues in Classical Greek Art." In *Theologies of Ancient Greek Religion*, edited by Esther Eidinow, Julia Kindt, and Robin Osborne, 249–80. Cambridge.

(2017). "Framing Divine Bodies in Greek Art." In *The Frame in Classical Art: A Cultural History*, edited by Verity Platt and Michael Squire, 392–424. Cambridge.

(2018a). *The Art of Libation in Classical Athens*. New Haven.

(2018b). "The Greek Libation Bowl as Embodied Object." *Art History: Special Issue: The Embodied Object in Classical Antiquity* 41, no. 3: 444–65.

Gaifman, M., and V. Platt. (2018). "Introduction: From Grecian Urn to Embodied Object." *Art History: Special Issue: The Embodied Object in Classical Antiquity* 41, no. 3: 402–19.

Gantz, T. (1993). *Early Greek Myth: A Guide to Literary and Artistic Sources*. Baltimore.

Gasparri, C. (1986). "Dionysos." In *LIMC*, 414–514. Zurich and Munich.

Gell, A. (1998). *Art and Agency: An Anthropological Theory*. Oxford.

Gianvittorio, L. (2017). "Introduction." In *Choreutika: Performing and Theorising Dance in Ancient Greece*, edited by Laura Gianvittorio, 25–36. Pisa.

Giuliani, L. (2013). *Image and Myth: A History of Pictorial Narration in Greek Art*. Translated by Joseph O'Donnell. Chicago.

Goette, H. R. (2001). *Athens, Attica and the Megarid: An Archaeological Guide*. London and New York.

Goldberg, M. Y. (1999). "Spatial and Behavioral Negotiation in Classical Athenian City Houses." In *The Archaeology of Household Activities*, edited by P. M. Allison, 142–61. London.

Goldhill, S. (1990). "The Great Dionysia and Civic Ideology." In *Nothing to Do with Dionysos? Athenian Drama in Its Social Context*, edited by J. J. Winkler and F. I. Zeitlin, 97–129. Princeton.

Goldman, M. L. (2015). "Associating the *Aulêtris*: Flute Girls and Prostitutes in the Classical Greek Symposium." *Helios* 42, no. 1: 29–60.

González, M. G. (2019). *Funerary Epigrams of Ancient Greece: Reflections on Literature, Society, and Religion*. London.

Gordon, R. L. (1979). "The Real and the Imaginary: Production and Religion in the Graeco-Roman World." *Art History* 2: 5–34.

Graf, F. (1980). "Milch, Honig und Wein: Zum verständnis der Libation im griechischen Ritual." In *Perennitas: Studi in onore di Angelo Brelich promossi dalla Cattedra di Religioni del mondo classico dell'Università degli Studi di Roma*, 209–21. Rome.

(2009). *Apollo*. London and New York.

Grand-Clément, A. (2013). "*Poikilia*. Pour une anthropologie de la bigarrure en Grèce ancienne." In *Anthropologie de l'Antiquité. Ancients objects, nouvelles approches*, edited by Pascal Payen and Évelyne Scheid-Tissinier, 239–62. Brepols.

(2015). "Poikilia." In *A Companion to Ancient Aesthetics*, edited by Pierre Destrée and Penelope Murray, 406–21. Malden, MA.

Greenblatt, S. (1980). *Renaissance Self-Fashioning from More to Shakespeare*. Chicago.

Greifenhagen, A. (1929). *Eine attische schwarzfigurige Vasengattung und die Darstellung des Komos in VI. Jahrhundert*. Königsberg.

Grethlein, J. (2016). "Sight and Reflexivity: Theorizing Vision in Greek Vase-Painting." In *Sight and the Ancient Senses*, edited by Michael Squire, 85–106. London and New York.

(2017). *Aesthetic Experiences and Classical Antiquity: The Significance of Form in Narratives and Pictures*. Cambridge.

Griffith, M. (2021). "Music, Memory, and the (Ancient Greek) Imagination." In *Music and Memory in the Ancient Greek and Roman Worlds*, edited by Lauren Curtis and N. A. Weiss, 25–62. Cambridge.

Griffiths, A. (1986). "'What Leaf-Fringed Legend...?' A Cup by the Sotiades Painter in London." *JHS* 106: 58–70.

Gruben, G. (1969). "Untersuchungen am Dipylon, 1964–1966." *AA* 84: 31–40.

Gunnarsdottir, S. (2023). "Ceramics and the Sacred in Greek Antiquity." PhD Dissertation, Yale University.

Güntner, G. (1994). *Göttervereine und Götterversammlungen auf attischen Weihreliefs: Untersuchungen zur Typologie und Bedeutung*. Beiträge zur Archäologie. Vol. 21. Würzburg.

Gurd, S. A. (2016). *Dissonance: Auditory Aesthetics in Ancient Greece*. New York.

Haas, G. (1985). *Die Syrinx in der griechischen Bildkunst*. Wiener musikwissenschaftliche Beiträge. Vol. 11. Vienna.

Hagel, S. (2009). *Ancient Greek Music: A New Technical History*. Cambridge.

(2014). "Ancient Greek Music on the *Kithara* and *Aulos*." Lund, Sweden: https://www.youtube.com/watch?v=4UWBoorsuHU.

Hagel, S., and T. Lynch. (2015). "Musical Education in Greece and Rome." In *A Companion to Ancient Education*, edited by W. M. Bloomer. Blackwell Companions to the Ancient World, 401–12. Chichester and Malden, MA.

Hamdorf, F. W. (1990). "Musik und Symposion." In *Kunst der Schale, Kultur des Trinkens.*, edited by Klaus Verneisel and Bert Kaeser, 238–46. Munich.

Hamilakis, Y. (2013). *Archaeology and the Senses: Human Experience, Memory, and Affect*. Cambridge.

(2017). "Sensorial Assemblages: Affect, Memory and Temporality in Assemblage Thinking." *CAJ* 27, no. 1: 169–82.

Hamilakis, Y., and A. M. Jones. (2017). "Archaeology and Assemblage." *CAJ* 27, no. 1: 77–84.

Harrington, K. (2015). "Privacy and Production: Sensory aspects of Household Industry in Classical and Hellenistic Greece." *Archaeological Review from Cambridge: Seen and Unseen Spaces* 30, no. 1: 63–69.

Harris, O. J. T. (2017). "Assemblages and Scale in Archaeology." *CAJ* 27, no. 1: 127–39.

Hartwig, P. (1893). *Die griechischen Meisterschalen der Blüthezeit des strengen rothfigurigen Stiles*. Berlin.

Haspels, C. H. E. (1936). *Attic Black-Figured Lekythoi*. Travaux et mémoires (École française d'Athènes). Vol. IV. Paris.

Hedreen, G. (1992). *Silens in Attic Black-Figure Vase-painting: Myth and Performance*. Ann Arbor.

(1994). "Silens, Nymphs, and Maenads." *JHS* 114: 47–69.

(2007). "Involved Spectatorship in Archaic Greek Art." *Art History* 30, no. 2: 217–46.

(2017). "Unframing the Representation: The Frontal Face in Athenian Vase-Painting." In *The Frame in Classical Art: A Cultural History*, edited by Verity Platt and Michael Squire, 154–87. Cambridge.

Heesen, P. (2016). "Meaningless, But Not Useless! Nonsense Inscriptions on Athenian Little-Master Cups." In *Epigraphy of Art: Ancient Greek Vase-Inscriptions and Vase-Paintings*, edited by Dimitrios Yatromanolakis, 91–118. Oxford.

Alexander, H. (2016). *Der Gott des Gelages. Dionysos, Satyrn und Mänaden auf attischem Trinkgeschirr des 5. Jahrhunderts v. Chr.* Image and Context. Berlin.

Henderson, J., ed. and trans. (2002). *Aristophanes. Aristophanes Volume IV: Frogs. Assembly Women. Wealth*. Loeb Classical Library 180. Cambridge, MA.

Henrichs, A. (1990). "Between City and Country: Cultic Dimensions of Dionysus in Athens and Attica." In *Cabinet of the Muses: Essays on Classical and Comparative Literature in Honor of Thomas G. Rosenmeyer*, edited by Mark Griffith and D. J. Mastronarde, 257–77. Atlanta.

Herington, C. J. (1985). *Poetry into Drama: Early Tragedy and the Greek Poetic Tradition*. Sather Classical Lectures. Berkeley.

Hermary, A. (1986). "Dioskouroi." In *LIMC*, 567–93. Zurich and Munich.

Himmelmann, N. (1998). "Some Characteristics of the Representation of Gods in Classical Art." In *Reading Greek Art: Essays by Nikolaus Himmelmann; selected by Hugo Meyer*, edited by William Childs, 103–38. Princeton.

Hobden, F. (2011). "Enter the Divine: Sympotic Performance and Religious Experiences." In *Sacred Words: Orality, Literacy and Religion*, edited by A. P. M. H. Lardinois, J. H. Blok and M. G. M. van der Poel, 37–57. Leiden.

(2013). *The Symposion in Ancient Greek Society and Thought*. Cambridge.

Hoepfner, W. (1976). *Das Pompeion und seine Nachfolgerbauten*. Kerameikos. Vol. 10. Berlin.

Hoffman, H., D. von Bothmer, and P. Truitt. (1973). *Boston, Museum of Fine Arts I*. Corpus Vasorum Antiquorum. Vol. 14 U.S.A. Mainz.

Hoffmann, H. (1997). *Sotades: Symbols of Immortality on Greek Vases*. Oxford.

Holmberg, E. J. (1992). *On the Rycroft Painter and Other Athenian Black-Figure Vase-Painters with a Feeling for Nature*. Jonsered.

Hölscher, F. (1981). *Würzburg, Martin von Wagner Museum II*. Corpus Vasorum Antiquorum. Germany 46, Munich.

Hopkinson, N., ed. and trans. (2015). *Theocritus, Moschus, Bion*. Loeb Classical Library 28. Cambridge, MA.

Hurwit, J. M. (1977). "Image and Frame in Greek Art." *AJA* 81: 1–30.

Immerwahr, H. R. (1964). "Book Rolls on Attic Vases." In *Classical, Medieval and Renaissance Studies in Honor of Berthold Louis Ullman*, edited by Charles Henderson Jr., 17–48. Rome.

(1973). "More on book rolls on Attic vases." *AntK* 16: 143–47.

Isler, H. P. (1970). *Acheloos: eine Monographie*. Schriften, hrsg. unter dem Patronat der Schweizerischen Geisteswissenschaftlichen Gesellschaft. Vol. 11, Bern.

(1981). "Acheloos." In *LIMC*, 12–36. Zurich and Munich.

Isler-Kerényi, C. (2004). *Civilizing Violence: Satyrs on 6th-Century Greek Vases*. Translated by Eric Charles de Sena. Orbis Biblicus et Orientalis. Vol. 208. Fribourg and Göttingen.

(2007). *Dionysos in Archaic Greece: An Understanding through Images*. Translated by Wilfred G. E. Watson. Religions in the Graeco-Roman World. Leiden and Boston.

(2015). *Dionysos in Classical Athens: An Understanding through Images. Translated by Anna Beerens. Religions in the Graeco-Roman World*. Leiden and Boston.

Jacquet-Rimassa, P. (1999). "Les représentations de la musique, divertissement du *symposion* grec, dans les céramiques attique et italiote (440–300)." *RÉA* 101, nos. 1–2: 37–63.

Janko, R. (1982). *Homer, Hesiod, and the Hymns: Diachronic Development in Epic Diction*. Cambridge Classical Studies. Cambridge and New York.

Johnston, S. I. (2002). "Myth, Festival, and Poet: The 'Homeric Hymn to Hermes' and Its Performative Context." *CP* 97, no. 2: 109–32.

(2013). "Demeter, Myths, and the Polyvalence of Festivals." *History of Religions* 52, no. 4: 370–401.

Jost, M. (1985). *Sanctuaires et cultes d'Arcadie*. Paris.

Judeich, W. (1931). *Topographie von Athen*. Munich.

Kahil, L. G. (1965). "Autour de l'Artémis attique." *AntK* 8: 20–33.

(1984). "Artemis." In *LIMC*, 618–753. Zurich and Munich.

Kaltsas, N. (2002). *Sculpture in the National Archaeological Museum, Athens*. Los Angeles.

Kane, B. (2014). *Sound Unseen: Acousmatic Sound in Theory and Practice*. Oxford.

Kansteiner, S., et al., eds. (2014). *Der neue Overbeck: die antiken Schriftquellen zu den bildenden Künsten der Griechen*. Berlin.

Karanika, A. (2014). *Voices at Work: Women, Performance, and Labor in Ancient Greece*. Baltimore.

Karavites, P. (1984). "*Spondai-Spendein* in the Fifth Century B.C." *L' Antiquité Classique* 53: 60–70.

Katsarou, S., and A. Nagel, eds. (2021). *Cave and Worship in Ancient Greece: New Approaches to Landscape and Ritual*. New York.

Kavvadias, P. (1897). "Τοπογραφικὰ Ἀθηνῶν κατὰ τὰς περὶ τιν Ἀκράπολιν ἀνασκαψάς." *Αρχαιολογική Ἐφημερίς*: 1–32.

Kaufman-Samara, A. (1997). "Οὐκ ἀπόμουσον τὸ γυναικῶν (Εὐριπ. Μήδ. 1089). Γυναίκες μουσικοί στα αττικά αγγεία του 5ου αι. π.Χ." In *Athenian Potters and Painters: The Conference Proceedings*, edited by John Oakley, W. D. E. Coulson and Olga Palagia, 285–95. Oxford.

Kéi, N. (2015). "The Floral Aesthetics of Attic Red-Figure Pottery: Visual Adornment and Interplay between Ornament and Figure." In *Pflanzen und Tiere auf griechischen Vase (Akten des internationalen Symposiums an der Universität Graz, 26–28 September 2013)*, edited by Claudia Lang-Auinger and Elisabeth Trinkl, 271–80. Vienna.

(2018). "Beneath the Handles of Attic Vases." In *Ornament and Figure in Graeco-Roman Art: Rethinking Visual Ontologies in Classical Antiquity*, edited by Nikolaus Dietrich and Michael Squire, 143–66. Berlin and Boston.

(2021). *L'esthétique des fleurs: kosmos, poikilia et charis dans la céramique attique du VIe et du Ve siècle av. J.-C.* Berlin.

King, L. S. (1903). "The Cave at Vari. IV. Vases, Terra-cotta Statuettes, Bronzes, and Miscellaneous Objects." *AJA* 7, no. 3: 320–34.

Kirk, G. S. (1985). "The *Homeric Hymns*." In *The Cambridge History of Classical Literature*, edited by P. E. Easterling and B. M. W. Knox, 69–75. Cambridge.

(1985). *The Iliad: A Commentary. Vol. 1: Books I–IV*. Cambridge.

Klöckner, A. (2001). "Menschlicher Gott und göttlicher Mensch? Zu einigen Weihreliefs für Asklepios und die Nymphen." In *Konstruktionen von Wirklichkeit: Bilder im Griechenland des 5. und 4. Jahrhunderts v. Chr.*, edited by Ralf von den Hoff and Stefan Schmidt, 121–30. Stuttgart.

(2010). "Getting in Contact: Concepts of Human-Divine Encounter in Classical Greek Art." In *The Gods of Ancient Greece: Identities and Transformations*, edited by J. N. Bremmer and Andrew Erskine. Edinburgh Leventis Studies, 106–25. Edinburgh.

Konstantinou, I. (1970). "Λευκέ Δελφική Κύλιξ." *Αρχαιολογική Ἐφημερίς*: 27–46.

Korshak, Y. (1987). *Frontal Faces in Attic Vase Painting of the Archaic Period*. Chicago.

Kossatz-Deissmann, A. (1988). "Hera." In *LIMC*, 659–719. Zurich and Munich.

(1992). "Memnon." In *LIMC*, 448–61. Zurich and Munich.

Kovacs, D., ed. and trans. (1999). *Euripides. Trojan Women, Iphigenia among the Taurians, Ion*. Loeb Classical Library 10. Cambridge, MA.

Kowalzig, B. (2007a). "'And now all the world shall dance!' (Eur. *Bacch.* 114): Dionysus' Choroi Between Drama and Ritual." In *The Origins of Theater in Ancient Greece and Beyond: From Ritual to Drama*, edited by Eric Csapo and M. C. Miller, 221–51. Cambridge.

(2007b). *Singing for the Gods: Performances of Myth and Ritual in Archaic and Classical Greece*. Oxford and New York.

(2013). "Broken Rhythms in Plato's *Laws*: Materialising Social Time in the Chorus." In *Performance and Culture in Plato's Laws*, edited by A.-E. Peponi, 171–211. Cambridge.

Kowalzig, B., and P. Wilson, eds. (2013a). *Dithyramb in Context*. Oxford.

Kowalzig, B., and P. Wilson. (2013b). "Introduction: The World of Dithyramb." In *Dithyramb in Context*, edited by Barbara Kowalzig and Peter Wilson, 1–27. Oxford.

Krauskopf, I. (1994). "Poseidon." In *LIMC*, 446–83. Zurich and Munich.

Kunisch, N. (1997). *Makron*. Forschungen zur antiken Keramik. Mainz.

Kunze-Götte, E. (2010). *Munich, Antikensamml ungen XV*. Corpus Vasorum Antiquorum. Vol. 87 Germany. Munich.

Kurke, L. (1997). "Inventing the "Hetaira": Sex, Politics, and Discursive Conflict in Archaic Greece." *ClAnt* 16, no. 1: 106–50.

(1999). *Coins, Bodies, Games, and Gold: The Politics of Meaning in Archaic Greece*. Princeton.

(2000). "The Strangeness of 'Song Culture': Archaic Greek Poetry." In *Literature in the Greek and Roman Worlds*, edited by Oliver Taplin, 58–87. Oxford.

(2012). "The Value of Chorality in Ancient Greece." In *The Construction of Value in the Ancient World*, edited by J. Papadopoulos and G. Urton. Cotsen Institute Papers, 218–35. Los Angeles.

(2013a). "Imagining Chorality: Wonder, Plato's Puppets, and Moving Statues." In *Performance and Culture in Plato's Laws*, edited by A.-E. Peponi, 123–70. Cambridge.

(2013b). "Pindar's *Pythian* 11 and the *Oresteia*: Contestatory Ritual Poetics in the Fifth Century BCE." *Classical Antiquity* 32, no. 1: 101–75.

Kurke, L., and R. Neer. (2019). *Pindar, Song, and Space: Towards a Lyric Archaeology*. Baltimore.

Kurtz, D., ed. (1989). *Greek Vases, Lectures by J. D. Beazley*. Oxford.

Kurtz, D., and J. D. Beazley. (1983). *The Berlin Painter*. Oxford.

Ladianou, K. (2005). "The Poetics of *Choreia*: Imitation and Dance in the *Anacreontea*." *Quaderni Urbinati di Cultura Classica, New Series* 80, no. 2: 47–58.

Laferrière, C. M. (2019a). "Hermes Among Pan and the Nymphs on Fourth-Century Votive Reliefs." In *Tracking Hermes, Pursuing Mercury*, edited by J. F. Miller and Jenny Strauss Clay, 31–48. Oxford.

(2019b). "Sacred Sounds: The Cult of Pan and the Nymphs in the Vari Cave." *ClAnt* 38, no. 2: 185–216.

(2020). "Painting with Music: Visualizing *harmonia* on Archaic Representations of Apollo Kitharoidos." *GRMS* 8, no. 1: 63–90.

(2023). "Education: Myth, Ritual, and Socialization." In *A Cultural History of Western Music: Antiquity*, edited by S. A. Gurd and Pauline LeVen. London.

(2024). "Gods." In *Imprints of Dance in Greek and Roman Antiquity/Improntas de danza antigua*. Madrid.

Lamb, W. (1930). *Cambridge, Fitzwilliam Museum I*. Corpus Vasorum Antiquorum, volume 6, Great Britain. Cambridge.

Lambrinudakis, W., et al. (1984). "Apollon." In *LIMC*, 183–327. Zurich and Munich.

Langridge-Noti, E. M. (2015). "'To Market, to Market': Pottery, the Individual, and Trade in Athens." In *Cities Called Athens: Studies Honoring John McK. Camp II*, edited by K. F. Daly and L. A. Riccardi, 165–96. Lewisburg.

Larson, J. L. (2001). *Greek Nymphs: Myth, Cult, Lore*. Oxford and New York.

(2011). "The Corycian Nymphs and the Bee Maidens of the Homeric Hymn to Hermes." *GRBS* 36, no. 4: 341–57.

Lavecchia, S. (2013). "Becoming like Dionysos: Dithyramb and Dionysian Initiation." In *Dithyramb in Context*, edited by Barbara Kowalzig and Peter Wilson, 59–75. Oxford.

Lawler, L. B. (1927). "The Maenads: A Contribution to the Study of the Dance in Ancient Greece." *MAAR* 6: 69–112.

(1964). *The Dance in Ancient Greece*. London.

Le Dinahet, M. T., and R. Étienne. (1991). *L'espace sacrificiel dans les civilisations méditerranéennes de l'antiquité: actes du colloque tenu à la Maison de l'Orient, Lyon, 4–7 juin 1988, Publications de la Bibliothéque Salomon Reinach*. Paris.

LeVen, P. (2013). "The Colors of Sound: Poikilia and Its Aesthetic Contexts." *GRMS* 1, no. 1: 229–42.

(2014). *The Many-Headed Muse: Tradition and Innovation in Late Classical Greek Lyric Poetry*. Cambridge.

Lewis, J. (2006). *Solon the Thinker: Political Thought in Archaic Athens*. London.

Lezzi-Hafter, A., and C. Zindel. (1991). *Dionysos, mythes et mystères: vases de Spina/ Mythos und Mysterien, Vasen aus Spina*. Kilchberg.

Lissarrague, F. (1990a). *The Aesthetics of the Greek Banquet: Images of Wine and Ritual*. Princeton.

(1990b). "Around the *krater*: An Aspect of Banquet Imagery." In *Sympotica: A Symposium on the Symposion*, edited by Oswyn Murray, 196–209. Oxford.

(1990c). "Sexual Life of Satyrs." In *Constructions of Erotic Experience in the Ancient Greek World*, edited by D. M. Halperin, J. J. Winkler, and F. I. Zeitlin, 53–82. Princeton.

(1995a). "Identity and Otherness: The Case of Attic Head Vases and Plastic Vases." *Source: Notes in the History of Art* 15, no. 1: Special Issue: Representations of the "Other" in Athenian Art, c. 510–400 B.C.: 4–9.

(1995b). "Un rituel du vin: la libation." In *In Vino Veritas*, edited by Oswyn Murray and Manuela Tecusan, 126–44. London.

(2013). *La cité des satyres: une anthropologie ludique (Athènes VIe - Ve siècles avant J.-C.)*. Paris.

Lonsdale, S. H. (1993). *Dance and Ritual Play in Greek Religion, Ancient Society and History*. Baltimore.

(1994–95). "Homeric Hymn to Apollo: Prototype and Paradigm of Choral Performance." *Arion, Third Series* 3, no. 1: The Chorus in Greek Tragedy and Culture: 25–40.

Lücken, G. v. (1972). *Schwerin, Staatliches Museum I. Corpus Vasorum Antiquorum*. Vol. 1 German Democratic Republic. Berlin.

Lullies, R. (1956). *Munich, Museum Antiker Kleinkunst IV*. Corpus Vasorum Antiquorum. Vol. 12 Germany. Mainz

Luschey, H. (1893). "s.v. φιάλη." *RE* Suppl. VII: 1026–30.

Lynch, K. M. (2011). *Symposium in Context: Pottery from a Late Archaic House Near the Athenian Agora*. Princeton.

(2015). "Drinking Cups and the Symposium at Athens in the Archaic and Classical Periods." In *Cities Called Athens: Studies Honoring John McK. Camp II*, edited by K. F. Daly and L. A. Riccardi, 231–72. Lewisburg.

Maas, M., and J. M. Snyder. (1989). *Stringed Instruments of Ancient Greece*. New Haven.

Mack, R. (2002). "Facing Down Medusa (An aetiology of the gaze)." *Art History* 25, no. 5: 571–604.

Mack, W. (2018). "Vox Populi, Vox Deorum? Athenian Document Reliefs and the Theologies of Public Inscription." *BSA* 113: 365–98.

Mackay, E. A. (2001). "The Frontal Face and 'You': Narrative Disjunction in Early Greek Poetry and Painting." *Acta Classica* 44: 5–34.

Männlein-Robert, I. (2007). *Stimme, Schrift und Bild: zum Verhältnis der Künste in der hellenistischen Dichtung*. Heidelberg.

Marconi, C. (2004). "Images for a Warrior: On a Group of Athenian Vases and their Public." In *Greek Vases: Images, Contexts, Controversies. Proceedings of the Conference Sponsored by the Center for the Ancient Mediterranean at Columbia University, 23–24 March 2002*, edited by Clemente Marconi, 27–40. Leiden and Boston.

(2017). "The Frames of Greek Painted Pottery." In *The Frame in Classical Art: A Cultural History*, edited by Verity Platt and Michael Squire, 117–53. Cambridge.

Marx, P. A. (1993). "The Introduction of the Gorgoneion to the Shield and Aegis of Athena and the Question of Endoios." *RA* Nouvelle Série, Fasc. 2: 227–68.

Maslov, B. (2016). "The Genealogy of the Muses: An Internal Reconstruction of Archaic Greek Metapoetics." *AJP* 137, no. 3: 411–46.

Matheson, S. (1984). "Two New Greek Vases for Yale." *YaleBull* 39, no. 2: 8–11.

(1988). *Greek Vases: A Guide to the Yale Collection*. New Haven.

(1995). *Polygnotos and Vase-Painting in Classical Athens*. Madison.

(2001). *Art for Yale: A History of the Yale University Art Gallery*. New Haven.

(2016). *New Haven, Yale University Art Gallery II*. Corpus Vasorum Antiquorum. United States of America 39. Darmstadt and Mainz.

Mathiesen, T. J. (1984). "Harmonia and Ethos in Ancient Greek Music." *The Journal of Musicology* 3, no. 3: 264–79.

(1999). *Apollo's Lyre: Greek Music and Music Theory in Antiquity and the Middle Ages*. Lincoln, NB.

Mayo, M. E., and H. S. Russell. (1998). *Ancient Art: Virginia Museum of Fine Arts*. Richmond.

Mayor, A., J. Colarusso, and D. Saunders. (2014). "Making Sense of Nonsense Inscriptions Associated with Amazons and Scythians on Athenian Vases." *Hesperia* 83, no. 3: 447–93.

McKay, K. J. (1967). "Door Magic and the Epiphany Hymn." *CQ* 17: 184–94.

McKirahan, R. D. (1994). *Philosophy Before Socrates: An Introduction with Texts and Commentary*. Indianapolis and Cambridge.

McNally, S. (1978). "The Maenad in Early Greek Art." *Arethusa* 11: 101–35.

Meillier, C. (1975). "L'épiphanie du dieu Pan au livre II de Daphnis et Chloé." *RÉG* 88: 121–31.

Melander, T. (2000). *Copenhagen, Thorvaldsens Museum I*. Corpus Vasorum Antiquorum. Denmark 9. Mainz.

Mertens, J. R. (1974). "Attic White-Ground Cups: A Special Class of Vases." *Metropolitan Museum Journal* 9: 91–108.

(1977). *Attic White-Ground: Its Development on Shapes Other than Lekythoi*. New York and London.

(2006). "White-Ground." In *Colors of Clay: Special Techniques in Athenian Vases*, edited by Beth Cohen, 185–238. Los Angeles.

Metzger, H. (1977). "ΑΠΟΛΛΩΝ ΣΠΕΝΔΩΝ: à propos d'une coupe attique à fond blanc trouvée à Delphes." *BCH* Supplement IV: 421–28.

Meyer, D. (2005). *Inszeniertes Lesevergnügen: das inschriftliche Epigramm und seine Rezeption bei Kallimachos*. Stuttgart.

Miller, J. F., and J. S. Clay, eds. (2019). *Tracking Hermes and Pursuing Mercury*. Oxford.

Mitchell, S., ed. and trans. (1989). *The Selected Poetry of Rainer Maria Rilke*. New York.

Mitropoulou, E. (1975). *Libation Scenes with Oinochoe in Votive Reliefs*. Athens.

Mittica, M. P. (2015). "When the World was Mousiké: On the Origins of the Relationship Between Law and Music." *Law and Humanities* 9, no. 1: 29–54.

Mojsik, T. (2011). *Between Tradition and Innovation: Genealogy, Names and the Number of the Muses*. Translated by Marcin Fijak. Akme. Studia Historica. Vol. 9. Warsaw.

(2013). "Some Reflections on the Muses and the Cult of the Dead." *Przeglad Humanistyczny* 2: 79–85.

Moore, M. (2010). "Hephaistos Goes Home: An Attic Black-Figured Column Krater in the Metropolitan Museum of Art." *Metropolitan Museum Journal* 45: 21–54.

(2016). "Sophilos, Inscriptions, and the Funeral Games for Patroklos." In *Epigraphy of Art: Ancient Greek Vase-Inscriptions and Vase-Paintings*, edited by Dimitrios Yatromanolakis, 185–202. Oxford.

Moore, M. B., and D. v. Bothmer. (1976). *New York, The Metropolitan Museum of Art 4*. Corpus Vasorum Antiquorum. United States of America 16. New York.

Most, G. W., ed. and trans. (2007). *Hesiod. Theogony. Works and Days. Testimonia*. Loeb Classical Library 57. Cambridge, MA.

Munn, M. (2006). *The Mother of the Gods, Athens, and the Tyranny of Asia: A Study of*

Sovereignty in Ancient Religion. Berkeley and Los Angeles.

Murray, O., ed. (1990). *Sympotica: A Symposium on the Symposion*. Oxford.

Murray, P. (2004). "The Muses and Their Arts." In *Music and the Muses: The Culture of 'Mousikē' in the Classical Athenian City*, edited by Penelope Murray and Peter Wilson, 365–89. Oxford and New York.

(2014). "The Muses in Antiquity." In *The Muses and Their Afterlife in Post-Classical Europe*, edited by K. W. Christian, C. E. L. Guest, and Claudia Wedepohl. Warburg Institute Colloquia, 13–32. London and Turin.

Murray, P., and P. Wilson, eds. (2004a). *Music and the Muses: The Culture of 'Mousikē' in the Classical Athenian City*. Oxford and New York.

(2004b). "Introduction: *Mousikē*, not Music." In *Music and the Muses: The Culture of 'Mousikē' in the Classical Athenian City*, edited by Penelope Murray and Peter Wilson, 1–8. Oxford and New York.

Muthmann, F. (1968). "Weihrelief an Acheloos und Naturgottheiten." *AntK* 11, no. 1: 24–44.

(1975). *Mutter und Quelle: Studien zur Quellenverehrung im Altertum und im Mittelalter*. Basel.

Nagy, G. (1990). *Pindar's Homer: The Lyric Possession of an Epic Past*. Baltimore.

(1999). *The Best of the Achaeans: Concepts of the Hero in Archaic Greek Poetry*. Revised ed. Baltimore and London.

(2013). *The Ancient Greek Hero in 24 Hours*. Cambridge, MA.

Nancy, J.-L. (1996). *The Muses*. Translated by Peggy Kamuf. Stanford.

(2000). *Being Singular Plural*. Translated by R. D. Richardson and A. E. O'Byrne. Stanford.

Naumann, F. (1983). *Die Ikonographie der Kybele in der phrygischen und griechischen Kunst*. Istanbuler Mitteilungen. Vol. 28. Tübingen.

Naerebout, F. (1997). *Attractive Performances: Ancient Greek Dance, Three Preliminary Studies*. Amsterdam.

(2015). "Dance." In *A Companion to the Archaeology of Religion in the Ancient World*, edited by Rubina Raja and Jörg Rüpke, 107–19. Chichester.

(2017). "Moving in Unison: The Greek Chorus in Performance." In *Choreutika: Performing and Theorising Dance in Ancient Greece*, edited by Laura Gianvittorio, 39–66. Pisa.

Neer, R. (2002). *Style and Politics in Athenian Vase-Painting: The Craft of Democracy, ca. 530–460 bce*. New York.

(2010). *The Emergence of the Classical Style in Greek Sculpture*. Chicago.

(2019). "Ancient Greek Vessels Between Sea, Earth, and Clouds." In *Vessels: The Object as Container*, edited by Claudia Brittenham, 6–49. Oxford.

Neils, J. (2000). "Others within the Other: An Intimate Look at Hetairai and Maenads." In *Not the Classical Ideal: Athens and the Construction of the Other in Greek Art*, edited by Beth Cohen, 203–26. Leiden and Boston.

(2001). *The Parthenon Frieze*. Cambridge.

(2004). "Vases on Vases." In *Greek Vase Painting: Form, Figure, and Narrative*, edited by P. Gregory Warden, 28–34. University Park.

Neils, J., and J. Oakley. (2003). *Coming of Age in Ancient Greece: Images of Childhood from the Classical Past*. New Haven.

(2004). *Striving for Excellence: Ancient Greek Childhood and the Olympic Spirit*. New York.

Nevett, L. C. (1994). "Separation or Seclusion? Towards an Archaeological Approach to Investigating Women in the Greek Household in the Fifth to Third Centuries BC." In *Architecture and Order: Approaches to Social Space*, edited by M. P. Pearson and Colin Richards, 89–112. London.

(1995). "Gender Relations in the Classical Greek Household: The Archaeological Evidence." *The Annual of the British School at Athens* 90 (Centenary Volume): 363–81.

(1999). *House and Society in the Ancient Greek World*. Cambridge.

(2011). "Towards a Female Topography of the Ancient Greek City: Case Studies from Late Archaic and Early Classical Athens (*c.* 520–400 BCE)." *Gender and History* 23: 576–96.

Nilsson, M. P. (1957). *The Dionysiac Mysteries of the Hellenistic and Roman Age*. Lund.

(1972). *Greek Folk Religion*. Philadelphia.

Nooter, S. (2012). *When Heroes Sing: Sophocles and the Shifting Soundscape of Tragedy*. Cambridge.

(2019). "Sounds of the Stage." In *Sound and the Ancient Senses*, edited by Shane Butler and Sarah Nooter, 198–211. Abingdon and New York.

Nordquist, G. (1991). "The *salpinx* as an Instrument of Eros and Dionysos." *Imago Musicae* 8: 61–72.

(1992). "Instrumental Music in Representations of Greek Cult." In *The Iconography of Greek Cult in the Archaic and Classical Periods: Proceedings of the First International Seminar on Ancient Greek Cult, Delphi, 16–18 November 1990*, edited by Robin Hägg, 143–68. Athens.

Nosch, M.-L. (2014). "Voicing the Loom: Women, Weaving, and Plotting." In *KE-RA-ME-JA: Studies Presented to Cynthia W. Shelmerdine*, edited by Dimitri Nakassis, Joann Gulizio, and S. A. James, 91–102. Philadelphia.

Oakley, J. H. (1990). *The Phiale Painter*. Kerameus. Vol. 8. Mainz.

(1997). *The Achilles Painter*. Mainz.

(2004). *Picturing Death in Classical Athens: The Evidence of the White Lekythoi*. Cambridge and New York.

Öhrman, M. (2018). "The Singing Loom: The Importance of Textile Production in the Roman Domestic Soundscape." In *Archaeoacoustics III: More on the Archaeology of Sound*, edited by Linda Eneix and Michael Ragussa, 143–50. Myakka City, FL.

(2020). "The Soundscape of Textile Work in the Roman World: Old Sources and New Methods." In *New Approaches to Ancient Material Culture in the Greek and Roman World: 21st-Century Methods and Classical Antiquity*, edited by Catherine Cooper, 183–200. Leiden.

Olsen, S. (2019). "Pindar, Paean 6: Genre as Embodied Cultural Knowledge." In *Genre in Archaic and Classical Greek Poetry: Theories and Models*, edited by Margaret Foster, Leslie Kurke, and N. A. Weiss, 325–46. Studies in Archaic and Classical Greek Song. Leiden.

(2020). *Solo Dance in Archaic and Classical Greek Literature: Representing the Unruly Body*. Cambridge.

(2021). "Narrating Neoptolemus: Dance and Death in Euripides' *Andromache* 1085–1165." In *Choreonarratives: Dancing Stories in Greek and Roman Antiquity and Beyond*, edited by Laura Gianvittorio and Karin Schlapbach, 156–79. Leiden.

Osborne, R. (2004). "Images of a Warrior: On a Group of Athenian Vases and Their Public." In *Greek Vases: Images, Contexts, Controversies. Proceedings of the Conference Sponsored by the Center for the Ancient Mediterranean at Columbia University, 23–24 March 2002*, edited by Clemente Marconi, 41–54. Leiden and Boston.

(2014). "Intoxication and Sociality: The Symposium in the Ancient Greek World." *PastPres* Supplement 9: 34–60.

Osborne, R., and J. Tanner. (2007). *Art's Agency and Art History*. Malden, MA.

Otto, B. (1984). "Dekorative Elemente in den Bildschöpfungen des Kleophrades- und Berliner-Malers." In *Ancient Greek and Related Pottery: Proceedings of the International Vase Symposium in Amsterdam, 12–15 April 1984*, edited by H. A. G. Brijder. Allard Pierson Series, 198–201. Amsterdam.

Otto, W. F. (1934). *Die Götter Griechenlands: Das Bild des Göttlichen im Spiegel des griechischen Geistes*. Frankfurt.

(1956, reprinted 1975). *Theophania: Der Geist der altgriechischen Religion*. Rowohlts deutsche Enzyklopädie. Frankfurt.

(1965). *Dionysus: Myth and Cult*. Translated by Robert B. Palmer. Bloomington and London.

Pache, C. O. (2011). *A Moment's Ornament: The Poetics of Nympholepsy in Ancient Greece*. Oxford.

Padgett, M. J. (2017). "Red-figure Hydria of Black-figure Shape." In *The Berlin Painter and His World: Athenian Vase-Painting in the Early Fifth Century B.C.*, edited by M. J. Padgett, 311–13. Princeton University Art Museum.

Pappas, A. (2012). "More Than Meets the Eye: The Aesthetics of (Non)Sense in the Ancient Greek Symposium." In *Aesthetic Value in Classical Antiquity*, edited by Ineke Sluiter and R. M. Rosen, 71–111. Leiden.

Paquette, D. (1984). *L'instrument de musique dans la céramique de la Grèce antique: études d'organologie*. Paris.

Parker, R. (2005). *Polytheism and Society at Athens*. Oxford.

Paton, W. R. trans. (1917). *The Greek Anthology, Volume III: Book 9: The Declamatory Epigrams*. Loeb Classical Library 84. Cambridge, MA.

Patton, K. C. (2009). *Religion of the Gods: Ritual, Paradox, and Reflexivity*. Oxford.

Pedley, J. G. (2012). *Greek Art and Archaeology*. 5th ed. Boston.

Peirce, S. (1998). "Visual Language and Concepts of Cult on the 'Lenaia' vases." *ClAnt* 17: 59–95.

Peponi, A.-E. (2009). "Choreia and Aesthetics in the Homeric Hymn to Apollo: The Performance of the Delian Maidens (Lines 156–164)." *Classical Antiquity* 28, no. 1: 39–70.

(2012). *Frontiers of Pleasure: Models of Aesthetic Response in Archaic and Classical Greek Thought*. New York.

(2013). "Theorizing the Chorus in Greece." In *Choruses, Ancient and Modern*, edited by Joshua Billings, Felix Budelmann, and Fiona Macintosh, 15–34. Oxford.

(2015). "Dance and Aesthetic Perception." In *A Companion to Ancient Aesthetics*, edited by Pierre Destrée and Penelope Murray, 204–17. Malden, MA.

Pellini, J. R., A. Zarankin, and M. A. Salerno, eds. (2015). *Coming to Senses: Topics in Sensory Archaeology*. Newcastle upon Tyne.

Petridou, G. (2015). *Divine Epiphany in Greek Literature and Culture*. Oxford.

Philippart, H. (1930). "Iconographie des "Bacchantes" d'Euripide." *RBPhil* 9, no. 1: 1–72.

Picón, C. A., et al. (2007). *Art of the Classical World in the Metropolitan Museum of Art: Greece, Cyprus, Etruria, Rome*. New York.

Pipili, M. (1988). "Herkyna." In *LIMC*, 264–65. Zurich and Munich.

Plaoutine, N. (1941). *Paris, Palais des Beaux-Arts de la Ville de Paris (Petit Palais, Collection Dutuit) I*. Corpus Vasorum Antiquorum. Vol 15, France, Paris.

Platt, V. (2010). "Art History in the Temple." *Arethusa* 43, no. 2: 197–213.

(2011). *Facing the Gods. Epiphany and Representation in Graeco-Roman Art, Literature and Religion*. Cambridge.

(2014). "Likeness and Likelihood in Classical Greek Art." In *Probabilities, Hypotheticals, and Counterfactuals in Ancient Greek Thought*, edited by Victoria Wohl, 185–207. Cambridge.

(2015). "Sight and the Gods: On the Desire to See Naked Nymphs." In *Sight and the Ancient Senses*, edited by Michael Squire. The Senses in Antiquity, 169–87. London.

(2016). "The Matter of Classical Art History." *Daedalus* 145, no. 2: 69–78.

(2017). "Introduction: Framing the Sacred." In *The Frame in Classical Art: A Cultural History*, edited by Verity Platt and Michael Squire, 384–391. Cambridge.

Platt, V., and M. Squire. (2017a). "Framing the Visual in Greek and Roman Antiquity: An Introduction." In *The Frame in Classical Art: A Cultural History*, edited by Verity Platt and Michael Squire, 3–99. Cambridge.

(2017b). "Getting to Grips with Classical Art: Rethinking the Haptics of Graeco-Roman Visual Culture." In *Touch and the Ancient Senses*, edited by Alex Purves, 75–104. London.

eds. (2017c). *The Frame in Classical Art: A Cultural History*. Cambridge.

Podlecki, A. J. (2014). "Aeschylus and the Early Philosophical Tradition." In *The Encyclopedia of Greek Tragedy*, edited by Hanna M. Roisman, 1–4. Chichester.

Pöhlmann, E. (1960). *Griechische Musikfragmente. Ein Weg zur altgriechischen Musik.* Erlanger Beiträge zur Sprach- und Kunstwissenschaft. Vol. 8. Nürnberg.

(1976). "Die Notenschrift in der Überliefenung der griechischen Bühnenmusik." *WürzJbb* 2: 53–73.

Pöhlmann, E., and M. L. West, eds. (2001). *Documents of Ancient Greek Music: The Extant Melodies and Fragments Edited and Transcribed with Commentary*. Oxford.

Pollitt, J. J. (1974). *The Ancient View of Greek Art: Criticism, History, and Terminology*. New Haven and London.

Porter, I. (2010). *The Origins of Aesthetic Thought in Ancient Greece: Matter, Sensation, and Experience*. Cambridge and New York.

(2013). "Why Are There Nine Muses?". In *Synaesthesia and the Ancient Senses*, edited by Shane Butler and Alex Purves, 9–26. London.

Pottier, E. (1881). "Bas-relief des Nymphes trouvé à Éleusis." *BCH* 5: 349–57.

(1895). "Deux coupes à fond blanc de style attique." *Monuments et mémoires de la Fondation Eugène Piot*. 2.1: 39–56.

(n.d.). *Paris, Musée du Louvre III. Corpus Vasorum Antiquorum*. Vol. 3 France. Paris.

Power, T. (2010). *The Culture of Kitharôidia*. Washington, D.C. and Cambridge, MA.

(2018). "The Sound of the Sacred." In *Sound and the Ancient Senses*, edited by Shane Butler and Sarah Nooter, 15–30. London.

Price, S. D. (1990). "Anacreontic Vases Reconsidered." *GRBS* 31, no. 2: 133–75.

Pryce, F. N. (1932). *London, British Museum VII*. Corpus Vasorum Antiquorum. Vol. 10 Great Britain. Oxford.

Purves, A., ed. (2018). *Touch and the Ancient Senses*. London.

Queyrel, A. (1985). "Un lécythe à figures noires avec Hermès, Apollon et des Muses." *AntK* 28, no. 2: 158–60.

(1988). "Les muses à l'école: images de quelques vases du peintre de Calliope." *AntK* 31, no. 2: 90–102.

(1992). "Mousa, Mousai." In *LIMC*, 657–81. Zurich and Munich.

Quincey, J. H., W. Ritchie, G. P. Shipp, and A. P. Treweek. (1959). "Notes on the *Dyskolos* of Menander." *The Australian Humanities Research Council, Occasional Paper 2*: 3–11.

Radermacher, L. (1931). *Der homerische "Hermesh ymnus"*. Sitzungsberichte (Akademie der Wissenschaften in Wien. Philosophisch-Historische Klasse). Vol. 213.1, Vienna.

Raja, R., and J. Rüpke. (2015a). "Appropriating Religion: Methodological Issues in Testing the 'Lived Ancient Religion' Approach." *Religion in the Roman Empire* 1, no. 1: 11–19.

(2015b). "Archaeology of Religion, Material Religion, and the Ancient World." In *A Companion to the Archaeology of Religion in the Ancient World*, edited by Rubina Raja and Jörg Rüpke, 1–26. Chichester.

Rapp, A. (1872). "Die Mänade im griechischen Cultus, in der Kunst und Poesie." *RhM, Neue Folge* 27: 1–22.

Reeder, E. D. (1995). "Containers and Textiles as Metaphors for Women." In *Pandora: Women in Classical Greece*, edited by E. D. Reeder, 195–298. Baltimore and Princeton.

Reitzenstein, R. (1893, reprinted in 1970). *Epigramm und Skolion*. Hildesheim.

Richter, G. M. A., and L. F. Hall. (1936). *Red-Figured Athenian Vases in The Metropolitan Museum of Art*. New Haven.

Ridgway, B. S. (1997). *Fourth-Century Styles in Greek Sculpture*. Madison.

Roberts, S. (1978). *The Attic Pyxis*. Chicago.

Robertson, M. (1992). *The Art of Vase-Painting in Classical Athens*. Cambridge.

Robinson, D. M., and S. E. Freeman. (1937). *Baltimore, Robinson Collection II*. Corpus Vasorum Antiquorum. U.S.A. 6, Mainz.

Robson, J. (2013). *Sex and Sexuality in Classical Athens*. Debates and Documents in Ancient History. Edinburgh.

Rösler, W. (1980). *Dichter und Gruppe: eine Untersuchung zu den Bedingungen und zur historischen Funktion früher griechischer Lyrik am Beispiel Alkaios*. Munich.

Rouse, W. H. D. (1902). *Greek Votive Offerings*. Cambridge.

Rocconi, E. (2015). "Music and Dance in Greece and Rome." In *A Companion to Ancient Aesthetics*, edited by Pierre Destrée and Penelope Murray, 81–93. Malden, MA.

Roy, J. (1996). "The Countryside in Classical Greek Drama, and Isolated Farms in Dramatic Landscapes." In *Human Landscapes in Classical Antiquity: Environment and Culture*, edited by John Salmon and Graham Shipley, 98–118. London.

Rudolph, K. C., ed. (2018). *Taste and the Ancient Senses*. Abingdon and New York.

Rüpke, J. (2011). "Lived Ancient Religion: Questioning Cults and Polis Religion." *Mythos: Rivista di storia delle religioni* 5: 191–204.

(2016). *On Roman Religion: Lived Religion and the Individual in Ancient Rome*. Cornell Studies in Classical Philology. Ithaca, NY.

Rutherford, I. (1993). "Paeanic Ambiguity: A Study of the Representation of the παιάν in Greek Literature." *Quaderni Urbinati di Cultura Classica, New Series* 44, no. 2: 77–92.

(2004). "Χορὸς εἷς ἐκ τῆς πόλεως (Xen. Mem. 3.3.12): Song-Dance and State-Pilgrimage at Athens." In *Music and the Muses: The Culture of 'Mousikē' in the Classical Athenian City*, edited by Penelope Murray and Peter Wilson, 67–90. Oxford and New York.

Rystedt, E. (1984). "Women, Music, and a White-Ground Lekythos in the Medelhavsmuseet." *Opus Mixtum: Essays in Ancient Art and Society* 21: 73–91.

Rzepkowski, K. (2012). "Stage Movement and Staging in Menander's *Dyskolos*." *Mnemosyne* 65: 584–96.

Santangelo, G. (1972). "L'"*incipit*" dell' "*Inno ad Apollo*" di Callimaco." *Giornale Italiano di Filologia* 3: 52–62.

Sarian, H. (1992). "Hekate." In *LIMC*, 985–1018. Zurich and Munich.

Sarti, S. (1992). "Gli strumenti musicali di Apollo." *Annali dipartimento di studi del mondo classico e del mediterraneo antico: archaeologia e storia antica* 14: 95–104.

Schachter, A. (1994). *Cults of Boiotia*. Vol. 3. London.

Schapiro, M. (1973). *Words and Pictures: On the Literal and the Symbolic in the Illustration of a Text*. The Hague and Paris.

Schefold, K. (1937). "Statuen auf Vasenbildern." *JdI* 52: 30–75.

(1992). *Gods and Heroes in Late Archaic Greek Art*. Translated by A. Griffiths. Cambridge.

Schmidt, E. (1909). *Der Knielauf und die Darstellung des Laufens und Fliegens in der älteren griechischen Kunst*. Münchner archäologische Studien - dem Andenken Adolf Furtwänglers gewidmet. Munich.

Schmidt, G. (2002). *Rabe und Krähe in der Antike: Studien zur archäologischen und literarischen Überlieferung*. Wiesbaden.

Schöne, A. (1987). *Thiasos: eine ikonographische Untersuchung über das Gefolge des Dionysos in der attischen Vasenmalerei des 6. und 5. Jhs. v. Chr.* Studies in Mediterranean Archaeology and Literature. Vol. 55. Göteborg.

Schöne-Denkinger, A. (2009). *Berlin, Antikensammlung XI*. Corpus Vasorum Antiquorum. Volume 86, Germany. Munich.

Schörner, G., and H. R. Goette. (2004). *Die Pan-Grotte von Vari*. Deutsches Archäologisches Institut Athen. Mainz.

Seaford, R. (2006). *Dionysos*. Oxford and New York.

(2013). "Aeschylus, Herakleitos, and Pythagoreanism." In *Tragedy and Archaic Greek Thought*, edited by Douglas Cairns, 17–38. Swansea.

Seebass, T. (1991). "The Power of Music in Greek Vase Painting: Reflections on the Visualization of *Rhythmos* (order) and *Epaoidē* (enchanting song)." *Imago Musicae* 8: 11–37.

Shakeshaft, H. (2022). "Beauty, Gods, and Early Greek Art: The Dedications of Mantiklos and Nikandre Revisited." *Art Bulletin* 104: 20–46.

Shapiro, H. A. (1987). "Kalos-Inscriptions with Patronymic." *ZPE* 68: 107–18.

(1989). *Art and Cult under the Tyrants in Athens*. Mainz.

(1992). "*Mousikoi Agones*: Music and Poetry at the Panathenaea." In *Goddess and Polis: The Panathenaic Festival in Ancient Athens*, edited by Jenifer Neils, 53–76. Princeton.

(1994). *Myth into Art: Poet and Painter in Classical Greece*. London.

(2004). "Dance." In *ThesCRA*, 299–343. Los Angeles.

(2009). "Apollo and Ion on Classical Athenian Vases." In *Apolline Politics and Poetics*, edited by Lucia Athanassaki, Richard Martin, and John Miller, 265–84. Athens.

Shapiro, H. A., M. Iozzo, and A. Lezzi-Hafter, eds. (2013). *The François Vase: New Perspectives*. Kilchberg.

Shear, T. L. (1937). "Excavations in the Athenian Agora." *AJA* 41, no. 2: 177–89.

(1938). "The Campaign of 1937." *Hesperia* 7, no. 3: 311–62.

Shelmerdine, S. C. (1995). *The Homeric Hymns*. Focus Classical Library. Newburyport, MA.

Siebert, G. (1990). "Hermes." In *LIMC*, 285–387. Zurich and Munich.

Simon, E. (1953). *Opfernde Götter*. Berlin.

(1969). *Die Götter der Griechen*. Munich.

(1976). "Ein nordattischer Pan." *AntK* 19, no. 1: 19–23, plates IV–V.

(1983). *Festivals of Attica: An Archaeological Commentary*. Madison.

(2004). "Libation." In *ThesCRA*, 237–53. Los Angeles.

(2009). "Silenoi." In *LIMC*, 450–52. Zurich and Munich.

Simon, E., M. Hirmer, and A. Hirmer. (1981). *Die Griechischen Vasen*. 2nd ed. Munich.

Sklar, D. (2001). *Dancing with the Virgin: Body and Faith in the Fiesta of Tortugas, New Mexico*. Berkeley.

(2008). "Remembering Kinesthesia: An Inquiry into Embodied Cultural Knowledge." In *Migrations of Gesture*, edited by Carrie Noland and S. A. Ness, 85–111. Minneapolis.

Smith, A. C. (2006). "The Evolution of the Pan Painter's Artistic Style." *Hesperia* 75: 435–51.

Smith, C. H. (1925). *Catalogue of the Greek and Etruscan Vases in the British Museum*. London.

Smith, H. R. W. (1943). *San Francisco, M. H. De Young Memorial Museum and California Palace of the Legion of Honor I*. Corpus Vasorum Antiquorum. Vol. 10 United States of America. Cambridge, MA.

Smith, T. J. (2010a). *Komast Dancers in Archaic Greek Art*. Oxford Monographs on Classical Archaeology. Oxford.

(2010b). "Reception or Deception? Approaching Greek Dance through Vase-Painting." In *The Ancient Dancer in the Modern World: Responses to Greek and Roman Dance*, edited by Fiona Macintosh, 77–98. Oxford.

(2014a). "Guess Who's Coming to Dinner? Red-figure Komasts and the Performance Culture of Athens." In *Athenian Potters and Painters III*, ed. John Oakley, 231–41. Oxford.

(2014b). "Revel without a Cause? Dance, Performance, and Greek Vase-Painting." In *Archaeological Approaches to Dance Performance*, edited by Kathryn Soar and Christina Aamodt, 85–94. Oxford.

(2014c). "Review: François Lissarrague: La cité des satyres. Une anthropologie ludique (Athènes, VI–Ve siècle avant J.-C." *Sehepunkte* 14, no. 3. http://www.sehepunkte.de/2014/03/23727.html. (2016). "Instant Messaging: Dance, Text, and Visual Communication on Corinthian and Athenian Vases." In *Epigraphy of Art: Ancient Greek Vase-*

Inscriptions and Vase-Paintings, edited by D. Yatromanolakis, 145–64. Oxford.

(2021). "Bodies in Motion: Dance, Gesture, and Ritual on Greek Vases." *Greek and Roman Musical Studies* 9: 49–84.

Sommerstein, A. H., ed. and trans. (2008). *Aeschylus. Persians, Seven Against Thebes, Suppliants, Prometheus Bound*. Loeb Classical Library 145. Cambridge, MA.

Sourvinou-Inwood, C. (1994). "Something to Do with Athens: Tragedy and Ritual." In *Ritual, Finance, Politics: Athenian Democratic Accounts Presented to David Lewis*, edited by Robin Osborne and Simon Hornblower, 269–90. Oxford and New York.

(2003). *Tragedy and Athenian Religion*. Oxford.

Speyer, H. (1932). "Zweifiguren-gruppen im 5. und 4. Jahr. v. Chr." *RömMitt* 17: 1–94.

Sporn, K. (2007). "Höhlenheiligtümer in Griechenland." In *Kult und Kommunikation: Medien in Heiligtümern der Antike*, edited by Christian Frevel and Henner von Hesberg, 39–62. Wiesbaden.

Sprigath, G. K. (2004). "Das Dictum des Simonides: Der Vergleich von Dichtung und Malerei." *Poetica* 36: 243–80.

Squire, M. (2009). *Image and Text in Graeco-Roman Antiquity*. Cambridge.

ed. (2016a). *Sight and the Ancient Senses*. Abingdon and New York.

(2016b). "Introductory Reflections: Making Sense of Ancient Sight." In *Sight and the Ancient Senses*, edited by Michael Squire, 1–35. Abingdon and New York.

(2018). "A Portrait of the Ancient Artist? Self-Portraiture in Graeco-Roman Visual Culture." In *Figurationen des Porträts*, 435–70. Paderborn.

Stansbury-O'Donnell, M. D. (1999). *Pictorial Narrative in Ancient Greek Art. Cambridge Studies in Classical Art and Iconography*, edited by H. A. Shapiro. Cambridge.

(2006). *Vase Painting, Gender, and Social Identity in Archaic Athens*. Cambridge.

Steiner, A. (2002). "Private and Public: Links Between *Symposion* and *Syssition* in Fifth-Century Athens." *ClAnt* 21, no. 2: 347–90.

(2007). *Reading Greek Vases*. Cambridge.

Steiner, D. (2021). *Choral Constructions: The Idea of the Chorus in the Poetry, Art, and Social Practices of the Archaic and Early Classical Period*. Cambridge.

Stewart, A. (1983). "Steisichoros and the François Vase." In *Ancient Greek Art and Iconography*, edited by W. G. Moon. Wisconsin Studies in Classics 53–74. Madison.

Svoronos, J. N. (1908–37). *Das Athener Nationalmuseum: phototypische Wiedergabe seiner Schätze*. Athens.

Tanner, J. (2006). *The Invention of Art History in Ancient Greece: Religion, Society and Artistic Rationalisation*. Cambridge.

Taplin, O., and R. Wyles, eds. (2010). *The Pronomos Vase and Its Context*. Oxford.

Thallon, I. C. (1903). "The Caves at Vari. III. Marble Reliefs." *AJA* 7, no. 3: 301–19.

Thomas, O. (2011). "The Homeric Hymn to Pan." In *The Homeric Hymns: Interpretative Essays*, edited by Andrew Faulkner, 151–72. Oxford.

Tolles, D. (1943)."The Banquet-Libations of the Gods." PhD Dissertation, Bryn Mawr College.

Topper, K. (2013). *The Imagery of the Athenian Symposium*. Cambridge.

Travlos, J. (1960). "ΧΡΟΝΙΚΑ: ΑΘΗΝΑΙ - ΑΤΤΙΚΗ." *ΑΡΧΑΙΟΛΟΓΙΚΟΝ ΔΕΛΤΙΟΝ* 16: 15–79.

(1971). *Pictorial Dictionary of Ancient Athens*. New York and Washington.

(1988). *Bildlexikon zur Topographie des antiken Attika*. Tübingen.

Trinkl, E. (2009). "Sacrificial and Profane Use of Greek Hydriai." In *Shapes and Uses of Greek Vases (7th–4th centuries B.C.): Proceedings of the Symposium Held at the Université Libre de Bruxelles, 27–29 April 2006*, edited by Athena Tsingarida, 153–71. Brussels.

True, M. (2006). "Plastic Vases and Vases with Plastic Additions." In *The Colors of Clay: Special Techniques in Athenian Vases*, edited by Beth Cohen, 239–49. Los Angeles.

Tsagalis, C. (2004). *Epic Grief: Personal Laments in Homer's Iliad*. Berlin.

Tsingarida, A. (2012). "White-ground Cups in Fifth-century Graves: A Distinctive Class of Burial Offerings in Classical Athens?". In *Red-figure Pottery in Its Ancient Setting: Acts of the International Colloquium held at the National Museum of Denmark in Copenhagen, November 5–6, 2009*, edited by Stine Schierup and B. B. Rasmussn. Gösta Enbom Monographs, 44–57. Aarhus.

Tuck, A. (2006). "Singing the Rug: Patterned Textiles and the Origins of Indo-European Metrical Poetry." *AJA* 110, no. 4: 539–50.

Tueller, M. A. (2008). *Look Who's Talking: Innovations in Voice and Identity in Hellenistic Epigram*. Leuven.

Ustinova, Y. (2009). *Caves and the Ancient Greek Mind. Descending Underground in the Search for Ultimate Truth*. Oxford and New York.

van Keuren, F. (1998). "The Upbringing of Dionysos on an Unpublished Neck Amphora by the Eucharides Painter." In *Myth, Sexuality, and Power: Images of Jupiter in Western Art. Papers delivered at the Georgia Museum of Art in connection with the exhibition Jupiter's loves and his children, February 8, 1997*, edited by Frances van Keuren, 9–22. Providence and Louvain-la-Neuve.

Van Straten, F. S. (1981). "Gifts for the Gods." In *Faith, Hope, and Worship: Aspects of Religious Mentality in the Ancient World*, edited by H. S. Versnel, 65–105. Leiden.

(1992). "Votives and Votaries in Greek Sanctuaries." In *Le sanctuaire grec: huit exposés suivis de discussions par A. Schachter...et al*, edited by Jean Bingen and Albert Schachter, 247–84. Geneva.

(1995). *Hierà Kalá: Images of Animal Sacrifice in Archaic and Classical Greece*. Leiden.

Vassilika, E. (1998). *Greek and Roman Art in the Fitzwilliam Museum*. Fitzwilliam Museum Handbooks. Cambridge.

Venit, M. S. (2006). "Point and Counterpoint: Painted Vases on Attic Painted Vases." *Antike Kunst* 49: 29–41.

Vermaseren, M. J. (1982). *Corpus Cultus Cybelae Attidisque*. Études préliminaires aux religions orientales dans l'Empire roman. Vol. 50. Leiden.

Vermeule, Cornelius, and Mary Comstock. (1988). *Sculpture in Stone and Bronze in the Museum of Fine Arts, Boston: Additions to the Collections of Greek, Etruscan, and Roman Art, 1971–1988*. Boston.

Vermeule, C., and D. von Bothmer. (1959). "Notes on a New Edition of Michaelis, Part III." *AJA* 63: 329–48.

Vernant, J.-P. (1985a). "Figuration de l'invisible et catégorie psychologique du double: le Colossos." In *Mythe et pensée chez les grecs: études de psychologie historique*, 325–38. Paris.

(1985b). "De la présentification de l'invisible à l'imitation de l'apparence." In *Mythe et pensée chez les grecs: études de psychologie historique*, 339–51. Paris.

(1989). "At Man's Table: Hesiod's Foundation Myth of Sacrifice." Translated by Paula Wissing. In *The Cuisine of Sacrifice Among the Greeks*, edited by Marcel Detienne and J.-P. Vernant, 21–86. Chicago.

(1990). "Figuration et image." *Métis* 5: 225–38.

Versnel, H. S. (2011). *Coping with the Gods: Wayward Readings in Greek Theology*, edited by D. Frankfurter, J. Hahn and H. S. Versnel. Religions in the Graeco-Roman World. Vol. 173. Leiden and Boston.

Vetta, M. (1983a). "Introduzione. Poesia simposiale nella Grecia arcaica e classica." In *Poesia e Simposio nella Grecia Antica*, edited by M. Vetta, viii–lx. Rome.

(1983b). "Un capitolo di storia di poesia simposiale. Per l'esegesi di Aristofane *Vespe* 1222–48." In *Poesia e simposia nella Grecia Antica*, edited by Massimo. Vetta, 117–32. Rome.

Veyne, P. (1990). "Images de divinités tenant une phiale ou patère: la libation comme "rite de passage" et non pas offrande." *Mètis: Anthropologie des mondes grecs anciens* 5: 17–29.

Vierneisel, K., and B. Kaesar, eds. (1990). *Kunst der Schale, Kultur des Trinkens*. Munich.

Vikela, E. (1994). "Die Weihreliefs aus dem Athener Pankrates-Heiligtum am Ilissos." In *MdI, Athenische Abteilung: Beiheft*, 1–248.

(1997). "Attische Weihreliefs und die Kult-Topographie Attikas." *AM* 112: 167–246.

Voutira, A. G. (1991). "Observations on Domestic Music Making in Vase Paintings of the Fifth Century B.C." *Imago Musicae* 8: 73–94.

Walters, H. B. (1927). *London, British Museum III*. Corpus Vasorum Antiquorum. Vol. 4 Great Britain, Oxford.

(1928). *London, British Museum IV*. Corpus Vasorum Antiquorum. Vol. 5 Great Britain. Oxford.

Walters, H. B., and E. J. Forsdyke. (1930). *London, British Museum V*. Corpus Vasorum Antiquorum. Vol. 7 Great Britain. Oxford.

Walters, H. B., E. J. Forsdyke, and C. H. Smith. (1893). *Catalogue of Vases in the British Museum, I–IV*. London.

Warford, E. (2019). "Performing Piety: A Phenomenological Approach to Athenian Processions." In *Ascending and Descending the Acropolis: Movement in Athenian Religion*, edited by Wiebke Friese, Søren Handeberg and Troels Myrup Kristensen, 23–41. Aarhus.

Weaver, B. (2009). "Euripides' 'Bacchae' and Classical Typologies of Pentheus' 'Sparagmos', 510–406 BC." *BICS* 52: 15–43.

Wegner, M. (1949). *Das Musikleben der Griechen*. Berlin.

(1973). *Brygosmaler*. Berlin.

Wehgartner, I. (1983). *Attisch weissgrundige Keramik: Maltechniken, Werkstätten, Formen, Verwendung*. Mainz.

Weingarten, J. (1985). "Aspects of Tradition and Innovation in the Work of the Zakro Master." *BCH, Supplément* 11, no. 167–80.

Weinreich, O. (1968). *Religionsgeschichtliche Studien*. Darmstadt.

Weiss, N. A. (2017). "Noise, Music, Speech: The Representation of Lament in Greek Tragedy." *AJP* 138, no. 2: 243–66.

(2018). *The Music of Tragedy: Performance and Imagination in Euripidean Theater*. Berkeley and Los Angeles.

(2020). "Ancient Greek *Choreia*." In *A Companion to Ancient Greek and Roman Music*, edited by Tosca A. C. Lynch and Eleonora Rocconi, 161–72. Hoboken, NJ.

(2023). *Seeing Theater: The Phenomenology of Classical Greek Drama*. Oakland, CA.

(2024). "Audience". In *Dance in Greco-Roman Antiquity/Improntas de danza Antigua*, edited by Zoa Alonso Fernandez and Sarah Olsen. Madrid.

Weller, C. H. (1903). "The Cave at Vari. I. Description, Account of Excavation, and History." *AJA* 7, no. 3: 263–88.

West, M. L. (1975). "Cynaethus' Hymn to Apollo." *CQ, New Series* 25: 161–70.

(1981). "The Singing of Homer and the Modes of Early Greek Music." *JHS* 101: 113–29.

(1982). *Greek Metre*. Oxford and New York.

(1992). *Ancient Greek Music*. Oxford and New York.

(1997). *The East Face of Helicon: West Asiatic Elements in Greek Poetry and Myth*. Oxford.

ed. and trans. (2003). *Homeric Hymns*. Loeb Classical Library 496. Cambridge, MA.

(2007). *Indo-European Poetry and Myth*. Oxford.

Wickens, J. M. (1986). "The Archaeology and History of Cave Use in Attica, Greece, from Prehistoric through Late Roman Times." 2 vols. PhD Dissertation, Indiana University.

Wiles, D. (1984). "Menander's *Dyskolos* and Demetrios of Phaleon's Dilemma." *GaR* 31, no. 2: 170–80.

(1991). *The Masks of Menander: Sign and Meaning in Greek and Roman Performance*. Cambridge.

Williams, D. (1993). *London, British Museum IX*. Corpus Vasorum Antiquorum. Vol. 17 Great Britain. London.

Williams, F. (1978). *Callimachus, Hymn to Apollo: A Commentary*. Oxford.

Wilson, P. (2000). *The Athenian Institution of the Khoregia: The Chorus, the City, and the Stage*. Cambridge.

Winkler, J. J., and F. I. Zeitlin, eds. (1990). *Nothing to Do With Dionysos? Athenian Drama in Its Social Context*. Princeton.

Winnington-Ingram, R. P. (1956). "The Pentatonic Tuning of the Greek Lyre: A Theory Examined." *CQ, New Series* 6: 169–86.

Wolf, S. R. (1993). *Herakles beim Gelage: eine motiv- und bedeutungsgeschichtliche Untersuchung des Bildes in der archaisch-frühklassischen Vasenmalerei*. Cologne.

Yatromanolakis, D. (2007). *Sappho in the Making: The Early Reception*. Hellenic Studies. Vol. 28. Washington, D.C.

(2016). "Soundscapes (and Two Speaking Lyres)." In *Epigraphy of Art: Ancient Greek Vase-Inscriptions and Vase-Paintings*, edited by Dimitrios Yatromanolakis, 1–42. Oxford.

Yavis, C. G. (1949). *Greek Altars: Origins and Typology, Including the Minoan-Mycenaean Offertory Apparatus. An Archaeological Study in the History of Religion*. Saint Louis.

Yioutsos, N. P. (2013). "Cave Dancing in Ancient Greece." In *Présence de la danse dans l'Antiquité-Présence de l'Antiquité dans la danse*, edited by Rémy. Poignault, 35–55. Caesarodunum. Clermont-Ferrand.

(2014). "Pan Rituals of Ancient Greece: A Multi-Sensory Body Experience." In *Archaeoacoustics: The Archaeology of Sound. Publication of Proceedings from the 2014 Conference in Malta*, edited by L. C. Eneix and E. B. W. Zubrow, 57–68. Myakka City, FL.

(2017). "Order in Ancient Greek Dance Rituals: The Dance of Pan and the Nymphs." *Dramaturgias. Revista do Laboratório de Dramaturgia* 5, no. 2: 212–34.

et al. (2018). "Archaeoacoustic Research on Caves Dedicated to Pan and the Nymphs in Attica, Greece." In *Proceedings of Euronoise*: 2169–74.

Young, W. J. and B. Ashmole. (1968). "The Boston Relief and the Ludovisi Throne." *Boston Museum Bulletin* 66, no. 346: 124–66.

Zanker, P. (1965). *Wandel der Hermesgestalt in der attischen Vasenmalerei*. Bonn.

Zorides, P. (1977). "Η σπηλία των νυμφών της Πεντέλης." *AEph (Chronika)* 116: 4–11.

INDEX

Note: page numbers in italics indicate figures.